Locating

Race/Class/Gender Connections

EDITED BY
Elizabeth Comack

WITH
Sedef Arat-Koc
Karen Busby
Dorothy E. Chunn
Judy Fudge
Shelley A. M. Gavigan
Lisa Marie Jakubowski
Kirsten Johnson
Patricia Monture-Angus
AND Laureen Snider

Fernwood Publishing • Halifax

Editing: Robert Clarke
Cover art: Judith Baldwin
Design and production: Beverley Rach
Printed and bound in Canada by: Hignell Printing Limited

A publication of:
Fernwood Publishing
Box 9409, Station A
Halifax, Nova Scotia
B3K 5S3

Fernwood Publishing Company Limited gratefully acknowledges the financial support of the Ministry of Canadian Heritage and the Canada Council for the Arts for our publishing program.

Canadian Cataloguing in Publication Data

Main entry under title:

Locating law

       Includes bibliographical references.
       ISBN 1-55266-008-7

1. Sociological jurisprudence. I. Comack, Elizabeth, 1952-

K376.L62 1999   340.1   C99-950012-0

Contents

Contributors

Sedef Arat-Koc teaches women's studies and sociology at Trent University. Her research is in the areas of Canadian immigration policy and its implications for women, feminist and Muslim women's discourses in Turkey, and transnational feminism. Her publications include two co-edited collections, *Through the Kitchen Window: The Politics of Home and Family* (1990) and *Maid in the Market: Women's Paid Domestic Labour* (1994), as well as a number of articles on women and immigration in Canada.

Karen Busby works as a researcher, teacher, and lawyer on sex equality law, especially laws relating to violence against women. She is an Associate Professor in the Faculty of Law at the University of Manitoba and has had a long association as a volunteer with the Women's Legal Education and Action Fund (LEAF) and other anti-violence organizations, including three years as a rape crisis counsellor. She was called to the Manitoba Bar in 1982.

Dorothy Chunn is a Professor in the School of Criminology and Director of the Feminist Institute for Studies on Law and Society at Simon Fraser University. Her publications include *From Punishment to Doing Good: Family Courts and Socialized Justice in Ontario, 1880–1940* (1992) and *Law as a Gendering Practice* (1999), co-edited with Dany Lacombe. Her current research projects focus on the historical regulation of sexuality and reproduction in the Canadian welfare state and on feminism, law, and social change in Canada since the 1960s.

Elizabeth Comack teaches in the Department of Sociology at the University of Manitoba. Her previous works include two editions of *The Social Basis of Law* (co-edited with Stephen Brickey), *Women in Trouble* (1996), *The Feminist Engagement with the Law* (1993), and several articles and book chapters. She has taught courses in the sociology of law and criminology for the past two decades.

Judy Fudge is an Associate Professor at Osgoode Hall Law School, York University, where she teaches courses on labour law and legal theory. She has written extensively on labour law, especially the legal regulation of women's work, as well as Canadian labour law history and legal theory from a Marxist perspective. She has worked with women's organizations and trade unions in the struggle for social justice.

Shelley Gavigan teaches at Osgoode Hall Law School, York University. A former legal clinic lawyer, she has twice been the Academic Director of Parkdale Community Legal Services, a community-based legal clinic in Toronto affiliated with Osgoode Hall Law School and the Ontario Legal Aid Plan. Her recent publications include articles analysing the legal regulation of lesbian parenting and the legal form of "spouse."

Lisa Jakubowski received her Honours B.A. (Sociology) and M.A. (Sociology) from the University of Western Ontario and her Ph.D. from York University. She is an Assistant Professor in the Department of Sociology at Brescia College (affiliated with the University of Western Ontario). Her teaching and research interests are in the areas of sociology of law, the sociology of "race" and racism, and critical pedagogy.

Kirsten Johnson is a doctoral candidate at the Centre of Criminology, University of Toronto. Her work includes *Undressing the Canadian State: The Politics of Porn from Hicklin to Butler* (1995), co-editor of *Wife Assault and the Canadian Criminal Justice System* (1995), and several articles in the areas of criminology and the sociology of law. She is completing a dissertation that examines Canadian legal cases of concealment of birth and infanticide in the twentieth century.

Patricia Monture-Angus is a Mohawk woman born and raised in London, Ontario, who now resides at the Thunderchild First Nation with her partner and their five children. She holds degrees from the University of Western Ontario, Queen's University, and Osgoode Hall Law School and teaches at the University of Saskatchewan. Her publications include *Thunder in My Soul: A Mohawk Woman Speaks* (1995).

Laureen Snider is a Professor in the Department of Sociology at Queen's University. Her main theoretical interest is in issues of social control and punishment, which she has explored in empirical studies of corporate crime, feminism, and new social movements. Her recent publications include "Toward Safer Societies" (1998), "Feminism, Punishment and the Potential of Empowerment" (1994), and *Bad Business: Corporate Crime in Canada* (1993).

Acknowledgements

Sometimes the work we do as academics feels like a chore, and other (thankfully, most) times it energizes and makes us realize how privileged we are to have the job we do. Readers of this book need to know what an energizing experience it has been for me to work on this project. It represents those things that academic work should embody: critical thinking and inquiry, a sharing of ideas, and supportive commentary and feedback.

While the book emerges from the desire to provide students with a sense of the sociology of law and of the kind of work now being done in this area, the approach taken in compiling this collection has been unique—not only because all of the essays have been written specifically for the book, but also because of the process that we used in compiling it. When I initially sat down with Wayne Antony of Fernwood Publishing to discuss what the book could look like, we began by listing the kinds of topics or issues to be included. When it came to determining the authors best suited to writing on those issues, several names easily came to mind. When contacted, all nine of the authors who have contributed to this project were very generous about taking the time from their hectic schedules (and, believe me, they *are* hectic) to write the essays. The authors were asked to speak to an issue on which they have an established expertise through their own research and writing. Each was given a set of guidelines within which to work and, in most cases, the essays were distributed to other authors for feedback and suggestions for revision. In the meantime, I took the liberty of writing a fairly extensive theoretical essay to introduce students to the different theoretical approaches in the sociology of law. I believe the result is a collection of essays that will not only inform the reader, but also provoke considerable discussion and debate around some very pressing issues that relate to how we locate law within the nexus of race/race/gender relations. For this I owe a great debt of thanks to each of the contributors.

The reader also needs to be aware that books of this nature would not be possible without the kind of commitment and dedication shown by a publishing company like Fernwood. I have witnessed first-hand the kind of hard work that goes into preparing a book for distribution: from the careful copy-editing of Robert Clarke, to Debbie Mathers' work in typing the changes to the final manuscript, to Beverley Rach's skills in setting the pages for printing and designing the book's cover, to Lindsay Sharpe's command of the distribution end, and to Jackie Logan's handle on the publicity. Ushering all of this along is the seasoned and down-to-earth approach of Fernwood's founder and guiding mind, Errol Sharpe, a man who puts his political convictions into practice and makes this business of publishing a humane endeavour. I would also make special mention of the work of Wayne Antony. Wayne not only acted in his capacity as publisher on the project (which includes overseeing all of the stages of the process), but his skills as a sociologist and critical thinker were also indispensable to me from start to finish. As well, I draw the reader's attention to the artwork on the book's front cover created by my dear friend, Judith Baldwin. This is the second time that Judith has put her talents to work for me in this capacity, and I commend her for her skill, energy, and vision.

Finally, I would like to acknowledge the work of the many academics who bring the issues of race/class/gender and social justice into their classrooms and expose them for students to discover, ponder, and rail against in the effort to generate consciousness and change. In this regard, one person (although he probably doesn't realize it) who has been instrumental in prompting me to do this book is Bernard Schissel of the University of Saskatchewan.

In keeping with the collective and political nature of this project, the royalties from the book will be donated to groups working for social justice.

Elizabeth Comack
December, 1998

Introduction

One of the primary concerns within the sociology of law has been to understand the "law-society relation." Underlying this concern is the belief that law has a distinctly *social* basis; it both shapes—and is shaped by—the society in which it operates. The main objective of this book is to explore this law-society relation or, as the title of the book implies, to *locate* law. More specifically, we propose that to understand the law-society relation, we need to place law within the nexus of race, class, and gender relations in society.

As individuals, our interactions and experiences are very much informed by our social positioning in society, and that social location is contoured and conditioned by three key elements: our race, class, and gender. But these three elements do more than specify "difference" between individuals; they are used to divide, separate, and categorize. In short, race, class, and gender constitute the *primary* bases on which inequality is produced and maintained—though they are not the only bases: (dis)ability and sexual orientation are two others.

Historically, inequalities of race, class, and gender have been an imbedded feature of Canadian society. It is a sad fact that our history is tainted by the systemic processes of colonization and forced dependency of First Nations people. This history includes the appropriation of their land, the transfer of their populations to geographical areas more often than not devoid of the natural resources needed to sustain traditional economic practices, and the forced removal of their children to residential schools, where physical and sexual abuse became an all-too-common practice in the drive to "assimilate" them to the ways of the supposedly "civilized" white society. This historical legacy is one that mainstream Canadian society is only beginning to comprehend fully in terms of its long-lasting effects on the lives of Aboriginal peoples and on their communities. As Geoffrey York (1990: xiii) notes, "Most Canadians are better acquainted with the history of native people in the eighteenth and nineteenth centuries than they are with the unsavoury realities of recent years." Consider the following.

- During the 1960s, what became known as the "Sixties Scoop" involved the removal of Aboriginal children from their families, communities, and cultures by child welfare agencies to be adopted into non-Aboriginal families. What began in the 1960s carried on through the 1970s and 1980s. Between 1971 and 1981 alone, over 3,400 Aboriginal children were shipped away to adoptive parents in other societies and sometimes in other countries (Hamilton and Sinclair 1991: 520).

- Aboriginal people constitute one of the poorest groups in Canadian society. While the poverty rate for non-Aboriginal families is 14 percent, nearly *half* of all Aboriginal families living on reserves— and *one-quarter* of those living off reserves—are below the poverty line (Battle 1998: 54; Oberle 1993: 5).

- Housing on reserves lacks the general facilities associated with an average Canadian standard of living: less than one-half of the houses (44 percent) have running water; 30 percent have indoor toilets; 33 percent have telephones; and 82 percent have electricity. In contrast, in Canada as a whole 97 percent of houses have running water and 97 percent have indoor toilets (Frideres 1988: 82).

- Life expectancy rates for First Nations people are 74 years for women and 67 years for men, compared to the Canadian average of 81 years for women and 74 years for men. Aboriginal infant mortality rates are more than 10.9 births per thousand, compared to the national average of 6.3 (*Globe and Mail* March 11, 1996: A6).

- The suicide rate for First Nations people is three times the national rate; for young people it is five to six times higher (Canada, Royal Commission on Aboriginal Peoples 1995: 1).

The experiences of other racialized groups who historically made Canada their home have been similarly marked by inequities and dispossession. At various points the treatment of the Chinese, Japanese, East Indians, Jews, and other groups has been characterized by both overt and more subtle forms of discrimination. Signs of discrimination continue to the present day.

- Individual acts of discrimination occur frequently in Canadian workplaces. In three consecutive surveys conducted in 1975, 1980, and 1991, the Canadian Civil Liberties Association found that most employment agencies surveyed in Toronto would agree to discriminate in their referral of employees. Therefore, racist employers could utilize such agencies to suit their prejudices. Of fifteen agencies surveyed, twelve agreed to comply with such requests from potential employers (Das Gupta 1996: 12).

- A study by Frances Henry and Effie Ginzberg (1985) found that when white and black applicants answered Toronto newspaper ads with similar resumés (for jobs in the retail food industry and retail sales, for junior managerial positions, and as unskilled labourers), white applicants received more application forms, encountered more helpful attitudes from potential employers, were more likely to be called for second interviews, and were offered more jobs. For every three job offers received by a white man, a black man received one.
- People of colour earn on average 7 percent less than white workers. Chinese-Canadian males earn 30 percent less than Canadian males overall, and Chinese-Canadian females earn 40 percent less than Canadian females (Das Gupta 1996: 7, 26–27).
- Black Canadians have experienced discrimination and exploitation not only in the labour market and workplace, but also in education, housing, and social services (Bolaria and Li 1988:196).

As a group, women have also encountered inequalities in the labour market and elsewhere. Women's wages, for instance, have historically been only a portion of what male workers earn and, despite advances in recent years, continue to lag behind men's. Historically, women were denied basic rights of citizenship—like the right to vote, to own property once married, and to hold public office. While most Canadian women won the right to vote in federal elections in 1918, Aboriginal women (and their male counterparts) could not vote until 1960 (and provincially in Quebec until 1969). The desperate economic situations of many Canadian women has resulted in what is referred to as the "feminization of poverty."

- Families headed by women are almost four times more likely to be poor than are families headed by men (their poverty rates were 39.7 percent and 10.6 percent in 1995, respectively) (Battle 1998: 53).
- In 1993, 56 percent of elderly women living alone in Canada were poor (*Toronto Star* August 9, 1995: A15).
- While women filled 72 percent of the new jobs created during the 1980s, they remain concentrated in lower-paid occupations in the clerical, sales, and services sectors and are more likely than men to work part-time (Battle 1998: 56).

- In 1995, women who worked full-time in Canada earned on average 73 percent of what men earned (an improvement over previous years, but mainly because men's wages fell by 2.2 percent in 1995). The wage gap is greater for married women and those with less education. As well, women of colour earned only 51 percent of what white men earned and 59 percent of what men of colour earned (*Globe and Mail* December 20, 1995, January 28, 1997; Das Gupta 1996: 7).

- A 1994 survey of 619 Canadian companies revealed that 377 of their 6,014 administrative positions—or only 6.3 percent—were held by women (*Winnipeg Free Press* April 2, 1997).

That class inequalities exist in Canada has long been recognized as "fact." What is perhaps less understood is the extent to which these inequities have been increasing in the past two decades in tandem with capitalist globalization, corporate restructuring and "downsizing," and the dismantling of the Canadian welfare state and its social programs. Consider the following.

- In 1995, 5.2 million women, children, and men—18 percent of the population—lived below the poverty line in Canada. Of the nation's seven million children under the age of eighteen, almost one-and-a-half million—or one child in five—lived in poverty in 1995. Some 30 percent of the children in Toronto—the city picked by the United Nations as the best place in the world to live—are subsisting below the poverty line (Battle 1998: 53–54; Laxer 1998: 3).

- Family incomes in Canada are dropping at the same time as the number of hours needed to support a household (45 hours a week in 1970 compared to 65-80 in 1991) and the number of female-headed single-parent families have increased dramatically. Between 1989 and 1996 the average family with children under eighteen suffered a $4,000 decline in income. The poverty rates of single mothers in Canada are now at record levels: 62 percent of single mothers live below the poverty line and make on average $2,834 less than they did two years ago (Brodie 1995: 20; *Globe and Mail* October 22, 1998: A12).

- The average income for the richest 10 percent of Canadian families in 1971 was $107,000—21 times that of the poorest 10 percent. By 1996 Canada's richest were making 314 times the average income of the poorest (*Globe and Mail* October 22, 1998: A11).

- Of the 100 largest economies in the world, 51 are now corporations. Wal-Mart, the number 12 corporation, is *bigger* than 161 countries, including Israel, Greece, and Poland (*Canadian Forum* 1997: 48).
- The wealthiest Canadian is Kenneth R. Thomson. In 1996 his personal wealth was estimated to be $8.2 billion. Following Thomson are the Irvings ($7.5 billion); Charles Bronfman ($2.9 billion); the Eatons ($1.7 billion); and Ted Rogers ($1.4 billion). None of the men who control Canada's five greatest fortunes is "self-made." All of them were born into their wealth and privilege (Laxer 1998: 79).

Recognizing that inequalities along race, class, and gender lines exist in society raises important questions, not the least of which concerns the role of law. What role has law historically played in generating today's inequalities? Is law part of the "problem" or part of the "solution" in alleviating inequities based on race, class, and gender? Can we use law as a mechanism or strategy to achieve substantive social change? The purpose of this book is to address these kinds of questions.

To engage in such an inquiry, we need some appreciation of the different ways of understanding or making sense of law and its location within society, and this is the task of the first essay, "Theoretical Excursions." Law's image of itself—or what Australian writer Ngaire Naffine (1990) refers to as the "Official Version of Law"—will be used as a backdrop to explore the different theoretical approaches that have emerged in the sociology of law to understand the law–society relation. As we will see, some of the approaches take the Official Version of Law as a given, some are more sceptical of its claims, and some reject it altogether. Exploring the reasons behind a particular theoretical stance regarding law tells us a great deal about how "society"—including its race, class, and gender dimensions—is understood within a theoretical perspective. In the process we can arrive at a better sense of the kinds of issues and questions that emerge in our efforts to locate law within its broader historical and social context.

The rest of the book is divided into three parts: "Racism and the Law," "Class Interests and the Law," and "Gender, Sexuality, and the Law." Carving out the race/class/gender dimensions of the law-society relation in this way, though, is very much an artificial construction. Just as individuals do not experience their race, their class position, or their gender in isolation from the other defining elements in their lives, so too it is difficult to separate these components for analytical purposes. As such, while the essays by Patricia Monture-Angus, Lisa Jakubowski, and Sedef Arat-Koc in the book's first part concentrate on how racism has been manifested in legal policies and practices, the authors also display a sensitivity to how class and gender figure into the matters discussed. In the same way, in the "Class Interests and the Law" section, Judy Fudge, Laureen Snider, and Shelley Gavigan focus on the connections between law and the class relations of society, while drawing out the implications of the issues they consider for race and gender. In the final section, on "Gender, Sexuality, and the Law," Dorothy Chunn, Karen Busby, and Kirsten Johnson explore issues relating primarily to the gendered nature of social relations, while also attending to their class and race dynamics.

Together, not only will these essays assist efforts to locate law, but they are also sure to generate new insights and understandings of the (inter)connections between the race, class, and gender dynamics of our society.

Theoretical Approaches in the Sociology of Law

Theoretical Excursions

© Elizabeth Comack[1]

Theory, in my experience, is not something that students embrace willingly. The concept usually conjures up images of very dry, abstract—not to mention boring—discussions that appear to have little relevance to our everyday lives. Before we begin our excursions into the theoretical approaches in the sociology of law, it is worth commenting on why we need to rethink the "bad rep" that theory holds.

To begin with, it might be useful to think of social theory as "a set of answers to questions we ask of social reality." What this suggests is that—far from being irrelevant to our everyday lives—social theory can clarify and inform our understandings of what we do on a daily basis and what goes on in the world around us. Whether we are aware of it or not, each of us already and regularly engages in "theory talk" on a regular basis. It invades our ways of making sense of why people do the things they do or say the things they say, whether it is with respect to our interactions with friends and families, the presence of crime in our communities, or the actions of political officials and governments. Theory, then, rather than being avoided, should be something that each of us closely interrogates. By doing so we have the potential to gain a clearer sense of not only our own but also other people's ways of making sense of the world.

Perhaps part of the reason for our resistance to "theory talk" is the tendency to see it as something static or unchanging. Far from it: social theories do not operate in a vacuum. Historically, social theorists and philosophers were very much motivated by what transpired in the world around them. Take Karl Marx as an example. The corpus of Marx's writing, which was largely concerned with formulating a theory of capitalist development, was inspired by the changes brought about by the industrialization of the nineteenth century and the often disastrous effects of those changes on ordinary people's lives. Similarly, contemporary theorists have been motivated by their desire to understand the effects on our lives of processes such as economic globalization, the breakdown of "community," and the increasing preponderance of violence. While poverty, inequality, social conflict, and suffering are by no means new phenomena, they can take on specific forms under different social and historical contexts. As such, any theorist who endeavours to make sense of such issues must be sensitive to the particular times and contexts in which they occur.

In the same way that theorists are influenced by what transpires in the world around them, it is also the case that, oftentimes, the theories that receive the most attention will be those that "mesh" well with the times. For instance, functionalism, at least in North America, was a theoretical framework that enjoyed considerable prominence in sociology during the 1940s and 1950s. Part of the reason for its popularity was its inherently conservative approach, which coincided with the politics of the Cold War era. With the increasing social and political conflicts of the 1960s, functionalism's popularity waned. Events such as the protests against the war in Vietnam, the Quiet Revolution in Quebec, and the increasing militancy and radicalism of student, racial, and women's groups generated questions and issues that functionalism, with its consensus-oriented assumptions about the social world, was ill-prepared to address. Consequently, other theoretical frameworks—such as liberal pluralism, neo-Marxism, and feminism(s)—gained prominence throughout the 1960s and 1970s. These approaches, with their greater attention to issues of power and conflict, opened the way for more critical analyses of social relations in the 1980s and 1990s. Interestingly, with the emergence of a new right politics in the 1980s functionalism (albeit in a revised form) reappeared within academia.

Theory is not "static" in one other sense. Theorizing is a cumulative enterprise; it builds on previous work. As such, individual theorists will not only be influenced by those who have gone before them, but also change and alter their theoretical perspectives over time in response to social developments, the challenges posed by other theorists, and their own critical self-reflection. For example, if we were to read the work that William Chambliss published in the 1960s (for example, Chambliss 1964), we would have the distinct impression that Chambliss was a liberal-pluralist thinker. By the 1980s, Chambliss's theorizing was decidedly more Marxist in its orientation (for example, Chambliss 1986). Similarly, Carol Smart's work has shifted over time from a socialist-feminist framework (Smart 1984) to a postmodern approach (Smart 1989, 1995).

These comments suggest the need to make an important caution in our discussion of the different theoretical approaches in the sociology of law. Here, in introducing some of the main approaches to understanding the law-society relation, I carve out different theoretical frameworks and discuss their main assumptions and premises with a view to highlighting their similarities and differences. Treating theories in this fashion runs the risk not only of oversimplifying them, but also of "fixing" them in time. What easily gets lost is the sense of "fluidity" that a theory may possess. In short, there is a danger of viewing each theoretical approach as static. As such, we need to treat the following discussion as a preliminary foray into the long and rich tradition of theorizing around law and society, keeping in mind that much more can be learned by reading the original texts and tracing an individual theorist's path as she or he endeavours to raise and answer some of the key questions that have guided the sociology of law.

The discussion is organized as follows. I begin with an elaboration of how law "sees" itself; the image it portrays in terms of its nature, role, and functioning in society. This is what Australian writer Ngaire Naffine (1990) refers to as the "Official Version of Law," and I use the Official Version of Law as a backdrop to explore the different theoretical approaches that have emerged in the sociology of law to understand the law-society relation. After considering the more traditional, mainstream approaches—functionalism, liberal pluralism, and Marxism—we look at the feminist frameworks—conservatism, liberal feminism, radical feminism, and socialist feminism. The essay concludes by considering two key challenges now confronting the sociology of law—racialized groups and the law, and postmodernism—before outlining some of the key questions pertaining to our investigation of the (inter)connections between law and the race, class, and gender relations in society.

THE OFFICIAL VERSION OF LAW

> The official version of law—what the legal world would have us believe about itself—is that it is an impartial, neutral and objective system for resolving social conflict. (Naffine 1990: 24)

As Ngaire Naffine suggests, "impartiality," "neutrality," and "objectivity" are the cornerstones of the modern legal system. They are symbolically represented in the image of the blindfolded maiden who holds the scales used to dispense justice. When we stop to think about it, this image speaks volumes about the messages that law endeavours to convey about itself. A "maiden" is a virginal young (white?) woman—presumably untouched, untainted, or uncorrupted. That she is blindfolded suggests she is not swayed or influenced by the characteristics of those who stand before her—she sees no class, no race, no gender distinctions. The scales she is holding connote the measured and precise nature of the decisions produced. But the Official Version of Law is reflected in elements other than the symbol of the blindfolded maiden. In both its form and its method, law asserts its claim to be impartial, neutral, and objective.

The form of law is partly reflected in its adherence to the adversarial system. Law is set up as a contest between two parties, each representing its own version of the events. In the criminal court, for example, the key actors are the Crown prosecutor, acting on behalf of the state, and the defence counsel, acting on behalf of the accused. The judge's task is to discern the "legally relevant facts" of the case—to find the "truth" about the matter brought before the court. In the process,

> Members of the Bench ... do not invoke their own personal beliefs of the rights or wrongs of an individual or a case. Nor do they operate with any particular set of social or cultural values. Instead, they are obliged to treat all who come before them in an unbiased fashion, fairly and dispassionately. To quote from the English judicial oath, the obligation on the judicial officer is to 'do right to all manner of people ... without fear or favour, affection or illwill.' (Naffine 1990: 24–25)

That judges are impartial in their deliberations is also reflected in the doctrine of the *separation of powers:* that is, that the legislature (which makes the laws) is separated from the judiciary (which administers the laws). This suggests that law is an autonomous, internally consistent system, divorced from the more political processes of the state. Further assisting in the impartiality and fairness of the proceedings is a distinctly legal mode of reasoning. This method is captured in the notion of *legal positivism.* Much like other sciences, legal positivism asserts that the focus of legal players is on facts and not values, such that legal method involves the application of the appropriate rule or test to those facts of the case that are deemed to be legally relevant. The result is a neutral, value-free, and objective science of law. In keeping with this view is the doctrine of *stare decisis*—or "to stand by decided matters." According to this doctrine, judges are bound to follow precedent. Developed under the common-law tradition of case law, precedent implies that "like cases are to be treated alike." Judges are to rely on previous cases in making their decisions, and lower courts must follow the decisions reached by higher courts. These principles are said to promote and ensure that law is predictable, consistent, and certain.

Perhaps the most central doctrine on which law is founded is that of the *rule of law,* which encompasses two broad claims. First, everyone is subject to the law, even the sovereign or ruler, since the law is presented as something separate and distinct from the interests of particular groups or classes. Second, the law treats everyone the same, as legal equals. "Equality of all before the law" and "blind justice" are thus the hallmarks of the rule of law (Hunt 1976: 178–87). The main effect of this particular legal form is to provide a barrier against the arbitrary exercise of the power of the state and a guarantee of the rights and liberties of individual citizens. As the English jurist A.V. Dicey explains it, "Not only with us no man is above the law ... but here every man, whatever his rank or condition, is subject to the ordinary law of the realm" (quoted in Naffine 1990: 48).

In both its form and its method, then, the law promotes an image of itself as fair, dispassionate, disinterested, and—above all—as *just.* In doing this, however, law presumes the existence of a particular kind of individual and a particular form of society. The subject of law is a universal, abstract person. As Naffine (1990: 51) notes, "If our legal system has been devised with a human being in mind, then that person is supposed to be a universal being, a human norm, someone who could be anyone functioning anywhere." Indeed, law's claim to impartiality is derived from its commitment to the view that it does not deal with different types of people, but with legal subjects, "and the way it does this is to abstract people from their particular contexts and examine the merits of their individual cases" (Naffine 1990: 52).

Naffine raises two challenges to law's claims. She suggests that the legal subject is not a universal being. Rather, "The legal person is endowed with a specific set of characteristics that are presented as universal ... he is deemed to be able-bodied, autonomous, rational, educated, monied, competitive and essentially self-interested" (Naffine 1990: 52). In short, law's preferred person is most likely to be a male who fits with the needs and priorities of a modern, industrial, competitive market society. Naffine also suggests that, although law professes to act "without affection or illwill" to all individuals, it does this by abstracting people from their social contexts or locations—the very aspects of their lives that might well make them different from each other. In other words, to make individuals equal before the law the law imposes upon them the characteristics of the abstract legal person so that they may be assumed, for legal purposes, to be free, capable, and competitive. If this sounds like circular reasoning, that is because it is.

Naffine's challenges to the Official Version of Law are instructive, because they raise the issue of whether law—or any mode of thought for that matter—can be completely valueless. Indeed, it is worth acknowledging that this image of law is historically specific, springing from Western societies. It emerged out of a particular set of philosophical and theoretical ideas—a combination of elements drawn from conservative and liberal social philosophies.

Conservatism, as a social philosophy, finds its roots in the writings of the seventeenth-century writer Thomas Hobbes, who argued for the existence of a "pre-social" being, or "man in a state of nature." Because "man" was characterized by his egoism, self-interest, and unlimited desire for personal gain, the state of nature was typified as a "war of all against all," as individuals sought to further their own interests. However, man's "saving grace" was that he also possessed reason, and reason told man that his interests would best be served by coming together to form a society. Men then struck a *social contract* with each other. In return for giving over a certain amount of power to a sovereign or central authority, men would receive security of their persons and property and thus be in better positions to realize their own self-interests. This social contract thus empowered the institutions of law and government to arbitrate the conflicts between individuals and to ensure an orderly, organized society. Hence the problem of the "war of all against all" was resolved. The main function of the state was to preserve the rights and freedoms of individuals to pursue their material interests, and with minimal interference from the powers that be. In the process, social order was maintained and upheld.

Liberalism is a social philosophy that emerged in the eighteenth century with writers such as Jean-Jacques Rousseau and John Stuart Mill. Liberalism places heavy emphasis on *rationality*, that is, on individuals' ability to think abstractly and objectively. As Naffine notes, this focus on rationality is part of a particular world view that sees the world in dichotomous terms, such as: rational/irrational; thought/feeling; objectivity/subjectivity; abstract thinking/contextual reasoning. Law adopts this dualism, and in each of these cases it gives preference to the former over the latter. In other words, "The rational, the intellectual, the objective and the abstract decision is the preferred and superior style of decision making" (Naffine 1990: 26).

At the core of liberal thought is the belief in the *rights and freedoms of the individual*. This is best reflected in Mill's dictum that "individuals should be free to pursue their own happiness so long as they do not infringe on the similar rights of others." The purpose of law, then, is to allow individuals to realize these inherent rights and freedoms. As Mill stated, "The only purpose for which power can be exercised over any member of a civilized community against his will is to prevent harm to others." In law's view, then, individuals are separate, autonomous beings—legal subjects—who must be held accountable or responsible for their behaviours.

To the extent that law's view of itself is not valueless but rather derives from particular philosophical ideas about human nature and conceptions of society, its claims to impartiality, neutrality, and objectivity become suspect. This is even more the case once we consider that the society in which law is located is one characterized by inequalities between groups and classes of individuals. Can we accept law's claims at face value? Or is a more sceptical approach warranted? In considering the three main theoretical approaches in the sociology of law, we will see that functionalism takes the Official Version of Law as a given, liberal pluralism is more sceptical of its claims, and Marxism rejects law's claims altogether.

TRADITIONAL APPROACHES IN THE SOCIOLOGY OF LAW

The functionalist approach

The functionalist approach dates back to the work of Emile Durkheim, a classical theorist of sociology who was writing at the turn of the century, but it became popular in North American sociology during the 1940s and 1950s with the work of Talcott Parsons. In criminology, it is reflected in the theories of Robert Merton (anomie theory), Albert Cohen (subcultural theory), and Travis Hirschi (control theory). Of all the approaches to the law-society relation, functionalism is the one most likely to take the Official Version of Law as a given. This is, in large part, because of a compatibility with the background assumptions that inform the theory.

Like the Official Version of Law, functionalism draws on elements of conservative social philosophy in formulating its image of human nature. Recall that, in the Hobbesian view, humans were possessed of unlimited desires and appetites that needed to somehow be controlled or brought into line to prevent a "war of all against all." In essence, we are, by our very nature, anti-social, self-interested, and egotistical, and it is only through our contact with society that we become social beings. In more sociological terms, we require the socializing influences of society. Through the socialization process, for example, we internalize or take as our own the norms, values, and beliefs—the culture—of society. In this respect, social control—both internal (through socialization) and external (by means of the police, prisons, etc.)—is necessary if society is to flourish.

Much like Hobbes, Durkheim was preoccupied with the question of what produces order in society. This is a key question in functionalist theorizing, and it helps to account for why so much of the focus of the functionalists is on those elements in society that produce order, stability, and harmony. In addressing this problem of order question, one of the basic assumptions that informs their work is the existence of a consensus or agreement in society on dominant norms and values. To use Durkheim's term, a "collective conscience" consists of the "totality of beliefs and sentiments common to the average citizens of the same society" (Durkheim 1964: 79). One implication to be derived from this is that *culture* is an important variable in the production of social order or integration.

As one of the so-called Founding Fathers of Sociology, Durkheim was intent on carving out an area of study that was distinctly sociological in both its subject matter and its method. Like other writers of his time, Durkheim was strongly influenced by developments in the natural or physical sciences. The impact of these developments are evident in Durkheim's work. In particular, Durkheim was an advocate of the positive method. Positivism is generally understood as the position that it is possible to adopt the laws and methods devised to understand the physical world and apply them to an analysis of the social world in order to arrive at the "truth" about human behaviour. In short, sociology was conceived of as a science, a social science. But the influence of the natural sciences is evident in other ways as well.

Theories that aim to understand the operation of different processes in society—like the law-society relation—are each premised on particular conceptions of what "society," at a fairly abstract or general level, "looks like." In formulating their conception or image of society, functionalists utilize an organic analogy. In other words (and here, again, we see the influence of the natural sciences), they theorize that society is very much like a living organism: it has evolved over time from simpler to more complex forms; it has a structure consisting of different parts; and each of the parts that make up the whole functions interdependently with one another. For example, much like the human body can be said to consist of different organs (the heart, lungs, stomach, for example) that carry out their own individual functions yet rely on each other to do their respective jobs (think of what happens when one of these organs stops working), the different institutions within society—such as the economy, family, religion, state, and legal system—can be said to perform specific functions that contribute to the maintenance of the social whole, each one functioning in harmony with the others. One implication of this conception of society is that, for analytical purposes, a particular institution (like the legal system) can be separated out and studied in isolation from the others by looking at its structure and functions (see, for example, Friedman 1977).

Because the focus of the functionalist approach is so heavily centred on the sources of order in society, it is an approach that cannot handle conflict very well. Conflict, when it is recognized, tends to be viewed either as pathological (in the sense of being temporary) or as functional. For instance, when social regulation does break down, and society's controlling influence on the individual is no longer effective, individuals are considered to be in a state of "anomie," or a condition of relative normlessness. Such a condition, however, is not endemic to society, because the prevailing tendency is towards stability and equilibrium. Likewise, functionalists are not well-equipped to handle an analysis of power. To the extent that they incorporate power into the analysis, they see it as a matter of *societal domination* or the power of society over the individual.

To say that functionalists are not well-equipped to handle an analysis of power does not mean that they are unaware of social inequalities. Rather, they understand inequality in a particular way, as both "natural" and "functional." Inequalities are natural in the sense that they emerge out of inherent or innate differences between individuals and groups (like those based on race or sex). Inequalities are functional because in a healthy and stable society individuals know their place; they have a duty to fit in and perform their assigned tasks. From the functionalist's standpoint, certain individuals are natural leaders. They possess the requisite skills and abilities to make decisions in the interests of society as a whole. One way to ensure that the most fit people carry out society's important tasks is to attach greater rewards and privileges to those positions. It follows that the people who occupy positions of power and privilege are those who are not only best suited to these roles, but also most *deserving* of the rewards attending to their station.

Because functionalists see culture or the normative system of society as a main source of social integration or cohesion, they necessarily see law as an important integrating mechanism. Indeed, for the functionalist, law both represents and reinforces the collective conscience of society. In applying the organic analogy, Durkheim suggested that law "plays a role analogous to that played by the nervous system in an organism. The latter has as its task, in effect, the regulation of the different functions of the body in such a way as to make them harmonize" (Durkheim 1964: 128). In much the same way Talcott Parsons (1980: 61) suggested, "The primary function of a legal system is integrative. It serves to mitigate potential elements of conflict and oil the machinery of social intercourse."

Durkheim's views on crime are also instructive. They not only provided the foundation for much of the later functionalist work in criminology, but also offer insight into the functionalist view of the modern state. Durkheim defined crime according to the sanctions imposed; that is, crime is an action that elicits punishment. The common characteristic of all crimes, regardless of the particular behaviours involved, is that they consist of "acts universally disapproved of by members of society" (Durkheim 1964: 73). Punishment against crime, according to Durkheim, takes the form of vengeance. Because crime shocks the collective sentiments of society's members, punishment provides a means of avenging the moral outrage aroused by the criminal. It is a means of defence for society and the collective conscience.

This is where the role of the state comes to the foreground. Because crimes are behaviours thought to be so serious that they threaten not just the victim but the entire society, it falls to the state, as the representative of the members of society, to take action against the offender. In this respect, functionalism conceptualizes the state as a *neutral force* operating on behalf of society as a whole. Its primary function is that of social control: ensuring individual conformity to the normative system.

This discussion of the functionalist approach gives us several clues as to why it is so compatible with the Official Version of Law. Given their similar philosophical roots, their adherence to the positive method, their view of inequality as unproblematic, and their image of both law and the state as neutral arbiters of social conflict in the interest of the common good, it is not surprising that functionalists take the Official Version of Law at face value. Indeed, because functionalism locates law as the institutional expression of the norms and values of the majority, the approach simply has no need to question law per se. For instance, with regard to criminal law, functionalists make no attempt to question the political nature of crime—to question whether definitions of "what is criminal" provide a means by which one segment of the population controls or manages another. Instead, their focus turns to the criminal offender and the question of the causes of an individual's inability to conform to the norms and values that everyone else in society deems acceptable.

In their efforts to theorize the causes of crime, functionalists have variously framed their explanations in terms of differing cultural beliefs (such as the existence of deviant subcultures), the social disorganization of inner city neighbourhoods, the absence of legitimate opportunities for realizing cultural goals, or the failure of the family to socialize children properly. Overriding these explanations is the assumption that crime is a *lower-class phenomenon*. Since the structure of the society goes unexamined, social problems like crime come to be viewed as the problems of particular groups or individuals who fail to fit into the requirements of the social order. Solutions proposed, therefore, tend to revolve around policies of resocialization or rehabilitation, increased social control (for example, more police), and harsher penalties for wrongdoing (such as lengthier prison sentences and capital punishment).

The liberal-pluralist approach
The liberal-pluralist approach finds its roots in the work of Max Weber, another classical sociological theorist who, like Durkheim, was writing around the turn of the century. It also reflects the influence of the Chicago School, a group of social psychologists (such as George Herbert Mead, Charles Horton Cooley, and W.I. Thomas) who worked out of the University of Chicago in the early twentieth century. In criminology, liberal pluralism is evident in Edwin Sutherland's differential association theory and in labelling and group conflict theories. In relation to the Official Version of Law, liberal pluralism does not go as far as the func-

tionalist approach in its outright acceptance of law's claims; it is more sceptical in its stance. Nevertheless, as we will see, there is a general compatibility between the two.

Liberal pluralists derive their thinking about human nature from eighteenth-century Enlightenment philosophers, especially Jean-Jacques Rousseau. They view humans as naturally competitive and power-seeking beings; everyone wants the most out of life and aspires to be number one. At the same time, however, individuals are possessed of certain innate human rights and freedoms that can only be realized through society. The task, therefore, is to ensure that the competition between individuals is fair and that society is organized in the way that is most amenable to realizing those rights and freedoms.

Like Durkheim, Weber devoted attention to the methodology appropriate to a scientific study of society. But whereas Durkheim took as his main point of departure the "social whole," Weber asserted that the starting point of investigation had to be the individual. Social behaviour could not be understood simply by observing it externally. Rather, the analyst had to pay attention to the *meaning* that individuals ascribe to their behaviour. As such, Weber's "interpretive sociology" is one that "considers the individual and his action as the basic unit" because "the individual is the sole carrier of meaningful conduct" (Weber 1968: 13).

In contrast to the functionalists, liberal pluralists do not make the assumption of a consensus on dominant norms and values in society. Instead, they see society as consisting of a plurality of competing interest groups, each one intent on realizing their particular interests. In Weber's sociology, for example, this competition for power occurs within the stratification order of society. Weber conceptualized stratification along three different dimensions. In other words, power in society derives from three different sources, and the amount of power an individual possesses is related to his or her standing along each of three *orders:* an economic order, which features classes; a social order, which features status groups; and a political order, which features parties. Since the sources of power are multidimensional, no one variable is seen as "determining." Liberal pluralism, then, promotes a multi-causal approach to understanding the sources of power differentials.

Liberal pluralism is better equipped than the functionalist approach to handle an analysis of conflict and power. But the approach sees conflict largely in *cultural* terms, as a conflict of interests between competing groups in society. It views power largely at the *interpersonal* level.

Weber defined power as the "probability that one actor within a social relationship will be in a position to carry out his own will despite resistance" (Weber 1968: 53). While the liberal view of society sees conflict and power as integral components, consensus is also prominent. Consensus is rooted in a belief in the legitimacy of the system in which the competition occurs.

These views on conflict and power help to shed light on the liberal-pluralist approach to inequality in society. While the functionalists are inclined to view inequality as the product of "natural" differences between individuals—and hence an inevitable feature of modern societies—liberal pluralists hold to a different view. They see the existence of a structure of inequality—that certain positions in society have more rewards and privileges attached to them than others—as an inevitable feature of modern society. In part, this belief stems from the liberal pluralists" view of human nature. They believe that because we are, by nature, power-seeking beings, we will inevitably be predisposed to compete with one another. In Weber's terms, even if we were to somehow dispense with the class structure of modern society, individuals would continue to vie with one another for status. As such, competition is a more or less permanent feature of social life. But while such structured inequalities are inevitable, liberal pluralists assert that a just society is one in which the competition for power and privilege is fair. That is, it is a society in which people should have an equal opportunity to compete for unequal rewards.

In this regard, liberal pluralists are inclined to view the state as an *impartial umpire* whose job it is to channel and adjudicate social conflicts. Different individuals and groups will compete with one another to use the state to their advantage in the realization of their own interests. A primary role of the state, then, is to provide the rules of the game by which this competition is played out.

While Durkheim's theorizing was directed towards the question of the problem of order, the main focus or problematic of Weber's work was to understand the peculiar features of capitalism as it emerged in Western societies. In contrast to his Marxist contemporaries, Weber argued that the search for a single causal factor—like the economic variable—was futile. The emergence of Western capitalism was to be understood, according to Weber (1958), as the result of an "elective affinity" between particular ideas and material interests. In this respect, a key connecting thread manifested in different spheres of capitalist society was an increasing *rationality*—in economic conduct, in religious ideas, and in law.

Liberal pluralists see law as an autonomous sphere in society. Law can (but not necessarily) be influenced by economic factors, and it can also influence economic activity. In Weber's terms, the form of legal thought that predominated in capitalist societies was one that came closest to his ideal type of "formal rational law," whereby law-making was based on principles that are autonomous, general, and universal, decisions do not differ from case to case, and there is no reference to moral, social, or other factors. In what is similar to the view of the state as an arena in which political power is contested, modern liberal pluralists view the law as one more form or dimension of power. According to Austin Turk (1980: 18), for example, law "is a set of resources for which people contend and with which they are better able to promote their own ideas and interests against others.... To say that people seek to gain and use resources to secure their own ideas and interests is, of course, to say that they seek to have and exercise *power*."

In contrast to the consensus-oriented view of the functionalists, then, liberal pluralists posit law as a reflection of power differentials in society. Accordingly, crime is not an inherent property of individuals but a *status* conferred on the individual by those who make and enforce rules. According to labelling theorist Howard Becker (1963: 9), "Social groups create deviance by making rules whose infractions constitute deviance, and by applying those rules to particular people and labelling them as outsiders." For the liberal pluralist, then, crime and deviance are *social creations*. As a result the emphasis within liberal pluralism is shifted away from etiology or the causes of criminal behaviour (as in the functionalist approach) and towards the processes by which particular acts come to be defined as criminal.

Becker, for example, went on in his work to argue that the process of creating deviance occurs much earlier than the application of labels to particular individuals. It is rooted in the inclinations of *moral entrepreneurs*, individuals in positions of power and privilege who take it upon themselves to arouse public concern and opinion around the need for new rules. In launching such moral crusades, moral entrepreneurs typically see their mission as a holy one, aimed at changing the behaviour of those less powerful in society. For liberal pluralists like Becker, then, "who gets defined as criminal" is ultimately a *political question*; it has to do with the nature of power relations in society.

By attending to the concepts of power and conflict, a liberal-pluralist analysis of the law-society relation offers a number of advantages over the functionalist approach. For one, it directs attention towards the question of the origins of law. Becker (1963), for example, was led to an investigation of the factors surrounding the passage of the 1937 Marijuana Tax Act in the United States. Platt (1969) studied the origins of the juvenile court in Chicago. Chambliss's work on the origins of the vagrancy laws "demonstrated the importance of vested interest groups in the emergence and/or alteration of laws" (Chambliss 1964: 77).

Another advantage is that, by attending to the political nature of crime, liberal pluralists have been led to investigations of how those who enforce and administer the law (police and judges) exercise their discretionary power. For instance, Piliavin and Briar (1964) and Cicourel (1968) engaged in groundbreaking research that documented the role of extralegal factors such as class, race, grooming, demeanour, and perceptions of the "quality of parental control" in the imposition of delinquent labels.

Finally, by shifting the focus away from the criminal offender towards the question of the social creation of crime, liberal pluralism helps to mitigate the lower-class bias found in the traditional functionalist accounts. The work of Edwin Sutherland (1961), for example, was instrumental in directing criminologists' gaze "up" the class ladder to examine the actions of white-collar offenders.

Despite these advantages, the liberal-pluralist approach has a limited explanatory power, primarily because of how it treats power and conflict. It fails, first of all, to adequately clarify the sources of power. In Turk's formulation, for example, society consists of relations between authority (those in dominant social positions) and subject (those in relatively powerless social groups). Liberal pluralists deem "how authorities become authorities" to be irrelevant. According to Turk (1969: 51), "It is sufficient that a social structure built out of authority relations exists." Moreover, the pluralistic view of society adds to the ambiguity of the approach. For theorists like Becker, it is enough to assert that the powerful enforce their rules on the less powerful: the old make rules for the young, men make rules for women, Anglo-Saxons make rules for racial minorities, and so on (Becker 1963: 17). The approach never does closely examine the specific structure of inequality in society.

While liberal pluralists have generated research on the operation of the criminal justice system (the use of police discretion, sentencing practices, and the like), their tendency to remain at the level of interpersonal relations has led to a failure to consider how the workings of the various social-control agencies are influenced by the overall structure and operation of the state in modern societies. As well, without an explicit and well-developed understanding of the political process, liberal pluralists simply tend to identify agents of the state as politically powerful moral entrepreneurs. Becker's analysis of the Marijuana Tax Act, for example, puts the onus of the Act on the moral inclinations of Harry Anslinger and the Federal Bureau of Narcotics, which leads two critics to ask: "What are the consequences of blaming government officials for the passage of restrictive laws? The answer is that the American political process and economic structure remain unquestioned with the problem being isolated to a few bad people. In the tradition of liberal muckraking journalism, it is either Joe McCarthy, J. Edgar Hoover or Richard Nixon who is seen as the source of the problem, rather than the underlying political or economic system" (Galliher and Walker 1978: 31).

Finally, the reluctance of liberal pluralists to single out any one variable as determining or primary leads to an eclecticism in addressing questions about the relation between law and other structures in society (especially the economic sphere).

Given the liberal-pluralist view of the law-society relation, to what extent does it mesh with the Official Version of Law? On the one hand, the two frameworks show several lines of congruence. Both adhere to the liberal belief in the inherent rights and freedoms of individuals to compete for material benefits and to realize their own happiness. Both envision law as an autonomous sphere; internally consistent, predictable, and rational. In both cases, law's impartiality or fairness—its legitimacy—derives from adherence to the rules of the game by which competition and conflict are played out. For liberal pluralists in particular, the fairness of the system derives from no one group being excluded from the exercise of power (by virtue of the democratic franchise). It is up to individuals and groups to mobilize and put pressure on the state to realize their best interests.

On the other hand, fissures begin to appear in this congruence with the liberal pluralists' assertion that law itself is a source of power and, as such, will inevitably reflect the power differentials of the wider society. To this extent, liberal pluralists open the way for a critique of the rule of law doctrine. If laws originate from the moral inclinations of the more powerful in society, and if agents of law (police and judges) utilize their discretionary power in ways that might disadvantage those with whom they come into contact, then is justice really blind?

In short, by attending to issues of power in their analysis, liberal pluralists generate a scepticism around law's claims. Nevertheless, while it opens the way for an analysis of power, liberal pluralism does not go so far as to question the actual form or structure of law. Law—or what Weber referred to as "rational legal domination"—provides a main source of consensus in modern capitalist societies: the rules of the game by which competition is played out. Nevertheless, liberal pluralism makes no attempt to explain "why particular claims to legitimacy are accorded legitimate status by those subject to them" (Hunt 1976: 114). In other words, liberal pluralism simply asserts that consensus exists; it does not question the *basis* on which it rests. Where does consensus come from? Why does everyone agree with the rules? Similarly, although liberal pluralists begin to call blind justice into question, they frame the analysis at the interpersonal level (as a competition or conflict between individuals and groups) and do not extend that analysis to the structure or framework of the society. Injustices may occur because of individual corruption, poor use of police discretion, or bad decisions of individual judges—but the system itself is basically sound.

In response to the perceived shortcomings of the liberal-pluralist approach, sociologists intent on studying the law-society relationship were increasingly drawn towards a Marxist analysis. Until the 1970s much of the work on the law-society relationship had centred around the study of crime. The shift to a Marxist perspective led to a different orientation. Because Marxism is a theoretical approach that directs attention to the broader structural features of society, it became increasingly evident that a more complete understanding of the phenomenon of crime required an investigation of the wider social, political, and economic factors impinging upon it. Consequently, the focus was no longer on crime per se, but on situating law (both criminal and civil) within the context of the role of the state in a capitalist society. In their examination of the law-society relationship, therefore, Marxists raised the issue of the class character of law under capitalism.

The Marxist approach

The Marxist approach dates back to the mid-nineteenth century and the writings of Karl Marx and extends into the twentieth century with the work of the neo-Marxists (such as Antonio Gramsci) and the emergence of the new left in the late 1960s. In criminology the 1970s saw the development of a radical or critical criminology that, in its initial stages, consisted of a critique of liberal pluralism (labelling and group conflict theories)—mainly for not going far enough in their assessment of the functionalist approach (see, for example, Taylor, Walton, and Young 1973). While functionalism can be characterized by its acceptance of the Official Version of Law and liberal pluralism by its more sceptical stance, the Marxist approach is notable for its rejection of law's claims.

While functionalists view human nature as anti-social and liberal pluralists see individuals as inherently power-seeking beings, Marxists view humans as basically good. The problem they see, though, is that people have created structures that limit the realization of our true potential, especially our creative capacity. Marx saw human beings as *homo faber* or "man the creator." What distinguished humans from other animals was their *labour power*—the ability to use their intellect to create and transform the world around them. In the Marxist approach, then, human nature is not the problem; it is the society and its structure that require scrutiny.

The Marxist approach starts from an assumption opposite to that of functionalism: instead of stability and consensus, society is characterized by conflict, antagonism, and exploitation. Moreover, in contrast to the liberal-pluralist approach, conflict is rooted not in cultural factors like "interests" but in the very structure of society. Key to the Marxist conception of society is the idea that the economic variable is the "determinant in the last instance." Marxists argue that if we are to arrive at an adequate understanding of society, our starting point must be an analysis of the nature of the prevailing economic system. In the Marxist conception, society consists of an *economic base* or *infrastructure* out of which arises the *superstructure* or other institutions and social processes of society (such as the legal, political, familial, and religious spheres). For Marx, the relation between the base and superstructure is dialectical: the superstructure arises out of the economic base but, once created, acts back to reproduce it.

Karl Marx was writing in the mid-nineteenth century, during a time when Europe was experiencing the full effect of early capitalist industrialization. To put it bluntly, Marx didn't like what he saw around him. While capitalism was the first system historically in which overproduction was possible, it was also the most exploitative. Marx reasoned that figuring out how to change the capitalist system meant studying it scientifically. He compared his work to that of a physicist in a laboratory. By researching the operation of capitalism, he could uncover the means by which it could be transformed. As such, Marx's work has been described as offering both a theory of capitalism and a theory of social change. Unlike other political economists of his day, he located capitalism as one system in a long historical chain of societal forms. Historically locating capitalism in this way opened up the possibility that it, too, could one day be replaced by a different form of society.

The Communist Manifesto, co-authored by Marx with Friedrich Engels, declares, "The history of all past society has consisted in the development of class antagonisms, antagonisms that assumed different forms at different epochs" (Marx and Engels 1998: 18). To understand this statement, we need a better sense of the Marxist conception of society.

According to Marx, people begin to distinguish themselves from other animals as soon as they begin to interact with nature and produce their own means of subsistence. As this productive activity takes place, different *modes of production* will develop over time. The mode of production essentially refers to how goods are produced and distributed in a society, which depends in turn upon the resources available in the environment and the level of skills and knowledge acquired. The mode of production will determine both the *means of production* (the tools and instruments used in productive activity) and the *social relations of production* (how individuals relate to one another in the process of producing). In class societies, the social relations of production yield two main groups: a *dominant class*, which owns and controls the material prerequisites for production; and a *subordinate class,* which, given that it does not own and control the material prerequisites, can only gain access to them by means of the dominant class. Because the dominant class is in a position to appropriate the surplus products produced by the subordinate class, the relation between the two classes is one characterized by exploitation and conflict.

Using his historical materialist method, Marx posited that different modes of production have predominated in different epochs, each with a particular configuration of class relations. Under feudal societies, for example, production was organized around agriculture, with land, ploughs, livestock, and the like comprising the means of production. The social relations of production under feudalism consisted of two main classes: the lords or nobility, who owned the land; and the serfs or peasants, who were legally bonded to the lords. The exploitative nature of the relationship between these two classes was revealed when, come harvest time, the serfs had to hand over the tithe or a proportion of the goods they produced.

Capitalist society is characterized by a different set of conditions and relations. Under capitalism the mode of production is centred around the production and exchange of commodities (things that have an exchange value). The means of production consist of the factories, capital, and machines necessary to engage in productive activity. The capitalist class (or bourgeoisie) owns and controls the businesses, factories, land, and capital, while the working class (or proletariat) must gain a livelihood by working for wages. The relationship is exploitative because, while the labour power of the workers produces the products and, hence, the surplus or profits of the production process, the capitalist possesses rights of ownership and can appropriate the surplus value that is produced.

Given the position of dominance of one class over another in the economic sphere, the other spheres and processes in society will be organized to serve the interests of the dominant class. In other words, within the superstructure the kind of legal system, the form of family, the nature of education, and the like will operate in accordance with the interests of the dominant class. In a Marxist approach, because the economic variable is viewed as primary, it becomes impossible to study other segments of society—like law—in isolation from the economic. Rather, law must be understood in relation to the economic sphere. The Marxist approach also sees inequality, conflict, and power in *structural* terms, as class inequality, class conflict, and class domination. Accordingly, consensus is not a "natural" condition; it has to be continually manufactured or created.

Marx's own writings did not include a coherent theory of the state, so that became an explicit task of later Marxist theorists. Generally speaking, these writers started from the fundamental observation that the state in a capitalist society broadly serves the interests of the capitalist class, an observation usually placed in the context of a passage in *The Communist Manifesto:* "The executive of the modern state is but a committee for managing the common affairs of the whole bourgeoisie" (Marx and Engels 1998: 3). From this similar starting point came two different theories of the state: the *instrumentalist* and the *structuralist*. Within the sociology of law, theorists used instrumentalism and structuralism to address the class character of law under capitalism.

Instrumental Marxism
The first of the two approaches to gain prominence, instrumental Marxism, takes Marx and Engels's statement to mean that, apart from very exceptional circumstances, the state acts *at the behest* or command of the capitalist class. This interpretation is based on the idea that the processes of the superstructure are determined by the economic base. As such, institutions within the state are tools that can be manipulated by the capitalist class as a whole. In essence, instrumentalists posited a direct correspondence between class power (ownership of the means of production) and state power. The principal support for this view consisted of inferring the power of the capitalist class from the class composition of the personnel holding key positions within the state (Miliband 1969; Domhoff 1970).

Within the sociology of law, the instrumentalists would argue that law itself is a weapon of class rule. The focus was on the coercive nature of law, whereby they saw law and legal order as a direct expression of the economic interests of the ruling class—a means of protecting property and consolidating political power. Some writers even went so far as to claim that capitalist class members were immune from criminal sanction (Quinney 1975; Chambliss 1975).

By directing attention to the linkages between class power and state power, instrumental Marxists called attention to the actions and behaviours of ruling-class members. In particular, the legal definition of crime came under close scrutiny, especially in the extent to which the criminal law excluded a range of behaviours harmful and threatening to members of society. This led to an examination of crimes of the powerful, including price-fixing, production of faulty consumer products, environmental pollution, and government corruption (see, for example: Goff and Reasons 1978; Snider 1978; Pearce 1976).

Instrumentalism was not without its shortcomings. For one, viewing the state as an instrument or tool of the ruling class does not allow for systematic analysis of how actions and strategies of various ruling-class groups are limited by constraints inherent in the structure of society. For another, to say that law is a weapon of class rule implies not only that the ruling class is a united whole, but also that it is so powerful that it will be able to ensure that the state will always legislate in its favour. While laws that ostensibly run counter to the interests of capital (in particular, anti-combines legislation) are sometimes weak in their wording and enforcement, instrumental Marxism cannot adequately account for a variety of other forms of legislation (such as employment standards, human rights legislation, and workplace health and safety legislation) that seek to place limits on the capitalist class and hence are not in its immediate interests. Finally, instrumentalism displays an insensitivity to the conditions and processes that legitimate democratic capitalist societies. Why, for instance, does a system that, according to instrumentalists, is apparently so biased and coercive also appear to so many as fair and just? Is the belief in "equality of all before the law" false? Are legal rights empty or illusory?

There is a need, in other words, to reconcile the assertion of the class-based nature of law with the existence of democratic ideals and principles that the legal order claims to uphold. Because instrumentalists portray legal enactments as unilateral declarations of a united ruling class, they do not adequately address this seemingly paradoxical nature of law.

Structural Marxism

By the late 1970s, Marxist theorists were moving away from the conspiratorial formulation of the instrumentalist approach towards a more structuralist account of the role of the capitalist state. In rejecting the notion of the state as an instrument or tool of the ruling class, structural Marxists put forward the view that institutions within the state provide a means of reproducing class relations and class domination under capitalism. They interpreted Marx and Engels's formulation to mean that, rather than acting at the behest of capital, the state acts *on behalf of* capital (Panitch 1977: 3–4). The role of the state is that of organizer in the long-term interests of capital and mediator of the conflicting relationship between capital and labour.

Structural Marxists saw the state, in carrying out its role as organizer and mediator, as performing particular functions, which were broadly subsumed under the headings of *accumulation* and *legitimation*. Accumulation includes activities in which the state is involved, either actively or passively, in aiding the process of capital accumulation (or wealth generation). In short, the state must try to create and maintain the conditions under which profitable accumulation of capital is possible. Legitimation refers to state activities that are designed to create and maintain conditions of social harmony—that is, "It must try to win the loyalty of economically and socially oppressed classes and strata of the population to its programs and policies, it must attempt to legitimate the social order" (O'Connor 1973: 79). The relationship between accumulation and legitimation is dialectical: nearly every agency or institution within the state is (often simultaneously) involved in both activities.

To carry out its role, the state requires a certain degree of autonomy, not from the structural requirements of the economic sphere, but from the direct manipulation of its activities by the dominant class (or fractions of it). In this way, the state is able to transcend the parochial interests of particular capitalist class members and thus ensure the protection of the long-term interests of capital (Poulantzas 1975). The relative autonomy of the state can therefore account for the presence of laws that favour workers (for example, legal limitations on the length of the working day, minimum-wage laws, and workplace health and safety legislation) and those laws ostensibly designed to control the actions of capitalists (such as restrictions on environmental pollution or unfair trading practices).

The structural Marxist emphasis on the role of the state as organizer and mediator—framed in terms of the dialectical interplay between the economic base and political and legal superstructure—led to more sophisticated analyses of law-making than those offered by the instrumental Marxists. William Chambliss (1986), for one, suggested that law creation was a response on the part of the capitalist state to crises and contradictions that emanate from the productive sphere. In other words, the basic conflict between capital and labour creates, in different historical periods, particular conflicts and dilemmas to which the state has to respond. One response is to create legislation. According to Chambliss, however, the laws that are created are not designed to resolve the basic contradiction, but only the conflicts and dilemmas that emerge from it. Law is only a "symptom-solving mechanism." Far from resolving the basic problems in the system, it creates the conditions for the emergence of new conflicts and dilemmas later on down the road (see also Comack 1991; Smandych 1991).

Whereas instrumentalists concentrated on the coercive nature of law, structuralists extended the analysis to include an examination of the ideological nature of law and legal order. Law was a means of both coercive and ideological domination—a part of the terrain on which *hegemony* is accomplished. Hegemony is a term used by Antonio Gramsci (1971) to refer to the "universalization of capitalist class interests"—the process by which the domination of the capitalist class is continually being (re)produced. Gramsci noted that the exercise of hegemony depends not solely on force but on a combination of force and consent. In this sense, even law, as part of the coercive side of the state, must work through ideology.

As an ideological form, law acts as a legitimizer of capitalist social relations. One way this is accomplished, according to structural Marxists, is in the form that law takes in a capitalist society; that is, the shape and structure of law under capitalism provide the appearance of equality. This effect is achieved, in large part, through adherence to the rule of law doctrine. Structuralists are quick to point out that the rights and liberties embodied in the rule of law are limited. While the pivotal point in the rule of law is "equality of all before the law," the provision of formal equality in the legal sphere does not extend to the economic sphere. Thus the law maintains only the *appearance* of equality, because it never calls into question the unequal and exploitative relationship between capital and labour. A quote from French novelist Anatole France points to this peculiarity of the legal form: "The law in all its majestic impartiality forbids both rich and poor alike to sleep under bridges, to beg in the streets and to steal bread" (France quoted in Hunt 1976: 184).

In essence, then, structural Marxists suggest that the law legitimizes the dominance of one class over the other by appealing to the very democratic principles that are thought to guard against such a bias.

In many respects, the structuralist approach offered a more powerful analysis of the law-society relation than did instrumentalism. Instead of a monolithic ruling class, structuralism recognized the existence of "class fractions" within the dominant class. The state, as such, was not simply an instrument or tool, but an organizer. Because consent was not an automatic condition, but had to be continually constructed, structuralists focused attention on the processes by which hegemony was realized. The attention to the ideological role of law enabled the structuralists to better reconcile the class-based nature of law with the existence of democratic ideals and principles (like "equality" and "justice") that the legal order claims to uphold.

Yet structural Marxism also had its limitations. For one, while instrumentalism was criticized for its overemphasis on capitalist class input into and control over the state, it could be argued that the structuralist account went too far in the other direction: it is the constraints and limitations of the structure—not human agency—that determine the direction of society. In a similar vein, the concept of relative autonomy has been criticized, in that the theory does not convincingly explain the specific factors that determine the state's degree of autonomy from economic relations. How is it, for example, that the law, as a relatively autonomous entity, succeeds in continually reinforcing and maintaining the capital-labour relation in a way that is functional for capital? As it stands, the focus on the accumulation and legitimation functions of the state leads to a kind of circular reasoning: any concessions made to workers are indicative of the legitimation function, while gains made by capital are attributed to the state's concern with maintaining capital accumulation.

The Marxist approach, then, is intensely critical of the law's claims to impartiality, fairness, and objectivity. From the Marxist perspective, the Official Version of Law is a form of *ideology*: a particular value-laden position that has the effect of legitimating a system of unequal social relations. Marxists also call into question the autonomy of law. While law may demonstrate its own internal cohesion, it is not separate or divorced from the economic sphere; that is, it is only *relatively* autonomous. Indeed, rather than being a value-free or objective enterprise, law is inherently political. For instance, Marxists note that the legal subject of law is actually a classed subject, in that law's underlying aim is to reinforce and maintain property relations. Alan Hunt (1976) makes the point that law does not distinguish between two kinds of property: "property for use" and "property for power." All individuals may have an interest in securing their own belongings (property for use), and so will consent to the law or see it as legitimate. At the same time, law also secures the rights of owners to use their property for power to appropriate the surplus from the production process. In essence, the law "treats the capital of the employer and the personal belongings of the worker as if they were the same thing" (Hunt 1976: 184).

The Marxist critique of the Official Version of Law stimulated debates over the potential for law as an agent of social transformation. While some Marxists went so far as to claim that the rule of law is a sham, others—like E.P. Thompson (1975)—suggested that for law to live up to its appearance as fair and just, it must at times truly dispense justice. In Thompson's view, insisting that law lives up to its ideal opens up the potential for change. Highlighting the contradictions and inconsistencies—the inherent tensions—built into the Official Version of Law offers the possibility of developing a "jurisprudence of insurgency" to undermine the social relations of capitalism (Brickey and Comack 1987).

During the 1980s, Marxist theorizing on law continued to be altered and reformulated (see, for example, Mandel 1986; Ratner and McMullan 1987; Glasbeek 1989; Snider 1989). Yet what was noteworthy about much of this work was that it framed the fundamental question or problematic in terms of class relations. By rooting inequality in the economic sphere, and by defining power in terms of relations between dominant and subordinate classes, the Marxist formulation went beyond the functionalist and liberal-pluralist accounts in clarifying the *systemic* nature of inequality and how it is reproduced at the superstructural level. In doing so, it effectively made other dimensions of inequality—specifically, gender and race—into contingent variables. This feature was not lost on many of the Marxist analysts, and as the 1980s drew to a close an increasing consensus grew among those working within this tradition that their fundamental problematic was in need of revision. The primary stimulus for the rethinking of the Marxist approach came from the challenge of the feminist movement.

THE FEMINIST FRAMEWORKS

Albeit to differing degrees, all of the traditional approaches that incorporated or responded to the Official Version of Law in their understandings of the law-society relation have come under criticism for their failure to speak adequately to the experiences of women. This has been true both in terms of women's positioning within the wider society as well as in their relation to law. In the last two decades feminism has made considerable inroads in challenging us to reconsider the traditional approaches to understanding the law-society relation as well as the claims that law itself makes in its Official Version.

Feminism can be broadly understood as both a body of knowledge and a political movement aimed at understanding and alleviating the inequality experienced by women in society. This body of knowledge includes a diversity of perspectives or frameworks. Each one interprets women's inequality in a particular way, and some of the frameworks have direct links to the functionalist, liberal pluralist, and Marxist approaches.

Conservatism

Conservatism is an approach that is concerned, quite literally, with "conserving" traditional gender relations in society. To this extent, conservatism does not offer a feminist analysis per se. While the approach acknowledges women's unequal position relative to men, it does not see that condition as a problem in need of remedy. Instead, the conservative approach understands women's inequality in society as both "natural" and "functional." It is natural in the sense that women and men are seen as having essential differences from each other, and these differences are rooted in biology. For example, men are "by nature" more assertive, outgoing, rational, aggressive, competitive, and logical. Women are "by nature" more passive, dependent, emotional, nurturing, caring, and sensitive. These differing traits provide the basis for a sexual division of labour in society; that is, the traditional division of labour between the public and private spheres, whereby women remain in the home and fulfill their supposed biological destiny as mothers and helpmates to their male partners, and men go out into the public sphere to perform the role of the breadwinner or economic provider for their families. Conservatives view the traditional division of labour as appropriate, not only because it reflects these natural differences, but also because it is functional for society as a whole. As such, gender inequality is taken as a given. Women are viewed as the weaker sex. They require the protection and guidance of men. That men may have more access to power and resources makes sense, in the conservative view, given the assumption of inherent biological differences between the sexes and the privileging of those traits associated with the male.

There is obviously an easy fit between this conception of gender roles and the functionalist approach. Organizing society along gendered lines is in the best interests of society as a whole. It follows from this view that any attempts to reorganize the sexual division of labour would only lead to anomie or disharmony. As such, conservatives—and their functionalist counterparts—tend to be anti-feminist. If anything, they cast the goal of the modern feminist movement to realize equality for women as threatening and disruptive to the natural order of society. As well, they make no attempt to question the Official Version of Law in terms of, for example, whether law may similarly privilege men over women.

Liberal feminism
Unlike conservatives, liberal feminists do not assume that men and women are different by nature. Instead, they see the sources of the difference as being not rooted in biology (sex) but as cultural (gender). Liberal feminists acknowledge that women are unequal in society, that women do not have the same access to power and resources as men. They attribute

the source of this inequality to two variables. One variable is *culture,* or the existence of gender roles that specify appropriate male and female aspirations and behaviours. They see the traditional gender roles as restricting women by keeping them in the home and out of the public sphere. The other variable is *socialization.* Males and females have been taught to conform to gender roles and to adopt identities based on culturally prescribed notions of masculinity and femininity. Liberal feminists are therefore concerned with realizing equality of opportunity for women. They believe that restrictive gender roles need to be redefined and women need to be "let in" to the corridors of public power and given their "equal share of the pie."

Liberal feminists share similarities with the liberal-pluralist approach, especially in their view of the state as an impartial umpire. They consider women to be an interest group intent on having their interests heard and realized. It follows that if they can put enough pressure on the state, those in charge will in turn make appropriate changes or reforms to provide women with equal opportunities relative to men. One of the areas in which liberal feminists have concentrated their energies is law. Like the liberal pluralists, they are sceptical of the claims made under the Official Version of Law, particularly in terms of legal equality. During the 1970s, when liberal feminism was especially prominent, it became evident that women were not, in fact, equal before the law. Several cases heard by the Supreme Court of Canada substantiated this belief.

The cases of *Lavell* and *Bedard,* both heard in 1973, involved a challenge to section 12(1)(b) of the Indian Act. Under this section, an Aboriginal woman who married a non-Aboriginal man ceased to be an "Indian" in legal terms, and both she and her children lost all claims associated with that status (for example, residence on a reserve, ownership of reserve property, participation in Band affairs). In contrast, an Aboriginal man who married a non-Aboriginal woman not only retained his legal status, but also conferred it on his wife and children. In 1973 the Supreme Court, in hearing the charge that section 12(1)(b) constituted sex discrimination and thus violated the Canadian Bill of Rights, denied discrimination in both cases. The Court stated, "No inequality of treatment between Indian men and women flows as a necessary result of the application [as opposed to the substantive content] of 12 (1)(b) of the Indian Act." The section was not abrogated until 1985.

In the same year as the *Lavell* and *Bedard* cases, the Supreme Court heard the case of *Murdoch* v. *Murdoch.* Iris Murdoch was the wife of an

Alberta rancher. Over the course of their twenty-five-year marriage she had worked with her husband on ranches for five years until they built up enough money to purchase their own ranching operation. After that her husband would regularly take a job for five months of the year, during which time she would run the ranch. The additional monies went into more land purchases, all in his name. In addition to the housework, cooking, and child care, Iris Murdoch "hayed, raked, swathed, mowed, drove trucks and tractors, and dehorned, vaccinated and branded cattle" (*Murdoch* v. *Murdoch* 1975: 443). After the breakdown of their marriage, she sought her share of the ranch assets. All of the Canadian courts that dealt with the case, including the Supreme Court of Canada (with the exception of Laskin J), held that Iris Murdoch was only a "normal ranch wife" and thus entitled to nothing. The main effect of this decision was to create an enormous public outcry from women's groups across the country. Within five years most provinces had changed their matrimonial property laws to allow for a more equitable division of marital assets.

Finally, the *Bliss* case, heard in 1978, involved sex discrimination in the Unemployment Insurance Act. Stella Bliss had been fired by her employer because she was pregnant. Shortly after the birth of her child, Bliss applied for unemployment insurance benefits. She was ready and able to work, but had not found suitable employment. Given the length of time she had worked before being fired, she would have qualified for regular unemployment benefits. However, the Unemployment Insurance Commission denied her claim, stating that Bliss was only eligible for pregnancy benefits—and the qualifying period was longer than that required for the regular benefits. After several appeals the case reached the Supreme Court, which ruled against Bliss. The Court held that Bliss was refused benefits not because she was a woman, but because she had been pregnant. As such, the discrimination arose not because of law, but because of nature.

The Supreme Court's apparent inability to recognize sex discrimination in law, along with the growing recognition of gender bias in other areas (such as the immunity of husbands under the rape law and the failure to consider wife abuse as a criminal matter) motivated liberal feminists to lobby for changes that would afford women formal equality before the law. In this regard, the passage of the Constitution Act of 1982 and the enactment of section 15 of the *Charter of Rights and Freedoms* in 1985 were seen as key victories for liberal feminists.

While the strategies advocated by liberal feminists went a long way towards challenging the inequalities that women confronted—particularly as those inequities are reflected in law—the approach is not without its limitations. For one, liberal feminism offers little in the way of an analysis of the structure of women's oppression in society. The approach views gender inequality more or less as a historical accident that can be rectified by the implementation of appropriate policies and strategies (such as affirmative action). For another, in centring on the need to let women into the public sphere, liberal feminists tend to accept the rules of the game as they are constituted—rules that are, by and large, male-defined and male-centred. To be successful in the system, for example, means that women must be more competitive, more aggressive, more individualistic—in short, more male. In effect the aim is to give women a greater share of the pie, without calling into question the nature of the pie itself. Liberal feminism can also be criticized for its middle-class bias. It amounts to a kind of career feminism that fails to speak adequately to and incorporate the experiences of working-class women and women of colour who have historically played a role in the public sphere by working in low-paying jobs (hooks 1981; Silvera 1989). For most of these women, aspiring to a career in law, medicine, or politics is simply not a part of their lived reality. As well, by centring attention on women's access to the public sphere, liberal feminism has a tendency to continue the practice of devaluing work done by women in the home. Such criticisms raise the question of whether the liberal-feminist goal of realizing formal equality before the law will take us very far, especially given the substantive inequality prevailing in the wider society.

Radical feminism
Radical feminism emerged in the 1970s largely as a critique of the liberal-feminist approach. The radical-feminist starting point was not one of letting women into the public sphere, but, rather, emerged out of a different concern. As the feminist movement gained momentum through the 1970s, more and more women came together to talk about their experiences. In the process, one of the silences broken down was around the issue of violence against women. Rape crisis centres and shelters for battered women were opened and almost immediately flooded with calls for help. The radical-feminist analysis of women's subordination, then, was very much fuelled by this discovery of the violence that women encounter at the hands of men (which, in part, helps to account for some

of the anger reflected in their work).

Radical feminism is premised on a particular image of men's and women's natures. Like the conservative approach, it assumes that men and women have innate or essential differences, and that these differences are rooted in biology. Men are by nature assertive, aggressive, and competitive. Women are by nature nurturing, caring, and sensitive. But radical feminists do a flip of the conservative approach. Whereas conservatives tend to value traits associated with the male (because these characteristics make for success in the public sphere), radical feminists are more women-centred and value traits associated with being female.

The radical-feminist conception of women's subordination in society goes deeper than the liberal-feminist view. Whereas liberal feminists talk about women's inequality, radical feminists are more inclined to talk about women's oppression. While liberal feminists aim for equality of opportunity of women, radical feminists call the structure of inequality into account. In particular, they single out *patriarchy*—the historical structuring of society by men and for men—as the main source of women's oppression. They understand patriarchy as a system of male domination that has kept women down, both literally and figuratively. Radical feminists argue that patriarchy transcends specific economic systems. As such, they locate capitalism as but one manifestation of male dominance; they cast its economic, social, religious, and political institutions as male-defined and male-centred.

While other feminist frameworks take their lead from various theoretical traditions, radical feminism claims to have no prior theoretical referent. As Catharine MacKinnon (1982) describes it, radical feminism is "feminism unmodified." According to MacKinnon, because men have historically held the power in society, they have been able to create the world in their own image. Society is male-centred; the male perspective is systemic or hegemonic. Patriarchy has so intruded into all aspects of women's lives that women must somehow break free. One of the methods that MacKinnon advocates is consciousness-raising: for women to get in touch with their true selves and with each other. Women thus need to become more women-centred, as opposed to the male-centred understandings that society engenders in us as we learn to see ourselves through the male gaze.

Not surprisingly, radical feminists such as MacKinnon argue that the state and law are inherently male. In terms of the Official Version of Law, what passes for objectivity, neutrality, and justice is really a male-centred or masculinist way of adjudicating. MacKinnon (1983: 644) states, for instance, "The law sees and treats women the way men see and treat women." Radical feminists have used this approach to understand law's treatment of rape cases (see, for example, Clarke and Lewis 1977; MacKinnon 1983). They also note how law is premised on the idea of the "reasonable man"—that is, the legal subject of law is a male. Women are "Other" in law's eyes.

Because radical feminism is an approach that is more structural in its orientation, the strategies it proposes for alleviating women's oppression are more fundamental in nature. Unlike the liberal-feminist approach, which calls for reform or more administrative changes in society, radical feminists advocate transformation or major structural change. One of the benefits of radical feminism is that it allows for an analysis of patriarchy, but in giving priority to male power as a focus of both theoretical analysis and strategies for change it encounters a number of difficulties. The approach has a tendency to promote an essentialist view of the differences between men and women; that is, men and women are by their very natures different species. Such an assertion comes close to the biology-is-destiny claims of the conservative approach. As well, by giving priority to patriarchy as the key source of oppression in society, radical feminists run the risk of excluding working-class women and women of colour from their purview. For those women, the ability simply to opt out of patriarchy (as writers like Sonia Johnson have advocated) is clearly limited. Moreover, such an assertion would imply that, in a women-centred world, inequalities of race and class would somehow disappear. Finally, since it is an approach that is so definitely women-centred, radical feminism effectively precludes men, especially the possibility of "feminist men" (a term that for most radical feminists is an oxymoron).

Socialist feminism
Socialist feminism is an approach that emerged in direct response to the problems encountered within traditional Marxism. While Marxism is attuned to the dynamics of capitalism and the historically specific social formations in which class relations emerge and persist, critics have nonetheless noted its inadequacies around the question of gender (Hartmann 1981). In response, Marxist feminist writers recast the Marxist framework to attend to the intersection between women's experience as workers and their position in the family, while still retaining the focus on class oppression under a capitalist mode of production. Socialist femi-

nists, however (partly under the influence of the radical-feminist approach), have engaged in a revision and reformulation of traditional Marxism to incorporate the interconnection between capitalism (class) and patriarchy (gender). Instead of giving theoretical priority to capitalism as a system of production, socialist feminists such as Zillah Eisenstein (1979) devised a dual-systems model that situates production and reproduction as two interrelated spheres at the foundation of society.

Traditional Marxist thought places its emphasis on the sphere of production, where the labour power of the worker is transformed to produce the surplus value or profit for the capitalist. Socialist feminists argue that an equally important labour process takes place in the sphere of reproduction. They see this reproductive or domestic labour as a necessary complement of the wage-labour/capital relation and argue that it involves four interrelated tasks: looking after adult members of the household (reproducing labour power on a daily basis); childbirth and childrearing; housework (cooking, cleaning, washing clothes); and the transformation of wages into goods and services for the household (making ends meet by shopping, sewing clothes, or growing and preserving food) (Luxton 1980: 18–19).

While all societies include reproductive labour, capitalism separates out the productive and reproductive spheres into public and private realms. In the process housework has become synonymous with women's work. Moreover, while productive labour (working for wages) generally takes place outside of the home, reproductive (or domestic) labour—previously integrated with the other labour of the household—has become devalued. Society considers it to be unproductive labour, because it does not directly contribute to the surplus value or profit of capital.

By focusing on the interrelationship between the productive and reproductive spheres, socialist feminism accounts for the specific nature of women's oppression in a patriarchal capitalist society. Its attention to class leads to analyses of women's work in both the productive and reproductive spheres. For example, although women have been entering the labour force in large numbers in recent decades, they have, by and large, been restricted to the lowest paid, most monotonous and least-secure jobs. In addition, because domestic labour continues to be relegated to women, those who work for wages carry the burden of a double day's work (Armstrong and Armstrong 1990).

Attention to gender leads to analyses of how men exercise control over women and women's sexuality. They do this both overtly and covertly: overtly through, for example, the medicalization of childbirth, the objectification of women's bodies in pornography, and violence against women (especially rape and wife abuse); covertly through monogamous heterosexuality, which has historically legitimated male control over children and property and reinforced the ideology that women are dependent on men for both their economic and sexual needs. Moreover, masculine dominance is maintained not only by the family and economic system, but also by the state, media, religious, and educational systems. Socialist feminists maintain that, like the class relations under capitalism, gender relations under patriarchy have both material and ideological dimensions.

One of the advantages of the socialist-feminist approach is that it allows for an understanding of how women confront a double oppression in patriarchal capitalist societies. To this extent, socialist feminism has the potential to move the analysis beyond the radical-feminist framework. "Career women" may experience systemic discrimination because of their gender, but they are also privileged by their class position. In addition, while socialist feminists acknowledge the need for women to become "women-identified" (much like Marx argued the need for the working class to become a "class-for-itself"), they do not preclude the possibility of working with men on a principled basis. Men as a group need to recognize that, while privileged by a patriarchal system, they too confront limitations. Conceptions of masculinity, for example, that subscribe to images of competition, aggression, and machismo invariably distort men's true potential and their ability to communicate with each other and with women (see, for example, Stoltenberg 1989). As well, unlike liberal feminism, the socialist-feminist approach does not continue to devalue the work that women do in the home. Rather, it locates this devaluation in the context of the capitalist distinction between productive and unproductive labour. In this respect, socialist feminism is better able to speak to the experiences of women in the private sphere.

Socialist feminism has also produced a different understanding of the role of the state and law under patriarchal capitalism. In an effort to move beyond the determinism found in some of the early structural Marxist formulations, socialist feminists such as Laureen Snider have promoted a conception of the state as a site of power—and of struggle and resistance. In this sense, the state is a *contested terrain* on which different groups and classes attempt to work through and towards their own interests and goals. In contrast to liberal-pluralist accounts, however, the state is not a level playing field. As Snider (1994: 80) notes: "Its shape (or tilt, to continue the geographic metaphor) reflects earlier struggles, and each new struggle is interpreted and resolved in light of the resolutions or compromises which preceded it.... The interests of non-dominant groups are reflected but not represented; the state attempts to contain counter-hegemonic views by organizing and privileging dominant ones at the expense of non-dominant."

Added to this, writers such as Jane Ursel (1992) have documented the specific role of the state and law in (re)producing patriarchal relations under capitalism. While patriarchy predates capitalism, capitalist systems, when they did emerge, incorporated and transformed the nature of patriarchal relations between men and women to suit the requisites of a productive system based on the exploitation of waged labour. According to Ursel, precapitalist society was characterized by familial patriarchy, based on the male as the head of the household. In a capitalist society, with the separation of home from work the male loses some of his power over to the capitalist. Yet in the same way that capitalism requires the state to organize and mediate productive relations, it also requires the state to organize and mediate reproductive relations. As capitalism develops, therefore, the state takes on the role of the patriarch—what Ursel refers to as *social patriarchy*—and passes laws and policies (for example, in the areas of marriage, child custody, reproduction, labour, and property inheritance) that maintain and reinforce the unequal relations between men and women. To this extent, like their Marxist counterparts socialist feminists focus on the class character of law, but add to this its gendered character. In this respect the Official Version of Law is one premised on a legal subject who is a propertied male.

Still, although socialist feminism has gone a long way towards addressing some of the inadequacies of other approaches, it is not without its own shortcomings. While it locates class and gender within the spheres of production and reproduction, it does not clearly include within its problematic other forms of inequality and difference, such as race. As well, because much of its analysis has remained at a fairly abstract or general level (in terms of investigating, for example, the role of the state in (re)producing patriarchal capitalism), socialist feminism has been open to charges that it promotes an overly structuralist account of social life—that as an approach it makes little room for individual agency. The view of the state as a contested terrain does open the way for analyses of forms of resistance that may be adopted by subordinated people, but it also privileges the state (and institutions within it, like law) as a site of struggle, to the neglect of other forms of resistance that people could adopt in their daily lives.

NEW CHALLENGES FOR THE SOCIOLOGY OF LAW

Theorizing on the law-society relation in sociology, then, has had a long and varied history dating back to the nineteenth century. In their efforts to locate law, different theorists have organized their work in relation to specific questions or problematics. For a functionalist such as Durkheim, the key was the problem of order. For Weber it was the desire to explain the unique features of Western capitalist societies. For Marxist writers, it was the class character of law. For feminists, it was the need to attend to the issue of women's inequality and oppression. In the process each of the approaches can be situated in terms of its acceptance (or rejection) of the Official Version of Law.

Because theorizing is not a static enterprise, different approaches predominated in the sociology of law at different times in history. As well, in varying degrees, each theory has undergone revision and refor-mulation in response to critiques from detractors, a theorist's own self-reflection, and events and changes occurring in the wider society. As such, the process of theorizing the law-society relation is ongoing. In-deed, the 1990s witnessed new challenges to how we think about and theorize the law-society relation. Among these are two important devel-opments: the need to (re)consider how race is situated within our theo-rizing; and the challenge posed by postmodern writers and their particu-lar way of approaching the Official Version of Law.

Racialized groups and the law

In recent years a number of events have raised awareness of the issue of racism as it applies to law and legal practice. In January 1990 a provin-cial inquiry into the Donald Marshall case in Nova Scotia completely exonerated Marshall, a member of the Mi'kmaq Nation, for any crimi-nal liability in the killing of Sandy Seale, a black Nova Scotian. Marshall had spent eleven years in prison for an offence he did not commit. The inquiry determined that racist attitudes were to blame for Marshall's wrongful conviction and that almost every stage in the criminal justice system (CJS) had failed Marshall—from the police to his defence coun-sel, the Crown prosecutor, the trial judge, and the Appeal Court justices (see Mannette 1992). The Marshall case raised serious questions about the rule of law as it applies to Aboriginal peoples. In a similar fashion, the release of the Aboriginal Justice Inquiry (AJI) report in Manitoba in 1991 provided evidence that racism is an inherent feature of our legal system.

The AJI report (Hamilton and Sinclair 1991) originated in response to two cases, one of which was the killing of Helen Betty Osborne in The Pas, Manitoba, in 1971 by a group of white boys who were out looking for a "squaw" one night. Osborne's body was found in the bush. She had been raped and stabbed fifty-six times with a screw driver. The justice system did not deal with the Osborne case until 1986, even though one of the boys involved had been bragging about the incident at a party in 1972. The other case was the shooting of J.J. Harper in March 1988 by a Winnipeg police officer. Within thirty-six hours after the shooting the Winnipeg chief of police exonerated the officer and later on an inquest accepted the officer's account of the events, even though at the time of the incident the police were looking for a twenty-two-year-old (Harper was thirty-six) who would most likely have been running, not walking, down the street (as Harper was). Although the police already had a suspect in custody, the officer decided to stop Harper anyway. The AJI heard testimony from Aboriginal people throughout the province about their experiences with the justice system. Like the Marshall inquiry, the AJI report stands as an indictment of the rule of law in Aboriginal affairs.

More recently the province of Ontario commissioned an inquiry into systemic racism in the Ontario criminal justice system. This was, in large part, in response to concerns among members of the black community about police-community relations. Between 1978 and 1997 police shot and killed at least thirteen black people in Ontario, and police bullets injured and, in some cases, paralyzed another six (James 1998: 158). The Commission found that Blacks stand a disproportionate chance of being charged and imprisoned in Ontario compared with Whites; and that this overrepresentation has skyrocketed within a period of six years, with 204 percent more Blacks jailed in 1994 than in 1986 (from 4,205 to 12,765 admissions), compared with an increase of 23 percent for Whites (from 49,555 to 60,929 admissions) (*Globe and Mail* January 16, 1996). Based on surveys of the general population, the Commission found a widespread perception among black, Chinese, and white Torontonians that judges do not treat people equally and that judges discriminate on the basis of race. Beliefs that judges discriminate on the basis of race were strongest among black respondents. As a participant at one of the public forums stated, "We have two systems of justice within the criminal justice system. One is for the majority group in our society—people who have money, connections, etc.—and the other is for the racial minorities" (Commission on Systemic Racism in the Ontario Criminal Justice System 1998: 200). Surveys of judges and lawyers, however, found strong resistance to any suggestion of racial discrimination in Ontario's criminal courts. It would appear that, while members of racial minorities call the Official Version of Law into question, members of the legal profession are not so inclined.

By documenting the experiences of Aboriginal people and people of colour in their encounters with the CJS, such inquiries not only raise questions about law's claims to be impartial, neutral, and objective, but also lead us to query whether the experiences and the standpoints of racialized groups have been adequately incorporated into our theorizing on the law-society relation. Each of the pre-eminent theories, for instance, reflects a particular understanding of "difference" when it comes to race. For instance, "race" itself is a term commonly used to refer to the colour of a person's skin: that is, the physical and biological features of particular groups of people. From this definition comes the view of race as a *biological* category or an ascribed characteristic on which difference is based. Starting from this point, some writers have gone on to suggest that the biological features that determine a person's race also determine mental and emotional capacities. This sets the stage for arguing the existence of racial hierarchies—with particular racial groups located at various points within the hierarchy based on their supposedly innate features and capacities.

Another view suggests that race connotes differing cultural characteristics between groups. As a term similar to ethnicity, race is understood as being based on certain socially selected cultural traits (language, or religious practices, for instance) and on people's sense of belonging to different racial or ethnic groups on the basis of these traits. From this perspective, difference is based on *culture*. More often than not, this difference is measured against the standard of the culture dominant in a society. Racial inequality, then, is understood in terms of the degree to which groups differ from the dominant social order. For instance, some racial groups are deemed to be less integrated into society, and their differing cultural traits are used to explain this lack of fit. This approach recognizes the need to alter people's beliefs or tolerance of difference (to counter individual prejudice and discrimination), but the main assumption is that the dominant social order is basically okay and that the problem is a lack of integration of particular racial groups. With the dominant culture taken as the norm, the solution proposed is typically one of assimilation of the so-called "out groups."

Yet another view sees race not as a biological or cultural construct but as a *social practice*. The focus here is on the social processes that help to define and maintain difference between groups on racial grounds. Race is thus understood in relational terms, not as a purely descriptive category. It has to do with the distribution of power in society. As such, the focus is on the institutional framework within which groups come to be defined as different and on the social interactions that emerge from that process. Racial inequality is thus located in the structural nature of the society in which racism operates. Those using this approach are more inclined to pose the question of "who benefits from racism?" They shift the focus from examining a particular racial group per se to exploring the institutional and social practices that construct and maintain these racial categories. This approach focuses attention not only on how individuals practise prejudice and discrimination, but also on the issue of systemic discrimination (practices supported by institutional power).

Each of these approaches can be connected to the mainstream theoretical approaches in the sociology of law: functionalism, liberal pluralism, and Marxism. Functionalists, for example, have typically approached the issue of Aboriginal peoples and the CJS by focusing not on the legal system but on Native people as a (relatively homogeneous) group. They would begin by noting the fact that Native peoples are disproportionately represented in Canadian crime statistics. According to the AJI report (Hamilton and Sinclair 1991: 87), while the national crime rate is 92.7 per 1,000, the rate for Indian bands is 165.6 per 1,000 (1.8 times the national rate). The rate nationally for violent crime is 9 per 1,000, while for Indian bands it is 33.1 per 1,000 (3.67 times the national rate). Functionalists would address these figures by asking, "What is wrong with Natives as a group?" Their task becomes one of developing explanations for this apparent deviance from the mainstream society.

Functionalist explanations have primarily been informed by the biological approach to race, with some recognition of race as a cultural category. Centring on the use of alcohol in Native communities, some writers have gone so far as to suggest that Native people—as a "race"—have a predisposition to alcoholism. Others have defined Native people as a deviant subculture, with the implication being that, in order to reduce the crime rate, Native people need to be reformed and assimilated into the mainstream culture. At bottom, the functionalist approach offers a restricted—and *racist*—interpretation of Aboriginal peoples' experiences with the CJS. By defining the issue as a problem "of" Native peoples, the law and the wider society remain unquestioned and unexamined.

Liberal pluralists are more inclined to approach the issue of Aboriginal peoples' experiences with the CJS in cultural and individualistic terms. Relying on the construction of race as a cultural category (and following labelling theory), liberal pluralists would begin to question the role of negative stereotypes and prejudice in the definition of Native peoples as more suspect by law enforcement agents. As an out group, Native people have been denied access to opportunities that would allow them full participation in Canadian society. Changing prejudicial attitudes of law enforcement officers through education and training, increasing Native representation on police forces and in the court system, and implementing more culturally sensitive practices (such as language interpreters) could resolve much of the problem "with" Native peoples. While liberal pluralism begins to recognize how racism is manifested at the individual or interpersonal level, it devotes little attention to its systemic forms. The system itself is basically sound. Problems such as Native peoples' overrepresentation in the CJS can be overcome through legislative and administrative changes and by increasing the equality of opportunity of Aboriginal peoples in society.

The Marxist approach takes a different tack, interpreting race as a social practice. Following the premises of Marx's theory, the focus is on the class position of Aboriginal peoples: their relationship to the means of production and their corresponding economic marginalization. By connecting race with class, Marxist analysts see the main issue as one of poverty. They understand Native crime rates and the high incidence of alcoholism and violence in Native communities not as a problem of or with Native peoples but as a reflection of the impoverished economic and social conditions of those living on reserves and in urban centres. Moreover, Marxists call attention to the history of racial oppression of Aboriginal peoples, including the processes of colonization, the role of the Canadian state in maintaining their position of economic dependency, and the benefits that the non-Native society has reaped from this exploitation. While the Marxist approach goes deeper in its analysis of Aboriginal peoples' encounters with the CJS (for example, by calling attention to the question of "who benefits?" and the systemic nature of racism and racist practices), it continues to interpret the issues largely in class terms. This raises the question of whether, by giving priority to class, the Marxist approach is able to fully accommodate and appreciate the experiences and standpoints of Aboriginal peoples—who may well not see their life experiences in only class-related terms.

For example, Patricia Monture-Okanee and Mary Ellen Turpel (1992) make the point that the Canadian criminal justice system is completely alien to Aboriginal peoples. The system is constructed with concepts that are not culturally relevant to an Aboriginal person or Aboriginal communities. Most Aboriginal languages, for example, have no word for "guilt." Given the tradition of an oral system of law, the notion of a written code of law is foreign to Aboriginal cultures. As well, the "impartiality" of judges under Canadian law runs counter to the Aboriginal conception of justice. Those persons with authority to resolve conflicts between Aboriginal people must be someone known to them, someone who can look at all aspects of a problem, not an unknown person set apart from the community in an impartial way. In response to the question, "How does an Aboriginal person experience the current justice system?" Monture-Okanee and Turpel (1992: 249–50) respond, "The overall perspective of an Aboriginal person towards Canadian legal institutions is one of being surrounded by injustice without knowing where justice lies, without knowing whether justice is possible." That response suggests that the Aboriginal and legalistic conceptions of justice have fundamental differences and will require not only a significant rethinking of what we have come to accept or assume as justice, but also an openness to listening to Aboriginal standpoints on this issue.

Functionalism, liberal pluralism, and Marxism offer, then, different and variable interpretations of race and racism as applied, for example, to Aboriginal peoples' encounters with the law. None of these approaches is entirely sufficient in theorizing the connections between racialized groups and the law. By defining Native peoples as a deviant group, functionalism amounts to a *defence* of racist policies and practices. Given its failure to locate the issue of racism in broader structural terms, liberal pluralism excludes consideration of many of the systemic processes that operate to (re)produce racism. Because it defines the issue primarily in class terms, Marxism can only take us so far in exploring the historical and contemporary processes and practices that have produced racial hierarchies and racialized understandings.

But what of the feminist frameworks? In the same way that mainstream theorists have been criticized for their inability to attend adequately to the question of race, feminists have been criticized for their inattention to difference and diversity, both within their theoretical frameworks and within political practice. Much of the impetus for this recognition came from the critiques offered by women of colour and First Nations women, whose experiences were not being adequately reflected in much of the feminist work.

Hazel Carby (1997), for instance, in an article aptly titled "White Woman Listen!" noted the troublesome nature of feminist theoretical concepts such as the family, patriarchy, and reproduction when applied to the lives of women of colour. While many feminist theorists have positioned the family as a key source of women's oppression, Carby (1997: 112) suggests that "during slavery, periods of colonialism, and under the present authoritarian state, the black family has been a site of political and cultural resistance to racism." Similarly, she points out: "Historically specific forms of racism force us to modify or alter the application of the term 'patriarchy' to black men. Black women have been dominated 'patriarchally' in different ways by men of different 'colours'" (115). In terms of reproduction, Carby asks, "What does the concept of reproduction mean in a situation where black women have done domestic labour outside of their own homes in the service of white families?" As well, Carby (120) comments on the sweeping generalizations found in much feminist work: "The generalizations made about women's lives across societies in the African and Asian continents would be thought intolerable if applied to the lives of white women in Europe and North America." In terms of law, recognition of the specific situations of women of colour goes a long way towards an understanding, for example, of the reluctance of women to call on the CJS for help in dealing with an abusive partner. As the Commission on Systemic Racism in the Ontario Criminal Justice System (1998) found, members of racial minorities often define the justice system as part of the problem, not part of the solution.

Carby's comments alert us to the need for historical and theoretical specificity in our efforts to situate racialized groups within our theorizing. As George Dei (1998: 303) notes: "Race is not a homogeneous or one dimensional category.... It is a social construct with changing meanings that are historically specific." More generally, we clearly need to think about the (in)ability of different theories to incorporate the diversity of people's experiences—in their encounters with law and in society, generally—and how that difference is both recognized and valued.

To single out this need to incorporate race and racism within our investigation of the law-society relation is not to suggest that racial oppression (in its various forms) is the only or primary form of oppression and inequality in society. But it does raise the question of how we are to understand the connections between race, class, and gender. As Roxanna Ng (1989: 10) notes, "There is a tendency to treat gender, race and class as different analytic categories designating different domains of social life." Yet that separation does not reflect people's actual experiences. As Patricia Monture-Angus (1995: 177–78) tells us, "It is very difficult for me to separate what happens to me because of my gender and what happens to me because of my race and culture. My world is not experienced in a linear and compartmentalized way. I experience the world simultaneously as Mohawk and as woman.... To artificially separate my gender from my race and culture forces me to deny the way I experience the world."

Rather than attempting to compartmentalize or to view race, class, and gender as additives (that is, race + class + gender), perhaps we can follow Rose Brewer's (1997) suggestion and begin to think about these concepts—and the relations they represent—as simultaneous forces (that is, race X class X gender).

The postmodern challenge
All of the theoretical approaches we have examined so far fall within what is referred to as Modernism or the Modern Age, which began in the nineteenth century. *Modernism* is basically a world view, a way of seeing and interpreting, grounded in positivist premises. In particular, the Modern Age disciplines of science (both the physical and social), medicine (including the "psy" professions), and law all rest on the assumptions that the positive or scientific method holds the key to the truth about human behaviour; that the knowledge produced by this method is characterized by certitude; and that the application of the scientific enterprise will inevitably serve progress. *Postmodernism* constitutes a rejection of these claims.

As a mode of thinking that challenges modernity, postmodernism disputes the view that science has the answers or is capable of revealing the truth; and truth is not seen as something that is "out there" and that science can therefore uncover or unmask. Nor is there one, inevitable, or definitive truth. Rather, postmodernists argue for the existence of many, often competing truths (with the various forms that science takes constituting particular "claims to truth"). Moreover, while modernity is characterized by the search for grand theories that could explain virtually all of human behaviour, postmodernists argue that such a project is doomed. As Carol Smart (1990: 194) argues, "We need to abandon the craving for a meta-narrative that will (at last) explain the oppressions and subjectivities of race, class and gender." Instead of formulating theories based on totalizing structures such as imperialism, capitalism, or patriarchy, postmodernists seek to rupture and disrupt the foundations of what we think we know. In the process, this approach "opens up the possibility that we cannot be certain of the outcome of any knowledge intervention" (Smart 1995: 212).

In contrast to modernist approaches that rely on the positive or scientific method, postmodernism adopts the method of *deconstruction*: a method of analysis that takes apart socially constructed categories in order to determine the makeup of a particular world view (Ristock and Pennell 1996: 114). Modernist thinking, for example, relies heavily on binary oppositions or dichotomous terms. Racism, for example, is a concept and a practice that is meaningless without the differentiation between white and black. Deconstruction illustrates how these differences are socially constructed and how the dominant category (whiteness) relies on the subordinate category (blackness) for its privilege and power.

Central to the method of deconstruction is the interrogation of discourses—the meanings and assumptions embedded in different forms of language use, ways of making sense of the world, and their corresponding practices. Discourses will vary according to the power effects accompanying them; certain discourses will attain a position of dominance in society. From this perspective, knowledge is not objective, but political. Knowledge production has to do with power, as power is productive of knowledge.

In formulating their approach, postmodernists have been particularly influenced by the work of Michel Foucault (1978, 1979a), who was especially intent on formulating a conception of power that did not succumb to what he saw as the deficiencies of the Marxist approach. Whereas Marxism focuses on capitalism as a system of production and on power as a commodity that is "owned," Foucault constructs a non-economic analysis of power. He displaces capitalism in favour of the "disciplinary society": the growth of new knowledges (like medicine and criminology) that came to constitute the "modern episteme" and to create not only new fields of exploration but also new modes of surveillance and regulation of the population. Foucault's focus is thus on the mechanisms of power (as opposed to Marx's focus on who holds the power). In opposition to the Marxist emphasis on power as oppressive or repressive (as in one class dominating over another), power can be creative and productive. For Foucault, "power is everywhere"; it is dispersed throughout society. It is neither an institution nor a structure, but is localized in different sites. Moreover, in taking on this conception of power a theorist no longer focuses attention on the state as a key centre of power in society. Instead, the state is *decentred* and the focus of analysis shifts to how forms of knowledge (discourses) claim to speak the truth and thus exercise power in a society that values this notion of truth. For instance, postmodernists would argue that making a claim to be a science is an exercise of power, because in doing so the approach accords other ways of knowing (knowledges) a lesser status.

In general terms, other theoretical frameworks in the sociology of law can be said to be geared towards explaining the authority and legitimacy accorded to law. These frameworks variously locate law's power as a reflection of normative values, group interests, class domination, or patriarchal relations. Postmodernists such as Carol Smart, however, approach the question of the power of law in a different way. In her book *Feminism and the Power of Law* (1989), Smart suggests that, much like the sciences, law is a form of knowledge and, therefore, of power. While relying on Foucault's approach, Smart takes it in a different direction. More specifically, Foucault's focus was on "power at its extremities" (where it is least law-like). He posited that with the advent of the disciplinary society, old forms of power—law and legal institutions in particular—were being replaced by new mechanisms of normalization or modes of disciplining members of the society. For this reason, according to Foucault, law was no longer a prime historical agent or mode of control. Smart, however, questions whether law is an old power that is declining as it is superseded by these other modes of power. Instead, she suggests that the "growing legalization of everyday life"—from the moment of conception (fetal rights) to the legal definition of death (euthanasia practices)—implies that law's power may actually be extending, rather than diminishing. If this is the case, theorists and researchers have all the more reason to interrogate law and its claims to truth.

Smart (1989: 9) suggests that law is like the sciences in that it has "its own method, its own specialized language, its own system of results." While it is not a science per se, law is able to make the same kinds of claims to truth as the sciences and, in so doing, exercise a power that is seen as legitimate. It does this not simply through judgments, but in the disqualification of other accounts. For instance, within the courtroom: "Non-legal knowledge is ... suspect and/or secondary. Everyday experiences are of little interest in terms of their meaning for individuals. Rather these experiences must be translated into another form in order to become 'legal' issues and before they can be processed through the legal system.... So the legal process translates everyday experiences into legal relevances, it excludes a great deal that might be relevant to the parties, and it makes its judgement on the scripted or tailored account" (Smart 1989: 11).

The process of the rape trial illustrates how people's experiences are translated within the legal process to become "legal relevances." From a woman's standpoint, rape is, more often than not, an experience of humiliation, degradation, and violation—of a terrifying ordeal. The rape trial, however, involves sifting through that experience to extract those "facts" of the case that law views as relevant to the determination of the guilt of the accused. For instance, did the woman in question consent? As a key witness for the Crown, is her testimony credible? Is there physical evidence to support her claim that it was rape? In this process, not only is the woman required to retell her experience so that the court can arrive at a just determination of the facts, but her body also becomes the stuff of evidence. For instance, a recent rape trial I witnessed at the Old Bailey in London, England, involved a woman who, prior to having been raped, was a virgin. During the trial the defence lawyer cross-examined a physician who had examined the woman shortly after the rape had occurred. A key focus of his questioning was whether there was physical evidence to suggest that the woman's hymen had been "breached"—and whether there was evidence (of tearing or abrasions) to substantiate that the intercourse was non-consensual. These criteria would surely be of doubtful relevance from the standpoint of the woman herself. For these and other reasons (see Smart 1989: ch. 2), the rape trial becomes a disqualification of women's experiences.

Smart's approach to law as a form of discourse that can make claims to truth leads her—like other postmodernists—to advocate deconstruction as her method: "to expose how law operates in all its most detailed mechanisms" (Smart 1989: 25). In other words, just as there is a need to decentre the state as a mechanism of power, so too is there a need to decentre law—perhaps not so much in theory (given that law continues to be a main focus), but in practice. According to Smart (1989: 164), "It is law's power to define and disqualify which should become the focus of ... strategy, rather than law reform as such."

Postmodernism represents a significant challenge to how we theorize the law-society relation. It has led many writers (myself included) to rethink the kind of work we do, the kinds of claims we make, and the ways of knowing we adopt. In this respect, many aspects of the postmodern approach carry considerable appeal—not the least of which are its implications for how we address the law-society relation.

For one, the Foucauldian conception of power is in many ways a liberating one. As Foucault reminds us, power is not simply a "thing," some property capable of being owned, possessed, or wielded. Nor is power a zero-sum game, whereby one side increases as the other diminishes. Using Foucault as his guide, Hunt (1991a: 106) defines power as "quintessentially relational; power is the capacity of social actors to realize aims in a relation of oppositions and resistances of others." Such a conception moves the analysis away from the tendency (found especially in some Marxist formulations) to view power as oppressive and the state as a monolithic, overdetermined, and all-powerful entity. As well, the approach decentres the state, as an object not only of theoretical inquiry, but also of political practice; it calls attention to the sphere of civil society and advocates a politics geared more to the local or community level. As Smart (1989: 7) describes it, "The mechanisms of power create resistances and local struggles which bring about new forms of knowledge and resistance."

Especially appealing about the postmodern approach is its implications for the study of law. Following the method of deconstruction, the task becomes one of unpacking the discourse of law to reveal the context in which it has been constituted and the biases it contains. Smart (1992), for instance, shows how law operates as a "gendering strategy." At different historical points, legal decisions and enactments have worked to produce a particular construction of Woman, not only in contradistinction to Man, but in terms of different types of Woman (the female criminal, the prostitute, the unmarried mother, the infanticidal mother). These constructions have had considerable reach in terms of their effects on women's lives and identities. In a similar way, Marlee Kline (1994) locates law as one of the discourses in which racism is constructed, reproduced, and reinforced in society. More specifically, she elaborates on how certain "ideological representations of 'Indianness'" (Kline 1994: 452) have historically been embedded in and expressed through judicial reasoning, and their import in the encounters between First Nations people and law. Such analyses go a long way towards explaining specifically how relations of race, class, and gender are (re)produced in society; and they deeply implicate the Official Version of Law in that process.

While postmodernism stands as an important challenge to our theorizing, several writers have questioned whether the postmodern turn constitutes—or requires—a complete departure from the more traditional, modernist approaches. As Hunt (1991b: 82) cautions, "Before embracing postmodernism too enthusiastically, we need to take cognizance of precisely what it is that is thrown out." One issue Hunt raises is that Foucault's work has displaced the concern with "totalizing structures"— like capitalism—with an "(under-theorized) new 'disciplinary' society in which capitalism, quietly, disappears" (Hunt 1991b: 82).

One implication of this move is that, in abandoning the notion of the existence of structures (like capitalism, imperialism, and patriarchy), we are left with the notion that "power is everywhere"; it is localized in different sites. Nevertheless, one could argue that there are good reasons for retaining the notion that social structures exist, not the least of which is that systems like capitalism *are* "totalizing structures" (Fudge and Glasbeek 1992). They condition and contour the economic, social, and political lives and identities of the individuals who move within them. Indeed, it is the very ways in which this "works" that need to be the subject of our theorizing.

To make the claim that capitalism (or patriarchy, or imperialism) is a totalizing structure that displays historically specific forms of control and regulation over people's lives does not, by definition, negate the role of social agency or the power of individuals within those structures. But it does suggest that people's actions, behaviours, and ways of knowing and perceiving their world will be very much influenced by their social positioning within it. While we need to acknowledge that individuals possess power and that they make choices, we must also keep in mind that power has a structural basis. It is unevenly distributed along a number of different axes—such as race, class, and gender. Choice, as a result, is never free or open. As Rosemary Hennessy (1993: 20) describes it, "The notion of choice has to be rewritten so as to make visible the systems of exploitation and oppression that affect the historical variability of particular positions to some subjects and not others as well as the possible movement of social subjects across and between them."

In the same way, in rejecting the notion of the state as the centre of power in society, postmodern writers like Foucault may go too far. Perhaps, while there is a need to resist seeing the state as *the* centre of power, the state still does play an important role in the operation and exercise of power in society. As Eisenstein (1989: 18) puts it, "To say that there is *a* state is not necessarily to accept that power is located only there, or even centred there, or always dispersed from there, but it is to say that the relations of power are sometimes concentrated there, even if, in contradictory and conflicting ways." The state could be said to *condense* the relations of power in society, and one of the ways it does so is through discourse.

Similarly, while postmodern analysis has the advantage of moving the focus of inquiry away from the purely structural features of the position or location of law and towards a more detailed consideration of the specific manner in which law operates as a discourse, it is also the case that law is more than just discourse. As a mechanism of power, legal practice has material effects on people's lives. This leads one to question the postmodern strategy of decentring law at the level of practice. This is an issue raised by Dawn Currie (1992: 76): "To de-centre law in our analysis is one matter, to de-centre it in real life is another." In her review of Smart's work, Dany Lacombe (1997: 147) poses this issue in a different way: "Using the game metaphor, I would say that Smart focuses on the result of the game: who won? who lost? What is missing from Smart's analysis are the moves the players made; the stakes they had in the game; the value of specific cards; the trump cards players used to effect a change of direction or to modify the stakes; the positions of players in the space of play, and the relative force of each player."

Postmodernism cautions against the call for "more law" to resolve the oppressions of different groups in society. It questions the extent to which engaging the state will result in giving over even more power to the agencies and institutions within it. Indeed, Smart (1989: 16) has argued that legal intervention can sometimes have a *juridogenic* effect; that is, "in exercising law, we may produce effects that make conditions worse." While we need to heed Smart's warning to be extremely cautious of how and whether we resort to law in formulating strategies for change, we must also remember that different groups and movements (such as First Nations, anti-poverty, gays and lesbians, and feminists) have already engaged law in their efforts to bring about substantive change. We will need, then, to continue making detailed analyses of the prospects—and pitfalls—of engaging the law.

CONCLUSION

Earlier I defined social theory as "a set of answers to questions we ask of social reality." As we've seen, the efforts of sociologists of law to understand or make sense of law and its location in society have led to the surfacing of many questions—and just as many, if not more, answers. Theorizing on the law-society relation is not a static but a continuing enterprise in which new questions emerge and new answers to old questions are formulated. In our further investigation of the law-society relation, and keeping in mind the (inter)connections between law and the race, class, and gender relations in society, we might consider three sets of questions that summarize these theoretical excursions into the different approaches in the sociology of law.

1. What "order" is law (re)producing? Whose interests are reflected in law?
2. Is law divorced from the play of politics, as the Official Version of Law would have us believe? Does law live up to its claims of fairness and equity? Does it, in practice, dispense justice?
3. If law is not living up to its ideal, how do we go about changing it? If law does, in fact, (re)produce relations of inequality and oppression in society, is it possible to use law as a mechanism for realizing substantive social change?

The essays which follow represent the work now being conducted on the law-society relation. Each essay addresses a specific aspect of one or more of these questions. Taken together, they should move us a long way towards understanding and clarifying law's location.

NOTE

1. Several people have been very generous in providing feedback on earlier drafts of this essay. Thanks to Wayne Antony, Vanessa Chopyk, Dorothy Chunn, Judy Fudge, Kirsten Johnson, Lisa Jakubowski, Bernard Schissel, Laureen Snider, and Linda Wood for helping me to make this a stronger piece than it would have otherwise been. It goes without saying, however, that any shortcomings of the essay are my own doing.

RACISM AND THE LAW

Introduction

Canada has often been described as a "nation of immigrants." Historically, the country was built up by means of large influxes of immigrant groups, including the prairie settlers who populated the West and the skilled and unskilled workers who took up positions in the great projects of industrialization in the urban centres. Unlike our American neighbour to the south, characterized as a "melting pot," Canada has been called a "mosaic," in which diverse racial and ethnic groups have been able to make the country their home while retaining their unique cultural traditions and heritage. The term often used to describe the Canadian experience is "multiculturalism."

This image of Canada as a diverse, multicultural—indeed, "racially tolerant"—nation has readily inspired national pride. It could be termed the "Official Version" of Canada's racial history. Nevertheless, the image belies the darker side of our history. For many Canadians—including First Nations populations—the historical experience has been characterized by racial intolerance, inequality, and injustice. Sensitivity to this feature of the Canadian historical record is imperative if we want to understand race relations in Canada and appreciate law's location in the perpetuation of racial inequalities. To this end, the essays in this part of the book explore the manifestations of racism (including law and legal practice) for different racialized groups in Canada.

In "Standing against Canadian Law," Patricia Monture-Angus speaks from her standpoint as a Mohawk woman to explain her impatience with Canadian law as a solution to the problems encountered by Aboriginal peoples. Her culture and gender not only inform her experiences, but also allow her—and, through her writing, us—to "see" Canadian law through a lens that penetrates the claims of law's Official Version to reveal how law has instead delivered the oppression of Aboriginal peoples. In doing this, Monture-Angus raises the issues of what transformative change means and whether law offers a site for its realization.

In a way similar to some of the postmodern writings on law, Monture-Angus's standpoint decentres law. She calls into question the legitimacy of the Canadian legal system as "the" mechanism for resolving disputes. Not only are there other viable mechanisms for dispute resolution, but the Canadian legal system has also historically worked to perpetuate rather than resolve disputes. Moreover, Monture-Angus argues that reforms to the criminal justice system—while giving the appearance of change—have not produced any such transformation. For instance, while some programs and accommodations (such as sentencing circles) have altered the experiences of individuals within the criminal justice system, the incarceration rates of Aboriginal people continue to soar.

Monture-Angus understands oppression as both an individual and a collective phenomenon. While resistance is a necessary strategy in response to oppressive conditions, given those conditions it is, in and of itself, insufficient. Monture-Angus discusses the processes and struggles involved in moving from victim to survivor, warrior, and teacher. Understanding Aboriginal peoples' experiences of oppression requires a methodology that allows them the space and the voice to speak their truths. Understanding how law is implicated in the oppression of Aboriginal peoples requires an analysis that is sensitive to systemic or structural racism. For instance, Monture-Angus notes that, while the amendments to section 12(1)(b) of the Indian Act removed some of its more blatant discrimination, the less visible and more deep-seated forms of oppression are left intact. In particular, the reserve system continues to operate as a way of dividing Aboriginal peoples from each other and from the land, and the reform leaves untouched the factors that have had a more far-reaching effect on Aboriginal women's lives than the items of 12(1)(b)—overt violence, residential schools, child welfare agencies. In this respect, Monture-Angus notes that preoccupation with 12(1)(b) parallels the agenda of the feminist movement (especially its liberal-feminist variant) and showcases the limits of formal equality in law as a strategy for realizing meaningful change.

Lisa Jakubowski's essay, "'Managing' Canadian Immigration," places the history of Canadian immigration laws in their political and economic context in order to reveal their explicitly racist nature. While labour-market demands (specifically, the demand for a plentiful supply of cheap labour) have historically been a major influence on immigration policies and practices, an overriding concern of the Canadian state was the control of immigration as capitalist industrialization proceeded. As Jakubowski shows, from the 1880s onward Canada's immigration laws and practices were informed by a "White Canada" policy that was "racist in orientation, assimilationist in objective." While restrictive legislation was used to limit the entry of Chinese, Japanese, and East Indian immigrants around the turn of the century, "race" became an explicit criteria for exclusion of the "least desirable" candidates (Jews, Blacks, and Asians) in the 1910 Immigration Act. Between the two world wars, the Great Depression gave the government a justification for further strengthening restrictions, and Jewish refugees fleeing Europe were met at Canada's door with the policy response of "none is too many" (Abella and Troper 1983). Only in 1962, when skills in relation to Canadian labour-market needs became the new selection criteria, was the "White Canada" policy rescinded. The implementation of the points system (enshrined in the 1976 Immigration Act) ostensibly ushered in a "formally colour-blind" immigration policy in Canada.

Yet Jakubowski questions whether this appearance of equality and fairness in contemporary Canadian immigration law matches up with the reality of immigration policy and practice. She argues that while in principle Canadian immigration law has shifted from being explicitly restrictive to non-discriminatory, in practice it reflects a more subtle and systemic form of discrimination. To investigate this further, she explores the "politicality" of law: that is, the ideological role law plays in reinforcing the image of Canada as an equitable and fair nation. Jakubowski locates law as a form of discourse that operates to secure the legitimacy of the state within a particular social order. Through the techniques of sanitary coding and equivocation, authorities remove the gendered, racialized, and class-based content of legislation, thereby creating an ambiguity that leaves the legislation open to manipulation by political actors. Through an analysis of recent immigration legislation, Jakubowski demonstrates how these techniques operate. For instance, her examination of the "family reunification" provision in Bill C-86 reveals a definition of "family" premised on an ethnocentric image of the nuclear family. That restricted definition runs counter to the experiences of immigrants from developing countries, where grandparents and other relatives play a more integral role in family life. Similarly, Bill C-86's "safe country" provision has the effect—without ever mentioning the word "race"—of restricting the admission of refugees from developing countries. In these ways, while the language of discrimination has been removed from the law, Canadian immigration law, policy, and practice remain racist and ethnically selective.

Sedef Arat-Koc's essay focuses on an issue in which class, gender, and race dynamics become readily apparent: foreign domestic workers and the law. In class terms, domestic labour has been relegated to a lesser status in capitalist societies. Understood in Marxist terms, domestic labour, because it is work performed in the private sphere of the home, does not contribute directly to surplus value and hence is deemed to be "unproductive" labour. That housework has typically been associated with "women's work" showcases its gendered nature. Historically, one of the ways in which families (when they were in a position to afford it) could fulfill their need for domestic labour was to hire women to perform the work; and that is where the race dimension of the issue comes into play. As Arat-Koc shows, racism has been a key factor in both the recruitment and control of domestic workers in Canada.

Arat-Koc suggests that, in the history of Canadian immigration, domestic workers from different source countries can be placed on a continuum in terms of the treatment they received. Since the turn of the century, as the source countries have moved further from Britain and Western Europe to the Third World, state regulation over domestic workers has become more coercive while work and living conditions have worsened. Initially, "preferred" domestic workers were women of British origin. Being of the "right" racial stock, they were considered as potential "mothers of the nation" who—under the careful scrutiny and control of social reformers—could both biologically reproduce the race and transmit British culture and "civilization" to future Canadians. When these "preferred" immigrants could not meet demands for domestic labour, the Canadian state turned its attention to other sources, including Scandinavia and Eastern Europe. The requirements of entry and working conditions of these workers differed, especially for refugee women recruited from the displaced person camps in Europe after World War II. Yet while the conditions and restrictions of British and Continental European domestics were infused with class and gender considerations, women of colour met with even worse treatment.

Even with the liberalization of immigration in the 1960s in the form of the points system, restrictions on the occupational demand categories have meant that domestic workers—especially those from Third World countries—have been unable to come to Canada as independent immigrants on a permanent status. Instead, the introduction of temporary work permits to meet the demand for domestic workers has created a new form of indentured labour. The most recent changes to immigration law—the Foreign Domestic Movement program and the Live-in Caregiver Program—represent a continuation of this pattern. As Arat-Koc notes, these programs have failed to produce any marked improvement in either the status or living conditions of domestic workers in Canada. Just as significant, the racism inherent in both the differential working conditions and the rationales surrounding evaluations of who is a "deserving" immigrant suggests that the principles of equality and fairness are absent when it comes to the situation of domestic workers from Third World countries.

Standing against Canadian Law: Naming Omissions of Race, Culture, and Gender

© Patricia Monture-Angus[1]

I have grown very impatient with Canadian law as a solution to problems that Aboriginal peoples, both as nations and as individuals, face in the Canadian mosaic. But to explain my conclusions and concerns about Canadian law and its impact on Aboriginal lives, I will need also to tell you how I situate myself against Canadian law as a Mohawk woman.

First of all, there is no single "Indian" reality. This is a formidable myth. It is a myth that has been accepted by all "mainstream"[2] disciplines that have an interest in studying "Indians." Professor Devon Mihesuah (Oklahoma Choctaw) articulates in her essay on American Indian women and history: "There was and is no such thing as a monolithic, essential Indian woman. Nor has there ever been a unitary 'worldview' among tribes, especially after contact and interaction with non-Indians, not even among members of the same group. Cultural ambiguity was and is common among Indians. Traditional Native women were as different from progressive tribeswomen as they were from white women, and often they still are" (Mihesuah 1998: 37–38). This discussion is, therefore, only one comment on the ideas (or story) of one person, a Mohawk woman.

My impatience is also grounded in the fact that, as a Mohawk woman, I do not accept Canadian law as *the* single, viable, and legitimate way of resolving disputes. My understanding is that Canadian law operates to perpetuate disputes. Consider how many Aboriginal claims—almost all the decisions recently heard by the Supreme Court of Canada—are resolved by the courts by sending them back to trial for a second time. This list includes cases heralded as great victories, such as *Sparrow* and *Delgamuukw*. Further, and more importantly, Canadian law from my standpoint is not the only option. I come from a peoples and a tradition that had rules and processes about dispute resolution that I experience as legitimate and viable. These rules and processes of dispute resolution are not simple, romantic visions of the past. They are present and viable in our communities today. I do not defer to the Canadian system any legitimacy solely because it is the only choice, because from my position it is not. Indigenous citizens of our nations have choices about dispute resolution traditions and mechanisms that are not necessarily available to Canadians.

As a Mohawk woman who came to study Canadian law, I am forever balancing the teaching, rules, and principles of both systems. This balancing act probably leads me to different understandings about the structure and shape of Canadian law. This is not a visibility that operates solely because I come from a "different" culture. It becomes visible because of both my tradition and gender, realities that operate concurrently in interlocking ways. Sherene Razack (1998: 58) concurs with this observation and explains the serious consequence of the misunderstanding that culture and gender are not separate realities:

> When women from non-dominant groups talk about culture, we are often heard to be articulating a false dichotomy between culture and gender; in articulating our difference, we inadvertently also confirm our relegation to the margins. Culture talk is clearly a double-edged sword. It packages difference as inferiority and obscures both gender-based and racial domination, yet cultural considerations are important for contextualizing oppressed groups' claims for justice, for improving their access to services, and for requiring dominant groups to examine the invisible cultural advantages you enjoy.

Understanding law from a place that is cultured and gendered offers advantages in my own understanding, but at the same time operates to the detriment in our position in the mainstream dialogue.

Part of the reason I feel advantaged is because I have a choice about legal systems. This has several consequences. I have never presumed that the Canadian legal system is the only system. Because I often "stand against" the principles on which Canadian law is founded, my position is critical. I do not take the principles of Canadian law for granted. Nor do I fail to see that the principles on which Canadian law is based are not absolutes. These principles were chosen. However, it is equally important to note that I will always defer to the standards of my first way to determine the value of participating in the Canadian legal system. At the same time, I recognize that the choice I exercise is not always possible. This choice is a reflection of the privilege of my legal education. A person facing criminal charges or child welfare actions or defending Aboriginal lands does not exercise such a privilege (nor would I if I were in any of those circumstances). At the same time that I engage in legal method, I am constantly assessing that law against my Mohawk understanding of law. It is not that I expect courts to become suddenly Mohawk; I am just looking for a significant degree of respect built on an understanding that is at least bicultural and gendered.

This is contrary to how I see Canadian courts and non-Aboriginal academics using Aboriginal legal discourse. When quoted (which is entirely all too infrequently), my words, like the words of other Aboriginal scholars, are used as cultural evidence and not legal method.[3] This reminds me of the caution I recently read: "When racism and genocide are denied and cultural difference replaces it, the net effect for Aboriginal peoples is a denial of their right to exist as sovereign nations and viable communities" (Razack 1998: 61).

When reading the Supreme Court of Canada's decision in *Delgamuukw*, I did not fail to notice that the eminent scholars the Court chose to quote were (significantly) all white men.[4] The failure to broaden the scope of their reading and reference (Matsudi 1988: 4–5) is most likely a reflection of the factums the lawyers presented to the courts. It is not that I think the Supreme Court of Canada should quote me. On a very personal level, I dread the day that this should ever occur.[5] It is, however, one of the notable but subtle ways in which Canadian law operates to exclude, omit, and deny difference. Or, if you prefer, it is how courts participate in perpetuating colonialism while ensuring that power— their power—continues to vest in the status quo.

The oppression embedded in the legal process ranges from the subtle to the overt and obvious. Several recent cases in Canada have criminalized the actions of pregnant women—one of them an Aboriginal woman—who were abusing alcohol or drugs. The social realities, including the historic oppression of Aboriginal peoples, are not realities that courts readily consider in their decision-making process. In a detailed analysis of the *Big Pipe Case* in the United States, where a Dakota woman found herself before the courts in just these circumstances, Elizabeth Cook-Lynn (Dakota) argues:

> There is evidence that women, thought by the tribes to be the backbone of Native society and the bearers of sacred children

and repositors of cultural values, are now thought to pose a significant threat to tribal survival. Indeed, the intrusive federal government now interprets the law on Indian reservations in ways which sanction *indicting* Indian women as though they alone are responsible for the fragmentation of the social fabric of Indian lives. As infants with fetal alcohol syndrome (FAS) and fetal alcohol effect (FAE) are born in increasing numbers, it is said that women's recalcitrant behavior (consuming alcohol and other drugs during pregnancy and nursing) needs to be legally criminalized by the federal system to make it a felony for a women to commit such acts. (Cook-Lynn 1996: 114–15)

These conditions—that the result of the tribal (that is, collective) oppression of Aboriginal peoples is now individualized within legal relations and that a greater burden is being placed on women for problems of social disorder and the resulting harms—also point to the inadequacy of an individualized system of law to resolve Aboriginal issues. The impact of the individualization of our legal relations moves Aboriginal nations further away from our traditions, which are kinship-based and collective. That women are the focus of these trends cannot escape our attention.

My impatience with law, with its theory and method, is grounded as well in the practical realization that long-term solutions are not available in Canadian law because of the very structure of that legal system. Granted, Aboriginal people are sometimes able to avail themselves of immediate solutions for the topical problems faced. Being represented by a counsel[6] who understands the history and being of an Aboriginal person may make a difference in a child welfare matter or the defence of a criminal charge. However, the consequence of being able to address immediate solutions is deceiving. It conceals that no significant change is occurring. I refuse to be satisfied with being better able to defend ourselves in small ways in particular circumstances as all that we can hope for.[7] This is one of the fundamental characteristics of oppression by assimilation. It appears as though change has occurred when it has not. This concern is even more pressing for women, especially for Aboriginal women who carry the weight of discrimination (race/culture) wound within discrimination (gender).

This impatience with Canadian law, conditioned on my understanding that it remains a problem for Aboriginal peoples and especially for

Aboriginal women, is not a conclusion that is widely shared. It is essential, therefore, to share the reasons why I have reached this conclusion.[8] I spent a good five years of my life as a student of law and another five years as a law professor. Despite leaving the law school a little more than four years ago, I am still reading cases and teaching about law. A preliminary examination of legal structure and theory clearly identifies that certain groups have not had an equal opportunity to participate in the process of defining social and state relations (including the law). Women, Aboriginal people, and other so-called minorities have not shared in the power to define the relationships of the institutions of this country (including the university, the law courts, criminal justice institutions, and social services).

CONSIDERING CHANGE: ABORIGINAL PEOPLE
AND THE CANADIAN CRIMINAL JUSTICE SYSTEM

I am interested in transformative change of the Canadian legal system; this is the kind of change that I consider significant. In Canada, much has been made of the many initiatives "for" Aboriginal people in the justice system. There are courtworkers, hiring programs, Native liaison workers in prisons, Elder-assisted parole board hearings, sentencing circles, and so on. All of these programs are mere "add-ons" to the mainstream justice system, and all of them operate on a shared presumption: if we can only teach Aboriginal people more about our system then that system will work for them and they will accept it. Many of the programs and developments are packaged as cultural accommodations. This should be recognized for what it is: a misappropriation of culture. The programs are really based on the notion of Aboriginal inferiority, and if we Aboriginal people just become more knowledgeable about the Canadian system, the problem is solved. Culture has been used to obscure the structural racism in the Canadian criminal justice system. The failure of the system is placed squarely on the shoulders of Aboriginal people and not on the system, where it really belongs. This is not transformative change, because transformative change requires structural change in the system when it is required and necessary.

Not only are the present reforms to the criminal justice system in Canada not transformative, but they have also not been fully successful. Because of my work in Canadian prisons (both men's and women's institutions), I do not question that the reforms have changed the incarceration experiences of Aboriginal people. This is an ameliorative and individual change in matters of criminal justice that is essential. However, real success would be demonstrated in decreased incarceration rates of Aboriginal people, which is not occurring. Aboriginal incarceration rates continue to increase, despite the new programs and accommodations. The collective experience of the justice system has not been transformed.

Much has been made of the establishment of sentencing circles in Canada. These circles, under the discretion of the judge, offer to the Aboriginal accused the opportunity to be sentenced in a community process (Ross 1996: 192–98, 246–47). But there is nothing intrinsically Aboriginal about these processes. We did not "sentence," and merely rearranging the furniture so we are sitting in a "circle" does not accomplish systemic or transformative change. Granted, a sentencing circle does borrow from Aboriginal traditions of dispute resolution as well as healing. Sentencing circles are accommodations of the mainstream process that may hold a better opportunity to provide a degree of comfort to community members, (Aboriginal) victims, and/or the Aboriginal accused. The sentencing circle may change the momentary experience of the Aboriginal person of criminal justice, but it does not really hold greater potential.

The concern that transformative progress is not being made is also visible in recent Canadian court decisions. In December 1997, when the Supreme Court of Canada released the decision in the *Delgamuukw* case, the central claim was the Aboriginal title of fifty-one hereditary chiefs of the Gitksan and Wet'suwet'en peoples. The decision was heralded as a great victory. I have difficulty with this conclusion, because the Supreme Court's decision was to return for retrial a case that had originally involved 374 days at trial and 141 days spent taking evidence out of court (Miller 1992: 3).[9] It is true that significant progress was made in the evidentiary rules, which had previously preferred the written document to oral history. These rules of evidence previously operated in Canadian law as a serious structural barrier to success in litigation brought by Aboriginal peoples. This diminishing of Aboriginal forms of history against non-Aboriginal written ways was a significant detriment in being able to bring Aboriginal claims forward. The Court opined: "Notwithstanding the challenges created by the use of oral histories as proof of historical facts, the laws of evidence must be *adapted* in order that this type of evidence can be *accommodated* and placed on an equal footing with the types of historical evidence that courts are familiar with which largely consists of historical documents" (*Delgamuukw* 1998: 49–50, emphasis added).

Granted, the Court's benevolent respect for the consequences of the exclusion of oral history and the accommodation of the rules of evidence represents a great victory. However, when we examine the language of the judiciary, a different picture emerges. The Court has "adapted" its own rules of evidence to "accommodate" oral history. This is the same pattern of nominal change that was noted in the discussion of the recent reforms to the criminal justice system. Here, the overall structure is not challenged, but just one unfortunate consequence of the evidentiary rules. If I believed that the only evidentiary rule that operated to the disadvantage of Aboriginal persons was this one, perhaps I would be more satisfied. The end result is that Aboriginal people walk away from this decision with lots more work to do. Every place where evidentiary rules do not fit with our ways must be brought to the courts for review. This will be both time-consuming and money-consuming. Nonetheless, I recognize that the decision in *Delgamuukw* may make this change easier to accomplish. Regardless, it still leaves the burden on Aboriginal people to continually challenge the system forced on us. Transformative change would require that courts or legislatures take it upon themselves to complete an ameliorative review with the intent of removing all such barriers existing in Canadian law.

Understanding Oppression and Resistance

This analysis of the problems in the structure of Canadian law has thus far been primarily focused on race and culture. But it is essential that gender (both male and female) be wound into this story. By the time I reached law school, I understood that much of my identity was shaped on the recognition that I was oppressed. I was oppressed as an Indian.[10] I was oppressed as a woman. I was oppressed as an Indian woman. I do not experience these categories of "Indian" and "woman" as singular and unrelated. The experience of Indian and woman is layered. My choice to go to law school was premised on my desire to fight back against the oppression and violence I had lived with as an Indian woman.[11] It was a journey of seeking solutions to both the immediate consequences and long-term impact of the criminal justice system on the lives of Aboriginal people I knew.

A decade ago I thought that ending my personal oppression only required the ability to fight back. I then saw that the best place for me to fight oppression Canadian-style was in law. I wanted to be a criminal defence counsel. What I learned during my law school years (and it has been a lesson frequently reinforced in the last few years) is that I am just too impatient for this kind of fighting back. Fighting back frequently only perpetuates the oppression, because all of your energy is directed at a "problem" you did not construct. When all of your energy is consumed in fighting back, transformative change remains elusive. This is one of the very real personal consequences of our inability to bring changes to the Canadian legal system that would make it truly inclusive.

Through the course of my legal education I began to learn that oppression is not of a unitary character. I experience it as both personal and collective (that is, directed at me not as an individual but as part of a people). I also experience oppression as layered. I now understand that the way I looked at the world back when I began to study law was naive or overly simple. Canadian law does not hold forth the hope or power to solve many of the issues that must be struggled with in our communities as the result of oppression at the hands of the Canadian state. Although the discussion here has focused on oppression—because oppression is what I feel as well as see in my daily life—it is essential to recognize that the oppression I have survived (and continue to struggle to survive on a daily basis) is the result of colonial beliefs and relationships. Colonialism is very easily understood. It is the belief in the superiority of certain ways, values, and beliefs *over* the ways, values, and beliefs of other peoples. Colonialism is the legacy that the so-called discovery of the Americas has left to the peoples who are indigenous to these territories. Colonialism is the theory of power, while oppression is the result of the lived experience of colonialism.

As a result of these colonial relationships, resistance became a key concept in understanding the relationship I held with law—and particularly with institutions of criminal justice—around and during the time of my law school days. I know that dictionary reading is not a sound academic pursuit or research methodology, but I thought it just might prove interesting (or an act of resistance/rebellion) and therefore a good place to start to understand resistance. Maybe I just wanted or needed the idea of resistance to be simple. I have lived resistance for a long time. For me a lot of complicated thoughts, ideas, and feelings are conjured up by that word, because so much of my life experiences are about resisting. I have often understood my life in terms of resistance. A lot of what I do in the university is about resistance.

The *Concise Oxford Dictionary* provided me with four beautifully simple definitions of resistance:

1. refusing to comply;
2. hindrance;
3. impeding or stopping;
4. opposition. (Fowler and Fowler 1974: 1059)

These definitional standards of "refusing to comply," "hindrance," "impeding," or "opposition" are not the concepts that I want to build my life on. They are not the concepts I would choose, if I had choice. I know I deserve more than refusing, hindering, or opposing. Mere resistance is not transformative. It often acts solely to reinforce colonial and oppressive relationships, not to destroy them. This is because resistance can be no more than a response to the power someone else holds. Responding to that colonial power can actually operate to affirm and further entrench it.

Sometimes resistance is still a necessary part of the First Nations' bag of survival tricks. I am not disputing that. But resistance only gains mere survival, and often the survival gained is only individual. I cannot—and I suppose will not—believe that the Creator gave us the walk, gave us life, to have nothing more than mere resistance. In my mind, resistance is only the first step, and it is a small step in recovering who we are as original peoples. Resistance is only a first step away from being a victim.

I have a particular understanding of being victim and of being victimized. Like too many other Aboriginal people, I have been a victim. I was a victim of child sexual abuse, of a battering relationship, of rape. In the First Nations women's community, that does not make me exceptional. I can tell you the name of only one Aboriginal woman in this country who I know for sure has not survived incest, child sexual abuse, rape, or battering. It is worse than that, because most of us do not survive just one single incident of abuse or violence. Our lives are about the experience of violence from birth to death, be it overt physical violence or psychological and emotional violence.

I also understand racism to be psychological and emotional violence (Monture 1993). Focusing solely on the physical aspects of violence both diminishes and disappears the full impact of violence in the lives of Aboriginal women. This is an important concept, and my hope is that it will be understood contextually. I offer this long quotation from the Task Force on Federally Sentenced Women—in which I participated—for just that purpose:[12]

> This survey report was prepared by two Aboriginal women *(Lana Fox and Fran Sugar)* who have been through the Canadian prison system. They gathered information for the study through interviews with 39 federally sentenced Aboriginal women in the community.
>
> The women spoke of violence, of racism, and of the meaning of being female, Aboriginal and imprisoned. They spoke of systematic violence throughout their lives by those they lived with, those they depended on and those they loved and trusted. Twenty-seven of the 39 women interviewed described experiences of childhood violence, rape, regular sexual abuse, the witnessing of a murder, watching their mothers repeatedly beaten, and beatings in juvenile detention centers at the hands of staff and other children.
>
> For many of the women, this childhood violence became an ongoing feature of life, and continued through adolescence into adulthood. Twenty-one had been raped or sexually assaulted either as children or as adults. Twenty-seven of the 39 had experienced violence during adolescence. However to these experiences were added the violence of tricks, rape and assaults on the streets. In addition, 34 of the 39 had been the victims of tricks who had beaten and/or raped them (12 of 39 had shared this experience and 9 had been violent toward tricks), some from police or prison guards. The violence experienced by these women is typically at the hands of men.
>
> The women also spoke of living with racism. Racism and oppression are the preconditions of the violence these women experience throughout their lives. (Correctional Service of Canada 1990: 63-64)

Both the forms of violence (physical, sexual, spiritual, emotional, and verbal) and how violence is inflicted on Aboriginal women are multifaceted. Violence is not generally experienced as a single incident. The violence is cyclical. All too often, violence describes most of our lives. Even when we manage to create a safe environment in which to live our individual lives, the violence still surrounds us. Our friends, sisters, aunties, and nieces still suffer. The violence becomes a fact of life and it is inescapable.

The methodology utilized by the Task Force on Federally Sentenced Women was an important component of the work that distinguished it from previous research on Aboriginal women. Culture was a significant concern of task force members involved in commissioning the research. As a result, the interviewers were not only Aboriginal women (of the same culture—Cree—as the majority of Aboriginal women who were serving federal sentences), but were also women who had previously served federal sentences. They, therefore, possessed a credibility among the population to be researched that most (academically trained) interviewers do not. Further, the research instrument was open-ended, which allowed the women interviewed to shape and tell their own stories. This was viewed as essential so as not to influence the research with non-Aboriginal and "straight"[13] views of incarcerated Aboriginal women. The interviewers were also central to the process of interpretation of the data, because they were able to contextualize the women's comments in their own experiences of incarceration. This methodology has been adopted in further research on Aboriginal women who have survived violence (McGillivray and Comaskey 1996).

Looking back, I now see how naive I was during the task force years. The task force embraced the philosophy of choices, which I was fully supportive of and thought was quite revolutionary at the time. But it did not work. While the words changed, the values and philosophy of "corrections" (that is, having the right to change a person because they committed a crime) were merely dumped into the new idea, of "choices." Further, I now see that this choices philosophy is basically a middle-class concept.[14] Not all women incarcerated federally have equal access to the means required to exercise good choices. This is particularly true for Aboriginal women, who have the least access to socio-economic resources of any group of women in this country. In contrast, with the exception of its chapter 2, the report was written by white women with at least middle-class access to services and middle-class experiences of the world. Although I do still think that the work of the task force held revolutionary potential, I would not agree to participate in future work in the same way.

The methodology I advocate involves the creation of a space (or spaces) for Aboriginal ways of knowing and understanding to occupy within more mainstream methodologies. Storytelling is a significant component of Aboriginal epistemologies (see Ladner 1996). How I understand Canadian law is influenced by the fact that I was a victim. This methodology does not advocate "objective" knowledge (if, in fact, such a thing exists) but holds that personal experience, when contributed carefully to research agendas, adds both quality and authenticity.

I led part of my life as a victim. I used drugs and alcohol to hide from how I felt and from the memories of the individual acts of violence. In a way, for part of my life, I agreed to be victim. Then I learned how to resist—just a little—the violence that surrounded me. Eventually I moved beyond the victim place and learned how to be a survivor. Victims (as juxtaposed to survivors) often allow things to happen to them (and, therefore, research on Aboriginal women should not revictimize them). This is not an argument that alleges that victims are responsible for the violence done to them. They are not. Survivors, however, have begun to take care of themselves and have begun taking charge of their lives. Recovery—moving from victim to survivor—is a gradual process. Unfortunately, there are still moments when racism, sexism, and/or colonialism continue to have the power to turn me into a victim again and I am immobilized.

Several years ago, maybe a little more, I got really tired of being a survivor. Just like I got tired of being a victim. I wondered for a long time, "Isn't there something more to life than victimization? Do I always have to be a survivor?" Just like I am now not satisfied with resistance as the most I can expect from life, with fighting back as the only mode of my existence, I was then not satisfied with being a survivor (Monture-Angus 1995: 53–70). Through reflection (and with the support of and many conversations with Elders and friends), I learned that we move beyond surviving to become warriors. This is the next "stage." I know this is not a linear process. Movement is not from one stage to the next with no going back. There is no graduation ceremony where the robes of victimization are shed for life. In my mind, I see it as a medicine wheel. The fourth stage is that of teacher. Teachers not only speak to the truth but they also offer ways in which we may change the reality we are living in.[15] As I am only beginning to see that there is a fourth stage, I am unable to comment on it fully.

Many of the women I know in my life are warriors, as they are able to stand up and speak their truth. There are some men, fewer than the women (in my experience), who are "true" warriors. That statement is not meant to amaze or anger. It is the truth as I see it in my community. It is with a great hesitation that I even use this word, "warrior."[16] I have used it because I have not been able to find one in English that is better. At the same time, I realize that my language has no word for "warrior." In 1990, in the *Indian Times* published in the Mohawk territory of Akwesasne, the following was said (and I sadly do not know what the equivalent woman's word in the language is or if in fact there is a need for one): "We do not have a word for warrior [in the Mohawk language]. The men are called *Hodiskengehdah*. It means 'all the men who carry the bones, the burden of their ancestors, on their backs'" (Johansen 1993: 66).[17]

For me, warrior is both an image of responsibility and commitment. Warriors live to protect, yes, but, more importantly, to give honour to the people. Being a warrior means living your life for more than yourself.

Warrior, in my mind, is not a man's word. It is not a fighting word. It is not a war word. Given what I have been told about many Indian languages, that you cannot use "he" or "she" in the same way that you do in the English language, I suspect that the word warrior is not gender-specific at all. Warrior is a "knowing your place in your community," "caring to speak your truth," "being able to share your gift," "being proud of who you are" word. Warrior, in the way I intend it, is not merely a resistance word. The way I have come to understand the warrior is as someone who is beyond resisting. Survivors resist. Resistance is one of many skills that a warrior might use. It is not their only way. Warriors also have vision. They dream for their people's future.

RESISTING THE INDIAN ACT

In offering the following discussion on the Indian Act, I hope to be able to provide an analysis that assists in our understanding of discrimination, oppression, colonialism, and possible forms of resistance. As long as the Indian Act [18] remains in force, colonialism remains a vibrant force in Indian communities, and I recognize the need for strategies of resistance. The Indian Act can never define who I am as a Mohawk woman, nor can it ever define who my children are as Mohawk and Cree. There is no identity in the Indian Act, only oppression and colonialism.

It is important to look at what the Indian Act has done to our identities as "tribal" people. Bill C-31[19] is an excellent and recent example. I think the next time that somebody tells me that they are a "Bill C-31

Indian,"[20] I am going to scream. There is no such thing as a Bill C-31 Indian. Once a bill passes into law it is not a bill anymore (maybe this is just a little quirk I have as a result of my legal education). Everyone running around calling themselves Bill C-31 Indians is saying (technically and legally), "I am something that does not exist." If we have to be "Indians" then let's all just be "Indians." I would prefer if we could be Mohawk or Cree or Tinglit or Mi'kmaq or Saulteaux. That is who we really are. That is the truth. It is important to reclaim who we are at least in our thoughts.

I want to reject the ideology of reserves as something of "ours" and as something "Indian." Reserves were not dreamed up by Indians. Reserves were a step—a rather long step, in my opinion—down the colonial trail. What really troubles me about this is that we as Indian people respect that piece of postage stamp silliness. We need to ask ourselves (and then remember the answer): Where did that reserve come from? When the Creator, in her[21] infinite wisdom, put us down in our territories, did she say, "O.K. Here's your postage stamp, Trish. You get to go live at the Six Nations reserve"? The Creator did not do that. She gave us territories. I am now living in Cree territory, territory shared with the Métis people. An Elder back home told me more than a decade ago to stop thinking and talking in terms of reserves. Instead, he said, think about your territory.

Nowadays, the Indian Act also allows for another clever little distinction between if you live on this little square piece of land called a reserve and those Indians who do not. You get certain "rights" or "benefits" if you live on the reserve and only if you live on the reserve.[22] You can be tax-free. You can have health benefits. You are eligible for education benefits. Even Indians now also measure "Indian-ness" based on the on-reserve/off-reserve criteria created by the Indian Act. When we think this way we are bought and paid for with those few trivial rights found in the legislation. If you live on 12th Street East in Saskatoon, forget it. You are not going to get any rights under the Indian Act because you do not live on the reserve. This is a problem that is not, at least initially, the fault of Indian people. One of the dangerous results of the federal government's Indian Act is how it divides (and that is a strategy of colonialism, because divided peoples are more easily controlled) our people from each other and the land.

It is even more disturbing to me that some Indians are going to see you as less Indian, as less authentic, if you reside off-reserve. This is incredibly narrow legal, social, and political thinking. It is one of the absolute seeds of oppression I must survive. We are mesmerized away from seeing our oppression in our efforts to ensure access to the nominal rights we have. In my mind, this means that the cost far outweighs the benefits under the Indian Act system. We spend untold amounts of energy (and money) fighting in political arenas and Canadian courts for a few "tax-free" and other assorted crumbs, rather than spending our energy shedding the shackles of our colonial oppression.[23]

Understanding the experience of women on the reserve exposes one way in which gender is important in this analysis. Many women have fled reserves because of the amount of gendered victimization they encountered there. In trying to escape the violence, part of their identity and access to that identity are torn away from them. Many of these women have not found better lives in the city (Hamilton and Sinclair 1991: 485; Dion Stout and Bruyere 1997).

Much literature has been written on the impact of the old section 12(1)(b) of the Indian Act, which stripped Indian women of their status upon marriage to a non-Indian.[24] In fact, a significant portion of the literature considering the contemporary situations of Indian women examines this discrimination once contained in the Indian Act. This is disappointing. The majority of Indian women were never affected directly by this section of the Indian Act. By 1996 approximately 104,000 persons were added to the Indian register as a result of the 1985 amendments to the Indian Act (Ponting 1997: 68). Not all of this number were women who were reinstated. Also included in this figure are the children (both male and female) of the women who "married out"; those who "voluntarily" enfranchised; families of enfranchised men; until 1951 those who resided outside Canada for five years or more; and professionals and university graduates. Even more interesting, I know of no study that considers the situation of non-Indian women who married into the community.[25] Perhaps my view is skewed because I was never victimized by these provisions. However, in my experience, Indian women's lives have been more significantly hurt by overt violence, residential schools, and child welfare agencies than they have by section 12(1)(b). My comments are not intended to diminish what I am certain was a very painful experience of being removed from one's community. But it is important to note that little academic interest and research remain in the areas that continue to have a specific and negative impact on Indian women beyond section 12(1)(b).

It is curious to consider where the preoccupation with former section 12(1)(b) comes from. One could postulate, for example, that it has come to the fore because it neatly parallels, albeit superficially, the agenda of the feminist movement. Women activists have long pointed to the unequal treatment of women in Canadian law. The *Lavell* and *Bedard* cases, which went to the highest court of the land, increased the visibility of this issue. Almost concurrently, national organizations of Native women were also forming. Many of these women were from urban areas and section 12(1)(b) had a negative effect on their lives.[26] The issue of loss of women's status was, therefore, available to the mainstream women's movement in a way that did not force non-Aboriginal women to step out of their comfort zones and directly into Indian women's lives and communities.[27]

Understanding the consequences of the feminist intervention in Indian women's lives is even more enlightening. Recently, I heard a CBC radio program in which two leaders of the women's movement were interviewed about the last few decades of change for women in Canada. One of the interviewer's questions focused on the relationship between Aboriginal women and "the movement." My pleasure at this question being on the interviewer's list quickly evaporated with the response. The women leaders bragged of the great success of the "coalition" in seeing the discriminatory provisions of the Indian Act removed and the women reinstated. The truth of the matter is that discrimination against women has not been removed from the Indian Act. This realization exposes the distance remaining between the women's movement and Indian women.[28]

There are several reasons for why the women's boast does not reflect the concerns of Indian women. First of all, the reinstatement process does not put Indian men and Indian women in the same position. Men who married out (largely because their wives gained status) continue to be able to pass their status on to the children and at least their grandchildren. Indian women who are reinstated only pass a limited form of status onto their children (under section 6(2) of the Act), and nothing remains for their grandchildren. The discrimination is not removed from the Indian Act, as many assert. It has merely been embedded into the act in such a way that it is less visible. Secondly, the women who were involuntarily disenfranchised because of their marriage to non-Indians do not receive any compensation for their loss of access to culture, ceremony, and language during the years that they were prohibited from living on the reserve; nor was this ever considered, despite the serious harm that was often done to them as a result. The effect of the 1985 membership provisions has, in addition, the more general result of making membership more difficult to gain, which means that the size of the status Indian population will probably diminish into the future. I do not join in the celebration of the 1985 amendments. The cost of women's partial reinclusion has been too great.

There are further reasons why it is premature to suggest that gender discrimination has been removed from the Indian Act. There has yet to be completed a systematic gender review of the legislation and the effects of the operation of the legislation to determine if women are systematically excluded from other "benefits" in the act. Certificates of possession, the system of property ownership on many reserves, are often only in the name of the male partner in a marriage. In the *Paul* and *Derrickson* cases, the Supreme Court of Canada disallowed the application of provincial matrimonial property law regimes on reserves.[29] Because the Indian Act is silent on the distribution of matrimonial property in cases of marriage breakdown, no matrimonial property regimes apply on reserves. This is a serious disadvantage to women. The 1985 amendments to the Indian Act only removed the most obvious and blatant discrimination against Indian women from the face of the legislation. It is inaccurate to translate this into an assertion that gender discrimination has been fully removed from the act.

The Indian Act has not just done damage to those of us entitled to be registered under that statute. It is because the Indian Act excluded from registration some people (such as the Métis) that some critics have argued that those excluded groups do not have any rights. They do not have the Indian Act and its colonized (twisted) form of thinking that a federal statute is the source of their rights. Rather, I think the Métis are "fortunate" because they do not have all that written colonization to hold them down. They, at least theoretically, have a clean "statutory slate." The Métis have neither treaty[30] nor the Indian Act to confine them. Their rights have not been as whittled away or tarnished by Canadian laws under the guise of granting rights or becoming civilized.[31] The separation of Aboriginal peoples by the kind of rights we possess is a strategy of divide and conquer, which is central in the process of colonization. The benefit from the strategy flows to the colonizer, because it is much too easy to control a people divided.[32] This is an ancient strategy of colonialism.

CLOSING THIS CIRCLE

In conclusion I want to first return to a discussion of methodology. When I finished law school I quite often described the feeling at graduation as the same feeling of relief combined with fear that I had after leaving an abusive man. It felt like I had been just so battered for so long. Finishing law school is an accomplishment, yet I did not feel proud of myself. I just felt empty. This feeling forced me to begin considering why I felt the way I did. It was this process that began to reveal the ways in which law is fully oppressive to Aboriginal people.

This process of self-reflection is an obligation that I have as a First Nations person trying to live according to the teachings and ways of my people. But it is much more than a personal obligation. It is a fundamental concept essential to First Nations epistemology (see Ermine 1995: 101–12). It is a methodology.

The realization that law was the problem and not a solution of transformative quality was difficult for me to fully accept, because it made the three years I had struggled through law school seem without purpose. I did not want to believe it. Think about everything that First Nations people have survived in this country: the taking of our land, the taking of our children, residential schools, the current criminal justice system, the outlawing of potlatches, sundances, and other ceremonies, and the stripping of Indian women (and other Indian people) of their status. Everything we survived as individuals or as Indian peoples. How was all of this delivered? The answer is simple: through law. For almost every single one of the oppressions I have named, I can take you to the law library and I can show you where they wrote it down in the statutes and in the regulations. Sometimes the colonialism is expressed on the face of the statute books, and other times it is hidden in the power of bureaucrats who take their authority from those same books.

Still, so many people still believe that law is the answer. The reason why Canadian law just does not fully work for resolving Aboriginal claims—including those fundamentally concerning Aboriginal women—is quite simple. Canadian courts owe their origin to British notions of when a nation is sovereign. It is from Canadian sovereignty that Canadian courts owe their existence. Courts, therefore, cannot question the very source of their own existence without fully jeopardizing their own being. Courts cannot be forced to look at issues about the legitimacy (or, more appropriately, the lack thereof) of Canadian sovereignty as against the claims of Aboriginal sovereignties. The result is that Aboriginal claimants (women, men, and nations) can never hope to litigate the issue that is at the very heart of our claims. This is what distinguishes much feminist litigation from Aboriginal "rights" litigation.

It is not just that the decisions of Canadian law are often the wrong decisions. It is more complex. I am interested in having a place, including a place in Canadian law, that feels right and fits right. This requires a place free from oppression. I cannot accomplish this through acts of (or a life of) mere resistance. The place I seek would not only allow me the space[33] and place to be a Mohawk woman, but also encourage me to be all that I am capable of being. It is a place that respects me for who I am as woman and for how I understand myself to be both a member of a nation as well as a confederacy. This is my dream.

NOTES

1. I am grateful to the Legal Research Foundation of New Zealand, whose visiting fellow program created the opportunity and space for me to again revise this paper. The section of this essay that deals with resistance was first published as "Resisting the Boundaries of Academic Thought: Aboriginal Women, Justice and Decolonization" in *Native Studies Review* (1997) 12(1).
2. I hesitate to use the word "mainstream," as by doing so I co-operate in the marginalization of my own people.
3. The most recent example (with all due respect) I have come across is in the work of Kent McNeil (1998: 37).
4. There is one scholar whose work I am not familiar with and cannot determine gender from the name.
5. Being quoted is a fear because, as it now stands, it would locate my scholarship within what I experience as the rigid judicial framework, which is both conservative and gendered away from me.
6. It is more likely that an Aboriginal person will be able to put themselves in this position. However, there is no guarantee that an Aboriginal person has learned the necessary things in a Canadian law school to carry this awareness. Perhaps this is a failing of how we educate lawyers in Canadian law schools, or perhaps Aboriginal culture and tradition do not belong in a Canadian institution. (This is a complicated issue; perhaps a topic for another paper.) It is also possible that non-Aboriginal persons may be able to situate their ability to practise law in such a way that they embrace the "difference" of an Aboriginal client. I think Canadian universities (including law schools) have done a much better job of developing education programs that assist non-Aboriginal people in accessing significant amounts of Aboriginal culture, tradition, and knowledge.
7. I mean no disrespect to the Aboriginal people who are able to sustain them-

selves in the daily practice of law. My point is simply to articulate one of the reasons, the structural reason, for why I do not have the patience for this kind of work.

8. I do not mean to suggest that I am the only "minority" scholar who has reached this conclusion. Please see, for example, the collection of papers edited by Adrien Katherine Wing (1997).

9. Please see *BC Studies: A Quarterly Journal of the Humanities and Social Sciences* 95 (Autumn 1992). This volume is a special issue titled, "A Theme Issue: Anthropology and History in the Courts." Its focus is the *Delgamuukw* decision at trial. Another excellent analysis of this case, Canadian law, and the discipline of anthropology is presented by Dara Culhane (1998).

10. Elsewhere I have explained: "I tell this story about naming because it is symbolic. Growing up 'Indian' in this country is very much about not having the power to define yourself or your own reality. It is being denied the right to say, 'I am!'—instead, always finding yourself saying, 'I am not!' In some places in the book, I have chosen to use the word Indian or First Nations, even recognizing that they can be viewed as excluding others. My experience is the experience of a person entitled to be registered under the Indian Act. Further, I have never been denied that right. These facts shape how I understand life, law and politics" (Monture-Angus 1995: 3).

11. Looking back, I understand both why "Flint Woman" (this is the Mohawk title of my first article, which was republished as the first chapter of my book *Thunder in My Soul*) emerged during my last years at law school and why a few years after leaving law school I wanted to move beyond the image I had created. "Flint Woman" is the one who fights back. However, more than a decade after graduating from law school, fighting back is no longer enough.

12. It is not my intention to appropriate the experiences of Aboriginal women who are federally sentenced. This was the first comprehensive study to collect and give voice to the stories of Aboriginal women and what they have survived. Further, I do not see a lot of difference between the lives of Aboriginal prisoners who are women and my life when the measure is what we survived growing up. Therefore, I do not judge their present circumstances or allow the experience to be an obstacle in creating friendships.

13. This term refers to individuals who have not been arrested and have never served terms of incarceration.

14. I am grateful to Stephanie Hayman of the Centre for Crime and Justice Studies, London, England, for bringing this concern to my attention.

15. I have a problem with a portion of the academic literature written by Aboriginal scholars (many of those who fit in this category, I would note, are men). Many of these scholars offer excellent critiques of colonialism, of where we have been, but offer little comment on where we should go.

16. I am not the first academic to borrow the imagery from our cultural experi-

ences and contexts. Please see Gloria Valencia Weber and Christine Zuni (1995).

17. Although Johansen is not a Mohawk or Aboriginal, the people of the community have supported his work. Douglas M. George (Kanentiio) states: "What was sorely lacking in previous books was a command of the facts *as the Mohawk people saw them.* Until Professor Johansen began his research, *no author had the trust and confidence of the Mohawk people* necessary to write about the events that are as sensitive as they are terrifying" (Johansen 1993: x; emphasis added). This criteria is far too infrequently considered in academia and the research generated on Aboriginal Peoples. It is indeed *on* the people—it is on our backs as it is without our consent, knowledge, and participation. Very few academics are even cognizant that their relationship with Aboriginal people and Aboriginal nations is a fact that must be considered. It is not as simple as returning the research to the community. This does nothing to displace the appropriation. Even well-intentioned researchers do not develop sustaining relationships, because the relationships are not in and of the community.

18. Whenever I discuss these particular sections of the Indian Act and its impositions on Indian women, I am reminded of a poem written by Lenore Keeshig-Tobias. Her poem, "(a found poem)," was borrowed (in part) from the Indian Act and creatively reconstructs former sections 11 and 12(1)(b). These two sections contained the gender discriminatory provision that disenfranchised women on "marriage out" (See Keeshig-Tobias 1983: 123–24).

19. Bill C-31 became law in 1985. It contains the provision allowing for the reinstatement of most individuals who were involuntarily disenfranchised by a variety of provisions in the act (including the women who married out), and it creates the ability for bands to assume some level of control over their membership.

20. As this discussion focuses on the Indian Act, I adopt the language (Indian) of that Act in this section of the paper. The Indian Act applies only to those entitled to be registered under section 6 of that act.

21. Careful! This is not evidence that I have embraced feminist critiques of the English language (and it is a lesson in presumptions). I use the female pronoun because, as one Elder taught me, the word for Creator in our languages is neither male or female. As so many people use the male pronoun when talking about the Creator, I have elected to always use the female in an effort to restore some balance into how we talk about the spiritual realm. Nia:wen Art Solomon.

22. When my family made the decision to move to my partner's reserve, I do not recall considering one of these "rights" or "benefits" as a reason to settle ourselves on the reserve. We moved to Thunderchild so our children would be raised with more family than just mom and dad. We wanted our

children to have a chance to learn the language. We moved to the reserve to free the children from the racism in the city so that they would have a place to be free and to be who they are. We moved back to the reserve to be in a relationship with our community in an effort to step away from the pattern of colonialism embedded in our life. We moved back to the reserve to establish a stronger relationship with the land of my partner's territory.

23. I do not "blame" Indians for this, as the central experience of colonial oppression is the fight for daily survival. When you are busy trying to feed your children and just to make it to the next day, it is very difficult to see the "big picture" painted by our collective and individual oppression. This is one of the "privileges" I have in my life. I am no longer fighting for basic daily survival.

24. See, for example, Kathleen Jamieson (1978); Lilianne Krosenbrink-Gelissen (1991); and Native Women's Association of Canada (1986).

25. I am grateful to Leona Sparrow for raising this issue with me.

26. The most comprehensive analysis of the Native Women's Association of Canada and their part in the lobby to see section 12(1)(b) repealed does not consider these factors. See the work of Lilianne Krosenbrink-Gelissen (1991).

27. For example, the Canadian Advisory Council on the Status of Women funded a study produced by Kathleen Jamieson (an Indian woman) in 1978.

28. I am not asserting that the involvement of all feminists or women's rights activists and Aboriginal women is inappropriate. An excellent bridge-building discussion of the violence against all women is provided in Laureen Snider's work (1998: 1–39). The work of Constance Backhouse (1991) also stands out in my mind as an example of feminist work involving Aboriginal women in an appropriate way.

29. For a fuller discussion, see Mary Ellen Turpel (1991: 17–40).

30. I mean no disrespect to the sacred nature of these alliances called treaties. However, one look at the situation of treaties in Canadian law and it becomes obvious why I hold such a view.

31. I do not believe that the individualized process for issuing script extinguished any "collective" land rights of the Métis. The script documents themselves are silent regarding extinguishment. In Canadian law, this is insufficient to create the extinguishment of land rights. With respect to our nation "lines," I will leave any further discussion for Métis citizens to write. To go further is to speak for the Métis (a distinct nation), and that is both unnecessary and improper.

32. This is not an argument in support of pan-Indianism. I have long believed we must organize around nation status (and/or perhaps treaty territories).

33. I am not talking about a "safe space," which would presume that there is space outside the safe space that is not safe. Conceding that much space is not an acceptable parameter for me.

"Managing" Canadian Immigration: Racism, Ethnic Selectivity, and the Law

© Lisa Marie Jakubowski

For centuries Canada has been identified as "a nation of immigrants" (Samuel 1990: 383) and by the early 1990s statistics were indicating that one out of every six Canadian residents was born outside of Canada (Immigration Canada 1992: 9). Given this multicultural population, it is not surprising that Canadian governments have publicly placed immigration in a positive light. We have been regularly reminded that the history of immigration has been a positive and unifying force for the country, that immigration helps us to prosper economically, and that, through our contact with diverse groups of people, we learn to become more tolerant and respecting of difference. This vision, however, can be misleading. Immigration has enriched Canadian society, but Canada has not always embraced the immigrant. Indeed, Canada is plagued by a history—albeit a lesser known history—of racist immigration laws and policies.

For decades Canadian immigration law was influenced by a racist-inspired "White Canada" policy. It was not until the 1960s, with the implementation of the points system, that a formally colour-blind immigration policy became the defining feature of the Canadian state's response to immigration. While, in principle, Canadian immigration law has moved from being explicitly restrictive to non-discriminatory, a closer examination of contemporary immigration patterns reveals that racism and ethnic selectivity have not disappeared. Rather, law, policy, and practice in the area of immigration now reflect a more subtle and systemic form of discrimination, particularly towards immigrants from the developing world.

The purpose of this essay is twofold: 1) to examine the early history of Canadian immigration laws and to contextualize these laws, both economically and politically, with a view to revealing their explicitly racist nature; and 2) to argue that, despite the *appearance* of equity and fairness in contemporary immigration law and policy, there is evidence of more subtle and systemic discrimination at work.

CANADIAN IMMIGRATION:
LOCATING THE ECONOMIC AND POLITICAL CONTEXT

Prior to 1968, Canada's overtly prejudicial immigration law was based on a "nationality preference system" favouring European immigrants (Simmons 1990: 141). Then, with the emergence of the more "liberal," "non-discriminatory" points system in October 1967, the characteristics of the potential Canadian immigrant began to change. Between 1968 and 1987 about 2.8 million immigrants from new origin countries in Africa, Asia, and Latin America arrived in Canada (Simmons 1990).[1] This new wave of immigration from Third World countries now constitutes two-thirds to three-quarters of the inflow to Canada (Simmons 1990; Citizenship and Immigration Canada 1996: 25; Young 1997: 5; Knowles 1997: 195).

Clearly, the law now enables more people of colour to come to Canada, but discrimination, in less obvious forms, persists. What is the relationship among "race,"[2] class, immigration, and the state? Does the presence of "new," visibly different immigrants expedite the persistence and advancement of capitalism in Canada? How does ethnicity factor into the equation? Obviously, links do exist between immigration and Canadian political economy, and many theorists (for example Basran 1983; Bolaria and Li 1988; Cappon 1975) have analysed the relationship between state immigration policies and Canadian capitalist development. The work of Simmons, for example, highlights how Canada's immigration and refugee policies are shaped by the prevailing economic context. Specifically, "The Canadian state has promoted immigration policies favouring relatively large inflows of immigrant workers during periods of economic expansion and more selective inflows of skilled workers, entrepreneurs and visa workers in periods of economic recession" (Simmons 1992: 13).

Still, there is more to the admission of immigrants than the demands of the labour market. Historically, *who* is admitted and *how many* are admitted have been determined by three, often competing, factors: the desire to populate Canada with British people (or those whose characteristics most resemble the British); the need to be respecting of, and attentive to, concerns of the international community; and economic conditions (Law Union of Ontario 1981: 17). In other words, the content and objectives of laws and policies have been shaped by a multiplicity of factors, including ideological and political considerations; international obligations; and economic requirements (Elliott and Fleras 1996: 290). In law creation, the relationship among these considerations, obligations, and requirements becomes increasingly more complex as the nation's population grows more diverse. But, over time, one goal has remained constant—maintaining immigration control.

NATION-BUILDING AND THE "WHITE CANADA" POLICY

Officially abandoned only in 1962, "White Canada" policies are deeply rooted in the mid-nineteenth century. As Hawkins (1989: 8) notes, these early origins "and indeed the whole lengthy episode of 'White Canada' is often downplayed, or clothed in discreet silence or simply not extrapolated from its historical context." Initially, immigration policies could be described as ethnically selective: "racist in orientation, assimilationist in objective" (Elliott and Fleras 1996: 290). Striving to preserve the British character of Canada, authorities directed their efforts towards excluding certain people from entry, while encouraging others to settle. Potential migrants were ranked into categories, with "preferred" immigrants being drawn from Great Britain, the United States,[3] France, and, to a lesser extent, Northern and Western Europe (Manpower and Immigration 1974: 4). When these recruitment efforts failed to produce the large numbers required to settle Canada's western prairie lands, the federal government extended its preferential policies to include other white immigrants— for example, Ukrainians, Italians, Poles, and Hutterites—previously classified as "non-preferred" (Henry et al. 1995: 72). Emphasis was placed on *white* immigrants because they were considered to be of "superior stock," more desirable and more assimilable than immigrants of colour (Elliott and Fleras 1996: 290). However, even with the expansion of the preferred categories to include more white immigrants, Canadian labour needs could not be met. In the 1880s thus began the recruitment of an "undesirable," visibly different source of cheap labour—the Chinese. It was during this time period that "race," in relation to Canadian immigration law and policy formation, first became an issue of significance (Henry et al. 1995: 72).

One of the central events triggering the immigration of the Chinese to Canada was the construction of the Canadian Pacific Railway (CPR). During the period of its construction (1881–85), the number of Chinese arriving in Canada rose dramatically (Bolaria and Li 1988: 105). Chinese immigrants were particularly attractive because of their large supply and cheap cost. While nation-building, the Chinese railway workers were tolerated by the white workers, as long as no other source of labour was available. When the CPR was completed, and Canada now had a surplus of labour, sentiments towards the Chinese presence changed. Accordingly, a conflict between business and labour arose.

It was clearly in the interests of Canadian capitalists to have this reserve army of labour. For the capitalist, the appeal of immigrant labour, in this case Chinese labour, resided in the apparent willingness of the immigrants to do undesirable work cheaply and in the opportunity to "weaken the organizational efforts and bargaining position of the dominant workforce" (Bolaria and Li 1988: 34; Portes 1978). The reaction of white Canadian labourers to the Chinese presence was less enthusiastic. The ultimate result was the emergence of a split-labour market.

According to Bonacich (1972: 549), a split-labour market produces a three-way conflict between the dominant class and two groups of labourers. The dominant business class strives to maximize profits utilizing the cheapest available sources of labour power. Through the process of super-exploitation (Cox 1948), the dominant class will replace higher-paid labour with cheaper labour. Bonacich (1980: 15) argues that because employers prefer to hire the cheaper labourers of colour, white workers fear and become hostile towards the more exploitable racial minorities. One way white workers can respond to this hostility and fear is to try to restrict the capitalists' access to cheaper labour through "exclusion" (Bonacich 1972: 554–57, 1976: 45).

In the case of exclusion, dominant white labour excludes the super-exploited workers of colour from full participation in the labour market by attempting to prevent this cheaper labour source from moving into a particular territory. The push by organized white labour to "control immigration" is one way of practising exclusion against certain visible minorities.

This pattern was clearly visible in the case of the Chinese labourers in Canada. Antagonistic towards, and feeling threatened by, these visibly different newcomers, white labourers began pressing the Canadian government to restrict immigration. Thus, when the nation-building projects, such as the construction of the CPR, were close to completion and the need for these cheap labourers diminished, the federal government began passing highly discriminatory, exclusionary pieces of immigration legislation (Henry et al. 1995: 72; Elliott and Fleras 1996: 290–91). A statement made by Prime Minister John A. Macdonald in 1883 provides the political and economic context of these legislative changes.

A Chinese person "was a sojourner in a strange land ... and he has no common interest with us," Macdonald said. He "gives us his labour and is paid for it and is valuable, the same as a threshing machine or *any other agricultural implement which we may borrow from the United States, or hire and return to its owner*" (quoted in Knowles 1997: 51; emphasis added).

Elements of restriction, first directed towards the Chinese in 1885 and subsequently towards all immigrants of colour, began appearing in immigration legislation from the 1880s onward (Hawkins 1989: 16). While the general term "race" did not emerge as a prohibitive/restrictive legal category until the Immigration Act of 1910, the federal government did pass specific regulations and pieces of legislation that were blatantly discriminatory towards certain racial minorities. In particular, it decided to take action against Asian immigration and devised different methods for "discouraging immigration" from China, Japan, and India (Law Union of Ontario 1981: 25). Among the legislation passed were the Chinese Immigration Act of 1885, the 1907 Gentleman's Agreement with Japan, and the Continuous Journey Stipulation of 1908—this last one directed towards India and the curtailing of East Indian immigration.

The Chinese Immigration Act of 1885 imposed a head tax on all Chinese men arriving in Canada—Chinese men only, because Chinese women and children were excluded from entry into the country. While the tax was set at $50 dollars in 1885 (SC 1885 c.71), it rose to $100 in 1900 (SC 1900 c.32) and to $500 by 1903 (SC 1903 c.8) (Bolaria and Li 1988: 107). But even with the tax the flow of Chinese immigration continued. Facing more and more pressure to eradicate this "immigration problem," the Canadian government passed the Chinese Exclusion Act (SC 1923 c.38), which served to prohibit Chinese immigration from 1923 to 1947 (Bolaria and Li 1988: 107).[4]

With respect to restricting Japanese immigration, the case was a little more complicated. Because the Japanese were allies of the British at the turn of the century, any action Canada might take against Japanese immigration had to be done without jeopardizing British-Japanese relations. Also, Japan had the potential to become a trading partner with Canada, so some degree of co-operation was considered desirable. Taking these factors into consideration, Rudolphe Lemieux, postmaster general and minister of labour, was sent to Japan to negotiate what came to be known as the Gentleman's Agreement: "Under the terms of this agreement, Canada agreed not to impose discriminatory laws against Japanese immigrants, but the Japanese government was to voluntarily restrict the number of people permitted to emigrate to Canada" (Law Union of Ontario 1981: 26).

In the case of India, William Lyon Mackenzie King, the deputy minister of labour, was not as successful in negotiations. India was clearly resistant to such restrictions, which left the Canadian government with a dilemma. Not wanting to cause rifts within the British Empire, Canada could not take direct, discriminatory action. How then could it more subtly control East Indian immigration? The solution was the Continuous Journey Stipulation of 1908. According to this regulation, immigrants who came to Canada "otherwise than by continuous journey from countries of which they were natives or citizens, and upon through tickets purchased in that country, may be refused entry" (Bolaria and Li 1988: 170). This particular regulation highlights the political nature of law. Because they were citizens of the British Empire, East Indians should have been entitled to immigrate to Canada, but the Continuous Journey Stipulation made this almost impossible. Specifically, at that particular historical moment, the only company that could provide transportation from India to Canada was the CPR. Thus, in order to achieve its exclusionary objective, the government issued the CPR express orders not to sell any "through tickets" to Canada (Law Union of Ontario 1981: 26). From the standpoint of law-makers and politicians, the stipulation was both functional and politically calculating.

The Act did indeed curtail Indian immigration to Canada after 1908. For example, in 1907 and 1908, a total of 4,757 East Indians immigrated to Canada. When the legislation became effective in 1909, the numbers decreased dramatically. In 1909 only six East Indians were admitted to Canada, while the total admission of East Indians to Canada between 1909–13 was twenty-nine (Bolaria and Li 1988: 169). In an effort to preserve its positive relations with the rest of the British Empire, the Canadian government ensured that the Stipulation did not *explicitly* bar any particular group of people from entry into Canada. Highlighting its politicality, the Continuous Journey Stipulation "amended the *Immigration Act* to allow the government to control East Indian immigration without having the appearance of doing so" (Henry et al. 1995: 73).

The now famous "Komagata Maru Incident" was an attempt by East Indians to challenge this racist policy. On May 23, 1914, a ship called *Komagata Maru* arrived in Vancouver carrying 376 mostly Sikh passengers. Because the ship had made numerous stops along the way to pick up people, the passengers were denied entry into Canada. Officials cited the Continuous Journey Stipulation. After a two-month standoff between East Indians and the Canadian Government, the *Komagata Maru* was escorted out of Vancouver Harbour by a naval ship. While the efforts of the East Indians failed during the summer months of 1914, to this day various East Indian organizations continue to demand compensation from, and an admission by, the federal government of wrongdoing in the incident of *Komagata Maru* (Elliott and Fleras 1992: 240; Bolaria and Li 1988: 171).

In essence, the Chinese Exclusion Act, the Gentleman's Agreement, and the Continuous Journey Stipulation were effective mechanisms for controlling immigration, ensuring that almost no Asians immigrated to Canada until after World War II (Henry et al. 1995: 73). Such mechanisms were consistent with the philosophy towards immigration that had emerged in the late nineteenth and early twentieth centuries: "Canada is situated in the North Temperate Zone.... The climate is particularly suited to the white race. It is the land of homes—the new homeland of the British people.... British people soon find themselves at home in Canada. It is a British country, with British customs and ideals" (from *Canada-The New Homeland,* as cited in Law Union of Ontario 1981: 26).

SECTION 38(C): CANADIAN XENOPHOBIA ENSHRINED IN LAW

The term "race" first emerged as a prohibitive/restrictive legal category in section 38(c) of the Immigration Act of 1910 (Hawkins 1989: 17). This section, amended in 1919 to include "nationality," is most representative of "White Canada's" xenophobia. In essence, section 38(c) created a class of immigrants considered to be "undesirable" for admission to Canada. Included among those who could be denied entry were "any *nationality* or *race* of immigrants … *deemed unsuitable* having regard to the climatic, industrial, social, educational, labour [conditions] … or because such immigrants are deemed *undesirable* owing to their peculiar customs, habits, modes of life, methods of holding property and because of their probable inability to become readily assimilated or to assume the duties and responsibilities of Canadian citizenship within a reasonable time after their entry" (emphasis added). By including section 38(c) in the Immigration Act, the government's discriminatory policies were enshrined in law—differential treatment based on "race" or nationality was firmly established as a government policy.

One form of differential treatment was the creation of a list of "preferred" countries, as Mackenzie King explained in a report:

> The policy of the [Labour] Department at the present time [1910] is to encourage immigration of farmers, farm labourers, and female domestic servants from the United States, the British Isles, and certain Northern European countries, namely, France, Belgium, Holland, Switzerland, Germany, Denmark, Norway, Sweden and Iceland. On the other hand, it is the policy of the Department *to do all in its power to keep out of the country ... those belonging to nationalities unlikely to assimilate and who consequently prevent the building up of a united nation of people of similar customs and ideals.* (quoted in Manpower and Immigration 1974: 9–10; emphasis added)

Most conveniently, the legislation of 1910 did not specify the "undesirable" nations. Instead, it gave immigration officials "wide discretion to exclude almost any prospective immigrant on the basis of race, national or ethnic origin or creed" (Henry et al. 1995: 73).

As Abella and Troper (1983) note, the hierarchy continued to reflect the preferences of earlier decades: 1) British and U.S. immigrants; (2) Northern and Western European immigrants; and—as a last resort—(3) Jews, Blacks, and Orientals. The third group comprised the least desirable candidates for immigration to Canada. They were acceptable only as long as they "were out of sight, risking life and limb in the mines and smelters of the west and north, holed up in lumber camps deep in the forest, or farming the more marginal areas of the western wheat frontier" (Abella and Troper 1983: 5).

What was particularly problematic for immigration officials was when these "undesirables" left the more rural and isolated areas and drifted towards the city. In this respect, Jews were "the worst culprits." They were "city people" who would not be kept on the farm. This "drift" towards the city became a rationale for the drastic immigration restrictions that emerged in the mid-1920s. By 1928, the deputy minister of immigration, W.J. Egan, ordered that Eastern European immigration be reduced by two-thirds. With the economy doing well, he used the following reasoning to justify the action: "Non-preferred country immigrants had drifted into non-agricultural work almost immediately upon arrival ... and [were] filling positions that might have been filled by immigrants from the Mother Country" (Egan, in Abella and Troper 1983: 5).

From the outbreak of World War I through to the Depression and World War II, Canadian immigration went through a long period of uncertainty (Manpower and Immigration 1974: 10). In response to the need to settle Western Canada, immigration had peaked at 400,870 in 1913. However, the unstable and uncertain conditions generated by the two world wars and the Depression resulted in fewer people coming to Canada, with immigration reaching an all-time low of 7,576 in 1942 (Elliott and Fleras 1996: 291). During these troubling political and economic times, anti-immigrant sentiments came to be embodied in extremely discriminatory and inhumane policies and practices.

The Depression, for instance, gave the government the justification it needed to further strengthen its already restrictive legislation. The new legislation reflected the intensified anti-immigrant sentiments among Canadians, who were generally of the opinion that immigrants were attempting to steal jobs from "more deserving" citizens. Basically, immigration from continental Europe came to a halt in March 1931 with the passage of Order-in-Council P.C. 695. By offering admission only to certain categories of people, the order made its ethnic, racial, and class biases quite transparent: "British subjects and American citizens with sufficient capital to maintain themselves until employment was secured; agriculturalists with sufficient means to farm in Canada, farm labourers with guaranteed employment, any individual engaged in the mining, lumbering or logging with assured employment in one of these industries; and the wives and children of adult males legally resident in Canada" (Knowles 1997: 115). The anti-immigrant sentiment in the country was so strong that Canada was not even prepared to distinguish between the "ordinary immigrant" and "the refugee." As Europeans were desperately fleeing Europe in search of refuge from the growing Nazi movement, Canada refused to open its doors.

During this time, the man responsible for enforcing Canadian immigration policy, Frederick Charles Blair, was particularly determined to keep Jewish refugees out of Canada. For Blair, "the term 'refugee' was a code word for 'Jew.' Unless safeguards were adopted, Canada was in danger of being 'flooded by Jewish people,' and his task was to make sure that the safeguard didn't fail" (Abella and Troper 1983: 8). A case in point is the now infamous "Voyage of the Damned." In 1939 the *S.S. St Louis* docked at a Canadian port carrying some 907 Jewish refugees. After being rejected by Cuba, various Latin and South American countries, and the United States, Canada was their last hope. But here, too, the Jewish refugees were denied entry (Abella and Troper 1983: 63-64), and the ship set sail for Europe, where many of its passengers would die in gas chambers and crematoria.

Beyond closing the door to new immigrants and refugees, the country also used deportation on a much more regular basis. New immigrants who had not yet obtained citizenship, who became unemployed, or "who got into any trouble" could be easily expelled from the country (Knowles 1997: 116). In some cases, even those innocent of wrongdoing were "persuaded" to leave. After the Japanese bombing of Pearl Harbor on December 8, 1941, over 20,000 Japanese-Canadians were evicted from their homes in British Columbia and sent to labour camps or farms in Alberta and Manitoba, or interned in detention camps/centres until the conclusion of the war (Knowles 1997: 124). At the war's end about 4,000 Japanese-Canadians (half of them Canadian-born—of whom two-thirds were Canadian citizens) gave in to the anti-Asiatic sentiments and government pressure, leaving Canada for Japan under the government's "repatriation" scheme (Knowles 1997: 124; Sunahara 1981; Ujimoto 1988).

Following World War II, immigration rates once again skyrocketed in response to a postwar boom in the Canadian economy. But even with an overwhelming need for labour, "discrimination and ethnic selectivity in immigration would remain" (Reimers and Troper 1992: 20). The "peacetime policy" (Manpower and Immigration 1974: 18) was unveiled in Prime Minister Mackenzie King's 1947 *Statement on Immigration*:

> With regard to the selection of immigrants ... I wish to make it quite clear that Canada is perfectly within her rights in selecting persons who we regard as desirable future citizens. It is not a "fundamental human right" of any alien to enter Canada. It is a privilege. It is a matter of domestic policy ... the people of Canada do not wish, as a result of mass immigration, to make a fundamental alteration in the character of our population. Large scale immigration from the Orient would change the fundamental character of the Canadian population.... The government therefore ... has no intention of removing existing regulations respecting Asiatic immigration unless and until alternative measures of effective control have been worked out. (King, in Manpower and Immigration 1974: 205)

Essentially, as this excerpt highlights, with the rejuvenation of immigration in 1947 came a return to the "policy, regulations and racial priorities of an earlier era" (Reimers and Troper 1992: 21). That is, policies were still racist in orientation, assimilationist in objective. Care would still be taken to ensure that those applicants from groups considered to be "most easily assimilated" —that is, "British subjects from the United Kingdom, Ireland, Newfoundland, New Zealand, Australia or the Union of South Africa, and also citizens of the United States (King, in Manpower and Immigration 1974: 203)—would be given preferential treatment during the admission process. To reinforce this xenophobic position, the Immigration Act of 1952 maintained the explicitly restrictive clause 38(c), although the category "race" was changed to "ethnic group" (Hawkins 1989: 17). Consistent with the exclusions outlined in the 1910 act, the Minister was given wide-sweeping discretion to prohibit or limit the admission of people on the basis of ethnicity, nationality, geographic origin, peculiarity of custom, unsuitability of climate, or inability to become assimilated (Reimers and Troper 1992: 25). Through the use of such discretion, the "national and racial balance of immigration would be regulated so as to not to disturb the existing *character* of the Canadian population" (Green 1976: 21).

ABANDONING THE "WHITE CANADA" POLICY— FACT OR FICTION?

From the Immigration Act of 1910 up to and including the 1952 Act, section 38(c) was the principal instrument through which the implicit "White Canada" policy on immigration was implemented. However, with the passage of new, non-discriminatory immigration regulations in 1962, the "White Canada" policy was, as Hawkins (1989: 39) notes, "virtually dead." These regulations officially ended racial and ethnic discrimination in the processing of independent immigrants, with *skills* or, more specifically, *skills in relation to Canadian labour market needs* becoming the main selection criterion (Reimers and Troper 1992: 32). This shift towards universal and equal treatment of all applicants was reinforced in the White Paper of 1966,[5] which proposed that all persons coming to Canada as immigrants would be subject to the same entrance standards, regardless of "race," ethnicity, religion, or country of origin.

These policy changes directed towards non-discriminatory treatment were not necessarily made in response to popular demand in Canada. As

Hawkins (1989: 39) suggests, change occurred because senior Canadian officials realized that "Canada could not operate effectively with the United Nations, or in a multiracial Commonwealth, with the millstone of a racially discriminatory immigration policy round her neck." But if "race," nationality, and ethnicity could no longer be used explicitly as a rationale for selecting immigrants, some other system had to be created that could be applied in a way that was "reasonably fair and objective." Accordingly, in October 1967, Canada developed the first immigration points system.

The purpose of the points system was to establish an "objective" assessment system for the admission of immigrants. The criteria for admission were education and training, personal assessment,[6] occupational demand, occupational skill, age, arranged employment, knowledge of French or English, relatives in Canada, and employment opportunities in the area of destination (Hawkins 1988: 405). The nine factors have a combined potential value of one hundred. An applicant who received fifty or more points was considered likely to settle successfully. An applicant who received less than fifty points was deemed unlikely to settle successfully (Manpower and Immigration 1974: 42).[7] While the original points system was revised in 1974, 1978, and 1985 (Hawkins 1988: 380), its intent remained the same: that is, immigration policy would be applied on "a universal basis which can be interpreted to mean that everyone seeking admission to Canada is assessed under the same set of standards regardless of race, religion or country of origin" (Green 1976: 42).

Although the establishment of "a formally colour-blind immigration policy" (Elliott and Fleras 1996: 292) made it appear as though racial discrimination had been eliminated, the evidence indicated the contrary (Henry et al. 1995; Bolaria and Li 1988; Malarek 1987; Green 1976). While the regulations no longer contained blatant discriminatory provisions, subtle discriminatory mechanisms remained. In the matter of immigration offices outside of Canada, for example, Green (1976: 43) noted that "as the government shifts from a national/ethnic-based policy to a universal admission approach, it would have to expand its overseas offices so that, in theory at least, right of review was equal for prospective immigrants regardless of their country of origin." But Green's (1976: 47–54) analysis of overseas expenditures indicated that from 1951 to 1969 the largest concentration of resources committed to the recruitment of migrants was in "developed," traditional source countries. Specifically, in the period 1951–57, 91 percent of total expenditures for recruitment went to developed countries and only 9 percent to less developed countries. In the years 1962–69, the distribution in resources remained largely unbalanced, with 78 percent of total expenditures for recruitment going to developed countries and 22 percent to less developed countries (Green 1976: 47). As Anthony Richmond observed, the country had "evidently no intention of abandoning the traditional preference for British immigrants" (quoted in Green 1976: 51).

The commitment, in theory, to the elimination of racial discrimination was more formally enshrined in the Immigration Act of 1976. Consistent with trends of past immigration law and policy formation, an interplay among several factors shaped the decision to include a non-discriminatory clause in the act. From an economic standpoint, Canada moved from "a dependence on unskilled manual labour toward a more highly educated and skilled workforce" (Henry et al. 1995: 76). Because of a decline in immigration from traditional source countries (due to postwar economic recovery), Canada opened its doors to "non-preferred" countries in search of economically suitable immigrants. From a more political and social standpoint, pressure to eradicate overt racism surfaced. Influences ranged from a newly implemented multicultural policy that recognized racial and cultural diversity in Canada to increasing pressure from well-organized, politically active, and increasingly influential minority groups, human rights activists, and lawyers, and from the international community (Henry et al. 1995). In response to the various influences, section 3(f) emerged:

> It is hereby declared that Canadian Immigration policy and the rules and regulations made under this Act shall be designed and administered in such a manner as to promote the domestic and international interests of Canada recognizing the need to ... *ensure that any person who seeks admission to Canada on either a permanent or temporary basis is subject to standards of admission that do not discriminate on grounds of race, national or ethnic origin, colour, religion or sex.* (Hawkins 1988: 426; emphasis added)

Under the act, all immigrants would be assessed according to "universal standards" designed to assess ability to "adapt to Canadian life" and settle successfully. Some analysts hailed the passage of this act into law in 1978 as an extremely positive and important moment in Canadian history. For instance, in the words of Freda Hawkins (1988: xv), "This marked the beginning of a new, more liberal and more cooperative era in Canadian immigration." But were these legislative changes, in practice, as positive as they appeared to be on paper? Despite the more universal system and the commitment, in theory, to equality, discrimination in less obvious forms persisted.

For instance, even with the 1976 act the distribution of immigration offices reveals a discriminatory policy. By way of example, "There are five immigration offices in the United Kingdom, but only three in South America, and only five in the whole of Africa, two of which are located in South Africa. The United States has ten offices, but India, with twice the population only has one" (Law Union of Ontario 1981: 46). The distribution of immigration offices following the passage of the act clearly indicated the historical preference for white European immigration. Furthermore, the wide use of discretion under the act and regulations allowed individual, biased officers to make discriminatory decisions.

The issue of "personal suitability" was one key to this discrimination. Under the original points system, this criterion—then known as "personal qualities"—was the only element that involved a subjective judgement on the part of the immigration officer. Within the original points system, this factor was worth fifteen points out of one hundred. On a scale of fifteen, immigration officers were to use their discretion in deciding on "a person's ability to become settled in a new country." This ability was based on the officer's perceptions of the applicant's adaptability, motivation, initiation, and resourcefulness (Manpower and Immigration 1974: 44). The criterion still exists within the points system, although it is now worth ten points out of one hundred and is called "personal suitability" (Young 1991a: 20).

The weighting of the personal qualities/personal suitability criterion might seem to imply a limitation on the immigration officer's use of personal discretion. But what is less well known is that the officer's discretion extended well beyond the "personal qualities" criterion. A further regulation granted officers the discretion to override the points system "in exceptional cases." A statement by Manpower and Immigration (1974: 50) outlined the department's justification for the inclusion of this regulation:

> Introduction of weighted selection factors in 1967 was a totally
> new immigration concept. It was hoped that totalling the units

of assessment awarded for each of the factors would indicate, within reasonable limits, the likelihood of most applicants' success or failure in becoming established in Canada. It was recognized, however, that it was impossible to cover every eventuality, and that the regulations should contain a mechanism for dealing with the exceptional case. Accordingly, when a selection officer is satisfied that there are significant circumstances affecting an applicant's prospects that have not been reflected in the assessment under the nine selection factors he is authorized, subject to concurrence of a designated senior officer, to accept or reject the applicant *irrespective of the number of units of assessment that may have been awarded.* (emphasis added)

This regulation continues to the present day. Specifically, section 11(3) of the immigration regulations "authorizes officers to exercise their discretion in respect of immigrants whose applications are unit-rated under the selection criteria, and to accept, or refuse to accept an applicant, whether the applicant achieves or does not achieve the number of units of assessment." The section points out that discretion is to be exercised "solely on the basis that the unit-rating does not accurately reflect an immigrant's chances of becoming successfully established in Canada" (Employment and Immigration Canada 1991: 07-90-6).

In principle, then, Canadian immigration law has moved from being explicitly restrictive to "non-discriminatory." But this preliminary review intimates that we must problematize—rather than unquestioningly accept—the claim that Canada's immigration law is "non-discriminatory." Although couched in the politically acceptable language of equity and fairness, does this automatically mean that the law is equitably applied to all potential immigrants at the point of entry? To address this question, and to highlight how racism and discrimination are manifested in more contemporary Canadian immigration law and policies, we will briefly consider Bill C-86 and *Not Just Numbers: A Framework for Canadian Immigration* (1997); and to better appreciate the complexities underlying the process of Canadian immigration law and policy formation, we will also consider the politicality of law.

THE ROLE OF LAW: "AMBIGUITY" AND THE POLITICS OF LAW
Laws exist for a reason. They are designed to help us maintain a socially ordered society, to give us a sense of security, to remind us that we live

in a just, fair, and equitable country. We only need look to the *Canadian Charter of Rights and Freedoms* to verify this. Section 15(1) of the *Charter* explicitly states: "Every individual is equal before and under the law, and has the right to equal protection and equal benefit of the law without discrimination based on race, national or ethnic origin, colour, religion, sex, age or mental or physical disability." In essence the basis of legitimacy within modern society is the law, and "on paper" Canada is indeed an equitable and fair nation. But what about in practice? When we examine the guiding frameworks of Canadian society, the question becomes more complicated.

Because Canada is distinguished by at least three philosophies—capitalism, liberal democracy, and multiculturalism—the process of state legitimation is complex. Clearly, these philosophies have their contradictions and competing goals. The dilemma for law-makers becomes how to reconcile the contradictions and to create laws and policies that will satisfy a more diversified constituency. This begins with the recognition that law is inescapably *political*. Law-makers recognize that law creation must address competing interests. Furthermore, the enshrinement in law of the interests of any particular group is the outcome of complex political negotiations. To facilitate this process of negotiation, symbolic ideals such as equity and fairness are embodied in the law. These symbols are so vague and all-embracing that "most members of society can accept or support them in some interpretation" (Cotterrell 1992: 103).

My own (Jakubowski 1997) documentary analysis of immigration law and policies provides concrete examples of this negotiation process. Specifically, an analysis of minutes from House of Commons Debates and meetings of the Standing Committee on Labour, Employment and Immigration around particular pieces of legislation—the Live-In Caregiver Program and Bill C-86—exposes the duality of law and, more precisely, its "equivocal" nature.

The documentary analysis takes as its starting point the "everyday world" of the organization (Smith 1987)—specifically, the federal government organization that in effect "manages" Canadian immigration. In the analysis I argue that the everyday world of the organization appears before us in the form of documents. Furthermore, our knowledge of this world is, to a large extent, mediated by various legal discourses that appear within these documents. The documents direct us to think about and view the world within predetermined conceptual boundaries that are not disruptive to the ruling order. Aiming specifically at acquiring legitimacy, the state (via law-makers) utilizes discourses designed to satisfy a diversity of interests: labour and capital, ethnic groups, and humanitarian organizations, to name just a few.

The deconstruction or unpacking of the documents' legal discourses places an emphasis on how law, as a text, produces competing messages, thereby enabling unequal practices such as racism and discrimination to persist with legitimacy. Herein lies the *duality of law*. The government may, for example, define legislative changes on matters pertaining to human rights as "gains" for the less advantaged populations. But these "gains" can simultaneously benefit those in positions of power by subtly reinforcing already existing systemic forms of inequality. This duality is particularly evident in various forms of anti-discrimination law—including Canada's Immigration Act.

To see legal discourses around immigration as "sanitary coding," as a rhetorical mode, is particularly effective. Sanitary coding is "the ability to communicate privately racist [and discriminatory] ideas with a discourse that is publicly defensible as non-racist [and non-discriminatory]" (Reeves 1983: 190). Basically, the discourse eliminates gender, race, and class categories in order to neutralize the text, which is thus cleansed of categories, explanations, evaluations, and prescriptions that have discriminatory potential. One of the most effective cleansing techniques is "equivocation" (Reeves 1983: 190–95). Briefly, equivocation involves the use of purposely vague and misleading terms in order to make the meaning, purpose, or intent of some claim deliberately ambiguous or confusing. Dummett's (1973: 185) analysis of the phrase "controlling immigration" illustrates this point: "At all times the propaganda in favour of 'controlling immigration' has been understood on every side to mean, 'cutting down on coloured immigration,' yet as with the wording of the law itself the defender of control can exclaim indignantly that he never mentioned colour but only the number of people coming into the country; while if he is attacked from the right, he can point out that everyone understood his remarks to refer to coloured immigration."

By using these devices to analyse the debates around legislative changes to immigration, it becomes clear how purportedly beneficial legislative changes can be used to perpetuate already existing forms of systemic discrimination.

Bill C-86 and Beyond:
Progressive Change or More of the Same?

Both Bill C-86 and the recommendations outlined in *Not Just Numbers* (LRAG 1997) reflect initiatives on the part of the federal Conservative and Liberal governments, respectively, to improve immigration law and policy. Each purports to be based on principles of non-discrimination, support for family reunification, and a humanitarian concern for refugees. Furthermore, both stress that immigration must continue to operate, economically, in the best interests of Canadians (see prefacing comments of *Managing Immigration* [Immigration Canada 1992]; *Not Just Numbers* [LRAG 1997: 1].

However explicit and reasonable these goals might be, both Bill C-86 and the recommendations outlined in *Not Just Numbers* have met with widespread criticism across Canada. Critics contend that both subtly reinforce discriminatory practices by favouring the rich, being racially and ethnically selective, having preferred countries and preferential types of immigrants, and favouring individuals from developed over developing nations. In both documents, standard criteria may be universally applicable to all people, but not all people have equal opportunity to meet the standard. The contents show an interplay among class, ethnicity, and race that creates a preferential category of immigrants, one that the majority of Canadians will be comfortable with.

Initiated by the Conservative government under Brian Mulroney, Bill C-86 was a complex and lengthy piece of legislation that represented the most extensive amendment to the Immigration Act since 1976 (Young 1992: 1). Indeed, Bill C-86 is an "immigration controlling mechanism." When introducing the bill, Immigration Canada (1992: 3) argued for the rather pressing need to develop new ways to "manage" Canada's immigration program, largely because "over the past decade, there have been growing large scale movements of people from one country to another." As an example, Employment and Immigration Minister Bernard Valcourt noted that the number of immigrants and refugees who gained admission to Canada had increased from 88,000 in 1983 to 250,000 in 1992 (Canada 1992, June 22: 12540). Furthermore, the majority were people of colour arriving from non-traditional (and therefore "less desirable") regions of the world.

These immigrants and refugees arrived when the climate of acceptance in Canada was less than ideal. Canadians were feeling far more vulnerable economically. They were developing a growing sense of mistrust and intolerance towards "outsiders" (particularly visibly different "outsiders") and were increasingly disillusioned and discontented with the government (Gallup Report 1992; *Maclean's* 1993: 42; Harper 1992: A24).The government, faced with a crisis of legitimacy, introduced Bill C-86 with the aim of balancing the needs of Canadians with Canada's reputation as an equitable, caring, and compassionate nation. To address the diverse concerns of Canadians, the government relied heavily on equivocation in the construction of Bill C-86.

Specifically, when introducing it, Valcourt presented Bill C-86 as the answer for *"managing immigration"* in the 1990s; the logic of sanitary coding, particularly the technique of equivocation, is easily applicable to the phrase "managing immigration." Drawing parallels between the phrases "managing immigration" and "controlling immigration" (Dummett 1973: 185), I would argue that "managing immigration" is a purposively vague and misleading phrase expressly designed to be confusing in its meaning, purpose, or intent. As an equivocal term, "managing" can have both "public" and "private" connotations. According to Reeves:

> The coexistence of public and private connotations, one announcing what ought to be mentioned, the other announcing what ought not to be mentioned, can be regarded as a kind of *code or cipher.* The underlying private message, however, is not secret in the sense that it is known only to a select few: most or all of the audience might recognize its presence and be able to decipher it with ease. *It is secret in the sense that the speaker is in a position to refute it.* (Reeves 1983: 193; emphasis added)

Publicly, the term "managing" takes on a benevolent tone, one that implies "taking care" of Canadians, "taking care" of immigrants, and that thereby protects the image of the Conservative government as a government with humanitarian values. Simultaneously, however, the private, coded meaning of "managing" is far less altruistic. Does "managing," as critics have argued, imply "controlling immigration from the developing world"? It is when politicians are challenged to account for their remarks that equivocation becomes crucial. Specifically, as Reeves (1983: 193) puts it: "The speaker may defend himself by denying the underlying message, and asserting that the public meaning should be taken at its face value. What he *really* said is there in public for all to see, and the private connotation is a product of his audience's minds, of their subjective connotations. And how can he be held responsible for others' subjective interpretations?"

From the standpoint of the government, there is an advantage to using equivocation in relation to the law. Ambiguity not only allows legislators to avoid commitment to any one constituency, but also leaves the legislation open to manipulation by legislators when it seems to be a politically feasible thing to do. Thus, when challenged to explain the phrase "managing," the government attempts to protect itself by giving different responses to varied interest groups. To defend itself against accusations of racism, for instance, the Conservative government could argue emphatically that the bill made no mention of "race" and therefore there was no violation of the *Charter of Rights and Freedoms* on this score.[8] When attacked from the other side by racists who say that Bill C-86 does not go far enough, Conservatives could argue that managing immigration can be taken to mean "controlling the immigration of people of colour." This approach is simply a more subtle, politically correct way of handling the problem in the current climate. This is what makes sanitary coding and equivocation so insidious—the real intentions of the politician cannot be unquestionably established (Reeves 1983: 204).

When it is trying to sell Bill C-86, how does the Conservative government negotiate the demands of varied interest groups? Here, in answering this question, I will limit my discussion to two areas: family reunification and the streamlining of the refugee determination process through the "safe" country provision. These areas again show the duality of law or, put another way, the literal versus "coded" meanings that are attached to the amendments. As we shall see, the equivocated use of "family" becomes a means of managing immigration.

On the question of "managing" families
According to the proponents of Bill C-86, there were to be "no limitations" on family reunification (see Canada 1992, June 22: 12540ff). But the perpetual reference to reunification "without limitations" is somewhat problematic, particularly among Canadians who have a less conventional understanding of the term "family."

In encouraging "unlimited" family reunification, the government was referring to immediate or nuclear family members. Bill C-86 does nothing for the extended family (Canada 1992, June 22: 12501 [Marchi],

12538-12539 [Mitchell], 12560 [Karpoff]). Grandparents, parents, and other more "distant" relatives were, in a sense, reduced to a "less than family" status by being processed in lower priority streams subject to annual quotas.

This restrictive definition was challenged by the Canadian Ethnocultural Council (CEC), The National Organization of Immigrant and Visible Minority Women of Canada (NOIVMW), and the Chinese Canadian National Council (CCNC), to name just a few. Thematically, the statements made by the CEC, NOIVMW, and CCNC showed many parallels. In essence, the message was that the multicultural nation within which we live has little recognition of, or tolerance for, diversified conceptions of the family.

By relegating all but nuclear family members to lower priority streams in the "management structure," the government adopted a Canadian-style (Knowles 1997: 193) definition of the family. "Unlimited family reunification" suddenly became "unlimited [nuclear] family reunification." Suddenly it appeared to be more difficult for certain kinds of relatives to be acknowledged as family. Given the difficult economic climate, the government was purportedly trying to better manage immigration by establishing a more appropriate balance between family class and independent immigrants; but arguably there could be more to the decision than balance.

An alternative interpretation is that with the more inclusive definition of family, the government had "little discretionary control" (Knowles 1997: 193) over the types of people who were entering the country under the family class. Furthermore, given the "new face" of immigration and the number of people arriving from non-traditional source countries, unlimited family reunification increased the probability that Canada would receive too many less developed, undesirable, economically unsuitable, less assimilable people who would disrupt the existing fabric of Canadian society. With a tilt towards more independent immigration via the points system, the country regains discretionary control and "management" strategies become more effective.

The key point, once again, is the equivocated use of the term "family." In a multicultural society, family connotes different things to different people. Therefore, do the government's efforts to better manage the family class mean taking better care of both Canadians and immigrants alike? Or do they mean controlling immigration from less desirable, developing world source countries? Only the creator of the amendment knows its true intention.

"Managing" refugees and the "safe country" provision

> Managing immigration really means, in a refugee protection
> context, denying protection to people who otherwise might be
> allowed and entitled to come as refugees. (David Matas, presi-
> dent of the Canadian Council of Refugees, in HC #5, July 30,
> 1992: 37)

From a practical standpoint, Bill C-86 is more concerned with controlling the influx of refugees to Canada than it is with protecting refugees.
The legislation downplays humanitarian concerns, and refugees become
simply another category of immigrants to be managed. One way that this
particular category of immigrants can be managed is through the use of
the Safe Country Provision, which, consistent with the approach as a
whole, is depicted as little more than code for "controlling immigration
from the developing world."

According to section 46.01(1)(b) of Bill C-86: "A person who claims
to be a Convention Refugee is not eligible to have the claim heard by the
Refugee division if the person … came to Canada, directly or indirectly,
from a country, other than a country of the person's nationality, or where
the person has no country of nationality, the country of the person's ha-
bitual residence, that is a prescribed country." Similar to the provision of
Bill C-55, this provision, in essence, prevents "refugee claimants from
entering Canada if they arrived from a 'safe country' which was prepared to grant them refugee status" (Knowles 1997: 198). The initial
purpose of introducing the Safe Country Provision was to prevent "asylum shopping"—that is, "coming to Canada from a position of safety as
a matter of personal choice" (Young 1991b: 1). The provision was attacked on two related grounds. First, the number of refugees entitled to
come to Canada would be drastically reduced, since at least 40 percent
come via the United States (Young 1991). Second, an estimated 95 percent of the world's refugees are in developing countries, and the Safe
Country Provision discriminates against people of the poor and the developing world (Wong in HC #5 July 30, 1992: 61). In his comments on
the racist nature of the provision, NDP immigration critic Dan Heap noted
that refugees from many African, Asian, and Central American countries
cannot come to Canada via direct air routes. They must come via Europe
or the United States, unlike refugee claimants from Eastern Europe or
the Soviet Union, who usually can take direct flights (Knowles 1997:

198; see also: HC #4, July 29, 1992; HC #8, August 12, 1992).

This particular provision of Bill C-86 bears a striking resemblance to the Continuous Journey Stipulation of 1908.[9] During the debates on the bill in 1992, the Jesuit Centre for Social Faith and Justice offered a hypothetical analysis of how—in more tangible terms—the Safe Country Provision would impinge on a refugee's ability to gain access to the Canadian system.

> If these changes had been in effect in ... 1991, the following situation could have resulted. In all there were 30,539 claims made in 1991. Of these, 19,111 were made at border points, with the balance being made by people who were already in Canada. Looking then, at the 19,111 claims made at border points, 14,780 were made by people who came through safe third countries, that is, the United States, European countries and Japan. All are countries which would no doubt end up on the list of prescribed countries. If all of these 14,780 border claimants had been ruled ineligible, then 48% fewer claimants would have been heard by the CRDD [Convention Refugee Determination Division]. (HC #10 Sept.15, 1992: 10A-27)

The ultimate effect of the legislation, then, without ever mentioning the word "race," is to control a particular dimension of the refugee population—"developing world" refugees, the majority of whom the government classifies as "visible minorities." As the Inter-Church Committee for Refugees suggests, historians correctly criticized the Continuous Journey Stipulation because it was used as a means of controlling what groups of people would be permitted to stay in Canada. They further contend that, on reflection, many historians will offer a similar criticism of the Safe Country Provision (HC #10 Sept. 15, 1992: 4A-58; 65).

The Safe Country Provision represents a classic example of sanitary coding. The text of the provision is cleansed of categories and explanations having discriminatory potential. By using the technique of equivocation, legislators have created a clause that is ambiguous in its meaning or true intent. This ambiguity allows politicians to address—yet remain non-committal to—the diverse concerns arising out of their various constituencies. For example, it is possible that the Safe Country Provision will be challenged on constitutional grounds. Specifically, does the provision discriminate on the basis of "race" or nationality, which would be in direct violation of section 15 of the *Charter*? In response, defenders of the provision could argue that the provision makes absolutely no mention of "race" or nationality and hence does not violate the *Charter*. Rather, they would argue, in an effort to keep out "system abusers" the government is simply trying to manage more efficiently the number and types of people who gain entry into Canada through the refugee determination process.

But, a politician could be asked, what is the underlying message? What is the "private" intent of the Safe Country Provision? Is it to control the immigration of people of colour? When the politician is challenged in this way, equivocation becomes essential; and however much the audience may see racism or discrimination in the provision, the politician is always in a position to refute the interpretation.

THE LIBERAL AGENDA FOR THE FUTURE: FINAL REFLECTIONS

After the Liberals came to power in the fall of 1993, little changed. Racial tensions remained high, unemployment was high, and Canadians became increasingly wary of "outsiders" (Knowles 1997: 199). Despite a similar political and economic climate, the Liberals promised an immigration policy with "new directions." But well into their term of office the new directions represented little more than "a continuation of a course charted by the Conservatives" (Knowles 1997: 201.). Despite promises to reassign top priority to the family class, Liberal policy reflected instead, a shift away from family reunification and towards immigrants who have "the education, skills, and language to adapt readily to the New Economy" (Knowles 1997: 200). Recruiting immigrants became an economic practice, as immigration officials aggressively·marketed Canada in places such as Hong Kong, Taiwan, and the Middle East with hopes of enticing entrepreneurs and investors to come to Canada.

Regarding the "management" of immigration, in what directions do Liberals seem to be moving? In 1997 the Legislative Review Advisory Group released *Not Just Numbers*, a report that made 172 recommendations on "the best future direction for Canadian Immigration in light of present challenges (LRAG 1997: 1). Key proposed changes include:

- proficiency in French or English for all immigrants, including family class immigrants; if applicants speak neither language, they will be required to pay an unspecified tuition fee to cover

the cost of learning the language (p.20);
- creating two laws: one for immigrants, geared to economic needs, and one for refugees to protect those seeking asylum (pp.1–2);
- denying refugee status to those who passed through, or first sought protection in a "Safe Third Country" (pp.26–27);
- expanding the definition of the family to include same-sex couples and common-law spouses (p.18), but still maintaining a "tiered" system that gives lower priority to extended family (p.19);
- requiring skilled workers to meet five core standards before being considered for admission: being between 21–45 years of age; having at least two years of postsecondary education; knowledge of French or English; skilled work experience; and self-sufficiency (pp.20–21).

The report drew scathing criticism from across Canada, and it is not clear how much of this advice Minister of Citizenship and Immigration Lucienne Robillard will accept. What is clear is that the recommendations reflect the priorities of an earlier era and will have a negative impact on applicants from non-traditional source countries in the developing world. Inconsistent with the reality of Canada's current immigration patterns, the new proposals favour wealthy, young, well-educated, English- or French-speaking people. Immigration lawyers suggest that "three out of every four people who have chosen to make Canada their home would be shut out under the new recommendations" (Murray 1998: B1). As a National Film Board of Canada video, *Who Gets In?* documents, the truth of the matter is that most of Canada's immigrant ancestors would not get into Canada today; and the irony is that most Canadians would not either.

In its earliest forms, then, Canadian immigration law was overtly prejudicial and based on a "nationality preference system" favouring European immigration. After 1962 came a shift towards universal, non-discriminatory treatment of all applicants applying for admission to Canada. The principle of equality is now embodied in section 3(f) of Canada's Immigration Act. While acknowledging these literal gains, the "non-discriminatory" Immigration Act is not as just and fair as it appears to be. The language of discrimination may have been removed from the law, but in less obvious ways immigration law is still racist and ethnically selective. Citizenship and Immigration Canada's *1996 Annual Report to Parliament* revealed that in 1994, "57.6% of our immigrants came from Asia and the Pacific Region, 13% from Africa and the Middle East and 9.3% from Central and South America, for a total of over 78%" (Young 1997: 5). While the number of new immigrants from non-traditional source countries remains high, these numbers suggest a bias in favour of immigrants from the developed world, people who may not be white but who are economically more "desirable," more "assimilable," and allegedly better suited to life in Canada than those from the developing world.

NOTES

1. According to de Silva (1992: 3–4), immigrants are classified as either "traditional" or "new" on the basis of their country of origin and skin colour. Although classification on the basis of these criteria is far from perfect, it appears to be "basically true" that, for the most part, "traditional" immigrants are white, whereas "new" immigrants are visibly different.

2. Throughout this essay I place the term "race" in quotation marks in formal acknowledgement of its uselessness as an analytic term (Miles 1989: 72; Guillaumin 1980: 39). "Race" is an ideological construction that has "profound meanings in the everyday world, but which has no scientific credibility" (Miles 1984: 232). I do not want to further reinforce the commonsensical understanding of this term. Instead, I wish to highlight that awarding analytical power to the word "race" or using it uncritically lends legitimacy to the misconception that "races" are real or correctly apprehensible. For a more detailed discussion of why the concept of "race" has been scientifically discredited, see Rex (1983).

3. In soliciting immigrants from the United States, the country took care to pursue only white immigrants. It made no attempts to recruit black Americans, for "blacks were widely regarded as being cursed with the burden of their African ancestry" (Knowles 1997: 90). More precisely, it was assumed that slavery had disabled Blacks—rendering them incapable of developing the qualities necessary for citizenship in a democracy.

4. Although the Chinese Exclusion Act was repealed in 1947, the only category of immigration open to the Chinese until 1962 was "sponsored relatives" of Chinese-Canadians (Bolaria and Li 1988: 118).

5. The White Paper of 1966 initially emerged in response to the postwar, unlimited sponsorship movement. The movement produced a largely unskilled workforce, incompatible with Canada's economic needs. This result—coupled with increasing unemployment—was, in the eyes of the government, cause for concern. Lack of immigration control could only exacerbate the

problem. For a more detailed discussion, see Hawkins (1988: 50ff).

6. In later versions of the points system "personal assessment" became "personal suitability." I discuss the problematic nature of this criterion in more detail later in the essay.

7. Under the current points system, an independent immigrant must receive seventy points before being considered to "have the potential to adapt successfully to Canada and be of benefit to this country socially and economically" (Young 1991a: 18).

8. Interestingly, Valcourt provided just such a response when he was accused by critics of "playing to the right" and attempting to reach the same constituency as the Reform Party. The Reform Party has repeatedly been accused of racism for its attacks on the immigration system (see Kirkham 1998). Although there are parallels between the philosophies of the Reform and Conservative parties on the question of immigration, Valcourt categorically denies any similarity: *"There's nothing, but absolutely nothing in C-86 that closely resembles the coded message of Preston Manning regarding Immigration"* (Valcourt in Thompson 1993: B7, emphasis added; see also Caragata 1992).

9. For further discussion of this comparison, see HC #4, July 29, 1992: 64–65, 73–76.

"Good Enough to Work but Not Good Enough to Stay": Foreign Domestic Workers and the Law

© Sedef Arat-Koc

Immigration law and policy, it has been said, often lag behind other laws and policies in the application of equality principles (WING 1985: 2). But in recent years Canadian immigration policies affecting foreign domestic workers carry an irony that goes beyond the unfortunate incapacity of the policies to keep up with other legal and political developments. Precisely during a time in Canadian history when citizenship rights have been generally improving for women, conditions have significantly deteriorated for domestic workers.

In line with other analyses (Bakan and Stasiulis 1997; Daenzer 1993; Villasin and Phillips 1994), I would argue that changes in the racial/ethnic composition of migrant domestic workers have played an important part in this deterioration. In the postwar period, when Canada's efforts to import domestic workers from the "preferred" sources of Britain and Western Europe failed, the country considered entry for women of colour from Third World countries as a last resort. The Caribbean (since the late 1950s) and the Philippines (since the mid-1970s) subsequently became the major sources of foreign domestic workers. Radical changes in immigration policies coincided with changes in the source countries, and together these conditions reduced the status of workers from permanent residents to temporary workers and resulted in a drastic loss of the rights of those immigrants as persons and workers.

Domestic labour has never enjoyed a high status in industrial capitalist society. As one of the organizing principles of modern society, the public/private split makes work performed in the home not only isolating for the people—almost entirely women—who perform it, but also invisible to the rest of society. The split also leads to the perception of housework as unproductive for the economy. Even when it is paid work, domestic labour is relegated to a low status in the labour hierarchy. Considered to be neither wives nor "real" workers, paid domestic workers occupy a contradictory and unfavourable social location. As working-class women they do not share the status of their middle- or upper-class mistresses. As workers in the private sphere they lack the status of other workers. Excluded from the organized labour movement, they have been denied the organizational opportunities, sense of solidarity, and protections and benefits provided by the labour movement (Fudge 1997).

In a sense, therefore, subordination has been an almost universal condition of domestic workers in industrial capitalism. Still, significant variations exist in the status and conditions of domestic workers on the basis of their race/ethnicity. Historically, the racial/ethnic location of domestic workers has been linked to their differential relationship to the Canadian state (as citizens or non-citizens) and the "Canadian nation." Racism has been central to the criteria for entry, the conditions of entry, the working and living conditions of domestic workers, and their rights of citizenship.

Whereas in Europe class and gender inequalities were the main determinants of relationships in domestic service, in Canada (as well as in other settler colonies) racial and ethnic inequalities played an important part. In addition to the effects of capitalist industrialization and urbanization on class and gender relations, the history of domestic work in Canada has been closely connected to histories of race and ethnic relations and immigration. Since the turn of the century, as typical source countries for domestic workers have moved further and further away from Britain and Western Europe, state regulation over workers has become more coercive, while work and living conditions have worsened.

British domestic workers coming to Canada at the turn of the century were regarded as "daughters of the Empire" and "mothers of the race." While their privileged status as members of the nation did not necessarily work to improve their conditions in domestic work, it did determine the nature and extent of the alternatives to that work. Even when British domestics were unable to improve their conditions at work, they could "vote with their feet" and leave domestic service for another employer or job, or marriage. In the case of domestics from the "least desirable" racial/ethnic backgrounds, such as black domestic workers, societal racism and/or direct state intervention in the form of immigration policies and regulations have restricted labour-market choices and undermined working conditions.

This essay looks at how inequalities on the basis of race and ethnicity—together with those based on gender and class—have historically shaped the policies and practices of the Canadian state in relation to domestic workers. It also demonstrates how the discriminatory treatment of domestic workers continues, albeit in different forms and with different types of justification, today.

DOMESTIC WORKERS IN CANADA: THE EARLY HISTORY

In Canada, as in other settler colonies, domestic service has historically been associated with forms of "unfree" labour. While much smaller in scale than the slavery characterizing the plantation system of the Southern United States, slavery did exist in Canada until its gradual elimination in the late eighteenth and early nineteenth centuries. The first Canadian slaves were Aboriginal peoples. Black slaves were also brought north from the United States by their employers, often United Empire Loyalists. Most female slaves were employed as domestic workers (Barber 1991: 3; Bolaria and Lee 1988: 165).

A lack of freedom and the subordination of the worker were not always typical conditions—and especially so in periods of Canadian history when domestic workers and their employers were not divided by class and racial inequalities. In the early nineteenth century, in rural areas in Canada and the Northern United States, local white women hired as domestics were "help" rather than "servants." Often a temporary form of employment, domestic work for these women was a way of contributing to their families' income and aiding neighbours in coping with the demands of illness, harvest season, or the care of numerous children. Employed by farmers and small shopkeepers, these workers shared the conditions and the tables of the families they worked for and "demanded treatment in accord with their status as a member of another family of 'independent worth'" (Barber 1991: 4).

The relatively favourable status of white domestic workers in the rural areas contrasted sharply with relations in propertied households in the cities, with their growing social distance between employers and employees. So significant were the differences in domestic workers' conditions in rural and urban areas that *The Canadian Settlers' Handbook* advised prospective domestics that they would enjoy "social amenities" in rural Canada, but that "no lady should dream of going as home-help in the cities, for there class distinctions [were] as rampant as in England" (quoted in Lenskyj 1981: 10).

From the mid-nineteenth century on, changes associated with urbanization, industrialization, and the growth of capitalism contributed to the development of a generally subordinate class position and unfavourable working conditions for domestic workers. The separation of the public and private spheres and the hierarchy associated with this separation coincided with the rapid development of domestic service as a women's job ghetto. Between the early and late nineteenth century, within a period of about sixty years, the number of women among urban domestic workers grew from 50 to 90 percent of the total (Lacelle 1987).

Further contributing to the decline in the status of servants was the availability of groups of vulnerable workers. Racialization and the consequent lack of alternative opportunities have historically created conditions of vulnerability for different groups of workers. In Canada and the Northeastern United States at certain times, groups of European immigrants perceived as inferior to the ethnically dominant population became a source of vulnerable labour. In the 1870s, for instance, Irish women who had fled economic desperation at home found almost no alternatives to domestic work in Canada. In all Canadian centres except Quebec City, female Irish immigrants were so highly represented among domestic workers that the service came to be identified with Irish women (Lacelle 1987). The term "servant," rarely used earlier in the nineteenth century to refer to white domestics, became commonplace as immigrants replaced Canadian-born whites as the dominant group of domestic workers (Rollins 1985: 51–52).

In the late nineteenth century immigration began to be used systematically to recruit and control domestic workers. This was a time when the demand for domestic workers increased, while the supply among Canadian-born women declined. The growth in demand corresponded to the high standards of housekeeping of a rising urban middle class during a time when household technology remained underdeveloped and housework extremely laborious. With industrialization and the opening up of new labour-market options—in factories, hospitals, offices, retail outlets, and schools—the supply of domestic workers declined. The conditions of domestic work, especially live-in service, were so unfavourable that Canadian-born working-class women refused to accept the jobs, even when the pay in other employment was lower. As Canadian-born women came to shun domestic service, the country made efforts to recruit immigrant women to meet the unabated demand. By the early twentieth century, more than one-third of domestic workers in Canada were foreign-born (Barber 1991: 7–8).

British domestic workers at the turn of the century: favoured by race, subordinated by gender and class

The demands of the labour market for domestic workers encouraged the recruitment of workers from abroad, but the dominant forces in Canadian society and the state were selective regarding the source countries for recruitment. In the period following Confederation, the state began not only to regulate immigration through legislation, but also to use immigration policy as the major means of actively controlling the composition of the Canadian nation then under construction. While recruitment of non-white immigrants for special labour-intensive projects did occur in the post-Confederation period—such as the use of Chinese workers during the building of the railway—the federal government enacted racist immigration legislation and regulations to quell non-white immigration.

A number of immigration schemes introduced in the late nineteenth and early twentieth centuries were specifically aimed at attracting white British women to Canada. In addition to the Canadian state, middle- and upper-middle class women from the social reform movement were actively involved both in planning the schemes and in the actual recruitment and settlement of British domestics in Canada. As much as wanting to find workers for middle-class homes like theirs, the social reformers doing female immigration work were interested in recruiting young, virtuous British "girls" who would be the future "mothers of the nation" (Roberts 1979).

In the early twentieth century British women constituted more than three-quarters of immigrant domestics coming to Canada, and the treatment of these domestic workers as a whole reflects a complex and contradictory articulation of privileges based on race and nationality and of disadvantages based on class and gender. On the one hand, British female immigrants were considered central to the project of nation-building in Canada. As women of the "right" racial/ethnic stock, they were desirable immigrants who were expected not just to biologically reproduce "the race," but also to transmit British culture and "civilization" to future Canadians. On the other hand, as working-class women or as impoverished gentlewomen, to do a working-class job in domestic service they were subject—in the process of recruitment, during travel, and during settlement—to the middle-class Victorian values and close scrutiny of social reformers.

Even though the society considered "culture-bearing" and "civilizing" as feminine attributes, it did not see these qualities as universally shared by all women. Sometimes eugenicist explanations were used to argue about the unsuitability of working-class women as immigrants. For instance, some commentators argued that many working-class women had "serious mental and moral disabilities" and that they were likely to end up in jails, hospitals, and asylums (cited in Valverde 1991: 126). The tension around the need for domestic workers and the anxiety about the suitability of working-class women as immigrants were partially resolved in the late nineteenth century with the availability in Britain of a huge "surplus" of "distressed" gentlewomen. These were single women from middle-class backgrounds who had been impoverished by economic circumstances or the death of spouses. At a time in Britain when an unfavourable male/female ratio limited women's marriage prospects and when white-collar jobs were not open to women, the options for these women were limited, making emigration to Britain's colonies a desirable option (Jackel 1982: xxi).

Even though British gentlewomen emigrating to Canada to do domestic work were of the "right stock" and came from a respectable class background, as poor, single women they could not be trusted by social reformers to maintain high moral standards. This was particularly a concern in view of the untamed moral character attributed to men and the temptations associated with "white slavery," such as a love for finery (Valverde 1991). Therefore, middle-class social reformers who were involved with emigration and immigration societies in Britain and Canada did not hesitate to recruit selectively and closely monitor and curtail the freedom of the chosen ones.

In addition to references and a personal interview, social reformers introduced into the recruitment process a compulsory medical examination, which was later extended to all immigrants (Lenskyj 1981: 8; Valverde 1991: 126). Horrified by conditions on steamships crossing the Atlantic, women's organizations also took on the responsibility of "protecting" and supervising single immigrant women during their voyage. Matrons watching over parties of women made sure that their charges did not waste their time or befriend unsuitable acquaintances. Once they arrived in Canada, women were taken into hostels and shelters supervised by women's groups before being accompanied to their final destinations (Roberts 1979). As one of the women recounted: "We all wondered if we were coming to a civilized country, for we were brought from the ship as though we were prisoners, and had to sit in a room, and hardly dared move, let alone speak. We were not allowed to bid goodbye to our friends we had made during the voyage, and in fact I think they thought we were heathens. Several passengers passed the remark as we were driven as cattle" (quoted in Lenskyj 1981: 9).

While claiming that their philanthropic immigration work was for the "protection" of immigrant women, and especially of their imperilled respectability, the middle-class women's reform groups did not hesitate to co-operate with authorities in the deportation of "unsuitable" immigrants. In what Valverde calls "philanthropic deportation," women immigration activists participated in the deportation of significant numbers of domestic workers in the name of preserving national health and morality (Valverde 1991: 122–27).

Segregation during the trip and in reception houses and women's houses limited domestics' opportunities to associate with other immigrants and workers and to learn about alternative job opportunities. Conditions in domestic service were sometimes so unfavourable that indenture became the only means of ensuring that domestics would stay with an employer. During the period between 1888 and the 1920s, when the government did not directly provide assisted passage, private agents arranged for advanced loans from employers that would tie domestics to them for a specific length of time. The Department of Immigration sometimes evaded legislation to fulfill its policing function. For example, around the turn of the century most of the provinces passed master and servant legislation aimed at protecting domestics from an exploitative contract they might have signed in order to immigrate. According to this legislation, contracts signed outside the province were not legally binding. The Immigration Department, aiming to enforce indentured status, avoided this legislation by having domestics sign a contract again upon arrival in Canada (Leslie 1974: 122).

Another group of immigrants arriving in the same period experienced the contradictory social location of being from the "right" racial/ ethnic stock, but belonging to the wrong class. These were "homechildren," child immigrants who came to Canada between 1868 and 1925. About one-third of them were orphans and the rest were unaccompanied by their parents. These "homechildren" came from the urban working class in Britain and had been removed from their families by philanthropic rescue homes and parish workhouse schools. Middle-class philanthropists, who "rescued" these children because they were horrified with the squalor of urban slums, also tended to romanticize rural life. The children were sent to rural households in Canada and Australia to help them acquire physical strength and achieve "spiritual salvation." As in the case of British gentlewomen, their immigration was favoured as essential for the protection of the "future progress of the Anglo Saxon race." Most of the 80,000 homechildren who came as immigrants to Canada were exploited as farm labour and domestic labour. Many were shunned simply on the basis of their class background, because they were suspected of potential criminal tendencies and moral and physical degeneracies. The immigration program that brought them to Canada was ended in 1925 after extensive lobbying by the Social Service Council of Canada and the Canadian Council on Child Welfare organizations, which questioned the legitimacy of Canada's "nation-building on the backs of children" (Parr 1980).

The treatment of British domestic workers and "homechildren" in Canada at the turn of the century demonstrates the complexity of relations involving gender, class, nationality, and race. Compared to the domestic workers from other racial/ethnic backgrounds who came before and after them, these groups enjoyed a privileged position with respect to their race and nationality. Common to both groups was their desirability as immigrants and their unquestionable place in the future of the nation. The social reformers' paternalistic treatment of the British domestics and the close scrutiny over their lives not only restricted their individual freedoms but also highlighted the class differences. Their treatment also reflected the dominant gender norms of the time.

In the case of the "homechildren," the exploitation by the families taking them on had to do with their class background as well as their vulnerability as children. Painful though their experiences were, however, their status as members of the nation gave them a certain advantage. Even though misjudgements about the nature of rural life and the goodwill of middle-class families had brought them to Canada, the decisions to send them here were still based on a well-meaning concern for the well-being of the children as members of "the race"—not simply on the labour needs of the families taking the children.

Despite the conditions both groups encountered in domestic work, their membership in the Canadian nation made it possible in the long term for many of them to "vote with their feet" and find viable alternatives to the crass exploitation of domestic work.

NON-BRITISH, EUROPEAN DOMESTIC WORKERS

As the Canadian state failed to fulfill its objectives to populate Canada and meet Canada's labour needs through an exclusively British source of immigration, the country sought out other sources of immigrants. In the late nineteenth century, the authorities considered Continental Europe and the United States the least objectionable alternative sources to Britain. Women from Scandinavian countries and Central and Eastern Europe came to Canada as single workers or as daughters of agrarian families settling in the prairies. A substantial increase in the number of non-British domestics occurred in the 1920s, and by the early 1930s as many as one-quarter of immigrant domestic workers coming to Ontario were from Continental Europe (Prentice et al. 1988: 222). In the mid-twentieth century, other sources, such as Southern Europe, also came into play.

Scandinavian domestic workers

In the early twentieth century Scandinavian countries were a favoured source of domestic workers, second only to Britain, and among Scandinavians Finnish women predominated. To encourage immigration of Finnish and other Scandinavian domestics, the Canadian government "bent immigration regulations, created special categories and made easier travel arrangements." Even in the midst of the Depression, in 1937, Canada started a special scheme to bring in domestics from this region (Lindstrom-Best 1986: 34, 36).

Almost all of the Finnish women who came to Canada in the early twentieth century found work in domestic service. In Winnipeg, for example, all Finnish women, except a few who worked in restaurants, were domestic workers. When native-born women and British immigrants were starting to move to other jobs in the labour market, Finnish women—despite the diversity of skills they brought to Canada—remained concentrated in domestic work, mainly because of language problems (Lindstrom-Best 1986: 35). Lindstrom-Best argues that Finnish domestic workers were "proud maids" who enjoyed a high status in the Finnish community and relatively favourable conditions at work. Because most women in the Finnish community in Canada were domestic workers, they experienced no negative comparisons of themselves and other women. Together they were able to build a proud collective image and work to improve working opportunities and conditions. Also contributing to their collective strength was the tradition of labour and socialist organizing that many Finnish immigrants brought with them to Canada. Many ethnic organizations served as labour locals. In addition, the Finns built "immigrant homes" in several cities and started employment services for domestic workers.

In this climate of class and ethnic solidarity, Finnish domestics were able to share information, object to low wages and bad working conditions, and therefore resist being treated as slaves. Even in their first years in Canada, many domestics were able to change jobs frequently (Lindstrom-Best 1986, 1988).

Central and Eastern European domestics

When the number of immigrants coming from the British Isles was insufficient to fulfill the defined objectives of populating Western Canada (thereby securing that territory against the United States) and developing an agrarian-based economy, the Canadian state was led to accepting immigrants from the non-preferred sources. The majority of Central and Eastern European domestics went to Western Canada, and in the 1920s the number arriving there from Continental Europe in general grew significantly. In Manitoba in 1921 the British made up 60 percent of immigrant domestics and the Europeans 30 percent. By 1931 the ratios were almost reversed (Barber 1987: 109).

Unlike the preferred British domestics, domestic workers from Continental Europe were not given assisted passage (Barber 1991: 16). Most domestics coming from Central and Eastern Europe were considered to be of "the peasant type"—that is, not familiar with the standards and equipment of housework in middle-class homes and therefore mostly suitable for rural households. Among them, though, one group of domestics was preferred for urban employment: the daughters of Russian Mennonites, women who came to Canada not as economic immigrants but as refugees and were themselves from servant-employing backgrounds.

While women reformers had concentrated their energy and attention on British domestics, most of the Central and Eastern European immigration took place outside of their control. Mennonites were able to establish Maedchenheim or Girls' Homes in several cities (for example, Winnipeg, Saskatoon, Vancouver, Regina, and Toronto). Similar to Canadian women's hostels for British domestics, places run by women reformers, the Maedchenheim offered temporary shelters for new arrivals and served as social centres. Unlike the Canadian women's hostels, but similar to the Finnish immigrant homes, these centres had no connections to employers and therefore worked to protect domestic workers. The Mennonite helpers would accompany the domestic to her place of employment, inspect the house with her, remove domestics from unfavourable working environments, and keep a blacklist of employers who would be refused domestic workers (Barber 1987: 112; Barber 1991: 16–18).

During and following the Great Depression, when many native-born women lost the few alternative sources of employment open to them, domestic work once again became the major employer of women. Despite the poor state of the economy, an increase occurred in the number of domestic workers in this period—largely because with the fall in wages and prices families with fixed or steady incomes could afford domestic workers (Prentice et al. 1988: 235–36). In addition to the usual supply of domestic workers from among single women, married women returned to domestic work on a live-out or sometimes live-in basis, while their unemployed husbands stayed home with the children (Barber 1991: 18). Central and Eastern European domestics who had come to Canada in the late 1920s faced special difficulties. They could only find work with low wages and bad working conditions (Barber 1991: 19).

After World War II the demand for domestic workers—following the trend in Canadian history since the nineteenth century—started to exceed the supply, and once again the Canadian state became involved in recruiting from foreign sources. Racism would play an important role in determining which of several vulnerable groups would be recruited. In the postwar period the first group of immigrant domestic workers came from among refugee women in the displaced persons (DP) camps in Europe. Between 1947 and 1952, Canada accepted around 165,000 displaced persons on the condition that they would work under one-year contracts in specific occupations—for wages and under conditions that were unacceptable to Canadians. Men were to be accepted as agricultural workers, miners, and loggers; women as domestic workers in institutions (as cleaners and kitchen workers in hospitals, sanatoria, orphanages, and mental institutions) or private homes (Barber 1991: 19; Danys 1986: 76–77). Humanitarian considerations were rarely a consideration in DP immigration, as the Canadian state not only specified the occupations in which refugees would work but also indicated ethnic and religious preferences. Even though the Department of Immigration never produced statistics to show ethnic and religious distribution, racist considerations are apparent in departmental memos. For domestic workers, a clear preference existed for those coming from the Baltic countries of Estonia, Latvia, and Lithuania. The authorities believed these women would be closest to the Scandinavians, who were preferred as domestics. A preference also existed for Protestants, even though they were a minority among DPs. Jewish women were considered to be an unsuitable source, because very few Jews had previously been in domestic service. The government would experiment, however, with a few Jewish domestics in Jewish homes (Barber 1991: 19–20; Danys 1986: 130).

The recruitment criteria reflected common gender and class assumptions long applied to domestic workers. The criteria seemed, however, to be more severe than in previous periods, given the conditions of refugees in postwar Europe. To qualify under the program, women had to be single or widowed, between eighteen and forty, and of "good average intelligence and emotional stability," and they had to go through strict medical examinations, which included tests for pregnancy and venereal diseases as well as X-rays (Danys 1986: 133). Those who qualified signed a contract to remain in domestic service for one year. Even though prospective employers also filled out a form specifying wages and conditions of work, they did not have to show this information to the domestic when she was hired (Danys 1986: 133).

Daenzer argues that the case of DP domestics constitutes a turning point in the nature and meaning of indenture for immigrant domestic workers. In this period the agreement to stay in domestic service for one year changed from a friendly "gentleperson's agreement" to a mandatory imposition (Daenzer 1993: 19). There were, however, no serious sanctions as yet for the non-fulfillment of contract. Another difference from the immigrant domestic schemes to follow was the ease with which domestics could change employers. Arthur MacNamara, the deputy minister of labour who designed the DP program, made it a policy that any DP who asked for a transfer was to be given one (Danys 1986: 157). Despite the relative flexibility of the program, though, most DP domestics fulfilled their contracts, usually with the same employers—not just to make a good impression as immigrants but also to not jeopardize the chances of the DPs still in camps (Barber 1991: 20).

Southern European domestic workers
When the relative scarcity of young single women in the DP camps was combined with the need for Canada to compete with other countries look-

ing for domestic workers, refugee domestics became only a temporary solution to the problem of supply. In the early 1950s Canada once again introduced assisted passage and made several not-so-successful attempts to recruit from the preferred areas of Great Britain and Western Europe. With the exceptions of Germany and Holland, the attempts remained futile. When the Cold War blocked off emigration from Eastern Europe, as a final resort Canada decided to experiment with countries in the least-preferred part of Europe: Southern Europe (Barber 1991: 21–23).

The approach of the Canadian state to Italian immigration in the 1950s demonstrates how the conflicting immigration priorities of meeting labour-market requirements and populating Canada with people of preferred races were played out. The dominant racist view equated Italians, especially those from the rural areas in the south, with hot climate, hot temperaments, dark skins, cultural backwardness, and undemocratic traditions "better suited to the ... 'fragile' politics of Latin America." Despite this perception, however, given pressures from business in the booming economy of the postwar period, the government decided that their presence could be tolerated if they could provide hard work and cheap labour in agriculture, mining, railway repair, and construction (Iacovetta 1986: 14). A program to bring in Italian domestic workers was started in 1951 and ended the following year after only 357 women were recruited.

The Italian domestic scheme was similar to the one used for refugee women from DP camps. Prospective employers in Canada would submit "orders" for domestic workers, and interested workers in Italy would sign contracts obliging them to stay in the designated occupation with the assigned employer for one year (Iacovetta 1986: 14). Even though Canada had reintroduced the Assisted Passage Loan Scheme for domestics from Western Europe and Britain, it initially refused to extend the plan to Italian domestics and instead tried to persuade the Italian government to advance passage fares (Iacovetta 1986: 15–16). The short life of the program had as much to do with the negative evaluation of domestics by both the employers and the state as it did with the lack of enthusiasm on the part of Italian women. The Canadians involved tended to see Italian domestics as ignorant, "primitive villagers" whose backward cultural background had failed to prepare them for the high standards and sophisticated technology of Canadian housekeeping. Even worse, perhaps, they found them to be feisty individuals who complained about working conditions, demanded to change employers, or simply left domestic work before the end of their contracts to work in the factories and/or join family members (Iacovetta 1986). These demonstrations of freedom could not be tolerated in a group of women who were not desired immigrants as "mothers of the race" or carriers of culture, but were brought into the country solely for the cheap labour they could provide, in jobs that Canadians—when and if they had the choice—would not do.

Less well-known postwar programs reached out to two other countries in Southern Europe (Greece and Spain). In 1956, during a period of otherwise restricted immigration from Greece, Canada started admitting Greek domestic workers, to be placed with Greek employers. The program lasted until 1966 and took in about 300 Greek women each year. A much more limited experiment involving fifty Spanish women in 1959–60 failed due to placement difficulties. The Spanish authorities wanted their people to be placed in Catholic homes, but most prospective employers in Canada were Protestant (Barber 1991: 22–23).

BLACK DOMESTIC WORKERS

In their treatment as domestic workers in, and future citizens of, Canada, women from different regions of Europe, arriving with and historically experiencing different levels of vulnerability, can be ranged along different parts of a continuum. But non-white domestic workers from other parts of the world stand alone at the far end of that continuum.

While Canadian policy and official opinion have rarely seen women of colour in Canada as good for anything else but domestic labour, in immigration policy they have been the last resort, only to be accepted if recruitment from British and other European sources failed. Since the 1960s the "liberalized" immigration policies do not show an express bias against domestics from non-European sources, and, indeed, in the last three decades women from the Third World have become the predominant source of immigrant domestic workers. Despite the apparent social and political acceptability of domestic workers who would have been unacceptable half a century before, racialized sexism and gendered racism are still alive and well in Canadian society and immigration policy.

Women of colour in Canada have been a source of domestic work during most of Canadian history, largely because they have been excluded from other possibilities in the labour market. Long after the abolition of slavery at the end of the eighteenth century, black women in Canada stayed in domestic work because it was their only option. When black women did finally find industrial employment during the labour shortage of World War II, they were subsequently the first group to be laid off (Brand 1991). Their case was similar to that of the Mi'kmaq women in Nova Scotia who, at the turn of the century, were excluded from industrial employment and considered suitable only for domestic work (Prentice et al. 1988: 121). In the postwar period, when Canada was considering the immigration of domestics from among European refugees, Canadian employers also made use of the cheap labour of "Canada's own displaced persons," the Japanese-Canadians (Light and Pierson 1990: 258).

Even though employers, if "desperate," would often accept cheap and docile domestic labour from any background, the political considerations determining immigration policy often dictated against an open door policy in immigration. As long as recruits could be found in the "preferred" and "not-so-objectionable" sources, Canada avoided nonwhite immigrants. The Immigration Act of 1910 (in a clause that was not removed until 1978) gave the government of Canada the legal power to discriminate on the basis of race. The clause said that the government could "prohibit for a stated period or permanently, the landing in Canada … of immigrants belonging to any race unsuited to the climate or requirements of Canada."

In 1911 Canada tried out a short-lived experiment with domestic workers from the Caribbean. Employers in Quebec, with permission from the government, arranged the immigration of about a hundred French-speaking domestics from Guadeloupe. Racist assumptions about black women's sexuality played an important part in the public's perception of these domestics. The press also fabricated stories and fuelled fears of immorality. When a second group of Guadeloupians applied for entry, even though the employers, in their own sexist, classist, and paternalistic way, had generally responded positively to the first group—finding the women preferable to fussy Canadian domestics—the government rejected most of the new candidates on the grounds of physical and moral unsuitability (Calliste 1989; Mackenzie 1988). During the recession of 1913–15, with a good number of unemployed Canadians now willing to do domestic work, the government deported many Caribbean domestics, arguing that they could become "public charges." Significantly, black domestic workers were, unlike their British counterparts, accepted only for their labour power and not as "permanent assets" that would contribute to the social and cultural life of Canada (Calliste 1989: 138).

Department of Immigration memos suggest that Canada lost interest in the importation of Caribbean domestics even as a temporary measure of expediency. The hope was that the world war would result in a "better" type of immigrant: "Canada would be adopting a very short-sighted policy to encourage the immigration of coloured people of any class or occupation. At its best it would only be a policy of expediency and it is altogether unnecessary, in view of the present upheaval in Europe, which will unfortunately throw upon the labour market a large number of women of a most desirable class" (quoted in Calliste 1989: 138). Long after the end of the short-lived Guadeloupe domestic worker arrangement, the alleged "immorality" of these women was still being used to explain the restrictions on Caribbean immigration (Mackenzie 1988: 128), and the immigration of black domestic workers was stifled until the 1950s.

In 1955, frustrated by unsuccessful attempts to secure domestic workers in Europe and under pressure from Caribbean governments and Britain, Canada finally introduced a scheme to bring in domestic workers from Jamaica and Barbados. Because the scheme involved a breach of the immigration regulations then in place, the government applied its order-in-council powers to the matter (Mackenzie 1988: 133). Rather than acknowledging its gratitude for receiving a much-needed and qualified workforce, the Canadian government reasoned that the scheme was a "favour" to the countries of emigration—an interpretation that provided a rationale for why Caribbean domestics were not eligible to apply for the interest-free loans under the 1950 Assisted Passage Loan Scheme. In what was significantly different from many prior programs, the Caribbean scheme required the sending countries to bear the responsibilities and the costs of recruiting, training, medically testing, and arranging for the transportation of domestics to Canada. To qualify under the program, women had to be unmarried, between twenty-one and thirty-five, and willing to do domestic work for at least a year with an assigned employer. When they arrived in Canada the domestics (who had already undergone extensive medical tests) were also subjected to gynaecological examinations (Mackenzie 1988: 134–35).

Through the tests for pregnancy and the emphasis on their single status, the Canadian government wanted to ensure that the members of the group would be in Canada solely for the purpose of filling a labour requirement; there was to be no sponsorship of spouses and children. Indeed, during the planning of the scheme the Canadian authorities contemplated a policy of temporary migration, instead of permanent landed status, for the Caribbean domestics. But the Canadian government decided against that move on a number of grounds. For one thing, it could be interpreted as a practice of forced labour and a blatant case of discrimination. For another, they reasoned that, unlike European domestics, the Caribbean women would—thanks to discrimination in the labour market—probably stay in domestic work past their one-year contract. Then, too, the government could always use "administrative measures" instead of blatantly discriminatory policies to prevent the domestics from moving on to other occupations and thus "abusing" the scheme (Calliste 1989: 143; Mackenzie 1988: 133). In an unusual deal made with the sending countries, Canada ruled that if Caribbean domestics were found unsuitable for domestic work, they would be deported to the country of emigration at the expense of the Caribbean government. They offered no definition of "unsuitable" in the agreement, thus implying that Canadian immigration officers could use unlimited discretion (Daenzer 1993: 53–54).

At least initially, general opinion held that the Caribbean domestic scheme was the most successful domestic program initiated in the postwar period (Mackenzie 1988: 136). Canada was receiving an overly qualified workforce at no cost to itself. Many of the women recruited were so highly educated that their emigration contributed to a brain drain from Barbados (Calliste 1989: 145). Despite their qualifications, the Caribbean women tended to stay in domestic service longer than European domestics arriving under similar schemes (Calliste 1989: 145).

Soon after the start of the Caribbean domestic scheme, immigration officials raised concerns when some domestic workers began to sponsor relatives. To them, the perceived deluge of sponsorship, with a consequent increase in the numbers of undesirable immigrants, meant the end of the program's usefulness (Mackenzie 1988: 138). One official stated: "The one unsponsored worker may meet someone's need for a domestic servant for a year or two, but the result may be ten or twenty sponsored immigrants of dubious value to Canada and who may well cause insoluble social problems.... I am greatly concerned that we may be facing a West Indian sponsorship explosion" (quoted in Satzewich 1989: 91).

Immigration officials were also disappointed because despite the discrimination in the labour market, Caribbean domestics proved to have a high mobility rate, enabling them to move out of domestic service. Once again, the government considered measures to pressure immigrant workers in domestic service. The deputy minister of immigration ruled against forceful tactics in this direction, arguing that it was "unfair in a free market economy to try to freeze anyone in a lowly occupation" (quoted in Mackenzie 1988: 139). Despite an ambivalence towards the continuing usefulness of the Caribbean domestic scheme—and fearing charges of racism from the black community in Canada and a breakdown in trade relations with Caribbean countries—the state continued the program until 1967, when the "points system" became the basis of immigration policy.

Non-racist immigration or "justified" discrimination? Foreign domestic workers under the points system
Immigration criteria were "rationalized" in the 1960s to make labour-market needs the basis for the recruitment of immigrants. In building on labour-market needs, the points system emphasized Canada's need for highly (formally) educated and highly skilled (as formally recognized) immigrants. This new system has been celebrated as marking a liberalization of immigration. It has been declared a form of recruitment that has ended discrimination on the basis of ascribed criteria such as race and sex. Ironically, however, the use of the points system has enabled the Canadian state to treat foreign domestic workers in the most unfavourable conditions legally possible in Canadian history since the abolition of slavery.

Because the definitions of "skill" and "education" in modern capitalist society approach domestic work as an unskilled type of work that women "naturally" do, domestic workers have been unable to qualify as independent immigrants under the points system. Still interested in a foreign supply of domestic workers, Canada started, in the 1970s, to introduce temporary programs to bring in domestics as migrant workers with no freedoms and rights of citizenship. Thus, indentured status for domestic workers—which in the 1950s was considered unacceptable in a free-market economy—became acceptable in the 1970s and has continued ever since. Even though the practice is seemingly "non-racist" and "legitimate" within the sexist discourses of "skill," "education," and the potentially "self-sustaining" immigrant, its acceptance raises questions for an otherwise liberal-democratic society.[1] In answering these questions, we need to note that the change took place at a time when it was apparent that women from the previously unwanted source countries in the Third World would constitute the major supply of foreign domestic workers in Canada for the foreseeable future.

THE CONTEMPORARY SITUATION

What distinguishes the contemporary status of foreign domestic workers from their past status is its temporary nature. The assignment of temporary status—as opposed to permanent resident or immigrant status—to domestic workers started in the early 1970s with the introduction of temporary work permits, and it continued under the domestic worker programs subsequently introduced in 1981 and 1992. In addition to giving domestic workers the message that their work and contributions to Canada are not significant enough to qualify them for permanent status in this country, the specific nature of temporary status and the regulations associated with it place particularly severe restrictions on the freedoms of domestic workers as persons and undermine, or damage, their working conditions.

Other than the formal, technical logic introduced by the points system and the sexist biases as interpreted through its criteria, social and political factors influenced the introduction of temporary status. In the late 1960s the Canadian demand for domestic workers began to increase, due to the increasing participation of middle-class women in the labour force and an insufficiently developed child-care system. Possibly, the increasing demand for domestic workers could have led to a more favourable environment for bargaining for better wages and working conditions. But the Canadian state's intervention to regulate the status and conditions of foreign domestic workers meant that conditions for domestic workers would, instead of improving, deteriorate below conditions in the nineteenth century.

Specifically, the Ministry of Immigration began to see the Caribbean Domestic Scheme as an inadequate means of helping to solve the shortage in domestic service. Many women who came to Canada under the program found their working conditions intolerable, and after fulfilling their one-year obligation they left the service for other work. Rather than providing the mechanisms to improve the conditions for domestic work and make it attractive to stay (for example, through extending and enforcing labour-standards legislation to domestic workers), the Canadian state opted for a solution that would force women to stay in domestic work.

The introduction of temporary work permits

In 1968 (and several times subsequently), without any explanation and supporting evidence for decreasing demand, immigration authorities arbitrarily lowered the rating for some categories of domestic work within the occupational demand category of the points system (Daenzer 1993: 75, 96, 113). This seemingly technical administrative procedure had an obvious racial dimension. Nursemaids and nannies, predominantly from Britain, continued to receive high points. Other categories of domestic work—predominantly filled by women from the Caribbean—received lower points. Given their countries' lack of formal training programs for nursemaids and nannies, Caribbean domestics could apply only in the other categories (Daenzer 1993: 76). The points system also assigned domestic workers low points for occupational skill, occupational training, and experience, even if they had years of practical training and experience in the field (Daenzer 1993: 116). As a result, most domestic workers—and especially those from Third World countries—could not meet the requirements of the points system to come to Canada as independent immigrants on permanent status. By 1978, five out of six domestic workers who came to Canada came as temporary workers (Daenzer 1993: 92), while many European domestics continued to enter as landed immigrants (Daenzer 1993: 95).

For domestic workers, temporary status meant a new and effective form of indenture. Temporary work permits allowed workers to stay in the country for a specified length of time (typically a year), doing a specific type of work, for a specific employer. The immigration program that applied to the majority of domestic workers from 1973 to 1981 treated them as "guest workers" with no rights to stay permanently in Canada or to claim social security benefits. Temporary work permits led to a revolving door situation. Although extension of the employment visa beyond the first year was common, the foreign worker would have to eventually leave Canada, to be replaced by other temporary workers. Temporary work permits typically rule out movement into other jobs, because the permit is issued only for a specific job. Regulations associated with work permits have made changing employers possible, but difficult. Such movement has been tied to receipt of a "release letter" from the former employer[2] (Arat-Koc and Villasin 1990; Toughill 1986); and mobility has been conditional upon the discretionary permission of immigration authorities, who have needed to be convinced about the seriousness of abuse in the employer-employee relationship.[3]

The main effect of the introduction of temporary status was the creation of a captive labour force. Unlike other workers who enjoy the basic freedom to leave a particular job or employer, a foreign worker on a temporary visa has only the freedom to return to her country of origin; and many Third World women who come to Canada out of conditions of economic desperation have no choice but to stay in Canada. Nancy Hook (1978: 107–8) reported that compared to Canadian workers, foreign domestic workers were more likely to live in the homes of their employers, to work more days per week, to work more overtime without pay, and to receive a smaller hourly wage.

Foreign domestic workers have paid a high price for services from which they could not expect to benefit. Even though their status in Canada has been unambiguously temporary, domestic workers on employment visas have been required to pay into the Canada Pension Plan as well as unemployment insurance premiums and income tax (equalling about one month's earnings a year), without being eligible to claim benefits. Revenue Canada calculated the total revenues from CPP and UIC premiums collected from foreign domestic workers between 1973 and 1979 to be more than $11 million (Task Force on Immigration Practices and Procedures 1981: 70). The nature of the employment visa has made access to unemployment benefits almost impossible, because the worker losing a job either has to find a new employer or leave the country. Benefits from the Canada Pension Plan have also been inaccessible, because the "guest worker" is expected to retire in the country of origin (Task Force on Child Care 1986: 121).

The Foreign Domestic Movement program
In 1981 a federal task force was established to study the conditions of domestic workers on temporary work permits. Its report recommended that the temporary work permit system be continued, but opportunities for permanent status be broadened (Task Force on Immigration Policies and Procedures 1981). The Foreign Domestic Movement (FDM) program, which came into effect later that year, made it possible for domestic workers who had worked in Canada continuously for two years to apply for landed immigrant status without having to leave the country.

While this was a step forward from the policies of the 1970s, it failed to address many of the problems of foreign domestic workers in Canada. First, the FDM continued to impose a two-year period of bonded service to be fulfilled by the domestic before applying for permanent status. In some ways, the FDM's entrenchment of a mandatory live-in requirement for all participants in the program strengthened the practice of indenture. Domestic workers who insisted on live-out arrangements would not only lose their right to apply for landed immigrant status but also not receive an extension on their employment authorization (Employment and Immigration Canada 1996: 17–18).

Another problem with the FDM was that it gave no guarantee for the granting of landed immigrant status. Applicants needed to meet immigration assessment criteria and demonstrate a "potential for self-sufficiency."[4] Because domestic workers continued to receive low points in the vocational preparation and occupational demand categories in their assessment for landed status (Task Force on Immigration Practices and Procedures 1981: 18–21), a number of requirements were imposed on them over and above those expected of other immigrants. These requirements included upgrading courses (with high foreign-student fees), demonstrating adaptation and integration into Canadian society (through volunteer work in the community), and proving financial management skills (through evidence of savings). Live-in domestic workers found it difficult to afford the time and the money to meet these requirements. Another problem has been that domestics with children and older domestics have faced special discrimination during assessments for immigrant status.

As a result of the conditions imposed by temporary status, foreign domestic workers have been denied basic freedoms that other workers— at least on a formal level—enjoy in modern society: the freedoms to choose and change occupations, to change employers, to have their own places to live, and to enjoy personal lives outside work and away from the direct control and supervision of employers. Moreover, the live-in requirement, as entrenched under the FDM, results in specific problems in working and living conditions. One of its major implications is the difficulty of maintaining clear boundaries between work and leisure—a difficulty that leads to very long hours of often uncompensated work.

According to a 1990 survey of 592 members belonging to INTER-CEDE, the Toronto Organization for Domestic Workers' Rights, only 35.2 percent of live-in domestics worked the regular workweek (in Ontario) of 44 hours; 40.3 percent worked 45 to 50 hours; 18.4 percent worked 50 to 60 hours; and 6.1 percent worked more than 60 hours a week (Arat-Koc and Villasin 1990: 6). The survey also found that a high percentage of domestic workers who performed overtime work were not compensated for it at the legally accepted rates. Among live-in domestics doing overtime work, only 33.7 percent received the legal compensation of $7.50 per hour or extra time off; 21.8 percent said they received some compensation but at less than legal rates; and an overwhelming 43.7 percent of those doing overtime work said they received no compensation whatsoever (Arat-Koc and Villasin 1990). Other consequences of the live-in requirement have been lack of privacy, restrictions on social and sexual life, greater vulnerability to sexual abuse, and variations in the quality of room and board—for which all domestics workers are required to pay a fixed amount to their employers (Arat-Koc and Villasin 1990).

The restrictions imposed by the FDM and, more generally, by temporary status have made it difficult for domestic workers to exercise even their albeit limited rights (for example, those provided for under labour-standards legislation in some provinces). The probationary nature of their status under the FDM has also tended to be intimidating, discouraging them from fighting for other rights or to improve existing rights (for example, the right to unionize and extending labour legislation to other provinces).

The overall effect of the 1981 change in immigration programs for domestic workers has been to create the possibility of an individual upward mobility of some domestic workers, while providing no structural solution to the problems of domestic workers in general. Ironically, to accumulate enough points to get landed immigrant status a domestic has to move out of domestic service altogether. The implicit message of immigration policies and practices is that domestic workers, as domestic workers, are "good enough to work, but not good enough to stay" in this country.

The Live-in Caregiver Program
In 1992 the Ministry of Employment and Immigration introduced several changes to the previous FDM program and renamed it the Live-in Caregiver Program (LCP), which remains the immigration program in effect for foreign domestic workers coming to Canada. According to the new policy, women intending to do domestic work are admitted to Canada on the basis of their education and training in the care of children, seniors, or the disabled. Specifically, the LCP requires successful completion of the equivalent of a Canadian Grade 12 education plus proof of six months of full-time formal training in areas such as early childhood education, geriatric care, and pediatric nursing (CEIC 1992).

The introduction of these new criteria raised concerns that many potential applicants from Third World countries would not qualify for entry. The requirement for Grade 12 is either an arbitrary or a deliberately racist criterion. In many countries, basic schooling only goes to Grade 10 or 11. As well, formal training in the areas of child, elderly, and disabled care is typically available only in Western European countries (DeMara 1992; *Domestics Cross Cultural News* June 1992). In 1993, responding more to concerns from employers about the decline in the number of workers arriving in Canada than to pressures from domestic workers' organizations, the Employment and Immigration minister introduced an amendment allowing the six months of formal training to be replaced by one year's experience in a caregiving area (Macklin 1994: 29).

The new program lifted some of the extra requirements placed by the FDM on foreign domestics for landed immigrant status (that is, having to do skills upgrading, volunteer community work, and demonstrate savings). To become a landed immigrant, a candidate must now only demonstrate a minimum of two years' employment as a full-time, live-in domestic worker. Also, domestic workers no longer need to obtain a "release letter" from their employers as a condition for changing jobs. But to receive a new employment authorization from immigration officers, domestic workers are still dependent on co-operation from their former employers, because they have to obtain a "record of employment" showing how long they were employed and detailing their earnings (CEIC 1992).

Despite amendments made in the qualifying requirements, and the elimination of some of the unreasonable requirements for landing, the LCP fails to bring any radical improvement in the status and conditions of foreign domestic workers in Canada. It has maintained two of the most oppressive aspects of the policies that had prevailed since the early 1970s: temporary status and the live-in requirement. Altogether, the LCP can be characterized as a program that requires more from domestic workers, without offering them more. It is a program designed to "enable Canadian employers to obtain higher qualified labour for less pay" (*Domestics Cross Cultural News* June 1992).

A historical analysis of immigration policies for domestic workers reveals a correspondence between the status of workers and working conditions and the background of the workers expected to do the work. The drastic changes in immigration policies since the 1970s, added to the more universal gender and class biases prevailing in societal judgements about the value of domestic work, indicate that the racial/ethnic and national backgrounds of the workers have contributed to making otherwise unacceptable practices of indenture seem reasonable to the general Canadian public.

Racism operates in contemporary immigration policies relating to domestic workers in at least two ways. First, it appears in the differential treatment received by domestic workers from different parts of the world: British and other European women were categorized as "nannies" and "nursemaids" and consequently qualified for immigrant status; while Third World women were categorized as general domestic workers and failed to qualify under the points system. Even when domestic workers from Western Europe participate in the same immigration programs, significant differences arise in how they are perceived and treated. Employers tend to see domestic workers from Western Europe—whether they have the formal qualifications or not—as "nannies" and therefore expect them to be involved only in child care, whereas employers expect Third World domestics to do both child care and general domestic work. Domestic workers from Western Europe are likely to get higher pay, better treatment, and recognition for their work (Cohen 1987; Macklin 1994).

Second, racism operates at a more structural level, through changes in the nature of immigration programs that are related to changes in the source countries for domestic workers. Even though race has been eliminated as an explicit criterion in selection of immigrants, racism operates in "commonsensical" ways in the new discourses. One of the modern-day discourses on race focuses on disparities in wages and standards of living between First and Third World countries. When the focus is on these disparities, emphasis shifts to the question of how much the immigrants want to be here rather than how much Canada needs them. In this discourse, immigration ceases to be viewed as a (much-needed) labour-recruitment mechanism and comes to be viewed as a system of "charity" from the First to the Third World.

When they speak about contemporary immigration policies on domestic workers, Canadian bureaucrats and politicians argue that foreign domestic workers, rather than being indentured, are "privileged." They suggest that the "special" immigration programs for domestic workers have given them an "opportunity" to come to Canada—something they would otherwise not qualify for under the points system.[5] On one level, this discourse reflects sexism in evaluations of who is—and who is not—a deserving immigrant. On another level, the choice of words such as "privilege" and "opportunity" to describe conditions unacceptable to most

Canadians is possible only because the reference point is, explicitly or implicitly, women of colour from Third World countries. Such language is hardly ever used in the case of domestic workers from Western Europe. When the mere "opportunity" of staying in Canada is assumed to be a "privilege" for immigrants from the Third World, it follows that domestic workers do not have a reason or right to complain, no matter what conditions they face in Canada. When these are the basic premises, the bureaucrats and politicians rarely use Canadian standards of equality and fairness to evaluate the working and living conditions of immigrants from the Third World (Arat-Koc 1992).

CONCLUSION

The Canadian state has played a contradictory role in the organization of domestic work. It has underregulated working conditions while overregulating the workers. On the one hand, the provincial labour-standards laws have either completely ignored the "private" sphere of the home or, at best, treated it unequally as a workplace, thereby failing to protect the workers. On the other hand, the federal government, with its jurisdiction over immigration, has overregulated the workers (Luxton, Rosenberg, and Arat-Koc 1990: 15).

In industrial capitalist societies, the public/private split and gender biases have tended to create obstacles in the conceptualization and treatment of the home as a "real" workplace. However, the anomalies between the conditions of domestic workers and other groups of workers have *increased* since the 1970s—which is particularly ironic because the same period has also seen a growing women's movement and the proclamation of multiculturalism as official state policy. This has also been a time, however, when the major source of domestic workers has moved from Europe to the Third World.

Any political efforts to improve the status and conditions of domestic workers in Canada will have to address the general gender and class biases regarding the value of domestic labour. In addition, and just as important, they will need to address the racism that implicitly justifies deplorable working conditions for Third World women. In recent times authorities have used immigration as a powerful tool for putting racism into effect in seemingly neutral and economically "rational" ways. The Canadian state has not simply acquiesced to power relations between domestic workers and their employers, but has played an active role in the construction of those relations of power and inequality. Struggles to improve conditions for domestic workers will, therefore, have to demand that the role of the state be changed from the overregulation to the *protection* of workers.

NOTES

1. For a discussion of some of the racist, sexist, and class-based discourses justifying such treatment, see Arat-Koc (1992).
2. Although Employment and Immigration spokespersons announced on a number of occasions that the practice of requiring release letters would be ended, a survey conducted among foreign domestic workers in Toronto revealed that as late as 1990 it was still common (Arat-Koc and Villasin 1990: 12).
3. The definition of "abuse" used by immigration officers sometimes proved to be flexible. Silvera reports the case of a Caribbean domestic who wanted to leave her employer for reasons of sexual assault. Because the assault did not involve sexual intercourse, her complaint was found to be not legitimate, and she was instead deported from Canada (Silvera 1981: 58).
4. Many workers who have had years of experience supporting themselves (and several dependents) find it very offensive to have to prove such potential: "I supported five children *before* I came here, and I've supported five children *since* I came here, and they want to know whether I can manage on my own?" (Mary Dabreo cited in Ramirez 1983/84).
5. This was how Barbara McDougall, then minister of employment and immigration, talked about the FDM program in her meeting with domestic workers at INTERCEDE in Toronto, October 28, 1990.

CLASS INTERESTS AND THE LAW

Introduction

In responding to the question of "whose 'order' is law reproducing?" many sociologists of law have focused attention on how class interests are embedded in law and legal practice. While some writers have stated this issue in bold terms—proclaiming, quite simply, that there is "one law for the rich and another for the poor" in societies such as ours—others have gone on to formulate more nuanced and detailed investigations of how law operates to (re)produce class inequalities and of the implications this recognition holds for ameliorating the hardships confronted by those denied the benefits of class privilege.

The essays in this part provide us with three different takes or angles on the law-society relation and its connection to law's class character. In "Legal Forms and Social Norms," Judy Fudge locates the Official Version of Law in its social and historical context in order to look at how law's claims to uphold the values of liberty, equality, and justice have been operationalized in limited or prescribed ways. Through a historical case study of the legal regulation of work in Canada around the turn of the century, Fudge undertakes a reformulation of the theoretical insights derived from the Marxist approach to the law-society relation.

In the early 1980s, when the Marxist approach—with its emphasis on the class character of law—was becoming more prominent within the sociology of law, several theorists were inspired by the work of Evgeny Pashukanis, a Soviet legal scholar who wrote in the 1920s (see, for example, Beirne and Sharlet 1980). Contemporary Marxist theorists adopted Pashukanis's "commodity form theory of law" to show how a particular legal form under capitalism—the creation of the "free" wage labourer at the level of exchange relations as a "bearer of rights"—operated to promote the "appearance" of equality in the legal sphere while obscuring the relations of inequality that emanate from the distribution of private property. As Fudge notes, Pashukanis's theory provides only a partial account of law's class character; it does not address the political form of the capitalist state (liberal democracy), the nature of economic relations at the level of production, or the complexity of legal norms and their content.

In addition, Fudge calls our attention to a key oversight in traditional Marxist formulations: that social relations are also *gendered*. Typically, Marxist theorists have understood production relations in terms of the class relations between workers and employers within the labour market and the workplace. In the process they have devoted little attention to the specific position of women within capitalist social relations and to the distinctive organization of families and households under capitalism. By broadening her conception of production relations to include the sexual division of labour, Fudge is able to show not only the differences in how men and women workers were treated under law as capitalist industrialization proceeded in Canada, but also the effect of gendered social norms on the emerging legal forms and norms.

During the period of capitalist industrialization in Canada (1870–1920), "status" (master and servant) was gradually supplanted by "contract" (employment) as the primary legal form for regulating the labour of male workers. Male workers not only achieved formal legal equality with their employers but also attained political status as "citizens." Yet, as Fudge notes, these achievements were both limited and made fragile by the contradiction between democracy (in the public/political sphere) and the hegemony of private property (in the private/economic sphere). Women, however, received different legal treatment: "status" and not "contract" governed their position and their labour within the home, reflecting the patriarchal nature of gender relations. As patriarchy was weakened by industrial capitalism (especially with the demand for a large supply of cheap labour), and as women began to challenge their legal subordination to men (using the liberal discourse of equality), a new form of legal regulation emerged to reinforce the sexual division of labour: "contract" was mitigated by "protective" legislation premised on women's subordinate position in the family, economy, and civil society. In essence, Fudge argues, women's subordination was reconstituted; it was no longer primarily legal but economic. The situation was especially precarious for domestic workers (who made up a large percentage of women wage labourers). As workers in private homes, their legal status was more akin to that of servant than employee.

As Fudge notes, it was not until the 1960s in Canada that women achieved formal equality in employment. Yet she cautions us not to give too generous a reading to this development. The sexual division of labour continues to persist in both the home and the workplace, and the legal norms of contemporary Canadian labour law continue to be male-centred. As well—as Pashukanis showed us—formal equality in the legal form continues to obscure the unequal relations emanating from the distribution of private property. In this respect, Fudge's historical analysis of the legal regulation of women's and men's work offers important insights not only into how law (re)produces both class and gender relations but also into the limits of formal legal equality, in and of itself, for addressing substantive social inequality.

In her aptly titled essay, "Relocating Law: Making Corporate Crime Disappear," Laureen Snider begins by noting that when it comes to the role of law in (re)producing class interests, even the most cursory application of the Official Version of Law to the anti-social and acquisitive acts of business demonstrates the overwhelming failure of law to impose meaningful limits on the offences of corporations. Indeed, attention to corporate crime draws out the *political* nature of law: how law emerges as both a product of and a response to contestation and struggle. Historically, to control corporate crime, workers, consumers, environmentalists, and other groups have succeeded in pressuring the state to produce laws and enforcement mechanisms (albeit ones that are relatively few in number and weak in nature). Yet, as Snider documents, the last two decades have seen these measures systematically repealed and dismantled. This has occurred, in her view, because of a successful *corporate counter-revolution.*

Snider situates this counter-revolution in the context of *globalization*: the increasing internationalization of not only the exchange but also the production of goods and services in the global market; and the corresponding transformation of increasing numbers of multinational corporations into transnational corporations. This trend, although "midwived" by governments, has led to a reduction in the ability of national governments to control events (Shields and Evans 1998; Brodie 1995). As a result, transnational corporations are now flexing their economic and political muscles—and with measurable effects. As Snider notes, levels of inequality and exploitation have been stepped up in recent years: the size, power, and profitability of corporations have dramatically increased, while the incomes and life chances of the majority of the population have declined.

An essential component of this corporate counter-revolution has involved getting rid of restrictions on corporate activity and profitability—including state laws and practices ostensibly designed to control (or at least regulate) the anti-social actions of business. Nation-states have been acquiescent in this process. For instance, under the discourse of "fiscal crisis" (McQuaig 1993; Workman 1996), the social safety net in Canada has been unwoven and the country declared "open for business." The items that Snider presents to showcase both the severity of the carnage done to workers, consumers, and the environment and the state's complicity in this action leave one wondering whether the struggle has been effectively "lost"—especially when labour unions, the traditional opponents of capital, are under increasing attack. Nevertheless, Snider sees some hope for resistance in the form of the counter-hegemonic struggles of progressive social movements. Armed with a "rights discourse" that essentially utilizes the logic of law's Official Version to demand basic legal rights (for example, to a safe environment, education, health care, a fair wage, and job security), progressive social movements have the potential to empower citizens, to challenge and resist the power of corporations, and to thereby open up new possibilities.

As various authors in this book point out, poverty not only is an ever-present feature of social life for a vast number of Canadian men, women, and children, but is also becoming even more so in recent years—especially with the move by provincial and federal levels of government to dismantle social programs intended to ameliorate the situation. In the face of this deepening crisis, significant theoretical and practical questions emerge for those of us concerned with assisting the casualties. Shelley Gavigan's essay addresses several of these questions by attending to the issue of what "access to justice" means for the poor and for those who practise poverty law.

Central to Gavigan's analysis is the need to attend to the theoretical framework surrounding our understanding of poverty and law's role in responding to it. When we inquire "who are the poor?" for instance, it becomes clear that women and their children are increasingly the ones hardest hit by changes and cuts to social programs. Yet to describe this situation as a case of the "feminization of poverty" and to locate its root causes in marriage breakdown or "deadbeat dads" misses the broader implications of women's poverty. It is not enough, Gavigan says, to simply look "within" the family or household (and the gendered ideologies and sexual division of labour represented there) to understand the factors associated with women's poverty. We also need to take into consideration the gendered (and racialized) nature of the labour market and the workplace. We need to recast poverty issues along lines that are attentive to gender *and* race *and* class.

Our understandings of poverty also inform legal practice and the delivery of legal services for the poor. Gavigan notes that not only have legal aid programs been typically premised on how the legal profession defines its role or mandate, but also the experiences of the poor have been defined in individualized terms (with corresponding legal solutions or remedies). Such an approach, according to Gavigan, neglects the complexity of the poverty issue and the need for diversity in fashioning appropriate legal responses. Attending to these factors requires critical reflection about the practice of poverty law—about ensuring that it is "client-centred" and that it speaks to the many and varied needs of people whose lives are conditioned and contoured by their gender, class, and race positioning in society. While law may not have all of the answers or solutions to respond to the plight of the poor, Gavigan maintains that it does offer one avenue of resistance and challenge to poverty.

Legal Forms and Social Norms: Class, Gender, and the Legal Regulation of Women's Work in Canada from 1870 to 1920

© Judy Fudge[1]

The Official Version of Law (Naffine 1990) provides an insider's view of a liberal legal system. It is the view shared, endorsed, and promulgated by most lawyers, judges, and law professors—the personnel who top the hierarchy of the legal system. It both prescribes the social values that a liberal society ought to uphold—at a minimum, liberty, equality, and individualism—and identifies the legal system as a key site for the realization of such values. While proponents of the Official Version may disagree among themselves about what "equality" means in a particular case or how it ought to be balanced against "liberty" more generally, such disputes are about the interpretation and application of legal principles and the design of legal institutions, not about the "justness" of liberal legality. The Official Version is based upon a normative acceptance of the liberal legal system's depiction of itself. As Hunt (1993: 31) states, the historical role of jurisprudence (a fancy term for official legal theory) is "to provide a socially persuasive account of the legitimacy of the existing legal order and through that the social order itself." In terms of the law-society relation, then, official legal theory starts from law and works out to society.

Instead of simply taking the Official Version of Law as a given, it is illuminating to adopt an external perspective on it.[2] What this requires is a suspension of judgement regarding the validity of the basic assumption of the Official Version: that the liberal legal system is the best way of resolving what is deemed to be the inevitability of social conflict. From an external perspective, the crucial questions are historical and sociological: why did a liberal legal system develop, and how did the liberal version of law come to be "official"? The starting point of this line of inquiry is society in general, and then the analysis moves to legal institutions, principles, and doctrines.

Marx adopted an external perspective when he examined the legal system, pointing to the importance of the economy and class in giving it both shape and substance (Marx and Engels 1968). This line of inquiry generated a critique of law from without, emphasized the connection between law and power, and suggested that the legal system is systematically biased in the resolution of conflict. Scholars following in Marx's footsteps have stressed the ways in which law perpetuates and maintains social inequality and the degree to which it resorts to coercion in order to do so.

Marxism provides an important challenge to, and critique of, the Official Version of Law, despite the fact that Marx never offered a full-fledged theory of law (Corrigan and Sayer 1981; Fudge 1991b). One important strand of scholarship inspired by Marx has been to show how an exclusive concentration on formal legal equality obscures the extent to which the law preserves and reinforces substantial social inequality. This strand is closely associated with Evgeny Pashukanis, a Soviet legal scholar who came to prominence after the Russian Revolution and was put to death by Stalin in 1937. What is distinctive about law under capitalism, according to Pashukanis, is its particular form: "Historical development is accompanied not only by a transformation of the content of legal norms and legal institutions, but also by development of the legal form as such" (Pashukanis 1978: 71, as quoted in Gavigan 1981: 4). Pashukanis regarded the creation of free wage labour as an exchange commodity as exemplifying the specific form of law under capitalism, one whose central construct is the "juridical subject" or the "legal person who is the bearer of rights" (Fine 1984; Gavigan 1981). He argued that all legal categories derive from relations between legal subjects. But while legal subjects are free and equal, this freedom and equality are formal and abstract. Ignored are the very different situations in which legal subjects as real human beings live within a society characterized by profound inequalities in the distribution of private property. Thus, the legal form obscures material inequality by emphasizing legal equality.

The commodity form theory of law under capitalism has made an important contribution to our understanding of how law is based upon, and reflects, class relations. But an exclusive focus on the commodity form obscures more than it reveals. Not only does it suggest that there is only one form of law, but it also isolates legal form from its content. While the commodity form captures the essential features of private economic relations, it misses many of the distinctive elements of liberal public law. The political separation of powers and the very distinct political philosophy underlying the rule of law cannot be reduced to the commodity form, and it is simply not possible to ignore the relationship between law and state in accounting for what is distinctive about liberal legality (Fine 1984). In short, what Pashukanis's theory of law fails to account for is the complex relationship between law and state in liberal capitalism.

During the prolonged shift from feudalism to liberal capitalism, the nature of the authority of the state changed from status to democracy. This is the historic achievement of liberalism. Under capitalism, liberal-democratic institutions, consisting of an independent judiciary, an elected legislature, and an administrative bureaucracy constrained by law, became the dominant, although not the exclusive, political form. Because workers are both legally and politically free in a liberal society, the state and the legal system mediate the conflict between labour and capital. Workers seek to have their interests represented both before courts and in legislatures. In this sense, the law is a site of class struggle and particular results, whether they are judicial decisions, administrative rulings, or statutes, must be understood in light of the balance of power between classes (Corrigan and Sayer 1985; Fine 1984).

But this does not mean that the liberal-democratic state is not a capitalist state. Its survival depends upon guaranteeing the conditions necessary for capitalist production: the private appropriation of surplus value (profit) by property owners. Democracy's writ only runs so far. The separation of the private realm of the economy from the public sphere of the state is embodied in private property (Corrigan and Sayer 1981; Fine 1984; Turkel 1988; Wood 1981). Private property, the realm of individual self-interest and choice, limits the scope of public authority and democratic accountability. In order to account for the distinctive nature of political authority under liberalism, which is democracy, as well as its limits under capitalism, we must pay attention to the content of law, especially private property, and not only to law's form. Expressed as an abstract legal right, private property equates an individual's ownership of her or his labour with the ownership of things.

A variety of legal institutions (including courts, tribunals, agencies, and legislatures) and legal norms have developed in liberal-capitalist societies during the twentieth century. Pashukanis's commodity form theory of law is unable to account for this complexity. However, this complexity, this legal pluralism, tends to hide the real nature of social relations. It tends to underplay the role of state law in exercising a centralizing discipline not only institutionally but also normatively (Hunt 1993). The ideal of the rule of law, according to which the ordinary courts are to have the final say as to the validity of legal and political decisions, exerts institutional pressure for consistency and coherence across different tribunals and areas of law. Moreover, the legal method's commitment to consistency and universality, embodied in the doctrine of precedent and its reverence for formal legal equality, exercises a dominance or hegemony that seeks to subordinate other normative traditions (Woodiwiss 1990). Thus, it is important to appreciate both the plurality of legal institutions and norms within liberal-capitalist societies and the special power of the state's legal system.

The commodity form theory of law has another problem: its focus on exchange relations rather than production relations. Because Pashukanis started his analysis of the legal form at the point at which labour power is exchanged in the labour market, he tended to overgeneralize the purchase of the independent juridic subject (Fine 1984; Gavigan 1981). Aboriginal people, women, and members of visible minorities have, for different periods and to different degrees, been denied the rights and privileges of legal personality and political citizenship granted to white, adult men in liberal societies (Corrigan and Sayer 1981). Only by examining the relations of production, which includes the production of human beings (as well as the production of other commodities that do not have the capacity for collective resistance), is it possible to begin to account for the relationship between legal forms and social norms (Fine 1984; Gavigan 1981; Hunt 1993; Picciotto 1979).

In what follows, I want to illustrate how the commodity form theory of law provides only a partial, and gendered, account of law. To do so, I shall build upon a traditional Marxist analysis of law as a commodity form by revising a recurrent flaw in traditional Marxism: a too-narrow conception of production (class) relations. If class is defined exclusively in terms of the relations between workers and employers within the labour market and workplace, women's position within, and contribution to, capitalist social relations is ignored. Obscured, too, is the distinctive way in which families and households are organized under capitalism. By broadening my focus to include legal forms and norms that pertain to women workers, my aim is to show how "status" was replaced by "protection" as the specific legal form of women's employment outside the home. I use a historical case study—the legal regulation of women's work from 1870 to 1920—to illustrate both the contrast in legal forms pertaining to men's and women's paid work and how social norms were gendered. The effect of the legal treatment of men and women workers was to perpetuate and reinforce a sexual division of labour in which women were subordinated to men. Moreover, the effect of these gendered social norms has been to maintain women's substantive inequality, despite the move to formal equality in the legal regulation of women's employment.

CAPITALISM AND CONTRACT: MEN WORKERS

Sir Henry Maine, a famous English legal scholar who held the Chair of Jurisprudence at Oxford University in the late nineteenth century, remarked that the crowning achievement of the English common law was the transformation from "status" to "contract," a change in legal and political authority that marked the transition from feudalism to liberal capitalism (Maine 1963). The shift also expressed the profound change in how productive relations came to be organized and legitimated under capitalism. Serfs occupied a particular social status, one in which they were legally and politically subordinate to their lords and masters. They owed their masters extensive duties, especially to labour on their behalf. In exchange, masters were required to ensure their serfs' well-being, even if it was unprofitable to do so. Master and servant law, which governed feudal productive relations, was paternalistic; it both accepted and promoted social relations of subordination. Together with marriage and paternity, in which the wife was subordinate to the husband and the child to the father, it comprised the essential domestic status relations (Blackstone 1979).

With the emergence of industrial capitalism in England in the late eighteenth century and its consolidation by the late nineteenth century, the legal form of the relations between producers and owners underwent a reconfiguration. The legal foundation of the new productive relations was the contract of employment, which in turn derived from the notion of free exchange via the medium of contract and the idea of exclusive use rights in private property. Contracts incorporated the prevailing liberal ideology of free agreement and individual choice. "Workers no longer existed as objects, the property of their masters, but were recognized as subjects having property in their own selves (work)" (Owens 1995: 43).

But this transition from feudalism to liberalism and status to contract was neither smooth nor seamless; it was contested and resisted. The notion of the free employment contract was infused with the older, feudal form of master and servant law. According to Fox (1974: 185): "Once the contract was defined as an employment contract, the master-servant model was brought into play—though not of course all the original aspects of it. The notion of the employer's diffuse obligation was clearly in decline. What was most important for the propertied classes was that element which legitimized the employer's prerogative. But along with this there was also carried over into the contract an expectation that the personal status characteristic of the master-servant model would remain."

The law underwrote this expectation, for the common-law courts implied into the voluntary agreement, the contract, duties on the part of the employee to obey the orders of, and to be faithful and loyal to, the employer (Glasbeek 1982; Owens 1995). While the employer was legally obliged to pay the employee for the duration of the employment relationship, the employer did not owe a duty of good faith to the employee. Moreover, employees' economic dependence upon employers reinforced the lingering legal subordination embedded in the contract by older notions of status. Since the business enterprise was their private property, employers had the legal right to control all that happened in the workplace and to reap the profits resulting from the employees' labour.

Between 1840 and 1880 the English common law was applied in what were to become Canadian courts, with the exception of those in Quebec, to regulate the relations between labour and capital. The symbiosis and tensions between contract and status in the legal form of the employment relationship were marked. Not only did Canadian courts follow their English forebears by implying duties into the contract of employment that resulted in workers' subordination to employers, but also the disparities in the employment relationship were exacerbated by the persistence of master and servant acts in several of the provinces (Craven 1981; Tucker 1991; Webber 1995). These statutes made it a criminal offence for an employee to quit work and stipulated imprisonment as the penalty. By contrast, an employer who failed to pay outstanding wages was only subject to a fine. In addition, when workers combined to resist the conditions imposed by employers, the common-law and criminal legislation operated to render their activities, if not their existence, unlawful (Chartrand 1984; Craven 1984; Tucker 1991). But however much the use of criminal law and coercive legislation may have dampened workers' collective resistance to exploitative employment relations, it neither stopped trade union organization nor put an end to strikes and other forms of industrial action.

The state, especially its democratic institutions, increasingly became the site of workers' struggles to obtain formal legal equality with their employers. By the 1870s, although Canada was still predominantly an agricultural country, it had undergone a period of state-building, urbanization, and increasing expansion of the manufacturing sector (Palmer 1992). The franchise was extended to greater numbers of working men as the property restrictions on the vote were lowered. Trade unions not only increased in size and number, but also began to intervene in the political process. Workers joined nine-hour-day leagues to reduce the length of the working day, elected their first candidates to federal and provincial office, and lobbied governments to enact favourable legislation in exchange for labour's support. Following the Tory federal election victory in 1872, the Macdonald government enacted the Trade Union Act, 1872, and the Criminal Law Amendment Act. These statutes provided trade unions with the imprimatur of partial legality by immunizing them from the common-law doctrines of criminal conspiracy and restraint of trade, which had made it unlawful for workers to combine to improve their terms and conditions of employment (Chartrand 1984, Tucker 1991).

The gradual achievement of formal legal equality in employment relations reflected the attainment of a new political status, that of citizen, for workers. The political rights of workers to participate in the electoral process ensured that, at the very least, the democratic institutions of the Canadian state would have to listen to their demands. Simultaneously, workers were transformed into independent legal persons, free and equal before the law. But this new legal status was both fragile and limited; it assumed a certain distribution of private property and a sexual division of labour. The slow emergence of the liberal state signalled the dominance of electoral democracy in the public/political sphere and the hegemony of private property in the private/economic sphere. The liberal state both recognized the rights of property owners and helped to create those rights by providing an apparatus, the common-law courts, to have property claims both vindicated and enforced. Market power was translated into political and legal influence through instrumental ties between private property owners and political officials, deep structural linkages, and pervasive and repeated expressions of the view that the interests of capital are coincident with those of the polity as a whole. While the liberal state must, of necessity, mediate the political demands of workers and employers, it can never completely resolve the contradiction between democracy and private property. In this context, not only do workers often lose, especially when engaging with less democratically accountable state institutions (such as the courts and the police), but their political and legal victories are often tempered by important concessions, both real and symbolic. For example, in Canada nearly every statute supportive of trade union rights and collective bargaining has been accompanied by restrictive measures designed to ensure responsible trade union behaviour, which generally has been defined to include respect for private property rights and a renunciation of the use of economic power for the purpose of promoting so-called "radical" economic and political objectives (McCallum 1996, Tucker 1991, 1995).

Not only did the social relations of private property undermine the significance of formal legal equality for workers, but also the legal status of free juridic subject was profoundly limited in its initial scope, applying predominantly to male workers of British origin. Excluded from formal legal equality, and many civil and political rights, were women and immigrants from outside the United Kingdom. In Canada in the 1870s, women were not considered to be legal persons equal to men, nor were they granted the rights of political citizenship until much later.[3] Until well into the twentieth century, the dominant legal form of women's work was not contract, but status.

PATRIARCHY AND STATUS: WOMEN WORKERS

Traditionally, most Marxist scholars who have examined the relationship between law and capitalism have emphasized the separation of direct producers from the means of production and the emergence of free wage labour. Contract supplanted status as the legal form for organizing the bulk of economic activity. This is why the commodity form theory of law has been so persuasive as a general account of law. It has fallen to feminists, however, to emphasize the flip side of that separation of producers from the means of production: the split between the site of procreation and daily and generational maintenance of the labouring population (the household and family) and the site of production (waged work and the workplace) (Picchio 1992). Rosemary Owens (1995: 43) notes, "The emergence of labour law in the 19th century as a category distinct from the old law of domestic relationships reflected the separation of home and work in the new industrial age." Within the home, the law of domestic relations, which was based on status, continued to be used to regulate the family. This was where the vast majority of women's work was performed. Thus, by focusing almost exclusively on the capitalist workplace, most theorists inspired by Marx have not only tended to ignore women's work and the distinctive nature of the legal form that regulated it, but also provided a too-narrow account of law.

Agricultural production was the predominant form of economic activity in pre-Confederation Canada, and all family members—men, women, and children—contributed directly to it. The household was the basic economic unit. Production within the household, which was mostly for the family's use, was largely organized and performed by women. As the market grew, more of women's production (food and clothing primarily) was sold in the market, but this work was still "confined to what could be performed within the household" (Cohen 1988: 11). This production gave women an economic base within the family, since they were generally agreed to be essential economic partners. Moreover, productive economic activity was compatible with the daily demands of caring for the human beings who made up the household.[4]

Work within the household did not translate easily into the emerging legal category of contract. Especially in situations in which one member of a family worked for another, the law reflected the significance of the family, not the individual, as the primary economic unit in a predominantly agrarian society. For example, a woman who did not receive the inheritance she expected after living for years with her father and caring for him brought an action against his estate claiming wages owed to her under an implied contract of employment. Describing her suit as "one of very dangerous tendency," Chief Justice John Beverly Robinson of the Court of Queen's Bench of Upper Canada commented: "This young woman could not be living anywhere else more properly than with her aged and infirm parent; and if she did acts of service, instead of living idly, it is no more than she ought to have done in return for her clothes and board, to say nothing of the claims of natural affection which usually lead children to render such service" (Craven 1981: 177, quoting *Sprague and Wife* v. *Nickerson* (1844), 1 UCQB 284).

By the turn of the twentieth century, however, the once-dominant form of family production was becoming a faint memory in most parts of Canada, as industrial capitalism and factory production superseded it. "Fewer and fewer households had the means to produce directly most of what they needed for survival, and few of those with a skill or a product to sell did so from their homes" (Armstrong and Armstrong 1994: 83).

Families became increasingly dependent upon uncertain and seasonable labour in staples and resource industries (Peikoff and Brickey 1991: 73). Men were forced to find employment for greater lengths of time, and women and children joined them in their search for waged labour. "Factories, workshops, department stores, and offices began to replace home-based production. Workplaces, work and workers became increasingly segregated" (Armstrong and Armstrong 1994: 83). Thus, what had been a general labour process was, as Seccombe recounts, "split into two discreet units: a domestic unit and an industrial unit. The character of the work performed in each was fundamentally different. The domestic unit reproduced labour power for the labour market. The industrial unit produced goods and services for the commodity market. This split in the labour process had reproduced a split in the labour force roughly along sexual lines—women into the domestic unit, men into industry" (Seccombe 1974: 6; quoted in Armstrong and Armstrong 1994: 84).

Industrial capitalism both strengthened and intensified the sexual division of labour. Waged work, which was increasingly necessary for household survival, was not easily compatible with domestic work, which was labour-intensive. Women historically had performed the largest bulk of domestic labour, especially child and elder care, and this did not change with industrial capitalism. Women's dependence upon men's wages deepened and expanded under industrial capitalism. Moreover, since domestic labour—commonly known as housework—was not paid work, it was not considered to have any market or economic value.

While the shift in the law of work relationships from status (master and servant) to contract (employment) was of profound significance to men, it had little effect on women. Rather, according to Owens (1995: 44): "The position of women in the family and through marriage was the primary determinant of their work relationships in law. Women's status in the family ensured that they remained the property of men, and women's work in the private sphere of the home was simply their matrimonial or filial duty." Women continued to be governed primarily by the law of domestic relations. Families were organized along status relations that were patriarchal, and the law both recognized and reinforced this form (Ursel 1992). Husbands and fathers were the heads of the households, and their control over wives, children, and household resources was institutionalized and legally enforceable. The system of coverture, in which a married women's legal personality and identity were subsumed within, and subordinated to, that of her husband, was a central element in patriarchal family relations. It meant that married women could not control the property they owned (only their husbands could), nor could they bring legal actions on their own behalf (Backhouse 1991: 177).

What was remarkable was the extent to which the duties owed by a wife to her husband were similar to those owed by the employee to the employer; wives were required to obey their husbands, as well as exhibit loyalty and fidelity (Owens 1995: 44). The lines of authority in marriage (husbands' control over wives) were, potentially, in conflict with the lines of authority in employment (employers' control over workers). Women who sought and obtained paid employment could, logically, be subject to two masters. This potential conflict in authority relations regarding women was resolved by elevating the importance of marriage for women over their employment in the hierarchy of legal relations. The system of coverture not only required that married women obtain the consent of their husbands in order to engage in employment, but that their husbands had the legal right to their wages (Backhouse 1991). For the minority of married women in Canada who worked outside the home, their husbands were the legal subjects of their employment contracts; the women, or more precisely, their labour power, were simply the objects of the contracts. "The wages-work bargain involving women's work was maintained as an exchange between men, citizens in the public sphere" (Owens 1995: 44).

But the formal legal subordination of contract and employment to status and marriage for married women was fragile and unstable. The logic of liberalism, with its emphasis on equality and liberty, is biased towards the extension of legal and political rights (Fudge and Glasbeek 1992). The legal subordination of women to their husbands did not fit well with the political discourse of liberalism. Women reformers exploited this contradiction in their struggle to be recognized as free and equal legal subjects and political citizens. Nor did these patriarchal vestiges of a pre-industrial society fit with the need for a large supply of cheap waged labour. The upshot of these tensions and pressures was the legislative abolition of the system of coverture. Between 1872 and 1907, married women's property acts were enacted in all common-law provinces except Alberta. As a result, a married woman's property, including her earnings, were at last hers (Prentice et al. 1988: 187; Ursel 1992).

FROM PATRIARCHY TO PROTECTION:
REGULATING WOMEN'S EMPLOYMENT

The revolution that swept away the legal foundation of patriarchy in the family by abolishing the system of coverture was not accompanied by a similar revolution in social relations. The sexual division of labour persisted, despite the erosion of the legal supports for patriarchy. While married women no longer had to obtain the consent of their husbands to accept employment and they had a legal right to the wages they were paid for their labour, very few married women were employed outside the home. By 1931, the earliest year for which figures are available, only 10 percent of women in the workforce were married and of all married women, only 3 percent were in the workforce. Moreover, the small proportion of employed married women were considered unfortunates, forced to find work because of the death, unemployment, or desertion of their husbands (White 1993: 12–13).

Until the 1960s employment was typically a young woman's activity, something she did before marriage and starting a family. There were several reasons for this. First, domestic labour, almost exclusively women's responsibility, was gruelling and time-consuming. Few married women chose to work outside the home unless it was absolutely necessary (White 1993: 12). Second, employers greatly resisted employing married women. In 1895, for instance, the Toronto School Board refused to hire either married women or women over thirty years old, despite primary school teaching being almost exclusively a woman's job (White 1993: 12; Phillips and Phillips 1993: 20). Third, women's wages were significantly less than men's, making it extremely difficult for women to support themselves, let alone any dependents.

For the period between 1881 and 1921, employment of women—married or not—was the exception, rather than the rule, even for young women. In 1901 women made up only 13 percent of the total labour force, increasing only by 2 percentage points by 1921. In that year, just under 20 percent of all women over fourteen years were employed (White 1993: 11). Despite the consolidation of industrial capitalism and the extension of free wage labour for men, the sexual division of labour persisted, such that the overwhelming majority of women were relegated to the home.

Moreover, even when women found paid employment, they tended to be confined to occupations "that were commercial counterparts to the work they had done in the home or on the farm. They would sew, clean, prepare food, teach, or keep boarders—jobs now done for pay where previously they had been done for the family" (Phillips and Phillips 1993: 15). At the beginning of the twentieth century, most women in paid employment were domestic workers, seamstresses, cotton mill workers, or "shop girls." The sexual division of labour in the family was replicated within the workplace, with women confined to the poorest paid and lowest positions in the occupational hierarchy. Even in those few instances in which men and women performed substantially the same work, women were paid substantially less than their male counterparts. Evidence presented to the 1889 Royal Commission on the Relations of Labour and Capital indicated that the average salesman was paid $10 to $12 a week, while a top-ranked saleswoman could only expect to earn $6 to $8 a week. Women workers rarely earned sufficient wages to support an autonomous household (Prentice et al. 1988: 127). In 1910, for example, a woman employed in manufacturing was paid on average only $5.44 a week—a figure that was at, or below, the minimum subsistence levels for a single person and only 57 percent of the average male manufacturing wage of $9.58 (Phillips and Phillips 1993: 15).

Women's employment in the newly industrialized nation elicited a number of contradictory responses both within and between different social groups. Employers, especially those engaged in light manufacturing (such as textiles, garments, biscuits and canning, and the retail sector), regarded women (and children) as a cheap source of labour. Appearing before the Royal Commission on the Relations between Capital and Labour in 1889, several employers stated that they were prepared to hire women so long as they were "docile, clean, quick, cheap and sober." They also made it clear that they hired women because it was "more profitable to us or we would not employ them"(White 1993: 38–39). But the short-term interests of some employers to increase their profits conflicted with the long-term interests of the capitalist class to secure a healthy, stable, and orderly labouring population. This concern was most consistently and powerfully expressed by the Canadian Social Reform Movement, whose leaders were largely drawn from the Anglo-Saxon protestant middle classes (Bacchi 1983).

Women's social reform organizations, especially the National Council of Women, played an important role in the social reform movement from the 1880s to the 1920s. Together with the churches and the medical profession—traditional bastions of male authority and privilege—they were concerned with protecting the moral and physical health of working-class women. Their emphasis on motherhood, combined with a concern to preserve racial purity, led them to conclude that women's employment was regarded as threatening the integrity of the Canadian nation. Restriction and protection were the solutions that social reformers endorsed for the problem of women's employment (Backhouse 1991; Ursel 1992).

Organized labour's position on the "problem" posed by women's employment was even more complex (Tucker 1990: 117). On the one hand, the low wages of individual male workers necessitated the employment of wives and children in order for households to survive. On the other hand, the lower wages paid to women and children created a downward pressure on men's wages in the competitive labour market (Ursel 1992: 77–78). Unlike capitalists, male workers faced an immediate dilemma. Consequently, as Peikoff and Brickey (1991: 74) summarize:

> [Trade unions] were torn between three different positions concerning women. As workers, unionists saw women as dangerous competitors. Thus, some unions openly advocated women's exclusion from the labour market. On the other hand, as trade unionists, men were committed to the protection of all workers, including women, and some opted for working class solidarity. As men, however, most union members also accepted the traditional moralistic definition of a woman's place as being in the home, as it ensured male privilege and familial order.

Trade unionists debated each of exclusion, protection, and equality as solutions to the problem of women's employment (Tucker 1990).

This range of responses to women's employment is not surprising, given that the "problem" was generated by the separation of maintenance and reproduction of the labouring population from direct access to the means of subsistence. Under capitalism, the wage became the primary mechanism through which most working people were able to purchase the resources necessary for survival (Acker 1988). However, there was nothing to ensure that wages were adequate to meet the subsistence needs of individuals, let alone the variety of existing households. Since the tension was inherent in capitalist social relations, any solution was bound to be temporary, precarious, and incomplete.

To a large extent, contradictions posed by women's employment were symbolic of the changes to social relations caused by the advent of industrialism in Canada. As White (1993: 43) points out, "Single women were a small and transient contingent of the labour force, while the vast majority of married women were dependent upon their men's wages." It was the shift from independent commodity production to wage labour, rather than women's employment per se, that seriously undermined the material basis for patriarchy. Women's paid employment, especially alongside men in factories, "not only undermined the privileged position of men in the labour market and at home, but also challenged their gender identity which was in part constructed around their ability to earn a family wage and to be independent at work" (Tucker 1990: 117–18). The employment also challenged the broader common sense in which women were regarded as naturally and properly belonging at home. In this way, society in general perceived women's employment outside the home as a threat to Victorian social order. The commitment to the domestic ideal of a woman's place within the home cut across class and gender lines, shaping the political and legal responses to women's employment. Women reformers, despite a minority of dissenting voices, endorsed special protection for women workers and the exclusion of child labourers (Backhouse 1991). So, too, did the majority of male trade unionists (Tucker 1990). The ideal solution was a combination of family wages for men, protection for women, and the exclusion of children.

The factory acts exemplified the latter two prongs of this solution. First introduced in Ontario in 1884, this legislation initiated the legal distinctions in employment between male labour, on the one hand, and female and child labour, on the other. It was one of the earliest examples of health and safety legislation in Canada, and it not only served as a model for subsequent legislation regulating employment in retail establishments but also established the legal precedent of focusing on women's sex—their reproductive capacities—rather than their economic needs, as a continuing preoccupation. The Factory Act of 1884 provided prohibitions on the employment of young children and restrictions on the employment of adolescents, but even these provisions were gendered. For example, the act prohibited industrial establishments from employing boys under the age of twelve and girls under the age of fourteen (Peikoff and Brickey 1991: 76). The factory acts focused on the possible adverse effects of work on women's health, offspring, mortality, and morality, requiring special consideration for women in the areas of sanitation and comfort. They protected women primarily as mothers, not as workers (Backhouse 1991; Chernier 1982; Creese 1991; Tucker 1990).

Protection was the predominant mechanism for dealing with the problem of women's employment alongside men in early industrial Canada, although examples of outright exclusion are embodied in legislation. In England in the 1840s, a report by the Children's Employment Commission made public the conditions and wages of women and children employed in mines, provoking a national outcry at the harsh and dehumanizing conditions of work. But instead of calling for the working conditions to be improved, reformers fixed upon the indecent, coarse, and unfeminine apparel and demeanour of the women and girl mineworkers. In response, the English Parliament enacted legislation prohibiting women and girls from working underground in mines. Although there were no similar exposés in Canada, the English laws were seized upon in British Columbia and Ontario, where legislation was passed banning women from working underground in mines. The Ontario legislation, enacted in 1890, went even further than its English precedent; it barred women from working in mines, even above ground, altogether. By contrast, Nova Scotia, which had the worst record of mine accidents in Canada, did not attempt to bar women from mines until halfway through the twentieth century (Backhouse 1991: 290).

But, of course, the absence of legislation excluding women from certain industries and occupations did not mean that women's employment opportunities were equal to those of men. Far from it: sex segregation remained the norm as employers had the legal right to discriminate against women workers until the 1960s (Ursel 1992).

While the enactment of factory legislation across Canada was a symbolic victory for social reformers and male trade unionists, it had little direct impact either upon the conditions of women's work or their access to paid employment. The acts were riddled with exemptions, provided low and inadequate standards, and were not effectively enforced (Backhouse 1991: 271–73; Tucker 1990: 111–14). Women workers gained very little from such legislative protection, nor did they suffer exclusion as a result of such sex-specific legislation. As Tucker (1990: 135) recounts, "labour market segregation limited the competitive threat posed by women and, in any event, the provisions of the legislation did not create a major disincentive for employers who desired to hire women."

But while it is unlikely that women suffered direct material losses from such protective legislation, its symbolic legacy for women was profoundly negative. The effect of the protective legislation in reinforcing women's reproductive role at the expense of their employment needs was evident, as Ursel (1992: 94) points out, even more in what the legislation omitted than in what it covered. Women who worked inside homes, whether in their own homes as pieceworkers or in other people's as domestic workers, were simply left out of the legislation. As well, the legislation did nothing about the problem of women's wages, which were both significantly lower than men's and not enough to provide support for even a single woman. According to Veronica Strong-Boag (1979: 158), such "legislation acknowledged female inferiority much more than it aimed at its elimination." Politically, it "institutionalized gendered discourses and practices which directly and indirectly restricted women's opportunities" (Tucker 1990: 136).

The issue of women's substandard wages was not addressed until the end of World War I. Then the concern was not so much with women's poverty, but rather with the storm of labour unrest that was building as the end of the war came into sight. Working people were dissatisfied with what they perceived as their unequal sacrifice for the war effort. The government gave factory owners, especially those who manufactured munitions, generous incentives to produce, while at the same time imposing restrictions on individual rights to bargain for higher wages or to quit an unsatisfactory job. Even before the war ended, reformers and trade unions challenged the idea that wage rates should be determined by individual bargaining. Demands for free collective bargaining and minimum-wage legislation increased. In 1917 Alberta became the first province to enact minimum-wage legislation. Remarkably, it provided for the same wage ($1.50 per day) to be paid to both men and women (McCallum 1996).

Despite the unprecedented levels of strike activity in 1918 and 1919, including the Winnipeg General Strike of 1919, neither the federal nor the provincial governments responded to workers' and unions' demands by enacting large-scale reform legislation to address the unequal relations between employees and employers. Instead, the political elites regarded the workers' turn to collective protest as a challenge to civil order, and they met the strike wave with repression and coercion. In this context, as McCallum (1996: 590) recounts: "Employers rejected proposals for a minimum wage for men, arguing that men's freedom to make their own contracts should not be restricted; but they accepted state intervention to ensure that the mothers of the race earned enough to feed themselves without being forced into prostitution."

Other provinces did not follow the Alberta precedent of providing across-the-board minimum wages for men and women workers. Instead, a much more modest—and sex-specific—technique was adopted. Led by Manitoba, the provinces (including Alberta, which fell into line in 1922) established administrative boards to set wages for female employees. They designed a wage standard that would provide a woman with a subsistence living in the event that she was entirely self-supporting and had no dependents (Kealey 1987). This benchmark failed to take into consideration the needs of women who were not dependent upon men but supported dependents, a category composed of a quarter of the women who had paid employment at the time minimum-wage legislation was enacted. The effect of this wage standard was to confine these women and their families to dire poverty (Creese 1991; Hobbes 1985; Kealey 1998; McCallum 1986; Russell 1991).

Moreover, the standard for women's wages contained in the minimum-wages legislation stood in direct contrast with the standard set for wages in fair wages resolutions. Such resolutions were adopted first by the federal government in 1900 as a response to the problem of "sweated" labour, which was symbolized by the horrible working condition of the children and women employed in the garment industry (McIntosh 1993). What fair wages resolutions and legislation did was impose a requirement upon businesses that entered into contracts with the government to meet certain minimum standards regarding wages and working conditions for their workers. However, these resolutions did little to improve working conditions for the most vulnerable workers, women and children in the garment trades. Instead, they applied primarily to men employed on railways and other public works central to government economic policy. Fair wages were to be living wages for male workers who supported a dependent wife and children (Kealey 1987; McCallum 1996; Russell 1991). By contrast, as the 1914 Report of Labour Conditions in British Columbia stated, "Employers stressed that women were not expected to have to live on their salaries and, therefore, women's wages had nothing to do with any notion of a living wage" (quoted in White 1993: 41). As well, when minimum wages were extended to men workers, they were higher than those required to be paid to women workers (Creese 1991; Ursel 1992).

Protective legislation had very little impact on improving the wages and conditions of women workers employed outside the home. Like the factory acts, minimum-wage legislation was riddled with exemptions and ineffectively enforced (Creese 1991; McCallum 1986). Furthermore, since the standards set for women's wages were so low, they most likely had little impact on increasing the cost of employing women workers. For these reasons, this form of legislative protection also probably did not directly result in the exclusion of women from paid employment. Once again, the effect of protecting women workers was to reinforce a specific understanding of the role of women. Thus, protective legislation must be understood in terms of its symbolism and ideological legacy. As status gave way to contract as the primary legal form for regulating productive relations, protective legislation served to reinforce the sexual division of labour under capitalism. "Through protective legislation that differentiated the conditions of hiring men, women and children workers, state intervention reinforced women's economic inequality, their maternal role and their dependence on a male breadwinner" (Creese 1991: 121).

WORKING WITHIN THE FAMILY: NO NEED FOR PROTECTION

Protective legislation pertained to women who worked alongside men outside of the home. It did not apply to the majority of women who worked for wages—domestic workers. Between 1871 and 1941 domestic workers made up the single largest category of paid female workers in Canada. They were also the only category of female workers designated as "desirable immigrants" by the Canadian government. But the desirability of these women immigrants was conditional upon their chastity and ethnicity (Cunningham 1991; Roberts 1988; Valverde 1991). Immigrants accounted for about one-third of the domestic workers in Canada until the outbreak of World War II. Of these, British subjects were the preferred category, since female domestic workers were brought to Canada not only to supply the high demand for household help, but also to provide a stock of wives for prairie farmers. While, initially, racial distinctions were constructed, using markers like nationality and language to exclude all but Anglo-Saxon immigrants, immigration policies changed in light of the profound demand for more people in Canada. Non-Anglo-Saxon European women also came to be recruited as servants. Racial distinctions became defined increasingly in terms of skin colour and European/non-European differences. Race, understood in these terms, continued to operate as a bar until the 1950s (Calliste 1991; Cunningham 1991).

Despite the fact that domestic workers were recruited to work and were paid wages (however low), their location within the family influenced how law categorized their employment relationship. Located in the home and associated with the realm of domesticity, domestic workers were, in some respects, attributed the status of a family member. For example, a master could receive a monetary award for damages against a man who seduced a female servant if he could prove that the female servant was previously of chaste character. The pregnancy of the servant was also considered a loss to the master, and the master could pursue this loss against the servant's seducer. This legal action, known as the tort of seduction, was also available to fathers and other male heads of household if their daughters or close female relatives were seduced. But when it came to the master's duty to provide medical care and services for the servant, the relationship was characterized at law as one of contract and not involving family status. Therefore, the master was not required to provide the necessities of life for the servant (Cunningham 1991).

While the contractual nature of the employment relationship was acknowledged in ways that did not benefit the domestic worker, the characterization of domestic workers as part of the family prevailed when they sought the protection of minimum-wage laws. Between 1913 and 1920 in Vancouver, Calgary, Winnipeg, Toronto, and Sydney, domestic workers' unions demanded the inclusion of domestic workers under the provincial minimum-wage statutes and the standardization of wages and hours (Cunningham 1991; Epstein 1983). In Ontario, the leader of the Liberal Party opposed the Farmer-Labour Alliance government's minimum-wage bill, which would have extended the proposed minimum wage to domestic workers, on the ground that domestic workers did not need such protection since they were provided with their food and keep by the employers they resided with. To ensure the passage of the minimum-wage legislation, the Ontario government simply excluded domestic workers from the scope of the bill. This move excluded domestic workers, the single largest category of female employees in Ontario, from minimum-wages legislation (Fudge 1997: 123).

Women who were employed within other people's homes faced the worst of what was generally a bad bargain for women workers. Domestic workers tended to be young, more often than not immigrants, with little or no training. Their legal status was extremely ambiguous; although employees, they were denied many of the protections available to other women workers. Thus, their wages tended to be even lower than the paltry standard set by minimum-wage legislation. Moreover, their hours of work were completely unregulated. Because they worked and lived within their employers' homes, receiving food and board in addition to wages, they were not seen as in need of protection. But since they were not kin, they derived little benefit from their location within the family. Thus, their legal status was more akin to that of a servant than that of either an employee or a family member. A former servant, recalling the 1880s, stated that when a girl was hired for a term, she was for that period "as much the property of her mistress as was ever a slave in the cotton fields of the south" (Prentice et al. 1988: 124). If a domestic worker lost her job, she also lost her home. The situation of these workers was extremely precarious, increasing their vulnerability to economic and sexual exploitation.

CONCLUSION:
DIFFERENT LEGAL FORMS AND GENDERED SOCIAL NORMS

The legal treatment of men's and women's employment in Canada during the period of industrialization (roughly from the 1870s to the 1920s) differed profoundly. For men workers, contract gradually supplanted status as the primary legal form for regulating their labour. Male workers exercised their recently secured liberal citizenship rights to throw off the shackles of legal subordination to property owners. By the end of the 1870s, the formal legal inequalities embedded in the master and servant acts and the criminal law were repealed. Contract replaced status as the legal device for regulating the employment relationship, and workers and employers were, generally, treated as legal equals by the law. Pashukanis's commodity form theory of law captures this development.

The story for women workers was much different. Status, not contract, governed their labour. Under patriarchy women were legally subordinated to their husbands. Until the mid-1880s, if employed outside of the home, married women had no legal right to their wages or to enforce their employment contracts; only their husbands had those rights. As patriarchy was weakened both by industrial capitalism (which eroded the basis for older social relations) and women's challenge to their legal subordination to men (which was fuelled and facilitated by the liberal discourse of equality, liberty, and individualism), a new form of legal regulation emerged to reinforce the sexual division of labour. In the case of women who worked outside the home, contract was modified by protective legislation, which focused on women's moral and physical vulnerability in employment. Such legislation "was premised on women's subordinate positions within the family, the economy and civil society" (Creese 1991: 122). Moreover, "in emphasizing special treatment for women and children, instead of protection for all workers, the factories acts did not directly contradict liberal ideals about the importance of citizens making their own agreements, because women and children were not full citizens anyway" (McCallum 1996: 583.) Women's subordination was reconstituted; it was no longer primarily legal, but economic. The different legal treatment of women from the men they worked alongside of in factories illustrates the extent to which the sexual division of labour and gendered social norms belied the notion of formal legal equality and reinforced women's social subordination to men.

Domestic workers faced an ambiguous, and detrimental, mix of contract and status as the legal categories regulating their work. As employees, not kin, they did not enjoy any of the legal benefits that accrued to family members. As women who worked within families, even though those families were not their own, they were denied the benefits of protective legislation available to women who worked outside the home. Despite the contradictions in the legal treatment of domestic workers, the overall message was clear—women's place was in the family, supposedly a "safe haven" within which they needed no additional forms of protection. In this respect, the legal status of domestic workers was equivalent to that of married women before the enactment of the married women's acts.

Women's struggle for legal equality went hand in hand with their struggle for political rights equivalent to those enjoyed by men. Gradually, and grudgingly, formal legal equality supplanted formal legal subordination for women in the political sphere (Prentice et al. 1988). But the legal form of women's employment was even more resistant to change. Legislation that began to remove employment barriers to women to work for wages was introduced in Canada in the 1950s, although the progress of legal equality was uneven. It was not until the 1960s that governments across Canada introduced legislation that prohibited employers from discriminating against women (Ursel 1992: 244–49).

Before a celebration of the transformation in the legal form of women's employment from protection to equality is warranted, it is necessary to attend to social norms, because social norms give content to legal forms. The sexual division of labour both within the home (where women do the majority of work) and the workplace (where women are crowded into low-paying, precarious jobs at the bottom of the bottom of the labour market) persists at the end of the twentieth century (Armstrong 1996: Fudge 1996a). The norms of contemporary Canadian labour law continue to be male (Fudge 1996b). Formal legal equality is not enough to address and remedy substantive and substantial social inequality. In this respect, both Marx and Pashukanis were right.

NOTES

1. I want to thank Elizabeth Comack, Harry Glasbeek, and Leah Vosko for their thoughtful and helpful comments on an earlier version of this essay and Shelley Gavigan for prompting me to take the question of legal form seriously. All errors and shortcomings are, however, my own.
2. H.L.A. Hart, in his extremely important and influential book *The Concept of Law* (1961), distinguished between internal and external perspectives on law. According to him, the internal perspective is adopted by officials of the legal system, while an external perspective is that of an observer (such as an anthropologist) who seeks to understand what the system's rules and functions are in a society.
3. World War I proved to be the precipitating event for the extension of the franchise to women. By the mid-1920s, voting rights in federal and the majority of provincial elections were granted to women. Quebec and the colony of Newfoundland were the only exceptions. The legal right to hold public office came later in many provinces—not until the 1930s (Prentice et al. 1988: 207–9).
4. As Ellen Meiksins Wood (1986: 16) points out, "Markets of various kinds have existed throughout recorded history and … people have exchanged and sold their surpluses in many different ways and for many different purposes. But the market in capitalism has a distinctive and unprecedented function. Virtually everything in capitalist society is a commodity produced for the market. And even more fundamentally, both capital and labor are utterly dependent on the market for the most basic conditions of their own reproduction."

Relocating Law:
Making Corporate Crime Disappear

© Laureen Snider

The study of corporate crime provides a dramatic illustration of the influence exerted over law by hegemonic class interests. We have seen this influence in other essays in this book, which show how difficult it is to apply the promises of Western legal systems embodied in the Official Version of Law: its claims of universalism and equality and the notion that justice is blind to class, race, and gender—in other words, to workers, people of colour and women, groups with little ideological and/ or economic power. But the most cursory attempt to use the Official Version of Law to explain the passage or enforcement of laws governing the anti-social, acquisitive acts of business quickly illustrates the overwhelming, and overt, failure of law to impose meaningful limits on the offences of corporations.

State law has consistently, though not exclusively or simplistically, accommodated the interests of Canada's economic elites, particularly when these elites act with unanimity on issues they see as important. In the last two decades, the few laws and weak enforcement mechanisms enacted to control corporate crime—themselves the product of a century of struggle by employees, consumers, feminists, environmentalists, and others—have been systematically repealed and dismantled. In direct contrast to state law in every other jurisdiction, which has become ever more intrusive and increasingly punitive (with rates of incarceration spiralling for all traditional offences despite falling crime rates) (Rothman 1995; Snider 1998b), laws governing corporate crime have become more lax and lenient, and many types of corporate crime have disappeared altogether from the law books.

This disappearance has not happened because corporate crime, defined as "white-collar crimes of omission or commission by an individual or group of individuals in a legitimate formal organization—which have a serious physical or economic impact on employees, consumers or the general public" (Box 1983: 20), has ceased to be a problem. The toll of lives lost, injuries sustained, species obliterated, watercourses decimated, savings and pensions destroyed, and life chances ruined by the various types of corporate crimes has dramatically increased with the advent of the global marketplace, the spread of capitalist workplaces and production to Third World countries, the new-found dominance of finance capital, and the decline in the power of the nation-state. It has happened, rather, because a successful *corporate counter-revolution* has succeeded in reversing progress towards a more egalitarian society by taking back "such gains as the working classes have made" (Glasbeek 1995: 112).

In the second half of the 1970s, the margin of profitability—that is, the surplus value accruing to capital determined by the difference between the all-in costs of production and the all-in profits of production (per unit)—began to decline. From roughly 1980 on, signalled by the election of right-wing governments under Ronald Reagan in the United States and Margaret Thatcher in the United Kingdom, the owners and controllers of capital and their allies in political, media, and knowledge elites have waged a highly successful campaign to increase the margin of exploitation, the absolute and relative profitability of capitalist enterprises. This campaign has meant decreasing the incomes and life chances of the bottom 75 to 80 percent of the population to benefit the top 1 to 2 percent.

Over the last twenty years, rates of inequality have dramatically increased. In the bellwether United States from 1977–89, the top 1 percent of U.S. families received 60 percent of after-tax income gains while the incomes of the bottom 40 percent went down, in real (absolute) as well as relative dollars (Miyoshi 1993: 738). In Washington, D.C. in the late 1990s, for example, the top 20 percent of families had incomes twenty-eight times higher than the poorest 20 percent. The bottom quintile took home an average of $5,290 per year, nearly $2,000 less than they received twenty years earlier (*Globe and Mail* December 23, 1997: A13). In Canada, between 1977 and 1991 the average total family income for the bottom fifth of families stood at $17,334 in 1996, a 6.1 percent share of the national income, the lowest in two decades, while the average income of the top fifth rose to $114,874, a 40.6 percent share, the highest in two decades (Statistics Canada 1997). Meanwhile the size, power, and profitability of corporations have dramatically increased. The total wealth of the world's 385 billionaires equals the combined incomes of 45 percent of the world's population, or 2.3 billion people (United Nations 1996). Corporate salaries, perks, and bonuses totalling $3 million a year for chief executive officers are not uncommon in Canada; in the

United States CEOs routinely get double and triple that amount (*Globe and Mail* May 5, 1998: B16, June 22, 1998: A1). Worldwide, the top 20 percent of the world's population increased their share of total global wealth from 70 percent in 1960 to 85 percent in 1991, and the share "enjoyed" by the poorest 20 percent actually *declined* from 1960 to 1991, falling from 2.3 percent to 1.4 percent (United Nations 1996). "The richest 200 largest corporations [now] have more economic clout than the poorest four-fifths of humanity" (Dobbin 1998: 74–75).

Getting rid of laws that control the acquisitive and anti-social acts of business, in general, and corporations, in particular, has been an essential component of this counter-revolutionary reversal. Historically, one of the main tasks of the nation-state has been to protect citizens from the harm caused by corporations. This was, however, a duty that capitalist states undertook with the utmost reluctance. Typically such laws were passed only after major environmental or industrial disasters made some sort of state response imperative (Snider 1991, 1993). Thus it is not surprising that national governments in the 1980s and 1990s, facing deficits and declining revenues (caused, in large part, by another successful corporate initiative, aimed at reducing the tax rates of corporations and the rich), were quick to repeal laws that restricted and criminalized potentially profitable acts and thereby annoyed the corporate sector. Indeed, corporate crimes—ignoring costly regulations on mine safety, not paying overtime wages, marketing drugs with harmful side-effects, conspiring to increase the prices of necessary goods—are always committed to increase profits or prevent losses (and they usually do). By abandoning efforts to prevent, monitor, or sanction such acts, the nation-state signals its acquiescence to corporate (and corporatist) agendas and acknowledges its inability (or disinclination) to protect its own citizens from the predations of the global marketplace. In the race to achieve maximal profitability, destroying profit-threatening measures such as environmental restrictions and the minimum wage shows that a country is, in the immortal words of former Prime Minister Brian Mulroney, "open for business." It signals that a century of struggle to use the laws of the nation-state to force capital to meet certain standards of behaviour and impose limits on the exploitation of human and natural resources has been abandoned.

This essay has two objectives: first, to document the disappearance of state law over corporate crime; and, second, to examine its significance. What are the implications for those who seek to force Western legal systems to live up to their promises of universalism and equality, their obligation to protect citizens from the harmful anti-social acts of senior executives in transnational corporations as well as biker gangs? And what does this disappearance say about the relations between state law and capital, or about the potential of law to challenge the corporate counter-revolution and promote a more equitable distribution of the spoils of capitalism in the developed world?[1]

THE DISAPPEARANCE OF CORPORATE CRIME

Item:

- Bolar Pharmaceutical Company admitted to selling adulterated and mislabelled drugs and lying to investigators from the federal (U.S.) Food and Drug Administration about the quality and origin of the medicines (*New York Times* March 24, 1991: 26; *Orlando Sentinel* February 28: A17).

- Mer/29 (triparanol), a drug developed by Richardson Merrell to reduce cholesterol levels, went on sale in the United States in 1960. When skin damage, cataracts, and changes in reproductive organs were reported in patients, investigation revealed that Richardson Merrell knew about these side-effects (through animal tests done in its own labs) but suppressed the damaging evidence (Clarke 1990: 205).

- Every year thousands of Canadians suffer adverse drug reactions; ineffective, impure, and unsafe drugs cause much human anguish and cost millions of dollars. From the Dalkon Shield (an intrauterine device that caused miscarriages, sterility, pelvic infection, and several deaths) to the Meme breast implant (a silicon gel coated with polyurethane foam that decomposed under certain conditions to produce a dangerous chemical; finally banned by Health and Welfare Canada in 1992), to defective heart valves and surgical gloves (more than half of the latex medical and surgical gloves failed quality tests): unmonitored, unassessed medical devices have "killed, mutilated, electrocuted, blinded, burned and injured hundreds, if not thousands, of Canadians" (Regush 1991: 9). Every year hundreds of new medical devices, products ranging from heart valves to incubators, are brought into Canada as part of a business worth more than $2 billion, with 300,000 medical devices produced by some 6,595 manufacturing companies, most of them in Third World countries (Regush 1991:16).

In the summer of 1997 Health and Welfare Canada closed down its research laboratories, known as the Bureau of Drug Research, eliminating sixty-eight jobs and saving the federal government $2 million (*Globe and Mail* July 11, 1997: A1). The government has also cut laboratories and programs in the food directorate, which sets standards for acceptable levels of chemical residues or growth hormones in food. The Bureau of Drug Research had been the agency responsible for investigating the safety and effectiveness of drugs sold in Canada, and for monitoring problems after medications were approved. Drug safety will henceforth depend on the validity of research conducted by pharmaceutical companies and on their truthfulness in reporting adverse findings and risks. This research is either conducted by scientists employed by these companies or on contract to them.

Item:
- *Taking Stock*, a report released by the NAFTA Commission for Environmental Cooperation, identifies seven Canadian facilities in the top fifty polluters in North America. A recent study of Environment Canada's Environmental Assessment process called it "a disaster." Standards and penalties are absent, and companies seeking cabinet approval for proposed developments (such as mining the Bedford Sea or logging old-growth forests) are free to shop for whatever industry-friendly scientists are available. The lack of standards allows scientists to "sell out to the highest bidder" (Nikiforuk 1997: 17).
- Canada has admitted its failure to meet the international obligations it agreed to at the Earth Summit in Brazil in 1992. Canada's output of greenhouse gases will *increase* by 10 percent from 1990–2000. Already it appears that Canada will not honour commitments to environmental protection made at Kyoto in December 1997 (*Globe and Mail* August 15, 1997: A-14; *Globe and Mail* October 4: D1; *Toronto Star* April 11, 1998: E-5; Gallon 1996).
- Less than 9 percent of Alberta's boreal forest remains; it is disappearing as fast as the Amazon rain forest (*Globe and Mail* June 22, 1998: A1).

In 1993–94 Environment Canada lost 30 percent of its budget under the Regulatory Efficiency Act passed by the federal Liberal government. In 1995–96 the budget was chopped from $705 million to $507 million. Staff was slashed from 10,000 to under 4,000 people, and in 1997 Environment was demoted from a senior to junior ministry (a loss of prestige and clout, plus staff and budget). In the seven-year period 1988–95 the department launched a total of sixty-three prosecutions for environmental offences for the whole of Canada, an average of 7.2 per year.

Item:

- Owners and operators of nearly half of all the underground coal mines in the United States have systematically tampered with coal-dust samples sent to federal safety inspectors and monitored to control black lung disease. More than 5,000 incidents of sampling fraud have been discovered thus far (*Washington Post* April 4, 1991: 1).

- Approximately 4,000 coal miners die every year from black lung disease; 4.5 percent of the workforce have contracted it (Cullen, Maakestadt, and Cavender 1987: 69).

- In 1992 the Westray Mine in Pictou County, Nova Scotia, exploded, killing twenty-six miners. Subsequent investigations showed that the owners of Westray routinely violated safety laws and failed to make essential repairs. Inspectors for the province of Nova Scotia provided advance notice of impending visits, routinely overlooked minor and major law-breaking incidents, and generally adopted the perspective of management, whose goal was to minimize the costs of production. Workers who reported unsafe conditions were seen, by both government and industry (and sometimes by their peers as well), as malcontents and rabble-rousers (Richard 1997; Comish 1993). By July 1998, all of the fifty-two non-criminal and three remaining criminal charges laid against the owners and managers of the mine and the government inspectors had been dropped (*Globe and Mail* July 1, 1998: A1; Jobb 1998).

Nova Scotia and almost all the other provinces have consistently cut the budgets and workforce of regulatory agencies charged with protecting the health and safety of employees. Self-regulation, a system that asks workers and managers to regulate themselves with minimal government oversight, has become the norm in virtually every industry (Tucker 1995b; Walters et al. 1995; Noble 1995). Between 1976 and 1993, almost 16,700 people died from work-related causes, an average of more than two deaths per day. The average annual rate of 7 per 100,000 deaths related to work (1988–93 data, all industries) is four times greater than the average homicide rate (which hovers around 2.2 per 100,000). Out of every 100,000 miners, 281 died as a result of their work in the 1988–93 period (Statistics Canada 1996; *Globe and Mail* August 10, 1996: A6).

Item:
- British Columbia has the highest fatality rates in Canada for on-the-job deaths in construction, forestry, and transportation, with deaths per 100,000 double and triple those of other provinces (Statistics Canada 1996).
- On July 17, 1997, British Columbia bowed to heavy, unrelenting business pressure and withdrew Bill 44, a law that would have increased the power of workers to refuse to work in unsafe conditions. The bill aimed at improving workplace safety by creating new rights for workers in service industries and strengthening laws in other areas. However, campaigns orchestrated by the Coalition of BC Business charged that the proposed law would scare off investment and increase (their) costs. The NDP government was vilified in the business press as a "crank government" conspiring with "Big Labour" to destroy small business and "enslave the private sector" (*Globe and Mail* July 17, 1997: B2).

Item:
- *Taking Stock* identifies Ontario as the third-biggest polluting jurisdiction in North America, behind only Tennessee and Texas in contributing to air, water, and land pollution. Ontario Hydro dumped at least 1,800 tonnes of heavy metals into Lake Ontario in the last twenty-five years. Smog alone kills 1,800 people per year in Ontario (*Globe and Mail* July 30, 1997; also January 13, 1997: A15, July 30, 1997: A3, August 19, 1997: A1, June 22, 1998: A1).

Fines against polluters in Ontario declined to $955,000 in 1997, the lowest in more than a decade, less than one-third of the 1995 amount. Since 1995 the province's Environment Ministry has lost 45 percent of its budget and 32 percent of its staff; the allied Department of Natural Resources has lost 19 percent of its budget and 30 percent of its staff (*Globe and Mail* June 22, 1998: A1). The number of charges laid against polluters has been cut in half since the Progressive Conservatives took office in Ontario in 1995, dropping from 1,640 in 1994 to 724 in 1996. The average fines on polluting companies dropped from a high of $3,633,095 in 1992 to $1,204,034 in 1997. According to Premier Mike Harris, many of

Ontario's rules frighten away investment because they are "extreme" (*Globe and Mail* November 14, 1996).

Item:

- Some two hundred people died when the appropriately named *Herald of Free Enterprise*, owned and operated by Townsend Car Ferries, went down in the English Channel in 1987. The accident occurred when the ferry left the dock before the bow doors were properly secured. Subsequent investigation showed that the crew piloting the ship, working on the bridge, had no means of communicating with those responsible for closing the doors in the bow. The company had rejected, in "authoritarian and contemptuous terms," requests from employees for a system of signal lights to remedy this dangerous situation (Clarke 1990: 203–4). That system would have reduced profits and increased costs. Investigations showed that the system would have added less than 1 percent to the price of a ticket.
- The subsequent legal report concluded, "A company could not in law be indicted for manslaughter" (Queen's Bench Divisional Court, October 6, 1987). In 1990 the British government awarded a peerage to the chairman of the company that owned the *Herald of Free Enterprise*, elevating him from Sir to Lord (Pearce 1993).

Item:

- On Sunday, December 2, 1984, a choking cloud of toxic fumes from the Union Carbide pesticides plant leaked through Bhopal, India. Methyl isocyanate and hydrogen cyanide gases burned the lungs of all who breathed them. By Monday morning, more than 2,000 people were dead. In addition, tens of thousands were left with wrecked lungs and impaired vision and subsequently developed cataracts, tuberculosis, breathlessness, and reproductive disorders. More than 5,000 have died in the intervening years (*Guardian Weekly* August 30, 1998: 24).
- Subsequent investigation found that Union Carbide, with declining markets for carbamate pesticides, cut costs by employing fewer staff, reducing the training time offered new employees, and cutting back on plant maintenance. Plant instrumentation and back-up systems were inadequate, workers were not properly trained or monitored, and the refrigeration plant was not powerful enough to cool the gases stored there.

- The company attributed the accident to incompetent employees and accused the Indian government of negligence (for failing to enforce its own regulations—which Union Carbide strove mightily to avoid). On February 14, 1989, the company negotiated a deal with the government of India (not with the victims) to pay $470 million in damages. India accepted the settlement even though it had originally requested the "anything but excessive" sum of $3.3 billion, roughly comparable to the $2.9 billion received by some 195,000 victims of A.H. Robbins's Dalkon Shield (an intrauterine device deemed responsible for "only" seventeen deaths) (Pearce and Tombs 1998: 211). However, the Dalkon Shield case was heard in U.S. courts, known for more generous settlements, and Union Carbide fought hard (and successfully) to keep the Bhopal case in India. The deal ultimately negotiated with the Indian government gave Union Carbide immunity from all future claims. In addition, it guaranteed that no criminal charges would be laid.
- It is no secret that corporations set up plants in the Third World to get away from regulation, because obeying regulatory laws adds to the cost of production. The chemical industry spends less than half as much on pollution and safety control in its overseas operations as it does in the United States (Pearce and Tombs 1998).

Corporate crime, then, causes injury and death. It is also incredibly costly, defrauding hundreds of thousands of people of millions of dollars. The average amount stolen annually by bank robbers makes up well under 5 percent of the totals stolen by white-collar and corporate criminals (Snider 1993: 4-5; Reiman 1994). Some recent examples of the harm done and losses incurred in financial corporate crimes follows.

Item:
- With the advent of global capitalism and the new-found dominance of financial capital, trillions of dollars circulate daily throughout the stock exchanges and currency markets of the world. Individual traders in these markets buy and sell thousands of shares each day, seeking to maximize their own profits and increase their personal fortunes. Traders, essentially unregulated actors, have the power to bankrupt individuals, companies, and countries—and have done so, in 1998, for instance, by driving the value of the Russian ruble down 90 percent in less than a week. In the mid-1990s, Indonesia, Japan

and many Asian countries, and Mexico suffered similar fates. The decision to "set capital free" and facilitate millions of untaxed, unregulated trades has destroyed the standard of living of hundreds of thousands of people in many parts of the world, producing starvation and revolution in some countries and the destruction of personal savings, destitution, and penury in others.

- Much of the harm done by these financial actors is not defined as criminal, but many countries have criminalized scams such as insider trading, falsifying records, failure to disclose, and outright fraud (as in the alleged "salting" of gold samples taken from the Busang site at Bre-X, inflating the value of Bre-X stock by millions of dollars and fleecing countless of innocent investors). While most stock-market traders are closely allied with multinational capital, "rogue traders" have the power to destroy centuries-old institutions, as Nick Leeson did at Barings Bank in the United Kingdom or Yasuo Hamanaka at Sumitomo Incorporated in Japan. Financial corporate crime has gone global. The BCCI bank, which imploded, causing an estimated $15 billion in losses, was organized to be off-shore everywhere. Corporations have always attempted to incorporate in jurisdictions with the lowest taxes and the fewest regulations, but the BCCI case shows the possibility of avoiding all nation-state restrictions.

The systematic removal of regulatory controls over financial institutions and stock exchanges has been a cherished component of those leading the corporate counter-revolution. Thus, after taking office in 1980 the Reagan government repealed regulations and fired regulators responsible for overseeing stock exchanges, such as the federal Security and Exchange Commission (SEC). Staff at the SEC fell by 300, while the number of securities requiring monitoring doubled from 1981–86. In the financial arena, the government removed a series of restrictions on institutions known as Savings and Loans companies, leading to the most costly series of corporate crimes ever, with estimated losses topping $500 billion (see below). This debacle caused some momentary re-regulation, but in 1994 the U.S. House of Representatives again loosened controls on banks, and in 1995 it tabled legislation to gut the SEC once again (Calavita, Pontell, and Tillman 1997).

Item:

- The S & L fraud, the collapse of the Savings and Loans companies, occurred after the counter-revolutionary drive of the 1980s repealed laws limiting the kinds of investments these companies could make and laws setting out minimum capital requirements to be maintained. The problem was compounded when federal insurance on losses was retained while federal regulators were removed.

- The most common frauds were of three types. *Hot Deals:* The owners of Savings and Loans institutions engaged in land flips, nominee loans, and reciprocal lending (huge sums were "lent" in return for deposits). *Looting*: Owners siphoned off funds, paid themselves huge salaries, took expensive holidays or bought yachts, women,[2] limousines, and other "luxury" goods from company money. *Falsifying Records*: False audits created the appearance that the companies were well-managed and fiscally sound. The case puts to the test the notion that such behaviour is rare in business, because every major accounting firm in the United States but one was implicated in the production of false, dishonest, and misleading accounts.

- Although estimated losses exceeded $500 billion, the mean loss per institution was put at $12,420,065; the estimated cost to each U.S. household at $5,000. A total of 284 Savings and Loans institutions went bankrupt, the bulk of them in Texas and California. Thousands of individuals lost their life savings, with most of the "little guys" recovering only a fraction of their money. The bulk of the federal insurance went to compensate "secured" creditors, typically large (corporate) institutions (Calavita, Pontell, and Tillman 1997; Zey 1993; *New York Times* June 10, 1990; *Observer* April 8, 1990).

Item:

- Competition/combines offences are anti-competitive practices designed to inflate profits through such deceptive practices as conspiracy to restrict trade, mergers and monopolies, predatory pricing, price discrimination, resale price maintenance, and refusal to supply. False advertising, an allied offence, refers to deceptive trade practices such as inflated claims about a product's effectiveness or misleading consumers by misrepresenting a product's regular price as a sales price.

- Combines, mergers, and monopolies were outlawed in Canada's first piece of corporate crime legislation, the Combines Investigation Act, passed in 1889. It was regularly amended and enlarged (though never effectively enforced) from that time until 1976.

- Shortly after its election in 1968, the Liberal government under Pierre Trudeau decided to strengthen the legislation and commissioned a white paper, the *Interim Report on Competition Policy*. The paper caused "all hell to break loose" (according to Ian Clark, the deputy minister of the department responsible at the time), as business and its spokespeople lined up to condemn the government's "radical" proposals for reform (which were really very modest). Three ministers of Consumer and Corporate Affairs were appointed and deposed in short order, and several versions of a bill, each weaker than the last, were put forth, but none passed.

- In January 1976 the legislation was split in two, and all efforts to reform laws on restraint of trade were dropped. An amended act was finally passed calling for increasing maximum fines for false advertising, extending price-fixing regulations to cover services (such as real estate or lawyers) as well as products, and prohibiting sales practices such as bait and switch, bid-rigging, and pyramid selling.

- In 1984 the new Conservative government under Brian Mulroney officially declared Canada "open for business" and appointed a "blue ribbon" committee to recommend revisions in legislation on mergers and monopolies.

- The committee consisted entirely of representatives of (big) business, from the Canadian Manufacturers' Association, the Canadian Chamber of Commerce, the Business Council on National Issues and, added later, the Grocery Products Manufacturers of Canada and the Canadian Bar Association. No labour or consumer groups were represented on the committee (but the deputy minister swore that the Consumers Association of Canada and "interested academics" were "also consulted").

- In 1986 the House of Commons passed new legislation abolishing the Combines Investigation Act. Its replacement, the Competition Act, had a different mission: "to improve and facilitate corporate operations," not to control or sanction conspiracies to restrict trade, drive up prices, or engage in monopolistic, predatory practices. To this end:
  - Criminal sanctions were *removed* from merger/monopoly sections.
  - The public interest" was *removed* as a criterion or directive to

be used in evaluating a proposed merger.

- A "compliance-centred" approach was adopted to deal with "clients" (who were no longer "offenders" suspected of "crimes").[3] The new goal of law was to provide a stable and predictable climate for business, with the promotion of business prosperity made key.

- Prosecutions for conspiracy, discriminatory and predatory pricing, misleading or deceptive practices, and price maintenance dropped from thirty-seven in 1982–84 and thirty-six in 1984–86 to twenty-three in 1986–88. By 1995–96, all regional offices of the Competition Bureau were terminated. The number of inquiries commenced dropped from eighty-two to eight in the four-year period from 1991–92 to 1995–96, the number of cases referred for prosecution dropped from fifty-five to seven, prosecutions declined from forty-four to seven, and convictions dropped from forty-three to fourteen (Canada 1997: 36). In spring 1998 a bill was introduced to further decriminalize misleading advertising and deceptive marketing practices (*Globe and Mail* May 5, 1998: B3; Canada 1998: 3).

- From 1986–89, 402 merger files were opened, twenty-six were "monitored," seven were abandoned, nine mergers were restructured, five went to the Competition Tribunal, and two were under appeal. By 1996–97, the Competition Bureau reviewed a total of 319 mergers, but only twenty-three were deemed problematic enough to require follow-up. In 1997–98 369 were slated for review (*Globe and Mail* March 30, 1998: B4), a record the *Globe* decries as "Cracking Down" by "Competition Cops" (Milner 1998; see also Snider 1993, 1978; Stanbury 1977, 1986–87, 1988; Canada 1989; Varrette et al. 1985; Goldman 1989).

Monopolistic markets have become a fixture of the developed world. They mean that the power of capital is increasingly concentrated in the hands of a small number of transnational corporations with monopolistic control over the lifestyles and life chances of most of the world's citizens. No representative citizenry elect the owner-controllers, and, increasingly, no public body regulates their actions or behaviour. Some fifty-one of the world's largest economies are not countries but corporations (Dobbin 1998; McQuaig 1998). In Canada in 1991, a mere ten corporations (excluding banks) made up more than one-fifth of the Gross National Product. Many of these are transnationals such as General Motors of Canada, Chrysler, Ford, and Imperial Oil; others such as Bell Canada, Noranda, George Weston, and Thomson are nominally controlled in Canada. Monopolistic, mammoth companies do not provide a commensurate number of jobs—the top 200 transnational corporations, with sales accounting for 28.3 percent of the world's GDP, employ less than 1 percent of its workforce (Dobbin 1998: 76). Nor do they pay a commensurate share of taxes—Nortel, for example, received "at least" $880 million in federal research and development tax credits, but paid a mere 0.4 percent of its total revenue back in income tax; as of 1996 it owed $213 million in deferred taxes (Dobbin 1998: 78).

WHY DOES IT MATTER?

Thus far, this essay has documented the harm caused by corporate crime and the virtual abandonment of attempts to proscribe or sanction the crime. The nation-state has, in effect, given up the struggle to control corporate criminals through law. The disappearance of corporate crime matters, but not because state law was ever particularly successful in punishing it. Given the power of the perpetrators and the collective weakness of the victims, the laws governing corporate crime have always been full of loopholes, the regulating authorities starved for funds, convictions few and far between, and sanctions totally incommensurate with the damage inflicted.[4]

The disappearance of corporate crime matters because this retreat is part of an ideological retrenchment whereby the ability to censure, monitor, or signal disapproval of the anti-social acts of capital is being lost. So too is the legal recognition of the harm caused by corporate acts. It matters because "the growing incapacity of sovereign states to control the behaviour of corporations" (Reiss 1992: 190) is a created event, not an inevitable, unalterable fact (McQuaig 1998).

And it matters because we are losing the data to counter the heavily promoted business claims that corporate crimes are no more than one-time accidents, committed by "good citizens" rather than "criminals." This argument is both beside the point and incorrect. It is beside the point because many traditional offences are equally unintentional, but in law intention is no defence *except* when the crimes of corporations are at issue. Drunk drivers who "didn't mean to hurt anyone" face charges of criminal negligence and long prison terms if convicted. It is incorrect because evidence of malice aforethought is plentiful in the annals of corporate crime: the executives at Ford who calculated that it was cheaper to pay off burn victims and bereaved families than to fix Pinto cars designed so that they exploded in flames when hit from the rear (Cullen, Maakestadt, and Cavender 1987); the thrift owners in the Savings and Loan debacle who bought companies in order to loot their assets and rob those who had trusted their savings to these men (Calavita, Pontell, and Tillman 1997); the insurance companies that exploited Aboriginal religious beliefs on the need to return the dead to their ancestral lands to sell fraudulent burial policies (Braithwaite 1995); the pharmaceutical companies that hid test results showing new drugs as unsafe, ineffective, or dangerous (Braithwaite 1984); the coal-mine owners who tampered with coal dust samples (Braithwaite 1985b); or the manufacturers of asbestos who knowingly exposed employees, their families, and neighbourhoods to asbestosis and similar cancers, systematically hiding test results and scientific studies from them (Gunningham 1984; for still other examples, see Coleman 1985; Green 1994; Punch 1996).

In the past, getting laws passed to proscribe the crimes of business has always required, in every country where this has occurred, decades of struggle. Resistance, publicity, political organization, and public education were among the tactics used in the nineteenth century by a wide array of interests and groups. The business class fiercely resisted the notion that any of its profit-seeking activities could be considered immoral or criminal. It balked at the principle of state law overseeing business practice, viewing this as an abrogation of the near-sovereign rights of ownership then enshrined in English common law. Those who owned the workplace and the tools of production were assumed to have the right to determine everything that went on in that workplace. If the owner did not want to pay more than ten cents a day, put guards on machinery, or provide safety equipment, lunch breaks, or clean, breathable air, the state had no right to interfere, the worker no right to protest (Paulus 1974; Carson 1970, 1980). When reformers ("rabble-rousers" and "communists," to the employer classes) began complaining about the number of workers losing arms, legs, and lives to unsafe machinery, about employees not yet twenty years old dying of lung diseases brought on by fibre-filled air in unventilated workplaces, or about women too weakened by eighteen-hour workdays in filthy factories to reproduce, discipline, or supervise their children (Ursel 1992; Marcus 1974; Tucker 1990), those in government were in a quandary. State policy throughout the nineteenth century was to ignore the costs of capitalism (which state legislators neither experienced nor saw, being mainly from privileged backgrounds themselves), celebrate its accomplishments, and use law to punish the feckless, inebriate, and larcenous—in other words, the poor and powerless. (The use and abuse of opium or marijuana by inferior races, prostitution, delinquency, and the genetic inferiority of "criminals" were all popular targets for criminalization.) But, by the second half of the century, it was becoming politically dangerous for legislators to ignore the mounting evidence of corporate carnage, when (male) workers were getting the right to vote and socialist notions were gaining adherents. It is also true that many parliamentarians—and some employers as well—were sincerely concerned about the pace of social change and the suffering of the "deserving" poor.

In Ontario, for example, industrialization grew rapidly from 1870 to 1900, bringing concomitant increases in the size of firms, the length of the workday, and the demands placed on employees. As sixty-hour workweeks became common, workers began to complain about the speed and intensity of production and the risks they were forced to take. Women and child workers became the focus of reform campaigns by upper-middle-class feminist and religious groups, because they not only endured the same conditions as men for even lower wages but also were often subjected to sexual harassment (Ursel 1992). (While sexual harassment was neither named nor criminalized at that time, it was nonetheless a fact of life for working women, who were shamed, blamed, and fired if they dared to complain.) Injuries and deaths on the job were common, but employees had no redress except the common-law right to sue their employers for damages. Because lawsuits required time, effort, and money, and workers laboured sixteen hours a day for wages too low to cover their daily necessities, few cases were brought to court. The few that were launched were generally unsuccessful, because the law presumed that, by "voluntarily" accepting a job, workers had also accepted the working conditions attached to that job, thereby forfeiting their right to object to these conditions (Austin and Dietrich 1990).

Changing this mindset and law took decades of demonstrations and government inquiries. A few muckraking media published pictures of mutilated workers and starving widows. A few crusading pastors wrote religious tracts and preached sermons on the human costs of industrialization. Workers demonstrated and first-wave feminists pointed out the toll on women's reproductive and social health. Ontario's Factory Act was finally passed in 1884, two decades after the first factory acts became law in Great Britain (Carson 1970, 1980). The immediate stimulus was a Conservative Member of Parliament, who became concerned that the employment of working-class women and children was causing a decline in their morals. Eventually the solid and impenetrable opposition of employers crumpled. The most prosperous industrialists, members of the Canadian Manufacturers' Association, came to see that the National Policy (the tariff imposed on all imported goods) meant that major producers like themselves would still be able to charge high prices and realize high profits. They began to see legislation as inevitable and switched from blanket resistance to compromise, with an emphasis on shaping the upcoming legislation in their own interests. This tactic resulted in a number of concessions to accommodate employer demands. Thus, the initial Factory Act covered only factories, not shops or other workplaces. It provided for a ten-hour day and a six-day week, and it set limits on compulsory overtime rather than forbidding it. Employers were directed to allow workers one hour per day for lunch and obliged to provide a room they could eat it in. Washrooms became mandatory, and women were to be provided with separate facilities from men. The act banned employment of boys under twelve and girls under fourteen and banned girls of age fourteen to eighteen from jobs in which their health was likely to suffer permanent injury. (Presumably it was fine for boys to be permanently injured; they were not seen as vehicles of reproduction.) Rudimentary ventilation and guards on certain types of machinery became mandatory (Tucker 1990). Over time these laws were strengthened and augmented, and conditions in the workplaces of Ontario gradually improved.[5]

This does not mean that most employers or major business organizations ever supported this kind of legislation. Small entrepreneurs and retailers were particularly vehement in their opposition because they, unlike the big guys, were often unable to pass increased costs on to customers or clients. In competitive markets they either had to operate more efficiently or forego some of their profits, and the National Policy tariff just increased their costs, forcing them to purchase more expensive manufactured products made in Canada. Sizeable segments of the business class continued to object to any and all government interference with their heretofore unchallenged right to determine the conditions and rewards of employment in "their" workshops. They accused politicians of selling out: "Employers felt that virtually the whole legislative programme put forward by organized labour and any favourable political response to it represented an attack on business interests" (Bliss 1974: 123). As Bliss (1974: 120) notes, "When Parliament began to make highly visible responses to labour pressure after 1900—establishing a Department of Labour, founding the 'Labour Gazette,' introducing fair wage provisions into federal work contracts, and giving a friendly hearing to Bills to institute the eight-hour day on Dominion public works—employers were outraged at how politicians had abandoned impartiality for fear of offending organized labour and in order to secure patronage." (Note that government was deemed to be acting with "impartiality" when it supported the interests of business; it was "biased" or partial whenever it did not.) Business saw every concession to employees or consumers as a backward move, an act threatening the productivity and competitive position of the capitalist class. The continued prosperity of this class, then as now, was deemed synonymous with the prosperity of the nation.

Not surprisingly, then, the victories of the employee classes were partial and fragile, and failures to get laws passed were more common than successes. In the early days spokesmen for the railroads argued against safety laws by telling the Royal Labour Commission that running along the tops of moving freight cars to apply brakes by hand was only dangerous when workers were careless or "not looking where they are going" (Bliss 1974: 59). The railway companies also argued that since the employees decided when to stop the train and the employees knew that applying the brakes required them to climb onto the roof of the cars, how could the railway companies be responsible if they fall off and get killed? It was the workers' decision to put on the brakes in the first place. In addition, they "knew about the hazards when they took the job" (Bliss 1974: 59). In the United States, "Between 1879 and 1906, 140 pure food and drug bills were presented in Congress and all failed because of the importance of the persons who would be affected" (Sutherland 1977: 45). Dozens of attempts to pass laws to protect consumers or workers were simply abandoned because of the overwhelming size and power of the corporate lobby. In the end the failures to legislate cost billions of dollars and hundreds, sometimes thousands, of lives (Coleman 1985: 151–92).

Governments, though, did not always cave in to business interests, and over the years in Canada these struggles created a new consensus about permissible standards of exploitation. The consensus was backed by state laws spelling out the minimum conditions that employers should provide and the minimum standards employees should accept. These new standards did not come about automatically or because employers suddenly decided to become "responsible employers." This does not mean all employers were unethical or lacked moral standards: their behaviour was not seen, by themselves or by mainstream political or religious authorities of the time, as irresponsible or unethical. Employing ten-year-olds in unhealthy workplaces for sixteen hours a day *was* ethical (as well as legal), because the ideological struggle that redefined the limits of ethical corporate behaviour was still in its infancy. This process of re-definition continued throughout the twentieth century, spurred by the growth of democratic socialism and the invention of the postwar welfare state. It resulted in a gradual improvement in the ethical and legal standards in the workplace and beyond—the progress now put at risk by the corporate counter-revolution.

The disappearance of corporate crime, then, matters because it has important ideological and symbolic effects. Criminalizing an act is a censure (Sumner 1983). Decriminalizing conveys the opposite message: that monopolizing the banking business or owning all the newspapers in a province or failing to maintain safe workplaces or pay employees a decent wage is no longer seen as a social problem. The perpetrators of such acts are henceforth inappropriate targets for social censure. They are not expected to "make amends" or "be ashamed of themselves," because they have not done anything blameworthy. The ideological process that shapes the social distribution of blame has exonerated these kinds of harmful acts and, therefore, the actors responsible for them.

When the exploitative acts committed by employers against employees are no longer identified or named, let alone measured, monitored, or sanctioned, they no longer "count" as crime. This is true literally as well as symbolically, and it has important implications. Making truth claims in modern society is contingent upon the ability to name a phenomenon and study it scientifically. This means that a school of knowledge claims can be developed around the phenomenon, that it can be studied by "experts" with advanced training in a "discipline" and described in ways that generate a set of claims to create what counts as knowledge in modern society (Foucault 1979b; Ericson and Haggerty 1997). The initial stage of the process through which sexual harassment gained credibility as a social problem, for example, involved naming and defining it. At that point its frequency could be documented, its incidence and effects statistically described and analysed. Then state law was created, and calls were made to secure increased public resources. Media attention, "survivor" accounts, and celebrity cases—important components of shaming, blaming, and punishing this new class of offenders—appeared.

The exact opposite process is underway with corporate crime. Removing state law, decriminalizing and deregulating, makes a behaviour less visible, more elusive. With the disappearance of state law, the victims of these acts (no longer "offences") have no one they can complain to, no state body from which to seek redress or justice. With no official body to validate complaints or record the frequency of occurrence, researchers or activists can no longer obtain incidence data. Corporate crime loses the sharp edge of legal definition, the public resources, and the social attribution of blame that accompany acts signified as crime.

Losing state definition directly sets back the job of the researcher or scientist, the knowledge professionals responsible for affixing the stamp of legitimacy to social problems. For corporate crime, these are the criminologists, sociologists, and law professors who originally "discovered" and named white-collar crime, then classified corporate crime as an important dimension of it. For these researchers, data sources, always problematic, have become more so. Major studies of corporate crime have always been based on the records of regulatory agencies or state departments of criminal justice (Shapiro 1985: 181; Edelhertz 1970). Information on the number of enforcement actions, the sanctions imposed, the decisions of courts and regulatory commissions, or the sentences imposed by criminal or administrative courts has constituted the most affordable and socially legitimate evidence available (for example, Wheeler, Weisburd, and Bode 1982; Clinard and Yeager 1980).[6] The only alternative to state data requires researchers to generate their own data, a herculean task. Not only does it require a massive research budget, but it also requires access to information. The average researcher has no way of forcing busy, high-status, socially important, and politically powerful actors or corporate bodies to reveal practices and predilections they have every reason to hide. With government regulations gone, and self-regulation, market incentives, and risk assessment replacing state officials and monitoring agencies, the amount and the availability of official, accredited data have dramatically declined. Determining the "dark figure" of corporate crime, assessing the "actual" number of offences that have occurred, and documenting the harm they have done all become more difficult.[7]

But securing the resources, access, and data to study offences by employees against employer has all become easier. Private foundations and consultants are competing for funds to study and document "white-collar crimes" of this kind, and the work of naming, blaming, and punishing the crimes of employees is flourishing. A prime example would be the discovery of a new "crime" committed by employees against employers. Named the "Theft of Time," it refers to unauthorized time that employees spend away from the primary work task. Advances in technology have made it possible to measure exactly how long employees spend in the washroom, or whether they take twenty minutes for coffee instead of fifteen or talk to customers longer than they should (time-management experts have charts specifying how many seconds employees "should" spend to complete a sale or find a phone number). Thus it is now possible to study and criminalize a new subcategory of employee-offenders, identify those most likely to commit this crime, and investigate the causes, incidence, and effects of their delinquency.[8] Soon there will probably be a test employers can administer to weed out "high-risk" employees, an addition to the plentiful array of screening tools (like those designed to test for drug use and "honesty"). New knowledge is also being created on other newly discovered employee offences. New computer crimes—for example, gaining "unauthorized entry" into corporate or government databases and "theft of software" (copying software "owned" by corporations into a personal machine)—have been criminalized. Massive public resources are now expended in passing laws, training enforcement agents, and educating scientists to create new knowledge about this new breed of criminal.[9]

The creation of new knowledge, then, is a *political* as well as a legal act, and corporate crime researchers are not the only group harmed by the disappearance of state law on corporate crime. Environmental activists, consumer spokespeople, feminists, and other counter-hegemonic social movements cannot call the state to account, nor can they provide numbers to back up their arguments without data and public access to it. If longitudinal data can no longer be gathered, it becomes impossible to show that certain companies are long-term offenders, recidivists, even career criminals and dangerous offenders. Labels such as these, derived from the master censure of criminal law, are particularly powerful. They attract media, state, and public attention. But establishing such claims requires access to "official" statistics gathered by "scientific disciplines"—the very data no longer collected, the knowledge no longer created. The process of policy formation is also set back. If state officials are unable to monitor workplaces or take preventative action, life-threatening factories or mines will be discovered only after disasters have occurred. Crimes that produce "only" injuries, or ambiguous illnesses with many possible causes, or workplace and environmental conditions that cause slow-developing cancers are unlikely to be detected at all, and they will certainly never be traced back to the corporate conditions that produced them. The harms caused by the anti-social acts of corporations, then, become once again, as in earlier centuries, the fault of careless individuals or unhealthy lifestyles.

Finally, the significance of the disappearance of corporate crime speaks volumes about the potential of state law to harness capital. The corporate counter-revolution illustrates how profoundly dependent the promulgation and enforcement of nation-state law is on the balance of powers operating within a society. Thus, where labour unions and/or social movements such as environmentalism or socialist feminism are strong (as in many Western European and Scandinavian countries), laws controlling the destructive but profitable acts of capital will also be strong, and downsizing and decriminalization will be resisted longer and more successfully. Where such groups and forces are weak, as in the United States and Canada, laws will be reluctantly passed, little enforced, and ignored as soon the spotlight of public attention shifts. With labour unions throughout the world under serious attack, ideologically and financially, the burden of maintaining the pressure on corporate capital falls, by default, on progressive social movements.

In general, this means that groups must use the individualizing, class-biased language of law and of rights discourse to press governments to provide broader rights for citizens, consumers, and employees. With all its drawbacks, the discourse of resistance (if not necessarily empowerment) is now that of risk (Ericson and Haggerty 1997). Citizen groups may get laws passed, or at least resist their dismemberment, by claiming legal rights to breathe clean air, drink pure water, and not be exposed to toxic materials and other dangers at home or work. Emphasizing government obligations to provide such "goods" provides a vehicle to resist deregulation in the short term, and to strengthen regulation in the long term. More counter-hegemonic strategies would include seeking broad-based rights to a fair wage, to job security, to high-quality health care, day care, and education. And certainly, in an era of global capitalism, international counter-hegemonic alliances are essential. The primary value of such struggles will be ideological, not legal—the goal is to challenge beliefs that employers can do anything they like to employees, communities, and countries in the interests of increasing profits for corporate stockholders. Such struggles reinforce agency. They empower people to become part of a self-fulfilling, beneficent prophecy: by challenging the idea that resisting global corporate power is futile, the limits of nation-state and citizen power are inevitably explored and expanded.

State law, then, has little power to resist corporate capital in the absence of strong, counter-hegemonic citizens' groups. Law is in no sense a "magic bullet." But the strategic importance of law in the modern state, its immense power as a censure, its ability to grab media attention and mobilize opposition, as well as build the membership base of movements, all make law a tool much too important to be ignored.

CONCLUSION

This essay argues that the disappearance of corporate crime signalled by the abandonment of state law is an event with massive political, legal, and ideological consequences. State law has not "kept pace" with the growth and development of corporate wealth and power (Wells 1993). Indeed, it has retreated, fled in ignominious defeat, ceded victory to corporate counter-revolutionary forces. For those who seek to create more equitable societies, this development represents a giant step backwards. It is one thing to argue that state law was inefficient—that governments seldom took effective action against corporations—and quite another to argue that they should jettison the capacity, and the legal obligation, to do so.

As we have seen, abandoning state sanctions has far-reaching symbolic and practical consequences. State laws are public statements that convey important public messages about the obligations of the employer classes (Ayres and Braithwaite 1992).[10] The situation is paradoxical indeed: while crimes of the powerful were never effectively sanctioned by state law, such laws are nonetheless essential to the operation of democratic societies.

NOTES

1. As noted, the spoils of capitalism are unevenly distributed from a worldwide perspective, and the disparity is getting worse, not better (United Nations 1996).
2. All the known perpetrators were men, although some women were peripherally involved (Calavita, Pontell, and Tillman 1997).

3. The most recent discourse switch has been the transformation of corporate criminals into "stakeholders" (Canada 1998: 3).

4. On this matter virtually the entire corpus of literature on corporate crime could be cited. In the U.S. literature the record has been documented in studies from Sutherland's (1949) classic *White Collar Crime* to Clinard and Yeager (1980), Shapiro (1984), Coleman (1985), and Green (1994); more international accounts are found in Box (1983), Clarke (1990), and Punch (1996). Recent studies go beyond description to explanation and reform (see, for example, Braithwaite 1995; Yeager 1991; Tombs 1996; and articles in Pearce and Snider 1995).

5. In countries in which such laws are absent, children are still being hired, and sixty-hour workweeks in dangerous environments are commonplace. As illustrated by exposés of working conditions in Nike and Nortel, in the *maquiladores* of Mexico, and the rug manufacturing workshops of India, companies provide healthy, safe workplaces only where forced to do so (Pearce and Tombs 1998; Dobbin 1998; Fudge 1998). So what will happen in First World countries when all state laws and sanctions have been replaced by "voluntary" agreements?

6. This dependence on available (state-collected) data also explains why so many recent U.S. studies of white-collar crime have documented almost no high-level corporate crime. No analysis that uses as its data source FBI data on prosecutions, for example, will unearth many CEOs of major corporations in the lists of offenders. Their power, their legal departments, and the insulating layers of bureaucracy in modern corporations all protect senior executives from becoming known to the FBI, much less charged. Thus such studies turn up the most powerless individual white-collar criminals, often black bank tellers who are assiduously pursued by law enforcement authorities for embezzling a few thousand dollars (see, for example, Weisburd, Cheyet, and Waring 1990).

7. Self-report data are not a satisfactory alternative in this area, because people are often not aware they have been the victims of negligence or fraud. Without state officials to investigate and publicize dishonest business practices, for example, victims identify "bad luck" or "accident" as causes. One of the few attempts to utilize this method is reported by Pearce (1990) in Islington (a suburb of London, England). Pearce found working-class victimization from corporate crime many times higher than revealed in official statistics.

8. If trends follow the now-standard route in traditional criminological literature, some enterprising investigator will next suggest that some employees have a genetic predisposition to steal time. Scientific resources will then be focused on isolating the particular gene responsible.

9. Massive sums are also spent designing technical systems to make such offences more difficult. The preferred method, the one deemed most cost-

efficient, is to eliminate the human employee entirely.

10. It is surprising that the citizens in so many democratic countries have allowed this to happen. Abandoning regulation and decriminalizing harmful acts were not achieved by state dictatorship in Canada. They came about through a public process, negotiated into existence. This does not mean everyone was consulted. It was largely a process of changing the minds of elites and of those citizens who vote. But, with the partial exception of environmental regulation (where active social movements were and are present), the disappearance of corporate crime never became a major news story.

Poverty Law, Theory, and Practice: The Place of Class and Gender in Access to Justice

© Shelley A.M. Gavigan[1]

In the 1970s community-based legal services clinics first appeared on the social and legal horizon in Canada. Lawyers, law students, and community advocates in these clinics sought to represent low-income clients and communities and advance their rights in ways that had never been tried before. Rather than simply being a "sharp legal thing" into which poor people bumped (Wexler 1970), the law was to be challenged, reformed—and perhaps even invoked—to address the aspirations and needs of the poor. Poverty began to be approached as a systemic and structural problem, not an individual failing or weakness. The problem to be tackled was poverty, including the barriers it posed and the misery it caused.

I was a clinic lawyer in the 1970s, and in 1983, after a few years in graduate school, I found myself supervising law students at Parkdale Community Legal Services, a storefront community legal clinic in downtown Toronto. During that year I often felt like a person with a bit part in the film and, later, television series *M*A*S*H*. With each crackle of the intercom, I imagined that our receptionist, the dedicated and indefatigable Dorothy Leatch (see Leatch 1997), would next say: "The choppers are here. They are bringing in the wounded." Had the war on poverty been only a skirmish?

I returned to Parkdale Community Legal Services in the late 1980s and again in the early 1990s, this time in the role of academic director responsible for the Intensive Programme in Poverty Law offered by Osgoode Hall Law School. I now had the responsibility of ensuring that the law students engaged in front-line legal services delivery developed an understanding of the phenomenon of poverty (including its causes), provided excellent legal services to their clients, and explored alternative strategies for lawyers to engage in law reform and social change. This felt like the enormous responsibility it was, and the way to proceed was not self-evident. For while the clinic's intercom and telephone system had improved, the choppers were still sending in the wounded. The social and legal problems of the poor people coming through the doors seemed insurmountable and resistant to change through the law. The search for explanations and appropriate legal strategies led me to lament, for neither the first nor last time, "the poverty of theory in poverty law" while I pondered the long-posed question: What is to be done?

Lawyers, activists, and academics who continue to be committed to the importance of poverty law and legal clinic practice know that the wounded are still arriving—thanks to new choppers in the form of neoliberal hatchet men who are forcing a dramatic restructuring of the foundation of Canadian social, economic, and political life. What were once heralded as universal social programs, available to all Canadians and designed to promote unprecedented levels of social security, are now under attack. Indeed, the principle of universal accessibility has been jettisoned, and social programs have been hollowed out (see, for example, Bakker and Scott 1997: 300–6; Cohen, Morrison, and Smith 1995; McQuaig 1993). The poor and the near poor have not been well served by the dramatic policy shift that has occurred. As Marjorie Cohen and her colleagues explain:

> Providing universal medical care, education, pensions, inexpensive transportation and communication systems, affordable housing, work at reasonable wages, and adequate child care are the things that make a decent life possible and keep large numbers of people out of poverty. During the past 10 years, even the programs which seemed secure because of their popularity have either been eliminated or weakened so badly that they are in danger of withering away. We have seen a steady erosion of programs and institutions, achieved through a thousand little budget cuts, tax changes, and hard-to-explain technical manipulations to existing legislation. (Cohen, Morrison, and Smith 1995: 9)

As long as clinic doors are able to stay open and clinics continue to be staffed, poverty law advocates will have the dubious honour of meeting first-hand the casualties and witnessing the implications of the new initiatives. But will they be able to do more than treat the wounded with temporary bandages? This is not a small question, for the choppers of the 1990s are less benign than those in *M*A*S*H*: not only are they sending in *more* wounded, they are taking away even the first-aid bandages.

The metaphors of war have long informed poverty law: the case-workers are front-line, they work in the trenches, their clients are "battered but not beaten" (McLeod 1987), and everyone—advocates, clients, and the communities served—feels besieged. Front-line legal clinic workers and the communities they serve attest that the once-heralded "war on poverty" of the 1960s, which facilitated the emergence of storefront law offices and community-based law, has given way to a "war on the poor" (Katz 1989). The problem now identified by politicians and pundits alike is not poverty per se. Rather, the poor themselves have now been targeted as the main cause of our economic woes.

For instance, in June 1995 a provincial election in Ontario ushered in a new Conservative government. The government struck swiftly: tax cuts for the well-off, welfare cuts for the poor. One of the first moves of the new government was to slash welfare benefits by 21.6 percent, impose harsh new eligibility rules on young people, narrow the definition of disability (Ellsworth 1997: 272–73), and, not surprisingly, implement an expansive and retroactively applicable definition of a "spouse in the house."[2] Without suggesting that legal changes inevitably yield measurable results, it is nonetheless possible to note some direct consequences of the 1995 welfare-law reforms:

- 500,000 children of families in receipt of social assistance were the direct victims of the 21.6 percent cut in social assistance rates (*Masse* v. *Ontario,* Factum of the Applicants 1996);
- over 10,000 recipients of social assistance were found to be ineligible as single persons or sole-support parents (*Falkiner* v. *Ontario* [Attorney General], Factum of the Applicants 1996);
- 89 percent of those who were cut off social assistance as a result of this new definition of spouse are women (*Falkiner* v. *Ontario* [Attorney General], Factum of the Applicants 1996);
- the vast majority (76 percent) were single parents whose children were also disentitled (*Falkiner* v. *Ontario* [Attorney General] Factum of the Applicants 1996); and
- welfare benefits for a single parent and one child in Ontario dropped from $14, 535 to $11,940 between 1995 and 1996; for a couple with two children, annual welfare benefits dropped $3,288 (NCW 1997–98: 32, Table 5).

Clearly, we are in the midst of a serious crisis, one that raises significant theoretical and practical questions about the role of law and legal advocates in responding to the situation of poor people in Canada. In this essay, I argue that poverty and poverty law need to be theorized because all legal practice—including legal clinic practice—has a theoretical foundation. I hope further to illustrate that a theoretical framework, whether articulated or not, inevitably shapes one's practice and engagement with law. In other words, the issue is not "theory versus practice" but, rather, "what theory and what practice?" In my view, the interrogation of this rather large question is best done through a series of smaller, though no less significant, questions, which I will attempt to answer.

1. Who are the poor? What factors have a bearing on why they are poor?
2. How should access to justice be defined and how should legal services be delivered?
3. Can the interests of the poor be advanced through the law, or is the law only a site of defensive struggle?
4. What sort of advocacy should a poverty law lawyer do? Is the role of the poverty law lawyer to organize against poverty?
5. What would legal clinic practice look like if it were informed by a theory linking race, class, and gender relations?

I do not claim to be the first to visit these questions, nor will I be the last. Nor do I purport to offer definitive answers. But I do want to argue for the importance of a clear and explicit theoretical framework for, and a broad definition of, access to justice for the poor. In the midst of this serious crisis faced by poor people and their legal advocates, my call for a revisiting of the theoretical premises of poverty law and for a rethinking of the contribution of feminist analysis to this area may seem ill-timed. I offer no apology. A commitment to principle and analysis is not something one can afford only when times are good, or at least not so bleak. A true testing ground of one's principles is not good times, but hard times. And, to be sure, these hard times will test poverty law advocates and their clients to their limits.

LOCATING THE POOR

1. Who are the Poor? What factors have a bearing on why they are poor?

There is no "official" poverty line in Canada; the closest thing to an "official" definition of poverty in Canada is the Statistics Canada "low income cut-offs." According to this indicator, a family household that spends more than 58.5 percent of its income on the basic necessities of food, clothing, and shelter lives below the "low income cut off" (Ross, Shillington, and Lochead 1994). As Table 1 shows, there are many different measures of poverty in Canada.

The 21.6 percent cut to social assistance rates in Ontario, which became effective October 1, 1995, places the household income for welfare recipients beneath even the insult of a "poverty line" drawn by the

Table 1
A Sample of Canada's Poverty Lines—1996

1996 poverty lines	1 person	4 person household
Statistics Canada low income cut-offs*	$16,061*	$31,862
Canadian Council on Social Development	$13,770	$33,330
Statistics Canada low-income measures +	———	$25,304
Provincial welfare Rates (Ontario)	$6,584	$15,428
* base year 1986; large urban centre (>500,000) + based on one-half of median family income with no geographic variations		

Source: The figures here are drawn from *Poverty Profile 1996: A Report by the National Council of Welfare* (NCW 1998a: 5–6) and *Welfare Incomes 1996: A Report by the National Council of Welfare* (NCW 1997–98: 32, Table 5). For other official and unofficial measures of poverty, see National Council of Welfare, *Poverty Profiles* (1996: 6).

neo-conservative think tank the Fraser Institute, which in 1994 placed the poverty line at $7,556 and $17, 542 for a single person and family of four respectively (Ross, Shillington, and Lochead 1994).

The poor in Canada are not a generic, gender-neutral category of unfortunate souls. While the majority of low-income families in Canada are headed by men (Battle 1994), women are more likely to experience the social and economic deprivation of poverty. In particular, women who are single mothers with children under eighteen experience "sky high" poverty rates of 91.3 percent (NCW 1998a: 41); rates that are disproportionate to their representation in the total population and the ranks of the poor (NCW 1998a: 21, Table 7, and Graph O: 34; Battle 1994: 151, 160). In other words, young single-parent mothers with young children have the highest poverty rate of all family types (NCW 1998a, Graph O: 34; see also NCW 1997: 32–34). The figures with respect to the elderly are telling: elderly poor unattached women (sixty-five and over) outnumber poor unattached men by a margin of six to one (NCW 1997: 32). As Diana Pearce (1985: 412) once observed with respect to similar U.S. figures: "It is not the lack of two adults [in a household] that is associated with higher rates of poverty, but the fact that it is a woman alone, struggling to maintain a household on her own, that is so highly correlated with poverty."

In Canada the economic privation of single mothers and their children is a long-standing matter of public record. In 1976 a federal report, *One in a World of Twos* (NCW 1976) reported that 85.5 percent of single-parent families were headed by women and 66 percent of these women and their children lived below the poverty line. As noted above, the National Council of Welfare has reported an increase in the poverty of single mothers that should alarm politicians and fellow citizens alike. Single-parent mothers continue to experience poverty rates many times higher than husband-wife families: "In 1998 the Council noted that families headed by single-parent mothers and 'unattached' people or people living outside families were among the groups of Canadians most likely to be poor" (NCW 1998a: 1)—an observation that appears verbatim in its report (1997: 1) of the previous year. The poverty rate for young single mothers (under twenty-five years of age) has leapt from 83 percent in 1995 to 91.3 percent in 1996, higher even than the disproportionately high rates for other single-mother-led households (NCW 1998: 35).

It is thus not surprising that women and children have been among the prime casualties of the changes and cuts to welfare benefits. Consider the following stories from the province of Ontario since the welfare cuts:

> **Kelly** is the sole-support parent of a one-year-old boy (still in diapers). After she graduated from university, she worked on a contract for the University of Toronto. After the contract was over, she was unable to find alternative work and received unemployment insurance benefits while she continued to look for work. When her unemployment insurance benefits ran out, she began to receive general welfare assistance. Her total income derived from welfare and child support was $1,221 per month; her rent for a modest one-bedroom apartment in Toronto was $700 per month. She shopped at second-hand stores, relied on the food bank, and paid for non-prescription medicines, trips to the dentist, and birthday presents out of her food allocation. On October 1, 1995, her social assistance benefits dropped to $957 per month. She was then left with $257 per month to feed, clothe, transport, and care for her son (*Masse* v. *Ontario,* Factum of the Applicants 1996: paras. 74–76).

> **Nancy** is a forth-three-year-old sole-support mother who left an abusive relationship. After the October 1, 1995, cuts to social assistance, she was left with $62 a month for food and clothing needs for herself and her nine-year-old daughter after paying rent and utilities. Nancy cannot afford to pay for school trips for her daughter, and despite careful budgeting she cannot provide her daughter with the fresh fruits and vegetables the child requires for a medical condition. Like those of Kelly, Nancy's efforts to find employment have been unsuccessful (*Masse* v. *Ontario,* Factum of the Applicants 1996: paras. 77–79).

> **Toni** has been a sole-support parent since her son, now sixteen years old, was eight years old. After October 1, 1995, her income was reduced to $957 per month. She had received a notice of rent increase from $725 to $882 per month. If the rent increase is implemented, she will be left with $120 per month to feed and clothe her teenage son and herself. Toni has a medical condition that prevents her from working, and her son has a learning disability and is hyperactive (*Masse* v. *Ontario,* Factum of the Applicants 1996: paras. 80–83).

The nature and extent of women's poverty are not new. Indeed, James Struthers places the poverty of women at the very heart of welfare law in the introduction to his history of social assistance in Ontario: "The origins of income security in Ontario began with motherhood. With the creation of mother's allowances in 1920, women became the first clients of provincial social assistance" (Struthers 1994: 19). Women's poverty— or, to be more precise, "widows' poverty"—was understood to be a private, familial problem, caused by the death of the primary male breadwinner. Deserving widows with young children were to be rewarded if they remained chaste and devoted to the important work of raising their children. Even so, other work was encouraged, as the women were not to be idle or comfortable. In Ontario mothers' allowances were paid at a rate that was intended to force women to find another source of income, but within a strictly circumscribed range. As Struthers (1994: 39) puts it: "Mothers were expected to work on a part-time basis to bridge the gap between their allowance and a basic level of adequacy for their families, and about 60 per cent of them derived income from a wide variety of tasks. Charwork, sewing and knitting, and keeping boarders provided the overwhelming source of extra funds for these mothers. Factory work, because it removed the mother from the home and supervision of her children, was explicitly discouraged."

The official explanations offered for women's poverty and the concomitant legislative provisions and government policies tended to assume, and inevitably have reinforced, women's marginal participation in the paid labour market and their primary responsibility in the home. Women's poverty became visible; women's work remained invisible whether within or without the home. But, as others have noted, the Canadian labour market is a changed and changing site. In 1988 the *Report of the Social Assistance Review Committee* observed: "The world of work has not kept pace with the tremendous changes in the composition and nature of families, particularly the changing participation of family members in the labour force. The most obvious and profound change has been in the role of women" (Ontario 1988: 92).

More recently, *The Canadian National Child Care Study: Parental Work Patterns and Child Care Needs* confirmed that most women (58.5 percent), even those with young children, were in the labour force or actively looking for work (Statistics Canada 1992: 23). The *Child Care Study* also found that the majority of families with preschool-age children were dual-earner families; "established images of family life no longer matching reality" (Statistics Canada 1992: 17). The *Transitions* report estimated that, by the year 2000, there will be equal numbers of men and women in the labour force (Ontario 1988: 92).

Although official figures indicate that women's households are heavily reliant upon government assistance as the source of income (and, indeed, more so than male-headed households), Statistics Canada reported in 1990 that two-thirds of female-headed households (66 percent) were dependent upon earnings as their source of income (Statistics Canada 1990: 106). Similarly, the *Transitions* report found, "Even with the many hardships poor women face—including delinquent child support payments, lesser access to contributory pensions, lack of affordable child care, and limited job prospects—only a third of the province's female-headed families require [or perhaps more accurately, receive] social assistance" (Ontario 1988: 30). However, more recent national figures reveal an increased reliance on social assistance: although "earned income is often the major source of income" for poor people and "the second most important source [46 percent] for poor single parent families led by women," social assistance was the major source of income for 68 percent of single-mother families (NCW 1998a: 66, Table 14). While unemployment is highly correlated with poverty, the National Council of Welfare (1998a: 38) reminds us, "Even 52 weeks of work a year does not always protect a person [or family] from poverty." For instance, in 1996, 81,000 Canadian families (7 percent of all poor families) were poor despite having two spouses together working 93 or more weeks (1998a: 38–39). In single-parent households, the average annual income from earnings for single-parent mothers was $7,629 (1998a: 67, Table 14).

As Parkdale Community Legal Services (PCLS) noted in an early law reform brief addressing employment standards legislation in Ontario, women's labour-force participation had more than doubled since the Second World War. Despite this, Parkdale Community Legal Services observed that women are still overwhelmingly segregated into specific industries and jobs noted for "low pay, little status and minimal prospects for advancement" (PCLS et al. 1989). And, as Judy Fudge (1991a: 77) states: "The feminization of the labour force [has been] matched by a complementary feminization of the labour market, the increase in jobs typically associated with women, jobs that are part-time, temporary, poorly paid and insecure." In 1995 the poverty rates of families in which the family head was employed in the female-dominated clerical and services sectors were 14.7 and 20.8 percent, respectively

(NCW 1998a: 40). Added to this, despite their increasing participation in the labour force, women continue to bear a greater burden than men do with respect to household labour and the caregiving for children and the elderly (PCLS et al. 1989). But, even more telling is the fact that whereas in 1980 earnings were reported as the primary source of income of 67,000 (or 35 percent) of all poor single-parent mothers, in 1996 only 19 percent (or 74,000) single-parent mothers had earnings as their primary source of income (NCW 1998a: 70, Graph AC). The unemployment of single mothers is clearly implicated in their increasing reliance on welfare as a source of income.

Some women have been especially hurt by these developments. While the textile and garment industries in Canada have traditionally been a female job ghetto, 36 percent of all workers there are immigrant women (Seward and McDade 1988; Ng 1993). Newly arrived immigrant women tend to be employed (in larger numbers than Canadian-born women) in the textile industries at jobs characterized by low wages, piecework, homework, and virtually unregulated working conditions (Seward and McDade 1988; Ng 1986). Aboriginal women's relationship to the labour market may be gleaned in part from their relatively low participation rate (which at 53.4 percent is lower than that of Aboriginal

Table 2
Principal Labour-Force Participation Sites for Aboriginal and Non-Aboriginal Women

	Aboriginal Women	Non-Aboriginal Women
	%	%
Management/administration	7.6	10.3
Social Sciences	7.1	3.0
Teaching	6.1	6.3
Medicine & health	6.1	9.1
Clerical	27.9	31.7
Sales	5.9	9.5
Service	25.6	15.8

Source: Canada, *The Report of the Royal Commission on Aboriginal Peoples,* vol. 4 (1996: 15, Table 2.4).

men, whose participation rate is 72.4 percent) (Canada 1996, vol. 4: 9) and their high rate of unemployment once they do enter the labour force: Aboriginal women experience unemployment rates that are twice that of non-Aboriginal women, and 60.3 percent of them had annual incomes of less than $10,000, as compared to 36 percent of non-Aboriginal women (Canada 1996, vol. 4: 15, Table 2.3). The principal labour-force participation sites of Aboriginal and non-Aboriginal women show differences as well as some similarities.

Aboriginal women and non-Aboriginal women alike find themselves located in jobs with low incomes, notably clerical and service jobs. Significantly, Aboriginal women have a higher participation rate in social sciences and are proximate to non-Aboriginal women in the field of teaching.

For Canadian women living with disabilities, the estimated 1994 poverty rate (based on 1986 data) was thought to be 29.5 percent, and for young women (aged fifteen to twenty-four), it was 34.5 percent (Ross, Shillington, and Lochead 1994: 41). The annual income of disabled women is as low as their poverty rates are high: in 1991, 35.3 percent had annual incomes of less than $5,000 and a further 18.5 percent had incomes of less than $10,000 per annum.

What all of this suggests is that a gendered division of wage labour and lower income for women in the labour force—coupled with women's predominant responsibility for child care and childrearing—are directly and significantly implicated in women's poverty. Race, immigration status, and disability are also clearly implicated. In short, the face of the poor in Canada is a female face: a single mother living on subpoverty-line income derived either from social assistance or low wages. What implications does this recognition hold for how we go about understanding or theorizing poverty? As the Royal Commission on Aboriginal Peoples observed in their report, "Statistics do not reveal why" (Canada 1996: 17).

Some feminists argue that the family household, with its overarching familial ideology, and a system of wage labour divided sharply along gender lines are the primary sites of women's oppression in Western capitalist societies (McIntosh 1978; Barrett and McIntosh 1982; Armstrong and Armstrong 1984; Pearce 1986). By "familial ideology" I mean "the range of dominant ideas and social practices, discourses and prejudices, common sense and social science, in which relations of gender and generation are held out and generally accepted to be best organized around and through a household of two adults of the opposite sex who (usually) have expressed a primary personal, sexual and economic commitment to each other and to care for and raise any children they may have. The family is often asserted to be the basic unit of society and is celebrated ... in quasi-sacred terms" (Gavigan 1995: 103). As I have argued elsewhere (Gavigan 1993), although a great many people and households do not live in this form of family, it is still held out as the model, the ideal, the prism through and against which all of us are measured in life and in law.

Despite a plethora of conflicting ideas and practices about work and family, these apparently discrete "sites" are inextricably intertwined; women's familial responsibilities are used as a rationale for their lower wages on the clearly ideological premise that their earnings are secondary and supplementary to the main, breadwinning income of a male wage earner. In my view, such a position suggests that the image of poverty is "phenomenal" in the Marxist sense. In other words, we need to analyse this outward "appearance" of poverty to uncover its underlying "essence"; the "real" relations that this appearance obscures. Women's poverty has as much to do with their unemployment and underemployment, the sites of their employment, and their limited access to good jobs, good child care, and employment benefits as it does with low or intermittent child support and familial responsibilities.

In addition, the concern with the definition, extent, and measurement of poverty is a concern directed at "outward" phenomena only. Although it is important to describe the economic facts of poverty (regardless of which is the best measure), the analysis of the statistics and their implications cannot rest with terms that speak of "poor families" or even "single-parent families." Even the terms "female-headed" and "male-headed" households imply that these households are essentially the same phenomena, or at least two sides of the same "household" coin.

The poverty that can be identified, described by some as the "feminization of poverty" (Pearce 1985), derives from underlying inequality. But what is expressed by the notion of the feminization of poverty? Is the poverty of single mothers caused by marriage breakdown and inadequate, intermittent, and unpaid support (as suggested by Lloyd Axworthy in his discussion paper, "Improving Social Security in Canada" [Canada 1994: 20–21])? To use the evocative phrase currently favoured by politicians, is the problem one of "deadbeat dads"—absent fathers who are not meeting their financial obligations to their children, thus forcing their families onto the welfare rolls? Or is the poverty of women and children within marriage and the family "most clearly exposed at marriage breakdown or divorce" because that is when "the economic vulnerability of women caused by marriage and the sexual division of labour is most clearly exposed"(Smart 1984: xiii)?

Thus, how we conceptualize the nature of the inequality of poor women is important. We need to recast "poverty" issues along lines attentive to gender, class, race, and ethnicity. Especially for those of us working in poverty law, attention to race, gender, and class relations and engagement with the problematics and politics of feminist, working-class, and racialized groups are prerequisites for our practices.

ACCESS TO JUSTICE

2. How should access to justice be defined and how should legal services be delivered?

Like the cutbacks to social programs generally, the funding of legal aid for the poor has come under attack in recent years. Indeed, no one who witnessed the legal aid funding crisis in Ontario during the early fall of 1995 can doubt that the Ontario legal aid plan was under serious threat (Schmitz 1995; Furlong and Schmitz 1995; Zemans and Monahan 1997).[3] Such crisis conditions occasion the need to (re)consider or rethink both the definition of those legal services and their means of delivery.

As terms, "legal services for the poor," "legal aid," and "poverty law" are often used interchangeably. To a great many lawyers and legal aid administrators, legal services for the poor mean criminal defence work, criminal legal aid. In my own experience as a lawyer in Saskatchewan in the 1970s as a clinic lawyer in a publicly funded, community-based legal services clinic, they also meant criminal defence work.[4] Nevertheless, in its report *Legal Aid and the Poor*, the National Council of Welfare (1995: 9–12) argues that legal aid programs emphasizing criminal legal aid do not address the legal needs of most poor people, including not incidentally, poor women (see also Mossman 1993; Ontario Family Law Tariff Sub-Committee 1992; Cossman and Rodgerson 1997: 796). This is particularly so because legal aid plans committed to delivering legal services on a "judicare" model assume the traditional structure of legal services and the traditional organization of lawyers, which means they take an individualized approach to the legal problems of the poor. Judicare is a form of legal aid that provides (limited) access to a (limited) range of private lawyers paid on a fee-for-service (or case-by-case) basis to represent an individual in courts. In Canada the delivery of legal aid—especially criminal legal aid—tends to be driven by either the legal profession's vision of how legal services are to be delivered (that is, on a fee-for-service basis by private lawyers) or cost-effective notions (that is, salaried lawyers in staff-delivery models, such as duty counsel). The image of the poor in these "legal aid" programs becomes blurred and imprecise, and the experience of poverty becomes abstracted into discrete legal problems or issues.

But the lives of poor people do not lend themselves to simple one-on-one legal solutions. Poverty law lawyers must have and hold onto an appreciation of the complex and central nature of poverty in the lives of their clients and need to acknowledge that the most significant struggles, defeats, and victories in their clients' lives are seldom, if ever, experienced in the courtroom. When a poverty law lawyer wins a welfare case or a landlord and tenant case, the best legal result is that the client is still on welfare or is still a tenant. Those victories are important, but they are hardly "transformative" of the deeper problems of the poor litigant. The lawyer may win, but the client remains poor. When Stephen Wexler (1970) wrote his pioneering "Practicing Law for Poor People," he argued that lawyers for the poor needed to take the reality of the lives and struggles of "the poor"—and not the law—as the focal point.

That focal point, though, is easily asserted but less easily comprehended. To begin with, poverty has no single expression, experience, or cause. Gender, race, disability, and being a young single-parent are significant relations in and through which poverty can be experienced, but a host of other conditions can also be identified, including injury at work, unemployment, depletion of natural resources, and regional economic disparities. It is imperative not to labour under the assumption that "poverty" is an easily graspable commodity. It also follows that poverty law varies according to context. In Ontario the definition of poverty law depends upon the position of the person asked. To a lawyer in a corporate law practice, it most assuredly means that poverty law is work that other lawyers do. At community legal clinics, it means social assistance, (un)employment insurance, income security and disability issues, landlord and tenant law, and mental health. In Toronto legal clinics, it has long meant immigration and refugee law. Clinic work also encompasses the rights and issues of injured, unorganized, and unemployed workers, the homeless and children, youth and the elderly. It has come to mean AIDS/HIV advocacy (Herman 1988; Shime 1994), environmental law, and clinics for specific communities such as the African Canadian Legal

Services, Aboriginal Legal Services, and Chinese and South-East Asian Legal Services for Metropolitan Toronto.

In Ontario no less than two provincial attorneys general from different administrations and, more recently, the chief justice of the province have vigorously defended the role of communities in community legal clinics. Former Attorney General Roy McMurtry, one of the clinics' early defenders, argued: "The clinics are in a position to take the law to those who need it most. It is almost trite to point out that a great many poor people have never been made aware of the right they enjoy under our laws.... The clinics, located in, and run by local communities, can reach out to advise people of their rights. They take the law to the people" (McMurtry 1982: 30–31). His successor, Liberal Ian Scott, agreed: "Clinics take the law directly to the people. They involve the community in setting service priorities. They ensure that problems are handled by persons with expertise in the subject matter.... They promote self-help, and they work actively in public legal education" (Scott 1985: 11–12).

Still more recently, McMurtry, as chief justice of Ontario, reaffirmed his support: "What distinguishes the [legal] clinics from other access-to-justice initiatives is their ability to respond in a community-specific manner to these needs.... Until Parkdale Community Legal Services [in 1971], these ideas had not been implemented" (McMurtry 1997: 429).

Whatever the breadth of "poverty law" and the elasticity of its scope, I do want to hold onto a conceptual distinction between poverty law and legal aid. Poverty law is poor people's law. Form and content aside, this means that the pivotal defining criterion is financial or economic. The difficulty in this, as Richard Abel (1985b: 405) once argued, is that "the category of beneficiaries defined by economic indices has no organic coherence, no necessary unity" (see also Mosher 1997: 921). While acknowledging the existence of many different perspectives on the meaning of poverty and many measures thereof, I would argue that economic indices, if probed and recast, reveal a coherence not often enough acknowledged. Class relations tell.

THE LAW: SWORD OR SHIELD FOR THE POOR?

3. Can the interests of the poor be advanced through the law, or is the law a site of defensive struggle only for the poor?

The discussion in the previous section raises an equally important question: what is or ought to be the objective of "poverty law" theory and practice? Poverty law advocates have been identified with the "access to justice" movement endorsed by former attorneys general McMurtry and Scott. But there has also been a long-standing and open critique of the legal system and of lawyers, coupled with a stated commitment to eliminate—or at least alleviate—poverty. The extent to which the law is implicated in poverty and the extent to which lawyers and the legal system ought to be involved and relied upon are rather contested. Abel (1985b: 491) has argued with some force that there is a dearth of unity of objectives in the access to justice movement and no clear sense of what "justice" is sought: some argue for creative use of law and the creation of new (legal) rights, whereas others express a commitment to "substantive justice" rather than formal or procedural justice.

It has long been an axiomatic theme in the law and poverty literature that access to justice must mean more than access to lawyers and courts (Wexler 1970; Gathercole 1982; Abel 1979; Ewart 1997). Abel suggests that the concern with formal justice and redistribution of lawyers' services reflects a lawyer's perspective, one internal to the legal system. It is his position that formal justice cannot be used as a vehicle for achieving social justice in a capitalist society. Indeed, he is convinced that the ideal of formal justice is unrealizable within capitalism: "Social justice is thus a prerequisite for formal justice" (Abel 1979: 7). Abel usefully examined the implications of various ways of redistributing lawyers' services (including deprofessionalization and informalism) to illustrate that— without a fundamental restructuring of social and economic relations— the impact of access or lack thereof is, at best, marginal. His work is particularly relevant for those engaged in poverty law, because he illustrates graphically the limitations of one approach encouraged in the poverty law literature: client self-help (Wexler 1970). Although the encouragement of self-help is framed as part of a commitment to empowering the previously powerless and in reaction against dependency upon experts and routine recourse to formality, Abel suggests that the result is the withdrawal of lawyers from people who, in any event, have had limited access to the profession. As well, "It may be impossible to restore to individuals the capacity to engage in self-help as long as they are opposed by adversaries who continue to employ legal representation" (Abel 1979: 11). Thus, this form of "empowerment" may be mythical at best and coercive at worst.

Although Abel's critique of the self-help or deprofessionalization movement is trenchant, he nevertheless evinces an ambivalence as to whether the law is an appropriate or important site for struggle (Abel

1985a). This ambivalence, in my view, derives from the contradictory nature of law within capitalism. For, although he insists that formal justice cannot precede social justice, he still argues that "the only source of power for the poor and disadvantaged [in U.S. society] is those rights derived from written law. The invocation of those rights is always a symbolic act, and the symbolic is always formal" (Abel 1985a: 382).

As the great British historian E.P. Thompson (1975: 263) was at pains to remind us: "The law may be rhetoric but it need not be empty rhetoric." Thompson (1975: 266) insisted that the equity and universality claimed by the rule of law in capitalist society are more than sham: "It is true that in history the law can be seen to mediate and to legitimize existent class relations. Its forms and procedures may crystallize those relations and mask ulterior injustice. But this mediation, through the forms of law, is something quite distinct from the exercise of unmeditated force. The forms and rhetoric of law acquire a distinct identity which may, on occasion, inhibit power and afford some protection to the powerless."

Even if we accept Thompson's position as theoretically sound, the question that remains is whether the law is the *only* form through which the powerful can be inhibited; and here the experience of poverty law practice can surely be invoked. For, while it may be that poor people can on occasion use the legal form to press a claim or defend themselves, still it is also crystal clear that they cannot confine themselves to legal forums. As Bob Fine (1979: 30) once argued, in a friendly critique of Thompson: "It is clear that the 'rule of law' does impose effective inhibitions on power. What remains at issue, however, is what kind of inhibitions, what are its limits, what is its base?... What must be resolved is the relation between inhibitions enforced by the form of law and by forms of extra-legal political organization."

POVERTY LAW ADVOCACY

4. What sort of advocacy should a poverty law lawyer do? Is the role of the poverty law lawyer to organize against poverty?
Here I want to turn to this important question of "extralegal political organization" by focusing upon and re-examining the pioneering work of Stephen Wexler (1970). Although based upon U.S. experience and published thirty years ago in a U.S. legal journal, Wexler's explicit critique of traditional lawyering and his attendant implicit critique of legal education continue to be relevant today. Wexler sought to expose the narrowness of both traditional lawyering (the solving of legal problems

and the one-to-one solicitor-client relationship) and the self-interest of the legal profession, including young lawyers oriented towards poverty law. For Wexler (1970: 1053), the legal problems experienced by the poor are "the product of poverty and are common to all poor people." Poverty, then, as the cause of the problems (and not the law), must be tackled and stopped. Lest poverty lawyers find the prospect of attempting to eliminate poverty daunting, Wexler (1970: 1053–54) insisted that lawyers abandon the notion of heroic white knighthood: "Poverty will not be stopped by people who are not poor. If poverty is stopped, it will be stopped by poor people. And poor people can stop poverty only if they work at it together. The lawyer who wants to serve poor people must put his skills to the task of helping poor people organize themselves.... Specifically, the lawyer must seek to strengthen existing organizations of poor people, and to help poor people start organizations where none exist."

Wexler outlined the tasks for poverty lawyers as being work primarily in the nature of information, education, and training lay advocates. Clearly he placed direct resort to law low on his agenda. Again, this is consistent with the theme in poverty law that legal victories do not amount to real victories and that legal change does not amount to social change (Gathercole 1982). He was concerned with avoiding the creation of "new dependencies" for the apparently already too dependent poor. The underlying question seems to be one of "who really instructs whom?" Related to this is a concern that poor people will look to lawyers for the solutions to all of their problems. (Is there historical evidence to warrant this concern?)

In my view this perception of the nature of the relationship between lawyers and their poor clients indicates Wexler's fear that lawyers for the poor could easily become agents of social control of the poor—a notion of lawyers not unique to him (see also Christie 1978; Ericson and Baranek 1982; cf. Cain 1983), but it does rather fly in the face of the professional ideology of lawyer as "advocate for" rather than "controller of" the client who retains the lawyer's services. The adequacy of this formulation needs to be interrogated, because we need to consider whether it is appropriate to think of all lawyers as agents of social control, or whether only certain kinds of lawyers dealing with certain kinds of clients fall within this category. Does media magnate Conrad Black's lawyer control him? Does control depend upon who possesses the greater economic power in the relationship?

It was, however, Wexler's call to organize that was both most challenging and most problematic. His insistence that lawyers essentially take a back seat in the poor people's organization is as critically important today as when he wrote it. It is troubling enough that lawyers and legal academics are disposed to the conceit that they hold the monopoly on knowledge about law. Lawyers also display a propensity to see themselves as experts on the world in general and all aspects of human affairs in particular. This, Wexler (1970: 1065) argued, imperils the organizations with and in which lawyers are involved: "The lawyer must help them do their thing, or get out." And yet, in his effort to bring home the importance of organizing, Wexler (1970: 1054) relied upon an example told to him by a "very successful welfare rights organizer," to illustrate "the 'proper' mentality for a poor people's lawyer":

> I found a recipient who worked hard at organizing, and was particularly good in the initial stages of getting to talk to new people. I picked her up at her apartment one morning to go out knocking on doors. While I was there, I saw her child, and I noticed he seemed to be retarded. Because the boy was too young for school and the family never saw a doctor, the mother had never found out something was seriously wrong with her son. I didn't tell her. If I had, she would have stopped working at welfare organizing to rush around to look for help for her son. I had some personal problems about doing that, but I'm an organizer, not a social worker.

Wexler conceded that this organizer had taken a very hard line and that the retelling of this story invariably makes listeners recoil. However, it is his view that the more that one can accept this organizer's model, "the more he [or she] can give poor people the wherewithal to change a world that hurts them" (Wexler 1970: 1054). This model reflects more than a hard line. It reflects a dearth of analysis. It implies that *real* organizing and *real* politics can only take place around issues "out there"—somewhere else. Although perhaps written before the most recent generation of feminists had begun to criticize the "public/private" split, the organizer lacked both imagination and vision with respect to organizing issues. From the brief example, it would appear that access to health care and child care could easily have been taken up. Beyond that, the organizer's ridicule of a woman who would "rush around looking for help for her son" most assuredly implicates him (her?) as part of a world that hurts the recipient and limits her ability to assist in change.

In embracing this organizer's model, Wexler made the mistake of equating individual legal right with individual human need. In his attempt to distance himself from the individualization and isolation of social relations that may result from invoking the law, the legal subject, and attendant individual legal rights, he failed to see that human needs are both individual and social. To sacrifice individual need without reflection and analysis is to imperil the success of a strategy for social change (see Petchesky 1985: 1–18).

I challenge Wexler's example of an "organizer's dilemma" not to eschew the place of organizing in poverty law but rather to endorse it; to insist upon its continuing relevance. Above all, an understanding of the face and place of the poor and a feminist analysis thereof can clarify the strategic position of organizing in poverty law. An analysis of the basis for the poverty of our clients, and an understanding of the interrelatedness of gender, class, race, and ethnicity must inform both legal and organizing strategies designed to get at the root(s) of the problem (see, for example, Cook and Watt 1987; Roberts 1996). Organizers must understand why they are committed to organizing and what they hope to achieve.

LEGAL CLINIC PRACTICE

5. What would legal clinic practice look like if it were informed by a theory linking race, class, and gender relations?

In this last section, I want to consider the implications of an insistence upon the centrality of gender both in poverty and poverty law. Can clinics deliver gendered services in the context of poverty law? If women are more at risk of experiencing poverty than men are, should legal clinics serve only women clients? Should legal clinics restrict their services to addressing the needs of single mothers who are employed in unorganized workplaces or are on social assistance? If access to child care is a central issue for both working and unemployed mothers, should this issue be incorporated into poverty law practices even if it does not fit neatly into current legal categories or casework?

Many legal clinics have turned their minds to gender issues in a number of important ways. For example, specialty mini-clinics have extended their hours of service and timing to accommodate the needs of women with children. Many clinics accommodate a request by a woman client to be served by a female lawyer, community legal worker, or student. Clinics are mindful of personal security issues when they attempt to telephone or correspond with women clients who are experiencing or at risk of domestic violence. These initiatives make an important contribution to enhancing access to justice for poor women.

Some clinics have made domestic violence a part of their work, and, indeed, some student clinics associated with law schools have divisions or cells they call "Women's Divisions" (Abell 1993; Carey 1992). They have compelling reasons for doing this, but, in my view, clinic case criteria or policies that characterize gender issues as "women's issues" risk blurring the class and race dimensions of poor women's life experiences. Poverty is not simply that part of the financial eligibility criteria that gets clients beyond the receptionist to see someone on intake. What we must keep in our sights is not the fact of limited financial resources, but the reasons behind that fact.

At the same time, rather than jettison the current areas of poverty law, I want to argue for the reconceptualization of the categories of "tenants," "workers" and "welfare recipients," "immigrants and refugees," and "sole-support parents" that challenges the implied gender and race neutrality of those clients. I am not unmindful of the fact that, for instance, clinic welfare clients are primarily women. This is not a coincidence, but neither is the explanation self-evident. If we can move beyond the appeal of the obvious, we will be better positioned to focus on what is to be done. We will be better able to respond, for instance, to the "deadbeat dads" sorts of government initiatives that consistently misrepresent and reinforce in the public mind that single mothers are poor because of unpaid child and spousal support or because they are promiscuous. Some of this thinking has begun to inform the shape of legal clinic practice at the clinic I am most intimately familiar with:

> For example, Parkdale students are urged to think through the relational nature of the inequalities they encounter in the client and community work: the majority of the Clinic's clients are women. In the workers' rights group, for instance, students meet women who are domestic workers, undocumented workers, workers who have been subjected to sexual harassment, and whose only access to employment is via the mechanisms of employment standards legislation. At PCLS one is able to articulate that women's rights are workers' rights. (Gavigan, 1997: 465)

CONCLUSION

Access to justice, then, must be broadly defined, theoretically informed, and attentive in practice to the interrelation, indeed interpenetration, of issues of class and gender relations. Poverty law advocates have never had the luxury of gender blindness in poverty law. and yet poverty law and access to justice have often been advanced and defended in gender-neutral terms. Paradoxically, while poverty law has been discussed in gender-neutral terms, poverty has long been identified as a women's problem. But, to describe the face of (women's) poverty is not the same thing as to analyse and explain why women are poor.

Early welfare-law reformers believed good women were poor because their husbands had died, and bad women were poor because they were morally unfit. Welfare reformers saw and believed what they wanted to believe, and welfare legislation reflected that vision. Women's poverty was thus legally entrenched. The poverty of women and children is related to, yet transcends, familial relations. Women are also poor because they are poorly paid, unemployed, or denied access to the labour force. And just as Ginger Rogers danced every step that Fred Astaire danced, only backwards and in high heels, so too do poor women experience all the dimensions of poverty that men do, while simultaneously raising, caring, and overseeing the education of their children and running their households. And, if we have not learned yet, we must struggle to remember that while women's poverty frequently finds expression in the legal system, the causes and solutions require theoretically informed extralegal solutions. Women's poverty may be of long-standing duration, but it is not inevitable. Its forms can and do change, as do the forms (legal and otherwise) through which it may be resisted and challenged. Class tells and theory matters in the practice and struggles of women, poverty, and law.

NOTES

1. An earlier version of this essay appeared as "Poverty Law and Poor People: The Place of Gender and Class in Clinic Practice," *Journal of Law and Social Policy* 11 (1995). I wish to thank Elizabeth Comack, Judy Fudge, and Karen Andrews for their careful and thorough comments, which greatly assisted me in revising the paper for inclusion here. This is for Janice Gingell and Norma Sim, great friends and great lawyers of the Saskatchewan Bar.

2. The history of welfare assistance for single mothers has been riddled with concerns about their sexual relationships to ensure that the women are liv-

ing alone as a single person and not with a spouse. Despite the gender neutrality of current legislation, which no longer refers to "men in the house" but rather "spouse in the house," women recipients of assistance are more directly affected by the changing definitions of "spouse" in welfare law. In Ontario, from 1988 until 1995, "spouse" for the purposes of welfare law included "a person of the opposite sex to the applicant or recipient who has resided continuously with the applicant or recipient for a period of not less than three years" (Family Benefits Regulation (O. Reg 366), s.1(1)(d)). In 1995 this regulation was amended to widen the definition of spouse to include a person of the opposite sex who is residing with the applicant or recipient if they have a mutual agreement or arrangement about their financial affairs and the social and familial aspects of the relationship amount to cohabitation. Additionally, for the purposes of determining a spousal relationship under Ontario welfare law, sexual factors are not to be considered or investigated. For a history of spouse in the house legislation in Ontario, see Little (1994); Gavigan (1993).

The constitutionality of this new definition of spouse was recently challenged by five welfare mothers in Ontario. After protracted litigation and lengthy delays, the welfare mothers won their case before the Social Assistance Review Board, which held that the equality and life, liberty, and security of the person guarantees of the *Charter of Rights and Freedoms* were violated by the new definition of spouse, and struck down the definition as unconstitutional (see S.A.R.B decision P1031-22, P122-25, P1026-05, Q0828-43, released August 14, 1998). The government filed an appeal of the decision.

3. The legal aid crisis in Ontario in the mid-1990s occasioned two major reviews: Zemans and Monahan (1997); Ontario Legal Aid Review (1997).
4. For a critical history of the Saskatchewan legal aid plan, see Abell (1993).

Gender, Sexuality, and the Law

Introduction

Over the past two decades a virtual explosion of interest and research has taken place in the area of feminist engagement with the law. As outlined in the essay "Theoretical Excursions," different feminist frameworks account for the nature and forms of women's inequality and oppression in society in relation to men, and each framework also incorporates particular strategies for addressing those inequities. Indeed, feminism has made its mark—not just in offering analyses of how structural and cultural constraints influence women's position in society—but also in its influence on state policies and practices. Following that contribution, this part of the book looks at the gendered nature of social relations, with each essay considering a particular area of concern, law's role in (re)producing gender inequalities, and the pitfalls and promises of using law as an avenue for change.

Dorothy Chunn begins by drawing out three main periods of social transformation in Canadian history, each one characterized by a particular kind of social organization and a corresponding state formation: industrial capitalism and the laissez-faire state; monopoly capitalism and the welfare state; and transnational capitalism and the neo-liberal state. As Chunn notes, each of these forms of social organization has been accompanied by particular patriarchal relations and models of the family: authoritarian, welfare, and egalitarian respectively. While significant differences exist between these familial forms, all are variations on the nuclear family form premised on heterosexual marriage, the sexual division of labour, and the separation of private and public spheres in society.

Chunn's main purpose is to show how feminists and the organized women's movement have played a key role in contributing to the transformations that have occurred. Specifically, in the late nineteenth and early twentieth centuries, "first wave" maternal feminists campaigned for reforms in family-related legislation and policies that helped to create the Canadian welfare state and entrench a welfare model of the family in law and social policy. Since the 1960s, "second wave" liberal feminists have influenced reforms based on an egalitarian model of the family, contributing to the dismantling of the welfare state. As Chunn notes, these reform efforts have had contradictory and differential effects, which are, in turn, mediated by race, class, gender, sexual orientation, and (dis)ability.

By drawing our attention to the different historical contexts and analytical frameworks of the feminist engagement with the state over family-related issues, Chunn allows us to better appreciate the contemporary challenges confronting the women's movement. In particular, in the current climate of "vampire capitalism" (in which globalization and corporate restructuring are reshaping women's structural position) and the advent of the neo-liberal state (with its concomitant retreat from the provision of social programs), both the situation confronting women as a group in Canada and the "playing field" on which activists endeavour to realize meaningful change have been dramatically altered. Chunn discusses the prospects for meaningful reform under these conditions. Those prospects, she argues, are daunting but at the same time possible.

Over the past two decades, the issue of sexual violence has been high on the agenda of women's groups in Canada. Indeed, concerted lobbying on their part has resulted in a series of legislative amendments to the *Criminal Code*—in 1983, 1985, 1992, and 1995. Yet, while Parliament has abrogated some of the most blatantly discriminatory laws, judicial decisions continue to reflect traditional cultural mythologies about rape (Morris 1987; Comack 1996b), including the idea that women and children lie about their experiences out of malice or delusion. Through her analysis of recent legal cases, Karen Busby shows us how these myths "work" in law, and how law's treatment of sexual violence cases thereby perpetuates women's and children's inequality—especially when the complainant is poor, disabled, Aboriginal, racialized, or lesbian.

More specifically, Busby's examination of sexual-violence prosecutions addresses the issue of how the Official Version of Law (specifically, the legal principles that law embodies) combines with rape mythologies to (re)produce gendered inequalities. In an approach similar to the postmodern view of law as a "discourse," Busby sees the law as a process that aims to seek the "Truth" about sexual violence. Nevertheless, she argues, this "Truth-seeking process" permits only *part* of the story to be told. As Busby documents, the combined effect of legal principles applicable to all criminal cases (the presumption of innocence, proof beyond a reasonable doubt, and the defendant's right to silence) and procedural rules applicable only to sexual violence cases makes the conviction of defendants unlikely.

Busby sensitizes us to two distinct aspects of the legal enterprise—

"law-as-legislation" and "law-as-practice" (Smart 1986)—and the tensions that can exist between them. For instance, while Parliament may be amenable to implementing reforms in sexual-violence laws through statute ("law-as-legislation"), it is still the case that the decisions of judges will have a determining effect on legal outcomes ("law-as-practice"). As well, the apparent sway of rape myths and misunderstandings on judicial reasoning suggests that, before meaningful, substantive change can occur to address the issue of sexual violence, we need to fix attention on those cultural and discursive practices that reside—not just within law per se—but extend beyond law's reach to the wider community.

Using the Supreme Court decision in *Butler* as her focal point, Kirsten Johnson demonstrates how criminal law has been complicit in constructing gendered (and class-based and racist) notions of sexuality and sexual freedom. To contextualize the *Butler* decision, Johnson summarizes for us the evolution of obscenity law in Canada. Historically, the criminalization of "obscenity" has been justified in functionalist terms—on the basis of its perceived threat to the moral order of society. The *Butler* case of 1992 has been heralded by some commentators as marking a distinct break with the past, in that the Supreme Court recognized that certain forms of violent pornography constitute a harm to society—and to women and children in particular. Nevertheless, Johnson cautions us against a too-optimistic reading of *Butler*. In particular she notes that, while organizations like LEAF sought to advance a feminist understanding of how pornography harms women's equality, the Court acknowledged this argument only in terms of a broader notion of harm to "society."

Even more worrisome is the record of the courts in deciding obscenity cases in the post-*Butler* era. Johnson argues that in the more recent cases the courts have continued to take gendered notions of sexuality for granted. While prosecutions of heterosexual pornography have typically resulted in acquittals, with the sexual content deemed "sex-for-fun," the obscenity provisions in the *Criminal Code* have been used repeatedly by customs officials to justify the detention of sexually explicit materials imported by lesbian and gay bookstores. Johnson's analysis, then, raises significant questions about the limits of using criminal law to promote either sexual freedom or ideas about sexual subjectivity that challenge the status quo.

Feminism, Law, and "the Family": Assessing the Reform Legacy

© Dorothy E. Chunn[1]

E ven a cursory retrospective reveals that institutions such as state, law, and family are not always and everywhere the same, either in a given society or in societies with similar histories. Rather, they are formed and (re)formed at particular transformative moments within the constraints of specific kinds of social organization (Garland 1985). In Canada three major periods of social transformation have occurred since 1840: the development of industrial capitalism and a laissez-faire state; corporate capitalism and a welfare state; and transnational capitalism and a neo-liberal form of state (Brodie 1995; Chunn 1992; Evans and Wekerle 1997; Moscovitch and Albert 1987; Panitch 1977; Ursel 1992).

These changes in capitalist organization and social relations have been accompanied by analogous transformations in patriarchal relations exemplified by the authoritarian, welfare, and egalitarian models of family respectively (Eichler 1997). Despite differences between them, all three models are variations on the nuclear or bourgeois family form that is premised on heterosexual marriage, the sexual division of labour, and the public-private split (Barrett and McIntosh 1982; Zaretsky 1976). Thus, it is the nuclear family form that has been, and continues to be, dominant in Canadian law and social policy related to the "private" sphere (Boyd 1997b; Brodie 1996; Eichler 1997; Luxton 1997; Pulkingham and Ternowetsky 1996).

Notably, analyses of socio-legal reforms that have contributed to transformations of state, law, and family in capitalist societies reveal that reform is an inherently contradictory phenomenon (Chunn 1992; Donzelot 1980; Garland 1985). Because they are always the outcome of political struggle and negotiation, reforms invariably generate both positive and negative effects, which, in turn, are mediated by gender, race, class, sexual orientation, and (dis)ability. On one hand, then, law and social policy help reproduce and perpetuate the status quo (and inequalities) by supporting particular forms of social and family organization. On the other hand, law and public policy are not simply unitary instruments of oppression that are the monopoly of white, bourgeois, heterosexual men (Boyd 1997b; Brophy and Smart 1985; Gavigan 1993, 1998).

Like their counterparts in other Western market societies (Dale and Foster 1986; Gordon 1990), feminists and the organized women's movements in Canada have played a major role in campaigns for legal and policy reforms and have therefore contributed to the transformations outlined above (Adamson, Briskin, and McPhail 1988; Bacchi 1983; Ross 1995). These campaigns have been very much informed by particular feminist explanations of why and how women are subordinated and the best means of bringing about change—explanations that incorporate distinct conceptions of the state, law, and family. During the late nineteenth and early twentieth centuries, first-wave maternal feminism (Bacchi 1983; Roberts 1979) was the dominant feminist influence on the family-related legislation and policies that helped to create the Canadian welfare state and to entrench a welfare model of family in law and social policy (Andrew 1984; McCormack 1991; Ursel 1992). Similarly, since the 1960s, second-wave liberal feminism has strongly influenced socio-legal reforms that are based on an egalitarian model of family and have contributed to the deconstruction of the welfare state in Canada (Boyd 1997b; Brodie 1995; Eichler 1997).

This essay assesses the role played by feminists in both the historical construction and the contemporary reordering of the Canadian welfare state through their successful advocacy of legislation and policies governing the "private" sphere of the family. In the first section I examine the implementation and contradictory effects of socio-legal reforms promoted by first-wave maternal feminists—reforms that reflected the shift from an authoritarian to a welfare model of (nuclear) family within the context of a developing welfare state. In the second section I outline the adoption and similarly mixed results of socio-legal reforms influenced by second-wave liberal feminists—reforms that have signalled the transition from a welfare to an egalitarian model of family within the context of an emerging neo-liberal state. In the final section I explore strategies that might enable Canadian feminists to obtain legislation and policies that will challenge the bourgeois family form at its ideological and structural roots and revitalize the movement to achieve substantive equality for all women.

FIRST-WAVE REFORMS: MATERNAL FEMINISM

In Canada and elsewhere, the catalyst for the emergence of an organized women's movement during the late nineteenth and early twentieth centuries was the legal invisibility of women, particularly married women. Legislation and policies governing families in laissez-faire states were based on an authoritarian model of the nuclear family, which gave husbands and fathers total legal control over their wives and children. Under the so-called "unity doctrine," a husband and wife became one person, and that person was the husband; a married woman thus became a mere extension of her patriarch-husband, with the same status as "an infant or institutionalized incompetent" (Kieran 1986: 41). Forcing poor and/or First Nations women to marry thus became a priority for authorities in the Canadian laissez-faire state (Backhouse 1991: ch. 1). While single women had more rights than their married sisters, a major impetus for the rise of first-wave feminism was a desire to end the legal subordination of women, especially white, middle-class women.

In Canada, maternal feminism was the first-wave feminist perspective that most influenced family-related law and policy. It was premised on the assumption that men and women are different but complementary in nature and that, therefore, they excel in "separate but equal" spheres of activity. Following from this assumption, the "masculine" traits of providing and protecting predispose men to enter the public sphere of production, while the "feminine" qualities of nurturing and caregiving make women uniquely suited to the private realm of reproduction. In their political work, then, maternal feminists embraced conceptions of state, law, and family and advocated reforms compatible with the assumption that women and men have sex-specific traits, capabilities, and needs.

The latter belief translated into an uncritical acceptance of the bourgeois family form. For maternal feminists, the "normal" family was a nuclear unit, based on a heterosexual marriage relationship, in which each member had a specific role. Husbands/fathers protected and provided for their dependants; wives and mothers nurtured and cared for other family members; children existed in a "natural" state of dependency on their parents. A "natural," sexual division of labour between the spouses mirrored the public/private split in society more generally (Chunn 1990; Gavigan 1988).

Along with adherence to the bourgeois family form, most maternal feminists initially accepted the nineteenth-century liberal notion of the state as a neutral arbiter of the common good. Only after some experience with the laissez-faire state did they begin to articulate the reformist view that safeguarding the common good might require state intervention on behalf of disadvantaged groups—such as women and children—to ensure that they received protection and support. In the words of first-wave feminist Nellie McClung (1976: 322): "More and more the idea is growing upon us that certain services are best rendered by the state, and not left to depend on the caprice, inclination, or inability of the individual."

For maternal feminists, law became the pivotal instrument of social engineering through which an interventionist state could address women's devalued status relative to men. They believed women were subordinate to men mainly because their central roles as wives and mothers within the family were not legally recognized. Thus, solving the problem did not require a revolution; rather, it involved merely the abolition of the unity doctrine and the implementation of legislation and policies that would give women legal rights in the private sphere of reproduction. To that end, maternal feminists supported women's suffrage—not to move women into the public world of business and politics, but because the right to vote would give women the political power to influence the men who made family-related law and policy.

Although first-wave maternal feminists did not challenge the sexual division of labour, they did "politicize the personal" through their efforts to acquire legal standing for women in their "proper sphere" of the family. They were especially concerned about reinforcing women in their motherhood role and keeping mother-headed families together in the midst of apparent "social disorganization" generated by the rapid industrialization and urbanization of Canada between 1880 and 1940 (Roberts 1979; Ursel 1992). From the 1880s onward, maternal feminists fought for legislation and policies that gave mothers and wives some rights when a marriage failed or when a male breadwinner was otherwise absent. In general, maternal feminists contributed to reforms that collectively shaped the welfare-state structures that regulated the private sphere of family or reproduction. In the process they helped to revamp the two-tiered, class-based system of family law that the English had transplanted to Canada. On the first level that related primarily to the propertied classes, the reform of divorce, custody, and property law benefited those middle-class and upper-class women who could afford legal counsel. On the second level, the reform of family welfare laws related to guardianship, maintenance, and support assisted some economically marginal women (Chunn 1992; Snell 1991).

A historical review of specific family-related legal and policy reforms advocated by maternal feminists in Canada illustrates these patterns. With regard to custody and guardianship law, for instance, Canadian courts consistently upheld the absolute right of fathers to legal control of their children under English common and statutory law throughout the nineteenth century (Backhouse 1991: ch. 7; Kieran 1986). By the turn of the century, however, feminists and other reformers had obtained legislation in a number of provinces that, to some degree, recognized the importance of women's motherhood role. In addition, an 1897 court decision in British Columbia laid the foundation for what became known as the "tender years" doctrine, by authorizing judges to award custody of children under the age of seven to non-adulterous mothers who were deemed "fit" parents (Backhouse 1991: 204). This principle, that "all other things being equal, a young child should be with its natural mother," came to dominate custody and guardianship decisions in the twentieth century and ended the presumption of automatic "paternal" right to children of a marriage.

By 1900 married women had also acquired new property rights. Under the unity doctrine, a wife was legally obligated to give all property acquired before or during marriage to her husband, including land, furniture, money, and even the clothes on her back. However, three successive reform "waves" during the nineteenth century led to the enactment of Married Women's Property acts, which introduced separate property regimes in some provinces, beginning with Ontario in 1884. The concept of separate property meant that both wives and husbands had the right to acquire, administer, and dispose of any personal property whether it was obtained before or during marriage; and if the relationship failed each partner kept what was hers or his (Backhouse 1992).

As with custody and guardianship, the authoritarian model of family that underpinned the unity doctrine allowed men to divorce or abandon their wives and children, leave them without any means of support, and still retain legal control over them (Kieran 1986: 49). From the 1880s onward, however, rapid industrialization and urbanization brought disproportionate numbers of women and children to cities in advance of their male breadwinners, and many of these mother-led families ended up destitute because their husbands/fathers never arrived. When the "feminization of poverty" became increasingly visible in urban centres, feminists and other reformers sought legislation that compelled men to support their dependants. Starting in 1888 with the Ontario Deserted Wives' Maintenance Act, most provinces enacted legislation that introduced a legal obligation on husbands and fathers to support their dependants after marital separation or face sanctions, including jail. After World War I, the provinces passed similar laws imposing a financial obligation on the putative father in cases of unmarried parenthood (Chunn 1992; Ursel 1992).

The post-World War I era also saw the state assume the financial role of husband and father for the first time through the payment of mothers' pensions/allowances in cases when a male deserter could not be found and when the male protector/breadwinner was absent from the family through death or mental or physical incapacity. Although "a broad spectrum of articulate, middle-class Canadians" had promoted such an income-support policy since the turn of the century, only the increase in mother-led families during the war, which fuelled a perception that the (nuclear) family was in crisis, provided a sufficient catalyst for implementing this reform (Strong-Boag 1979: 25). "Deserving" women were awarded allowances to help them fulfill their "natural" domestic role by enabling them to engage in part-time rather than full-time outside employment or to earn wages without leaving home. Recipients of pensions/allowances were considered to be state employees and expected to supplement their government salaries with other earnings (Strong-Boag 1979: 27).

Contradictory and differential effects of first-wave reforms
Like all reforms, the family-related legislation and policies promoted by first-wave feminists had both intended and unintended consequences in practice. On the positive side, women benefited from the reforms in a number of ways.

First, they received explicit legal recognition of the work that women perform in their role as mothers (and, to a lesser degree, as wives) and a concrete acknowledgement that the "private" sphere of reproduction was important and should be taken into account when a marriage ended through separation, divorce, or mutual agreement. Specifically, the tender years doctrine assisted many women in their attempts to gain custody or guardianship of their children. Likewise, the reform of Canadian divorce laws in the postwar decade meant that, by 1930, middle- and upper-class women could obtain a divorce on the same grounds as men (adultery) (Snell 1991). Similarly, desertion legislation and enforcement mechanisms, such as family courts, gave women without means the legal assistance to obtain spousal and child support (Chunn 1992).

Second, reforms such as the provincial mothers' pensions/allowances policies represented some recognition of state responsibility to oversee the well-being of the disadvantaged and, if necessary, to contribute materially to their subsistence rather than leaving the burden to families and charities in the private sector or to local governments. During the interwar period, increasing numbers of women received state salaries. In British Columbia, for example, the number of mothers or foster mothers receiving allowances rose from 636 in 1919–20 to 1,751 in 1938–39, and the amount expended by the province increased from $612,645 in 1927–28 to $790,101 in 1938–39 (Strong-Boag 1979: 26, 28–30).

Finally, although statistics are incomplete, feminist-supported laws and policies to shore up the nuclear family arguably left poor white women and children without male breadwinners at least marginally better off than they might otherwise have been. For instance, the early family courts in Ontario collected substantial sums for women and children, as did the government official who handled unmarried mothers' cases (Chunn 1992). Clearly, separate property regimes also saved some women from the destitution that previously befell many wives when a marriage ended (Backhouse 1992; Kieran 1986: ch. 7).

In retrospect, however, the negative effects of first-wave-inspired reforms are obvious. Since they took the nuclear family as a given, maternal feminists promoted reforms that sanctified rather than challenged that model, thereby helping to entrench in law and policy a definition of family as one based on heterosexual marriage, a sexual division of labour, and the public/private split. Privileging "the family" and women's role in it reinforced their subordination to, and dependency upon, men in several ways.

Historically, heterosexual marriage has been premised on a sexual double standard: women, but not men, must be chaste before and monogamous during marriage. The family-related legislation and policies obtained by maternal feminists and other reformers all incorporated and therefore reinforced this double standard. Whether women applied for custody, maintenance, or mothers' allowances, they were routinely scrutinized for sexual purity and moral fitness. "Uncondoned adultery" by a wife automatically barred her from obtaining spousal maintenance after marital breakdown and was a ground for the rescinding of existing support orders (Chunn 1992). Likewise, moral laxity disqualified women as "deserving" recipients of mothers' allowances or of other public financial assistance. Moreover, under the so-called "man in the house" rule, if a woman resided with a man she became ineligible for state benefits because authorities assumed that he must be supporting her; the same rule did not apply to men (Little 1994; Strong-Boag 1979). Thus, women who adhered to the sexual double standard were rewarded; the morally "undeserving" were punished through the loss of their children, denial of financial assistance, and even criminal prosecution (Gavigan 1993; Martin 1992).

The failure of maternal feminists to attack the sexual division of labour meant that legal and policy reforms gave married women more power within the family—not so much in their own right as women, but because of their role in social reproduction, particularly as mothers (Brophy and Smart 1985: ch.1; Chunn 1992). Thus, women's unpaid, intrafamilial motherwork, wifework, and housework (Rosenberg 1990: 58–61) were assumed, and the economic dependency of women within marriage remained intact, ultimately to be underlined by cases such as *Murdoch* v. *Murdoch,* which revealed a basic weakness of separate property regimes. The Murdochs were Alberta ranchers who separated in 1968 after twenty-five years of marriage. During that time Irene Murdoch had done not only domestic work but also enough ranch work that her husband did not need to hire a ranch hand. When she sued for half-interest in their property, cattle, and other assets, the Supreme Court of Canada decided that Irene Murdoch was entitled to alimony but had no claim to the property, because she had not made "a direct financial contribution" to the ranch. The unpaid work she did for twenty-five years was "the work done by any ranch wife." In short, Mr. Murdoch held the title to "his" property, and Irene Murdoch could not claim a share of it under the existing separate property regime in Alberta (Kieran 1986: 142).

Maternal feminists also espoused legislation and policies that reinforced the idea of "separate spheres" and, hence, the public/private distinction so central to the liberal state. Since "the family" fell on the private side of the divide, they strongly advocated the use of state power to enforce the "privatization of the costs of social reproduction" (Fudge 1989) by holding individual men legally responsible for maintaining their dependants even after marital separation or divorce. Thus, a woman would be maintained in her "natural" role as caregiver and housekeeper when a male breadwinner was no longer part of the family unit. The problem with privatized responsibility was that, despite the considerable sums of money collected on behalf of women and children by state agencies such as family courts, the majority of men defaulted on or were chronically in arrears with their support payments (Chunn 1992). Moreover, even when the state assumed some direct financial responsibility for social reproduction through such policies as mothers' allowances, the emphasis remained on individual family units and case-by-case assessment of eligibility (Little 1994).

Finally, the differential effects of the legislation and policies supported by first-wave feminists must be underscored. Maternal feminists focused solely on differences *between* women and men and, hence, on sex/gender comparisons, and they did not examine differences *among* women and *among* men generated by race, ethnicity, class, sexual orientation, and (dis)ability. As a consequence, the family-related reforms they promoted were premised on assumptions that reflected primarily the experiences of white, middle-class, heterosexual women (and men). Not surprisingly, then, it was precisely such women, and to a lesser extent their counterparts in the "respectable" working classes, who were best able to adhere to the "norms" governing the nuclear family and who benefited most from law reforms related to custody, property, and support. The reforms did help some white women among the working and dependent poor, especially single mothers, but the price of assistance from the paternalistic state was increased surveillance and scrutiny of family life (Chunn 1992; Little 1994). Lesbians, women of colour, Aboriginal women, and (dis)abled women remained invisible in the pertinent statutes and public policies. Moreover, most First Nations women living on-reserve did not live in nuclear family units and were governed entirely by the federal Indian Act. Therefore, provincial legislation and policies related to marriage, matrimonial property, maintenance, and other family matters were irrelevant to their lives (Turpel 1991). Likewise, First Nations women have been embroiled more often in guardianship battles with the state than with the fathers of their children (Monture 1989; Monture-Angus 1995).

Notwithstanding the negative and differential impact of the reforms they advocated, first-wave maternal feminists played a major role in transforming a family law system that accorded married women no rights into one in which women had rights based on their status as wives and mothers. Together with other reformers, they undermined the authoritarian model of family that underpinned legislation and policy in the laissez-faire state and helped entrench the welfare model of family that underpinned legislation and policy in the interventionist state. The resulting system of family-related law and policy remained intact until the 1960s and 1970s, when another generation of feminist reformers came of age under very different social, economic, and political circumstances.

SECOND-WAVE REFORMS: LIBERAL FEMINISM

Second-wave feminism was one of many organized, equality-seeking movements that emerged in Canada and other liberal democracies during the 1960s—a period of welfare-state consolidation, prosperity, and rising expectations among traditionally marginalized groups. Unlike some other groups, however, women were not a minority of the population and most had acquired basic civil and legal rights. The impetus for second-wave feminism was the realization that gaining legal visibility had not ended women's subordination to men. On the contrary, existing law and policy had codified the dependency of women on men. Thus, if women were to be free, it was necessary to repeal inherently paternalistic legislation and policies based on a welfare model of family and state. It was also necessary to implement socio-legal reforms premised on an egalitarian model of family and the principles of gender neutrality and formal equality in both the public and private spheres (Adamson, Briskin, and McPhail 1988).

Liberal feminism was the second-wave feminist perspective that most influenced family-related law and policy. Like maternal feminists, liberals focus on sex/gender comparisons, but they assume "sameness," not "difference." Following this assumption, women have the same capabilities as men, yet few develop their full potential because they are socialized to adopt the "feminine" role of caregivers and housekeepers and, if they do enter the public realm, most do not have the same opportunities as men. For liberal feminists, then, the key to women's liberation was for women to become more like men through (re)socialization and participation in the world of men. Thus, liberal feminists embraced somewhat different conceptions of state, law, and family than their maternal feminist predecessors, and they advocated reforms compatible with the assumption that there are no sex-specific traits, capabilities, and needs (Boyd and Sheehy 1986).

Nonetheless, liberal feminists continued to embrace the maternal feminist view of the nuclear family as the "norm" and assumed that most women would marry and bear children. Unlike first-wave feminists, however, they made a direct link between "liberation" and women's economic independence. Therefore, while they accepted the bourgeois family form, liberal feminists implicitly challenged the idea of separate spheres and the sexual division of labour by arguing for the movement of married women en masse out of the home into paid employment. Once women were economically viable, equality with men would follow (Boyd and Sheehy 1986).

In contrast to maternal feminists, second-wave liberal feminists viewed the paternalistic welfare state as a cause of women's continued subordination, and they embraced a more classical liberal conception of the state as a mediator or umpire, particularly in the public sphere. Liberal feminists assumed that once women gained the same access and opportunity to compete in the public sphere as men, the state would not treat their interests any differently from those of men. Like their first-wave precursors, however, liberal feminists believed that discrimination against women could be removed through a process of incremental reform without any fundamental restructuring of social institutions (Boyd and Sheehy 1986).

Consequently, second-wave feminists retained the maternal feminist emphasis on law as a major vehicle for achieving and guaranteeing women's equality. In Canada, the *Report of the Royal Commission on the Status of Women* (Canada 1970) established the second-wave reform agenda for the next two decades. A quintessentially liberal-feminist document, the report emphasized the implementation of gender neutrality and formal equality in law and policy and based on these principles set out numerous recommendations for reform that would collectively make women's equality with men a reality. Overall, liberal feminists helped bring about an overhaul of the family-related law and social policy that maternal feminists had fought for and, thus, contributed to a restructuring of the Canadian welfare state (Andrew and Rodgers 1997).

Whereas maternal feminists fought to enhance the position of women within the family, their second-wave successors wanted legislation and policies that would allow flexibility and interchangeability of roles for women and men in both the private and public spheres. Beginning with the implementation of a federal Divorce Act in 1968, Canada's family law system was extensively (re)formed and now incorporates an egalitarian as opposed to a welfare model of (nuclear) family (Eichler 1997). Legislation and policies are based on principles of gender neutrality and formal equality, and there are no rights to custody, property, and financial support based on sex (Mossman and MacLean 1986, 1997).

Current family law and policy related to parenting, for example, rest on the assumptions that women are no more predisposed than men to care for children and that fathers and mothers are equally capable of parenting. As the introduction to the 1979 B.C. Family Relations Act stated, the new law was designed to recognize "the changing roles of spouses" and to "place parents on more equal footing in custody and access disputes." Therefore, when a marriage ends, children should be placed with the parent who can best serve their interests. The gender-neutral "best interests of the child" principle thus displaced the tender years doctrine that gave preference to fit mothers of young children in custody and access decisions (Boyd 1989a).

Parental-leave policies also incorporate the notion of equal parenting. A 1990 amendment to the Unemployment Insurance Act (now the Employment Act) allows either parent to take ten weeks' leave following the birth or adoption of a child. The rationale for parental leave is the reduction of work-family conflict and the potential for changing the sexual division of labour both at home and in the workplace (Evans and Pupo 1993; Iyer 1997).

Today the principles of gender neutrality and formal equality also govern federal and provincial marital property laws. Following the 1973 Supreme Court of Canada decision in *Murdoch*, women's groups joined with other reformers to rectify the weaknesses in legislation based on the concept of separate property regimes. Now the division of marital property is based on the principle of equalization incorporated in a deferred community property regime. As a general rule, separate property rights exist so long as a marriage is intact but, if the relationship ends, all marital property is shared equally between the spouses (Steel 1985). Moreover, the concept of property has been expanded greatly to include "virtually anything of which one could conceive," including such assets as pensions and academic degrees (Morton 1988: 260).

With regard to financial support, contemporary family law is based on the principle of spousal self-sufficiency and equal parental responsibility for maintaining children. Gone are the sex-specific clauses in the divorce, desertion, and other family-related legislation promoted by first-wave feminists that imposed a legal obligation on men to maintain wives and children and required women to be non-adulterous to qualify for support. Current legislation applies not only to legal marriages but also to common-law unions and, in British Columbia, to same-sex relationships of at least two years' duration. The courts assume that in most cases of marital breakdown each spouse can attain economic independence and contribute financially to the upkeep of their children. Therefore, spousal support is viewed as unnecessary or as short-term assistance awarded for the sole purpose of allowing a dependent partner to become self-sufficient. As stated in *Maw* v. *Maw*: "Absent an agreement to maintain, only where self-sufficiency is not possible can there be a lifetime obligation to support."

Since the 1960s, however, the increasing number of people, primarily women and children, who are impoverished following a marital breakdown has generated court decisions and public policies aimed at ensuring the payment of spousal and child support that is awarded. The historical pattern of default on support orders did not disappear when new provincial family relations laws were enacted during the 1970s and 1980s, and several provinces (including British Columbia, Manitoba, and Ontario) created maintenance-enforcement programs to reduce the astronomical rate of non-compliance. Such programs are state-ordered collections on behalf of persons who are not receiving spousal or child support; for example, an individual who consistently fails to make payments without good reason may have his or her wages garnisheed.

Notwithstanding these reforms, family welfare law still incorporates sex-specific assumptions about morality and the family unit. The "man in the house" rule—now the "spouse in the house" rule—remains in the social assistance legislation of every province. While ostensibly gender-neutral, the spousal rule almost always is used to disqualify women who live with men from receiving benefits (Gavigan 1993, 1998; Martin 1992; Mossman and MacLean 1997).

Contradictory and differential effects of second-wave reforms
The overhaul of family-related legislation and policies achieved, in part, by second-wave feminists has generated effects no less contradictory and differential than those produced by socio-legal reforms enacted through the efforts of first-wave feminists (Andrew and Rodgers 1997; Busby, Fainstein, and Penner 1990). On the positive side, family law based on the principles of gender neutrality and formal legal equality ended the blatant sexual discrimination and enforced dependency embedded in the old desertion statutes and mothers' allowances legislation. For example, the new family relations

acts did not contain adultery clauses, and thus women were no longer held accountable to a sexual double standard.

Parental leave also reinforces the feminist critique of the sexual division of labour. By enabling fathers to assume child-care responsibilities in the private sphere, the policy helps to undercut the pervasive belief that women "by their nature" are predisposed towards, and better at, "motherwork" than men (Rosenberg 1990). Similarly, the policy has the potential to improve women's position in the public sphere because they can remain attached to the paid labour force on leave while they stay home to care for a child, rather than leaving the ranks of the employed altogether (Evans and Pupo 1993; Iyer 1997).

Another positive result of second-wave family law reforms was the increased recognition of women's economic contribution to marriage through the implementation of deferred community property regimes for the spousal division of family assets upon marital breakdown. Redefining property to include social benefits such as pensions and intangible assets such as academic degrees has benefited many women: those who, like Irene Murdoch, had never been part of the paid workforce when divorce ended a long-time marriage; and women who periodically left the labour force and/or worked part-time to accommodate child-care responsibilities during a marriage (Keet 1990; Steel 1985).

Finally, the family-related socio-legal reforms promoted by second-wave feminists have recognized, to some degree, different types of cohabitation; specifically, that many heterosexual and same-sex common-law relationships resemble legal marriages. Now the maintenance sections of the provincial family relations acts apply to heterosexual, common-law unions, and, in British Columbia, to same-sex relationships. In addition, a precedent-setting 1997 Ontario Court of Appeal decision in the case of *M. v. H.* upheld the claim of a lesbian for spousal support from her financially better-off former partner. The appeal court accepted M.'s argument that the Ontario Family Law Act discriminated on the basis of sexual orientation because it did not apply to same-sex partners, one of whom was dependent upon the other when the relationship ended. If the Supreme Court of Canada upholds the appeal court's decision in *M. v. H.*, the door will be open to define same-sex unions as common-law unions in all family law provisions governing support (Gavigan 1998).

While family property law still applies only to married couples, heterosexual and, in British Columbia, same-sex common-law couples are able to use constructive trust doctrine when dividing property at the end of a relationship. In 1992, for example, the B.C. Supreme Court found that Michael Forrest and William Price "lived in a lengthy, sexually faithful relationship for thirteen years" that was "tantamount in all respects to a traditional heterosexual marriage." Therefore, Forrest, who had assumed a homemaker role, was entitled to a share of Price's assets (*Vancouver Sun* November 5, 1992: B1). This judgment has obvious implications for other cases involving same-sex couples who dissolve a long-term relationship (Duclos 1991; Gavigan 1995).

Although few regret the repeal of legislation and policies rooted in paternalism, feminists have been confronted with the unpleasant reality that implementing formal legal equality in family law and social welfare did not end women's structured dependency, and actually intensified it in some instances upon marital breakdown (Andrew and Rodgers 1997; Busby, Fainstein, and Penner 1990). But why and how does legislation based on an egalitarian model of family and principles of gender neutrality and formal equality continue to help reproduce and sustain women's inequality? Liberal feminists did not foresee that strict adherence to the principle of formal equality in the absence of substantive equality inevitably produces unequal outcomes; treating unalikes in the same way merely perpetuates differences. In short, like maternal feminists before them, liberal feminists ultimately failed to challenge the ideological and structural roots of the bourgeois family form. This failure to interrogate prevailing assumptions about the normality of heterosexual marriage, the sexual division of labour, and the public/private split was reflected in legal practice where decision-making about custody, property, and spousal/child support often has been detrimental for women.

Overall, child custody law based on gender neutrality and formal equality has given fathers more power to lay claim to their children than they had before the law was changed, and with no corresponding increase in their caregiving obligations. Since the 1970s the percentage of cases in which mothers retain sole custody of children after a separation or divorce by agreement with the fathers has dropped, joint (legal) custody arrangements have gone up, and, in contested cases, men have a good chance of "winning" (Bertoia and Drakich 1993; Boyd 1989a: 845). Likewise, since the late 1980s, judicial decisions in cases involving disputes over access of non-custodial fathers to their children often have favoured fathers over mothers (Bourque 1994; Boyd 1997b; Taylor, Barnsley, and Goldsmith 1996). These trends reflect the combined influence of ideologies about family, motherhood, fatherhood, and equality on judicial interpretations of the "best interests of the child" principle (Boyd 1989; Drakich 1989).

Taking the nuclear family based on heterosexual marriage as the norm, many judges assume that it is in the best interests of children to have ongoing contact with two opposite-sex, biological parents, and they conceptualize former spouses and their children as a "post-divorce family" (Boyd 1997b). In Canada and elsewhere, they are handing down judgments about custody and access based on assumptions that children must have a father in their lives and that contemporary men are equally involved in parenting their children (Drakich 1989). Such decisions not only privilege the nuclear family form, but also ignore other pertinent factors: some fathers are bad role models, and most fathers do not contribute equally to the care of their children prior to divorce (Bourque 1994; Boyd 1997b; Taylor, Barnsley, and Goldsmith 1996). Moreover, studies of fathers' rights advocates show that they do not want sole responsibility for children or an equal division of child care and responsibility. Instead, they want equal status as legal parents, which really is a demand "to continue the practice of inequality in postdivorce parenting but now with a legal sanction" (Bertoia and Drakich 1993: 612).

The judicial privileging of marriage also bodes ill for a lesbian who leaves a heterosexual union and ends up in a custody dispute with her former husband. A review of the outcomes in contested cases involving young children after the implementation of gender-neutral law reveals that, regardless of her parenting abilities, a lesbian mother almost always loses custody to the father unless she appears to fit the norms of the "good" mother—white, middle-class, and heterosexual (Arnup 1989; Boyd 1998). The B.C. Supreme Court decision in *Elliott* v. *Elliott* is one of the most explicit judicial statements on the need for mothers to be, or appear to be, heterosexual (Sage 1987). Mr. Elliott gained custody of his seven-year-old daughter, who had been living with her mother, because Ms. Elliott had established a live-in relationship with a lesbian partner. Clearly equating the "best interests" of the child with a heterosexual family environment, the court said: "Whatever one might accept or privately practise, I cannot conclude that indulging in homosexuality is something for the edification of young children" (Sage 1987: 1, 8).

Ideological assumptions about motherhood, fatherhood, and the sexual division of labour strongly influence judicial interpretations of the "best interests" principle as well. On the one hand, the idea that women's primary work is the altruistic care and nurture of other family members means that judges often equate best interests with the stay-at-home mother. Therefore, a woman who engages in full-time or part-time paid employment to support her children may be viewed as abandoning them to pursue her own selfish interests and lose custody to her husband, especially if he has a new homemaker-wife, a housekeeper, or some other surrogate mother to look after the children (Boyd 1989, 1997a). On the other hand, the idea that men's primary work is to protect and materially provide for other family members means that fathers need only to demonstrate some interest in parenting or do some child care to be seen as "super dads," while the work that many women perform routinely is expected and therefore not specifically noteworthy.

Similar thinking influences judicial application of the "friendly parent" provision in the Divorce Act, which directs courts to operate on the principle that children should have as much contact with each parent as is in their "best interests." The onus clearly is on a mother to facilitate contact between children and their father, even if he has been physically or sexually abusive. Otherwise the mother risks losing custody for being unco-operative and putting her own interests before those of the children (Boyd 1989; Rosnes 1997). In *LiSanti* v. *LiSanti*, for example, the wife took her children to a women's shelter to escape the alleged abuse of her husband, who was then awarded interim custody of the children. According to the court, Mrs. LiSanti's "abrupt departure" was "a complete denial of the husband's custodial rights," and "the best interests of the children, were they ever first considered by her, would have militated against such a result." Thus, although Canadian law contains no presumption in favour of joint legal custody, women often are forced to accept de facto or formal joint custody arrangements with fathers (Bourque 1994).

The same ideologies of family, work, and equality have governed judges' interpretations of the ostensibly gender-neutral principle of self-sufficiency in decisions about spousal and child support. Clearly, the courts have tended to assume that women and men are equally capable of being self-supporting after marital breakdown, and they have interpreted self-sufficiency not based on a previous standard of living but on earning any sort of living at all. Therefore, although marriage puts most women in a position of economic dependency (both in the family and in the market), the courts have not considered the substantive inequality in the post-divorce economic situations of most women relative to men, and they expect both spouses to achieve financial independence either immediately or in a very short time after the marriage ends. This condition naturalizes the sexual division of labour that "causes" women's economic dependency. Thus, until recently, women's unpaid domestic labour and the wage gap between women and men engaged in paid employment have been largely invisible in judicial decision-making about spousal and child support. Yet many older women have been full-time home workers, and many more women have had interruptions in their paid employment and/or have worked part-time to care for children during a marriage, with obvious impact on their earning potential after a separation or divorce (Keet 1991; Morton 1993). Moreover, in 1994, even women with full-time, full-year paid employment made only 70 percent of the earnings of their male counterparts in Canada, and among all earners that year women made 62 percent as much as men (Luxton and Reiter 1997: 204; Evans 1998).

Not surprisingly, women are still much more likely than men to be plunged into poverty when a marriage ends, and the feminization of poverty has increased significantly along with the divorce rate since the 1950s. In 1951, one in every twenty-four marriages ended in divorce; by 1990, one couple divorced for every 2.4 who married (Mossman and MacLean 1997: 119). On the issue of financial responsibility for an ex-spouse who does not attain self-sufficiency, the Supreme Court of Canada has adopted two contradictory positions since the mid-1980s. In cases in which the spouses themselves agreed to set a time limit on support payments, the court generally has applied the so-called "causal connection test," which requires the spouse requesting an extended period of support to demonstrate "that he or she has suffered a radical (and unforeseen) change in circumstances flowing from an economic pattern of dependency engendered by the marriage" before it will intervene (Bailey 1989). Because causal connection is difficult to establish, the court generally has treated the spousal agreement as a binding contract and emphasized the principle of self-sufficiency and independence.

In contrast, when the dependent spouse would otherwise become a state dependant on social assistance, the Supreme Court has been willing to intervene in cases in which court-ordered spousal support has existed. The 1992 Supreme Court decision in *Moge* v. *Moge* accepted the claim of the ex-wife that her former husband, who had not lived with her for many years, should continue to pay spousal support. For the first time a Canadian court was swayed by the argument that women's unpaid contributions to a marriage, such as domestic labour and child care, typically were undervalued in spousal support awards and this under-valuing is linked to the feminization of poverty as divorce and separation increase. Thus, "the responsibility for women's poverty should rest wherever possible with a man with whom they have had a recognized relationship" (Boyd 1996: 176–77).

Clearly, family law reforms promoted by liberal feminists and implemented since the 1960s have continued the historical emphasis on the "privatization of the costs of reproduction" (Fudge 1989). This individu-alized focus in law and policy has reinforced the public/private distinction and contributed to the impoverishment of women and children (Boyd 1997b). For example, the maintenance-enforcement programs established in some provinces have reduced the default rate on support payments, and the federal Child Support Guidelines adopted in 1997 have set out minimum levels of support; but neither policy can eliminate or even sub-stantially ameliorate poverty, because both spousal and child support awards are generally so low (Eichler 1991; Pulkingham 1994). Empha-sizing individual responsibility for the "personal" also pre-empts the crea-tion of new social programs. The use of tax exemptions and/or credits for child-care expenses incurred by parents perpetuates the idea that so-cial reproduction is a private rather than a public concern (Eichler 1997). Moreover, social reproduction remains primarily women's work, because the financial rewards for the work of caring for children are so low that men have no incentive to change the sexual division of labour (Ferguson 1998; Iyer 1997).

Like their first-wave precursors, liberal feminists did not anticipate the differential impact of the family-related legislation and policies they promoted. Again, white, middle-class, and upper-class heterosexual women and, to a lesser extent, their counterparts in the more affluent sectors of the working class have benefited the most from the reordering of family law since the 1960s. Poor women and/or women of colour, Aboriginal women, lesbians, and women with disabilities have been dis-proportionately unable to use legislation and policies based on gender neutrality and formal equality (Andrew and Rodgers 1997; Boyd 1997b).

Class differences are important in relation to property, for instance. A deferred property regime is of little relevance to many couples who have no property to split when their relationship dissolves. Or, if com-mon property exists, it is most often a house with a mortgage, so there is nothing to divide except mutual debt. Similarly, child and spousal sup-port obligations imposed on the working poor may mean that two families are impoverished rather than one (Mossman and MacLean 1997).

Child-care policies generate the same disparities. During the 1980s only slightly more than 50 percent of pregnant women in paid employment claimed maternity benefits under unemployment insurance, probably because the benefit was so low that only women and/or couples with a good income to begin with could afford to do so. The situation is even worse under the Employment Insurance Act. Because the benefit remains low (about 55 percent of average insurable earnings), eligibility now is based on hours and not on weeks worked, and the maximum weekly payment has been reduced (Iyer 1997: 187). Tax credits and exemptions for child care also are most helpful to more affluent professional women and couples who can afford to hire domestic workers or to support a stay-at-home mother (Macklin 1992). None of these programs is especially accessible for single, low-income parents, most of whom are women and/or members of racial and ethnic minorities. Moreover, the growing reliance of affluent families on poor women of colour to provide child care has created conflicts among feminists about the exploitation of some women by other, more privileged women (Arat-Koc 1990; Bakan and Stasiulis 1997).

Undeniably, second-wave feminist support for individualized solutions to the problem of women's subordination has helped some women. At the same time it is painfully apparent that a diversity of Canadian women face difficulties that simply were not part of the picture of women painted by the 1970 Royal Commission on the Status of Women (Andrew and Rodgers 1997; Bannerji 1993; Herman 1994; Monture-Angus 1995; Razack 1998; Wendell 1996). The negative and differential effects of family-related reforms promoted by second-wave feminists reflect, in part, some "fatal flaws" of the liberal-feminist approach.

First, liberal feminism does not problematize the state, law, and family. Liberal conceptions of these institutions—the state as "umpire," law as the protector of equality rights, the family as nuclear and private—are taken as givens. They are viewed as homogeneous rather than differentiated and contradictory, timeless as opposed to historically and culturally bounded. Because of a singular focus on enabling women to act and be the same as men, liberal feminism also tends to conceptualize sex and gender in terms of a simple nature/nurture dichotomy. Since biology is not destiny, it is differential socialization of women and men on the basis of biological characteristics that has created sex inequality, which, in turn, is sustained through discriminatory law and policy.

This conceptualization of gender equates socialization with passivity (that is, the individual is acted upon), assumes that socialization is the same for all women and for all men, and ignores the contexts of socialization. Thus, liberal feminists do not see the need to analyse the structural embeddedness of patriarchal relations in state, law, and family; the different forms and content of patriarchal relations in different types of social organization; or how differences generated by race, ethnicity, class, sexual orientation, and (dis)ability shape the social construction of gender. Consequently, they cannot explain the state's role in (re)producing gender relations and the privatization of the reproductive sphere or how patriarchal discourses and ideologies are reflected in and (re)produced through law.

Second, the liberal-feminist explanation of women's subordination is premised on a conceptualization of inequality as "unequal opportunity and access to the world of men." From this perspective, the liberal, capitalist state is basically sound, and achieving equality for women is a matter of addition and subtraction: (re)socialize women to be more "masculine" and men more "feminine"; move women into paid labour; and implement reforms to entrench and guarantee sex equality. Although it implicitly challenges the sexual division of labour, this approach to women's liberation rests on an acceptance of the public-private split and leaves it intact. Simply moving women into paid work does not lead to equality. Most women straddle the production-reproduction divide, and they confront structured inequality on both sides: low-paid clerical and service work and unpaid domestic work (the double day). This structured inequality cannot be rectified by piecemeal reform and (re)socialization. Women's oppression can only be eradicated through systemic change that will not only challenge patriarchal ideologies and discourses but also transform the bourgeois family form that sustains them.

PROSPECTS FOR "REFORM" IN THE NEO-LIBERAL STATE

The problem for feminists is how to mount such a challenge in the current climate of neo-liberalism. While liberal feminism helped to create the reform agenda for the second wave of the women's movement during the 1970s and 1980s, the nature of both the productive process and the state has undergone transformations. "Vampire capitalism" has replaced welfare capitalism through globalization—which entails the radically increased mobility of capital and the international organization of production and distribution—and through restructuring—which involves the reordering of national economic, social, and political systems in keeping with the values of globalization and transnational capital (Cohen 1997: 30). In Canada, as elsewhere, this highly gendered development has brought about significant changes in social relations and women's structural position as well as a very different landscape for the feminist engagement with the state to address women's subordination. The "playing field" has been transformed, and even the limited redistributive gains made by second-wave feminists are now being attacked and eroded. Feminists find themselves engaged in "politics on the margins" as they try to defend what is left of the welfare state that they critiqued so strongly in the past (Brodie 1995).

A central task for feminists is to challenge the neo-liberal idea that now pervades public culture of "the 'inevitability' of the market as the main regulator of social life" (Cohen 1997:30). With the best of intentions, to achieve equality for women second-wave liberal feminists promoted legislation and policies based on a non-interventionist state, gender-neutral law, and an egalitarian model of the nuclear family. The neo-liberal twist on these conceptualizations of state, law, and family—embodied in notions of the genderless international citizen and privatization—has rendered structured inequality and women/gender invisible. While an anti-feminist backlash has diluted and even erased the feminist impact on contemporary law and policy, many feminists continue to see law and the state as critical sites of struggle against the new world order (Adamson, Briskin, and McPhail 1988; Brodie 1995; Gavigan 1993; Razack 1991). Nonetheless, it is also clear that socio-legal reforms per se cannot end women's subordination; women cannot litigate their way to substantive equality. Therefore, feminists must think carefully about the unintended as well as intended consequences of the reforms they advocate and strategize about how they can inject potentially transgressive proposals for family-related law and policy into the political and public cultures (Boyd 1997b; Luxton 1997).

Specifically, feminists need to engage with state power at all levels, defend what remains of the welfare state, and advocate reforms that challenge and subvert the bourgeois model of family. While there is no blueprint for change, feminists could pursue a number of existing proposals for family-related legislation and policies that would contribute to the implementation of a "social responsibility" model of family; one that focuses on "minimizing inequalities that are the result of being married or being a parent instead of on [formal] equality" (Eichler 1997: 130). In the area of custody and access, replacing the "best interests of the child principle" with the "primary caregiver presumption" could benefit some women. However, primary caregiving would have to be defined and the principle applied in a way that recognized the routine, ongoing motherwork performed by women without penalizing them if they do not meet the expectations of "good motherhood" encapsulated in the bourgeois model of family (Boyd 1997b: 272).

Other reforms would challenge the "privatization of the costs of reproduction" (Fudge 1989). For instance, the total elimination of the sexist and paternalistic elements in welfare law—particularly the "spouse in the house rule"—would improve the financial and legal position of sole-support mothers (Gavigan 1993, 1998). Ending the current policy of provincial governments, whereby any child support beyond a minimal amount received by a welfare recipient automatically is deducted from social assistance payments, would also benefit many women and children. An even more comprehensive reform would entail the implementation of a state-subsidized system of child support that would guarantee a minimum income, not only to lone-parent families, but also to parents in low-income families regardless of marital status. This reform would address the issue of child poverty, which cannot be resolved through child and spousal support payments alone (Eichler 1997: 155–56).

Legislation and programs recognizing the inextricable links between women's paid and unpaid work and explicitly challenging the sexual division of labour would also help establish social responsibility for re-production in Canada. While policies such as pay and employment equity aimed at creating equality of opportunity for women (and other equity-seekers) may benefit those who have "good" jobs in the public sector or in large firms, they do nothing for the majority of people entering the current, deteriorating labour market—people who only have equal opportunity to find "bad" jobs. To address the inequalities women confront in both the home and paid employment we need reforms to labour law and policy that recognize the gendered nature of work and the political will of the state "to regulate the labour market in a way that minimizes competition and exploitation at the bottom" (Fudge 1996b: 261–63). In addition, specific policies, such as a national day-care plan that is not implemented through contracting out to private, non-unionized agencies, would help to socialize the costs of reproduction and to address women's inequality. Similarly, reforms to maternity and parental leave programs that raise the monetary benefits and increase the length of the leave period would make them accessible to those women (and men) who cannot afford to take leave under existing programs (Iyer 1997).

Obtaining legislation and policies based on a social responsibility model of family would go some way towards the deconstruction of the neo-liberal agenda and the regressive conceptualizations of state, law, and family that underpin it. Working alone and in alliances with other equality-seeking groups, feminists can mount powerful ideological and political resistance to the status quo. The market as social regulator is not inevitable. Substantive equality for all women and men can be achieved.

NOTE

1.   I am indebted to Elizabeth Comack for her insightful comments and suggestions, her collegiality, and her patience. Thanks also to Karen Busby and Kirsten Johnson for their input on an earlier draft of this essay. What appears here is a different version of a chapter in Nancy Mandell and Ann Duffy (eds.), *Canadian Families: Diversity, Conflict and Change,* 2nd edition (Toronto: Harcourt Brace & Co. Canada, forthcoming).

"Not a Victim until a Conviction Is Entered": Sexual Violence Prosecutions and Legal "Truth"

© Karen Busby

The last two decades have seen a massive increase in public awareness of male violence against women, largely because of the work
of the feminist anti-rape movement. This awareness led to multifaceted
approaches to ending the violence, including the development of counselling services and shelters; ensuring that women have the economic
ability to leave abusive men; improved health care; and, of course, demands that the criminal justice system take women's stories about violence seriously. This essay is about sexual violence prosecutions with a
specific emphasis on how the law justifies certain practices in sexual
violence trials.

Readers must keep in mind that the criminal justice system is not the
only, or even the most important, sector for naming and ending male
violence against women. Women know this. Only about 6 percent of all
incidents of sexual assault—including only 11 percent of more serious
assaults, such as those involving a weapon—are reported to the police
(Roberts 1994).[1] Feminist activists, including feminist academics, are,
at best, ambivalent about the utility of relying on a coercive state to counter
violence against women. Some argue that "the very legal process ...
creates its own order of damages for the abused child or woman. It is
glaringly obvious that the criminal law does not provide a remedy to
sexual abuse; it is increasingly obvious that it causes harm" (Smart 1989:
161). Others argue that women should be in a position to demand that
the system also works for us. As Nancy Matthews (1994: 152) notes:
"Two disjunctures intersect in the movement: for white women, between
the expectation of police responsiveness and police inaction on violence
against women; for women of color, between knowing the lack of police
responsiveness and the desire to demand this as a basic right. The anti-
rape movement demand for police responsiveness *on this issue* became
the dominant approach because it addressed both of these concerns" (emphasis in the original).

Various legal principles—including foundational rules governing all criminal proceedings, laws on what acts constitute sexual offences, and evidentiary and procedural rules specific to sexual offences—work *against* the likelihood of securing a conviction in sexual violence cases. In particular, laws specific to sexual violence offences have reflected and perpetuated women's and children's inequality, and these inequalities are compounded when the complainant is poor, disabled, Aboriginal, racialized, or lesbian. While some of the most blatantly discriminatory laws have been abrogated by legislation, sexual violence laws were founded on rape mythologies, and these beliefs remain deeply insinuated in many judges' reasoning about sexual violence. That most egregious myth—the belief that women and children frequently lie about sexual violence out of malice or delusion—underpins all of the other myths and has never been expressly repudiated by a Canadian judge (Scott and McIntyre 1997). These myths are sustained even though there is no evidence in Canada that the incidence of false reports is higher for sexual offences than for other offences. New mythologies, like the spectre of therapy-induced memories, are conjured up and relied upon in decision-making by the Supreme Court of Canada without evidence or context (*R. v. O'Connor* 1995, *R. v. Carosella* 1997). Judicial pronouncements like these, especially when they emanate from Canada's highest court, have a special power for lawyers: if a judge says something is true, then it is. Lawyers will, for example, cite a judicial pronouncement as authority for a "fact" rather than give an academic reference. Lower courts are also required to apply the legal principles established by higher courts.[2]

In this essay, I describe and examine law's justification or "Official Version" (to use the expression coined by Ngaire Naffine [1990] and discussed in Elizabeth Comack's opening essay here) for why it uses certain legal principles to arrive at its very particular version of the "truth" in sexual violence trials. In particular, I examine the interaction of legal principles, which foster partial and incomplete fact-finding, and rape mythologies, which perpetuate inequalities. The Official Version is so much a part of the terms of reference or methodology of legal professionals that it becomes an unquestioned or natural process, whereas non-lawyers are more likely to recognize the contingency and other flaws of law's account of itself—but they run the risk of being branded by legal professionals as uniformed and unfair if they call the Official Version into question. An examination of these interactions provides the foundation for a more in-depth consideration of other connections between law, sexual violence, and inequality.

FOUNDATIONAL RULES OF CRIMINAL LAW

The important principles underlying the Official Version of Canadian laws on criminal procedures include the idea that criminal convictions are extremely serious and therefore should only be obtained if there is a very high degree of certainty that an offence was committed; and that police should be restrained from using coercive tactics during investigations. Following this, three foundational rules apply in all criminal cases: 1) the person charged (the defendant) is presumed innocent until the charge is proved; 2) the Crown must prove the offence "beyond a reasonable doubt"; and 3) the defendant has the right to silence.

1. Presumption of innocence

Anyone charged with a criminal offence is presumed to be innocent. The Crown has the burden of proving both that the defendant did the acts that amount to an offence and that the defendant intended to commit the acts. To satisfy the intention element in sexual assault cases, the Crown must prove not only that the defendant intended to commit a sexual act but also that he[3] intended to do it in the absence of consent. Evidentiary gaps or weak evidence on any element of the offence will result in an acquittal. Conversely, there is no presumption that the complainant is telling the truth. As one judge said, "One is not a victim until a conviction is entered," because the use of the term "victim" is inconsistent with the presumption of innocence (*R*. v. *Seaboyer* 1992).

2. Proof beyond a reasonable doubt

The Crown is also held to a strict standard in proving the case: the judge or jury must be convinced "beyond a reasonable doubt" when all the evidence is assessed together that the defendant committed the alleged acts. If there is a doubt, the defendant must be acquitted. The Supreme Court of Canada recently stated in *R*. v. *Lifchus* (1997) that jury instructions should include a statement like the following: "Even if you believe the accused is probably guilty, that is not sufficient. In those circumstances, you must give the benefit of the doubt to the accused and acquit because the Crown has failed to satisfy you beyond a reasonable doubt."

In civil cases, such as those in which an injured person seeks financial compensation from the person responsible for the injury, the standard of proof is "balance of probabilities"; that is, which of the parties is to be believed more. In contrast, criminal cases are *not* to be decided on the basis of a credibility contest. The Supreme Court of Canada held in *R. v. W.(D.)* (1991) that when a complainant gives evidence that the defendant denies, the judge or jury is to weigh the evidence using these tests: "First, if you believe the evidence of the defendant, obviously you must acquit. Second, if you do not believe the testimony of the defendant but you are left in reasonable doubt by it, you must acquit. Third, even if you are not left in doubt by the evidence of the defendant, you must ask yourself whether, on the basis of the evidence which you do accept, you are convinced beyond a reasonable doubt by that evidence of the guilt of the defendant."

These tests are strictly applied. In *R. v. Scott* (1997), involving a charge of sexual assault with a weapon, the trial judge found the complainant to be "extremely credible" and stated that he was "impressed with her honesty" and that she did not exaggerate or show vindictiveness. He found the defendant's credibility to be "in question." The trial judge concluded: "If I had to choose between the two, I would unhesitatingly accept the evidence of [the complainant] and, therefore, I find the Crown has proven its case beyond a reasonable doubt." The defendant was found guilty. This verdict was overturned on appeal and a new trial ordered because the last statement, according to the appeal court, indicated that the trial judge improperly decided the case on the basis of a credibility contest.

The "reasonable doubt" standard in sexual violence cases falls well short of a positive response to the question "Is she lying?" Rather it approaches, "Are you convinced about her version of the events?" Therefore, if the defence lawyer can undermine a complainant's credibility in some way or make the case that a different interpretation of the events is possible, a "reasonable doubt" may exist and the defendant should be acquitted. Most commonly, something about the complainant's character will compromise her credibility as a witness. In *R. v. Adams* (1995), for example, the evidence was clear that the complainant had agreed to engage in sexual activities with the defendant, but the judges who heard or read the rest of the evidence described it as confusing and contradictory. She testified that she was threatened with a sword and was forced to perform sexual acts. He testified that she was a prostitute, that he did not want to have sex with her when he discovered she was pregnant, and that she robbed him of $900 and, when confronted, she became hysterical and attacked him. What the judges did *not* note in the formal reasons is interesting: the complainant's denial that she was a prostitute, her evidence that she received a wound at the defendant's hand that required stitches to close, and that she fled from the hotel room in her underwear—information I only found in a newspaper article about the case (Bindman 1995). The trial judge found that neither the complainant nor the defendant was "completely reliable," but gave no explanation for these findings on credibility (and, by law, an explanation is not required). With no independent verification of the events, the benefit of the doubt had to go to the defendant, and he was acquitted. Did the stereotype of the "extortionate prostitute" aid the defendant in this case?

In some historic abuse cases (that is, cases in which the events giving rise to the charge occurred years before the charges were laid) it is not unusual for the judge to state that he or she believes the complainant's evidence but nonetheless has some doubt arising from the defendant's sworn denial and the absence of corroborative evidence. The defence strategy in historic cases is to argue that, because of the passage of time, the evidence is too weak to satisfy the reasonable doubt standard. In *R. v. A.J.G.* (1998), the judge found that the complainant was reliable and had no ulterior motive in laying a complaint against his father. The judge even stated, "I am satisfied that the accused may well have compelled the complainant to ... perform fellatio and sodomized him." Nonetheless, the judge acquitted the defendant, stating "I do not have the degree of certainty required to support a criminal conviction because of the inherent difficulty for any witness to recall and relate accurately events said to have occurred more than 30 years previously and the difficulty for an adult to relate events which are said to have begun at the age of 3. To rest the entire burden of the Crown's case upon such evidence is not safe." Some judges have acknowledged that "such a result is often unsatisfying but is unavoidable" (*R. v. Finley* (1998). Such an acknowledgement rings hollow in the face of the Supreme Court of Canada's assertion that "one is not a victim until a conviction is entered."[4]

Cases involving recovered memories are not likely to meet the "reasonable doubt" standard and, for this reason, are rarely prosecuted. The Ontario Court of Appeal held in *R. v. E.F.H.* (1996) that "we are mindful of the fact that this type of case, perhaps more so than any other, carries with it the potential for a serious miscarriage of justice." *E.F.H*, a rare recovered memory case in which a conviction was obtained, illustrates how difficult such cases are to prosecute. The complainant had repressed memories of sexual abuse until shortly after the birth of her first child. She had been sexually and physically abused by her alcoholic father from a very young age until just after she reached puberty. The trial judge (*E.F.H.* 1994) determined that he first had to be satisfied that the memories were not falsely induced by external sources (like counsellors or self-help books) or were not the internally driven product of an emotionally disturbed person's imagination. Because the father/defendant had testified at trial and denied that the acts had occurred, the judge had to determine the credibility of his evidence. The judge found that he was "incredible" because he lied about certain provable facts, such as his alcoholism and whether he was physically abusive of his wife and other children. But even these two findings (memories were not falsely induced and the defendant was lying) were *not* sufficient to sustain a conviction.

On an appeal affirming the trial decision (*R.* v. *E.F.H.* 1996), the appeal judge described recovered memories as inherently frail in the context of a criminal prosecution and therefore in need of support by confirmatory evidence. The Court of Appeal recognized that "corroborative" evidence (that is, evidence which is independent of the complainant which directly supports the complainant's story) cannot usually be found in sexual violence cases because the acts occur in private and that, in this case, corroborating medical evidence (such as pregnancy and an illegal abortion at age twelve) would have been obliterated by the birth of the complainant's children. However, the trial judge's findings respecting "confirmatory" evidence (that is, independent evidence that indirectly supports the complainant's story) were somewhat reluctantly upheld by the appeal court (leave to appeal to the Supreme Court of Canada was denied). This evidence included information such as her mother finding blood stains on the complainant's underwear prior to puberty, a hemorrhage after a tonsillectomy, which had no medical explanation but was consistent with fellatio, and recovered memories that could be independently verified (such as the father's killing or injuring family pets, which other family members confirmed but the father denied, and the dimensions of the closet where she had hidden from her father).

Without the confirmatory evidence a conviction would not have been sustained in the *E.F.H.* case. While the duration and viciousness of the assaults in the case provided the evidentiary trail requisite for a conviction, the appeal court found that the bizarre nature of the alleged acts (such as fellatio after a tonsillectomy and a repression of an abortion), in and of themselves, gave cause for heightened concern about a wrongful conviction. This finding creates a Catch 22—the confirmatory evidence has to be consistent with the sexual assaults (and not something else), but not so bizarre that it seems incredible. The reasonable doubt standard is, indeed, a difficult one to meet.

3. Right to silence

In law's account, "Perhaps the single most important organizing principle in criminal law is the right of an accused not to be forced into assisting in his or her own prosecution" (*R. v. P.[M.B.]* 1994). A defendant cannot be compelled to testify at his own trial, nor can evidence he has given in a previous proceeding be used against him. Moreover, no adverse inference can be drawn from the failure to testify, unless it is the uncommon case in which the defendant is in the unique position of offering an explanation about an unusual fact. Evidence obtained in violation of the right to silence rule cannot be used at trial even in very serious cases (like murder), except in rare circumstances.

The right to silence extends to the investigative stages of the proceedings. Thus, for example, any statements made by the defendant to the police (or others in authority) will be scrutinized to ensure that they were made voluntarily and taken only after the defendant was advised of the right to a lawyer. If there is any hint that the police used coercion or deception in taking the statement, the statement will be rejected. In *R. v. Moreau* (1986), the police took the complainant to the hospital and then arrested the defendant. The police told the defendant that the medical examination would conclusively determine whether a sexual assault had taken place. After receiving a positive answer to the question—"Doctors can tell for sure, can they?"—the defendant confessed to sexual assault. His conviction was overturned on appeal because the confession was obtained by deception: a medical examination cannot prove with certainty that an assault has taken place.

While fingerprints can be taken of anyone charged with an offence, and search warrants for property can be obtained relatively easily, it is more difficult to obtain body samples from a defendant for DNA testing. Legislation introduced in 1995 to permit and regulate the taking of DNA samples from the accused has been subject, so far unsuccessfully, to *Charter* challenges. Bodily samples (like hair or saliva) obtained without the defendant's consent and either prior to the 1995 legislation or in a manner that is not in accord with it violate the unreasonable search and seizure provisions of the *Charter* and cannot be used in evidence. Even a tissue discarded by a suspect while in custody attracts *Charter* protection (*R. v. Stillman* 1997). By law's account, no adverse inference can be drawn from a failure to give a sample except in accordance with the legislation, as such an inference would be contrary to the right to silence rule.

Few feminists would disagree with the principles underlying the foundational rules of the presumption of innocence, proof beyond a reasonable doubt, and the right to silence given the abuses that would flourish in the absence of such rules. At the same time, these rules also have the effect of creating a truth-seeking process, including the trial, which is partial to the defendant and only permits part of the story to be told. The process by which law arrives at the "truth" falls well short of the methodological standards required by other disciplines.

THE ROLE OF THE CROWN ATTORNEY

Crown attorneys represent the state; they do not represent complainants. With the exception of personal records applications (discussed later in this essay), complainants do not have the status of a party to the proceedings and, even if they could afford it, complainants cannot have independent legal representation in court in criminal cases. While some Crown attorneys are sensitive to the experience of trauma complainants, it is not their role to counsel complainants. Moreover, many Crown attorneys have such high caseloads that they have little time to prepare witnesses for trials (often they only see the file the night before the trial), and even less time to keep complainants informed about the progress of the prosecution. Plea bargains (that is, an agreement between the Crown attorney and the defendant's lawyer that the defendant will plead guilty if the Crown will either drop some charges, reduce the charges, or agree to recommend a lighter sentence than the offence might otherwise attract) usually occur without any input from complainants, and they may not even be informed that a guilty plea has been entered and a sentence pronounced (McGillivray 1998).

The Crown attorney's role is not to obtain convictions. It is to ensure that the evidence in the case is presented fairly. Police lay charges if they have information that suggests there are reasonable and probable grounds to believe that an offence has been committed. The standard for taking a case to trial is higher: the Crown attorney can only proceed when there is a reasonable chance of conviction based on admissible evidence. If they are of the view that this higher standard is not met, they must stay the charges and cannot proceed to trial even when, for example, a complainant wants the case to be heard. If an acquittal is entered, the complainant has no say in determining whether it should be appealed and, if an appeal is made, she cannot participate in the appeal. In law's Official Version, a complainant has no interest in the outcome of criminal proceedings.

THE SPECIFIC ELEMENTS OF SEXUAL OFFENCES

Generally speaking, a defendant in a sexual violence case will be found guilty if the Crown proves beyond a reasonable doubt that he (and not someone else) committed the offence and that the acts amounting to the offence with which the defendant has been charged did occur and the complainant did not (or could not) consent to the acts. The defendant may be found not guilty if he can prove diminished responsibility arising from, for example, insanity. Sexual violence prosecutions in which the defence involves either the defendant's identity or sanity are uncommon. Whether the acts constitute an offence is sometimes in issue, particularly in historic cases. But, in most cases, consent is the contentious issue if the complainant was more than fourteen years of age at the time of the incidents (inaccurate memory is the usual defence for offences against children). Although very few recovered memory cases are prosecuted, when they are several issues arise. Is there a possibility the memory is false? Is the defendant credible (if he testifies)? And are the recovered memories confirmed by other evidence?

1983 Criminal Code *amendments*

The *Criminal Code* provisions on the precise acts necessary to a finding of criminal culpability in sexual offence cases have been subject to revisions by Parliament in 1983, 1985, and 1992. But because the law that applies is the law in effect at the time of the acts giving rise to the charges, the former laws continue to be applied to some historic cases. Thus, for example, for events occurring prior to 1983, proof of vaginal-penile penetration is a requirement in rape cases, and husbands cannot be charged with raping their wives. Some judges are of the view that a pre-1983 rape conviction requires not only an unwilling complainant but also forcible intercourse, which requires some evidence of resistance by the complainant (*R. v. O'Connor* 1998; Łoś 1994).

As sexual offences now only require that there be some sexual element to the acts, proof of the acts themselves (apart from issues of credibility) is not usually problematic in cases in which the events took place after the 1983 amendments. For example, the New Brunswick Court of Appeal held, in *R. v. Chase* (1984), that grabbing a woman's breasts did not constitute a sexual assault because breasts, "like a man's beard," were secondary sexual characteristics, and it overturned the conviction. The evidence also established that a forty-year-old man had entered the home of a fifteen-year-old girl, uninvited, and grabbed her. He said, "Come over here, don't hit me. I know you want it." She had prevented him from touching her genitals. This decision was overturned by the Supreme Court of Canada (1987), which held that a sexual assault is committed in circumstances of a sexual nature such that the sexual integrity of the victim is violated.

1985 Criminal Code *amendments*
Until 1985, sexual offences against children focused on whether the complainant was "of previously chaste character" and applied, in most cases, only to females. The 1985 *Criminal Code* amendments, which mainly concerned offences against children, are gender-neutral and based on a combination of age, power dynamics, and specific activities. For example, consent is not a defence to any sexual offence charge if the complainant is under twelve; if the complainant is twelve or thirteen, consent is not a defence unless the defendant is less than two years older than the complainant. A person who is in a position of trust or authority, or with whom the complainant is in a relationship of dependency, who engages in sexual activity with someone between fourteen and seventeen commits an offence. "Procuring" and other prostitution-related offences attract harsher sentences if minors are involved.

In the age-based cases, the judges still sometimes discount the harm flowing from the offence. For example, in *R v. Bauder* (1997), the Manitoba Court of Appeal commented in a sentencing appeal that "the [twelve-thirteen-year-old] girl, of course, could not consent in the legal sense, but nonetheless was a willing participant. She was apparently more sophisticated than many her age and was performing many household tasks including babysitting the accused's children. The accused and his wife were somewhat estranged." This statement is even more shocking in that the girl never testified, because the defendant entered a guilty plea. All three of the appeal judges who heard the case had no problem simply agreeing with defence counsel's unsupported assertion that the twelve-year-old was a "willing participant." As Anne McGillivray (1998: 381) notes, "myths abounded" in the *Bauder* case:

> Sexual abuse does not hurt; children are not believable; children should be spared the trauma of testifying at whatever cost to the administration of justice and to their own sense of justice; and sophisticated little girls ensnare innocent men, jail-bait to the last: "willing," "sophisticated" and consenting, leading men on, playing grown-up, bullying them. That the law says they cannot consent factually or legally is a minor problem in myth making.

1992 Criminal Code *amendments*
When consent or memory is the contentious issue, the defence lawyer's likely strategy will be to raise some doubt about whether the complainant is telling the truth. A complainant's credibility can be undermined by, for example, showing bias, prejudice, bad character, inconsistent previous statements, impaired capacity to recall, or possibly false memories. While feminists have attempted to limit how credibility attacks can be mounted against complainants (see the section here on special evidence rules for sexual violence cases), another strategy has been to redefine the legal meaning of "consent" by imposing positive obligations on parties to obtain voluntary agreements and imposing age restrictions on some activities.

The 1992 amendments to the *Criminal Code* (often referred to as Bill C-49) redefined the "consent" element in sexual assault law to be the voluntary agreement of the complainant to engage in specific sexual activity at a specific time, rather than, for example, whether she offered a sufficient degree of resistance or whether she consented on a previous occasion. This amendment is intended to shift the factual and legal issue at trial away from what the defendant might have thought to what the complainant actually said or otherwise communicated at the time of the incidents. By this law, initiators of sexual activity should no longer be able to rely upon stereotypes or fantasies about women or even their knowledge of specific complainants' sexual lives to assume consent, but rather have the positive obligation of determining whether the real, present woman is agreeing on the particular occasion to sexual activity. For greater specificity, the 1992 amendments also provide that no consent is obtained if a third party purports to make the agreement; the complainant is incapable of consenting; the accused induces consent by abusing a position of trust, power, or authority; or the complainant expresses by word or conduct a lack of agreement to engage or to continue engaging in the activity.

The Crown is required to prove that the defendant knew that the complainant was not consenting or that he was being reckless about whether she consented or not (*R. v. Sansregret* 1985). Therefore defendants can rely on the "honest-but-mistaken belief in consent" defence: the defendant testifies that he "honestly" believed that the complainant was consenting to the acts in question. Prior to 1992 the test was whether the defendant himself honestly believed this, and his belief could be based on, for example, his information on the sexual history of the complainant or even his own ideas about the "kinds" of women who would consent. While there had to be an "air of reality" to his assertion, it was irrelevant whether she was, in fact, not consenting or what a "reasonable person" watching the events would have believed about consent. The 1992 amendments limit the mistaken belief defence by restricting it to situations in which the defendant actually took "reasonable steps" to ascertain that the complainant was consenting. This change places the burden on the defendant to substantiate his claim of belief in consent. The bill also eliminates the defence altogether when the defendant was intoxicated or wilfully blind to the complainant's non-consent.

Research by Meredith, Mohr, and Cairns Way (1997: 42) on the first three years of Bill C-49 could not identify any "impacts of the Bill C-49 amendments concerned with consent as a defence in sexual assault cases," except the requirement that the defendant demonstrate that he had taken "reasonable steps" to determine if the complainant was consenting. Therefore, while the 1992 amendments on consent and mistaken belief in consent represent a significant theoretical shift in the elements of sexual assault, it is a shift that, at best, is slow to be integrated into the day-to-day reasoning of courts in these cases.

GENERAL EVIDENCE RULES

Some of the facts that need to be proved in sexual violence cases include the elements of the offence, such as "Did he obtain her voluntary agreement?" and "Did he take reasonable steps to ascertain whether she was consenting?" As well, in law's Official Version the credibility of a witness is also something that can be proved or disproved, and is always an issue. Information is admissible in court if it is relevant and reliable.

While there is usually a high degree of consensus on what information is relevant, it must nonetheless be recognized that this determination, especially on credibility issues, will be influenced by a judge's experience and social location. Judges in Canada are still predominately male and from upper-middle-class origins. Overwhelmingly, they are white, heterosexual, and able-bodied (except for age-related disabilities, such as visual impairments). As one Supreme Court of Canada judge said, a credibility determination "is a decision particularly vulnerable to the application of private beliefs.... There are certain areas of inquiry where experience, common sense and logic are informed by stereotype and myth" (*R. v. Seaboyer* 1991).

R. v. Brown (1994) provides a good example of how experience and common sense inform credibility findings. Defence counsel argued that the complainant, who was thirteen at the time of the incidents giving rise to the charges, should not be believed because, if she had been abused as alleged, she would not have maintained contact with the defendant (her best friend's father) and that, if she had been bruised and bleeding as alleged, she would have gone to a doctor. The trial judge's rejection of these arguments, presumably based on her common sense and experience, was criticized by the appeal court, which stated that a trial judge cannot reject such arguments out of hand unless there is *expert* evidence that would explain the complainant's conduct. Implicitly the appeal court judges' view of "common sense" was that a thirteen-year-old would have taken the initiative to end all contact with the defendant (and therefore her friend) and taken herself to a doctor.

Reliability

Various evidence rules have been developed to try to ensure the reliability or competence of witnesses, that is, their ability to tell the truth. For example, courts will not receive the testimony of children under fourteen under oath unless it is first established that the child understands some notion of a moral obligation to tell the truth and has the capacity to perceive, remember, and communicate events. In the rare cases in which a mature minor or adult has a mental disability that affects his or her reliability, expert witnesses may be called upon to give evidence about the impact of the disability on the memory, perception, or ability to communicate. In her analysis of trial transcripts in *R. v. Mohammed,* Sherene Razack (1998: 142) describes the effect of questioning a complainant (who had a mild mental disability) about her disability: "It was quickly established that Lisa did indeed have some understanding that she was under oath to tell the truth, but her competence was possibly acknowledged at the expense of her credibility, as she explained to the court in childlike phrases that she knew God would punish her if she lied."

Relevance: Prior convictions
General evidence rules exclude information that may be relevant if the probative value (that is, light that the evidence might shed on the case) is outweighed by a competing concern flowing from its use in criminal proceedings. Thus, for example, the Crown cannot enter evidence of a defendant's prior convictions or character unless the defendant testifies or otherwise raises these issues, for example, by having others testify that the defendant was not the sort of person who could have committed the acts. How does the law justify this rule? The fact that the defendant has committed crimes in the past or that he is generally regarded as a bad person is of little relevance, for it does not tell the judge or jury much about whether he committed the specific acts in issue. Moreover, it is unfair to require the defendant to account in the course of a criminal trial for every previous wrongdoing. Finally, such an inquiry would lengthen trial proceedings considerably. However, if a conviction is obtained, prior offences are relevant to the issue of sentence and therefore such evidence can be received at a sentencing hearing.

Even if the defendant does testify and thereby puts his own credibility in question, the judge can restrict questioning on character, including criminal record. What is law's justification for this rule? As one appeal court judge stated, "Generally, previous convictions [against a defendant] for violent offences such as sexual assault do not directly reflect on honesty and truthfulness and, depending on the circumstances of the case, have limited probative value in assessing credibility" (*R. v. Charland* 1996).

The rules on character evidence do not apply with the same force to other witnesses, including complainants. The defence frequently uses character evidence, including cross-examination on criminal records, to undermine complainants' credibility. Law justifies this double standard on the ground that witnesses are not being tried and therefore do not risk the serious consequences of a criminal conviction.

Relevance: Similar fact

Another exclusionary rule concerns "similar fact evidence," which is information that the accused has committed acts on other occasions that are similar to the subject matter of the charge before the court. Like evidence on the defendant's character, similar fact evidence is not admissible because such evidence has the severely prejudicial effect of inducing the jury to think of the accused as a "bad" person who has a propensity to commit such acts, but the evidence possesses little relevance to the precise issue of whether the accused committed the particular act described in the charge. In other words, by law's account, the fact that someone has committed other acts of sexual violence does not tell us much about whether he committed the assault that is the subject of the charge. There is an exception to this rule: the evidence can be received if the similar acts "are so unusual and strikingly similar that their similarities cannot be attributed to coincidence" (*R. v. C.[M.H.]* 1991).

Two examples illustrate how the similar fact rule might apply. In *R. v. Smith* (1915) the defendant was charged with murdering his first wife after his second and third wives died in the same manner as the first: drowning in the bathtub. As it was unlikely that the unusual manner of the three deaths could be attributed to coincidence, evidence on the manner of the deaths of the second and third wives could be received to support an inference of foul play. However, as *R. v. Khan* (1996) demonstrates, the application of the "unusual and strikingly similar" rule is not always straightforward. In that case, the defendant's sister was found dead in a deep freezer with tranquillizing drugs in her system. The cause of death was asphyxia. Three years later, the defendant's new wife was found dead in a bathtub, again from asphyxia, and again with drugs in her system. Both women were heavily insured by the defendant, and he was the beneficiary. The Manitoba Court of Appeal held that the two charges of murder against the defendant should not have been heard at the same trial because, by law's account, the evidence adduced on one count was not probative of the other count. Moreover, the evidence in one case could give rise to improper inferences about the kind of person the defendant was and, therefore, was highly prejudicial.

While similar fact evidence can be admitted in child sexual abuse cases, the exceptions overtake the already narrow "so unusual and strikingly similar" rule, with the result that such evidence is unlikely to be admissible in many child sexual abuse cases (including historic and recovered memory cases). For example, the evidence is unlikely to be received to show that the *modus operandi* of the defendant is the same, because it is unlikely that the *modus* will be significantly different from that used by many abusers (for example, "He told me never to tell anyone"; "It only happened when Mom was not home"). Therefore, the evidence is not probative. On the other hand, if the "so unusual" test is met, the Catch 22 described in *E.F.H.* (1996) could come into play: its bizarreness is cause for heightened concern about its credibility. As well, the Supreme Court of Canada said in *R. v. Burke* (1996) that similar fact evidence should be regarded with suspicion if there was any opportunity for collusion or collaboration to concoct the evidence between the complainants or a complainant and another witness giving similar fact evidence. Such contact opportunities would be the norm rather than the exception, because they would include, for example, cases in which the complainants are relatives, are participating in civil actions, were involved in the same organizations or institutions, or come from the same geographical area.

Special Evidence Rules for Sexual Violence Cases

For centuries the special evidence rules have applied to sexual violence cases. The rules, as formal principles or by judicial application, have permitted far greater range for attacking the complainant's credibility than is permitted in other criminal cases.

John Wigmore (1970: 736), whose treatise on evidence law has been called the single most famous work in any field of law, stated: "Modern psychiatrists have amply studied the behavior of errant young girls and the women coming before the courts in all sorts of cases. Their psychic complexes are multifarious and distorted.... One form taken by these complexes is that of contriving false charges of sexual offences by men. The unchaste mind finds incidental but direct expression in the narration of imaginary sex incidents of which the narrator is the heroine or victim.... The real victim, however, too often in such cases is the innocent man." He went on to advocate that sexual offences ought not to be prosecuted unless a psychiatrist had testified as to the complainant's ability to tell the truth.

Wigmore's assertion was not good science (Bienen 1983) when first asserted in 1934, and although the paragraph quoted here was repeated in all subsequent editions of the work, the psychiatric examination of complainants did not become a general requirement for sexual violence prosecutions as suggested. However, the thinking underlying his proposition—that women and children frequently lie about sexual violence out of delusion or malice—remains deeply ingrained in sexual violence law. Until the 1983 *Criminal Code* amendments, for example, the law required that a complainant's testimony had to be corroborated (that is, directly supported by independent evidence) before a conviction could be entered for some sexual offences. For other sexual offences, a judge had to warn a jury that it was dangerous to convict in the absence of corroboration.

While corroboration is no longer required for any sexual offences and the jury warnings do not have to be given, the *Adams* and *A.G.J.* cases demonstrate that the absence of corroborative evidence can still be fatal to a prosecution. Similarly, if a complainant failed to tell someone about the assault at the first reasonable opportunity after it occurred, the "recent complaint" doctrine required judges to tell juries that this failure supported a strong presumption of unreliability. The belief underlying this rule—and freely described as such by judges in law's official account—was that women would fabricate complaints if given time to think them up in order to protect their reputations against allegations of consensual but extramarital sex. While this doctrine was also abrogated in 1983, it re-emerges in cases in which judges draw negative inferences from a complainant's failure to obtain a medical examination immediately after an assault (Feldberg 1997).

Abolition of the formal discriminatory evidence rules makes little practical difference, as demonstrated in cases like *Adams* and *A.J.G.,* as to whether a complainant's account is accepted. But, as described in the next two sections, the most egregious special evidence rules are those permitting defence lawyers to question a complainant about her sexual history and the emerging practice of defence access to complainants' personal records.

Sexual history evidence

At common law, a complainant in a sexual violence case could be questioned about her sexual history because, according to law's official explanation, this information was relevant to her general credibility (unchaste women were less worthy of belief) and to whether she consented (unchaste women were more likely to consent to the acts giving rise to the charge than chaste women). These two uses of sexual history—often referred to as the "twin myths"—and the discriminatory logic underlying them were so firmly embedded in Canadian law that it took specific legislative amendment in 1983 to remove them from the law, and even these amendments were subjected to a constitutional challenge in the *Seaboyer* (1991) case. The Supreme Court of Canada also repudiated the laws on the "twin myths" of sexual history evidence in rejecting this part of the constitutional challenge in *Seaboyer*.

i. The *Seaboyer* case

In *Seaboyer,* the Court also struck down the 1983 *Criminal Code* amendment that restricted the admissibility of evidence on the complainant's sexual history to three circumstances: testimony by someone other than the accused stating that it was he (and therefore not the accused) who committed the acts in question; to give evidence of sexual activity on the same occasion to support a mistaken belief defence; or to rebut evidence adduced by the Crown on the complainant's sexual reputation (for example, she is a nun and therefore would not have consented). The Court now stated that the complainant's sexual history might be relevant and admissible in other, additional situations. By way of illustration only, the Court gave these examples: to explain the complainant's physical condition; to prove bias or motive to fabricate; to establish similar fact conduct on the part of the complainant; and to support a mistaken belief defence. While the Court predicted that it would be an exceptional case in which the evidence would be admitted and expressed confidence that judges were now free of the biases that characterized an earlier age, the guidelines were so open-ended that they would encourage defence attempts to admit the evidence and ensure the success of such attempts.

The *Seaboyer* decision outraged people across Canada, and that outrage mobilized demands for Parliament to act (McIntyre 1994). Parliament responded with the 1992 amendments (often referred to as Bill C-49), which stated in its preamble that a complainant's sexual history is rarely relevant and its admission should be subject to particular scrutiny, bearing in mind the inherently prejudicial character of such evidence. The bill makes it clear (again) that the evidence cannot be used to support the inference arising from the twin myths respecting character and consent. It also stated that the evidence had to be of specific instances of sexual behaviour, relevant to an issue at trial, and of significant probative value that was not substantially outweighed by the danger of its prejudice. Bill C-49 has been subjected to a constitutional challenge (*R. v. Darrach* 1998), scheduled to be heard by the Supreme Court during the 1998–99 sessions.

ii. Indirect uses of sexual history

In some situations, defence counsel does not need to solicit direct evidence on a complainant's sexual history, but rather can rely on stereotypes held by judges and juries about the sexuality of certain "kinds" of women. The judge in the *Adams* case, for instance, seems to have been influenced by the defendant's testimony that the complainant was a prostitute (an allegation she denied, but a factor that, in any event, should not have had any bearing on her credibility). Questions concerning a complainant's manner of dress at the time of the assault are routine. In *R. v. Ewanchuk* (1998), one appeal court judge stated, "It was a hot summer day and both [the complainant and the defendant] were wearing shorts and T-shirts. Underneath her shorts and T-shirt, the complainant wore a brassiere and panties." Later he sarcastically stated that the complainant did not present herself for the job interview offered to her by the defendant "in a bonnet and crinolines." Other wholly irrelevant details about the complainant's sexual life managed to find their way into the judgment, including that she was a seventeen-year-old mother of a six-month-old baby and that she shared an apartment with her boyfriend and another young couple.

Judges often note that a complainant did not appear to be vindictive (for example, the *Scott* and *A.J.G.* cases). Implicit in such comments is that if complainants fail to maintain an appropriate demeanour (a presentation fraught with race and class implications) under cross-examination they may be perceived as vengeful. Razack (1997), in her analysis of the *R. v. Mohammed* case, notes that after the defence lawyer challenged a mentally disabled complainant's reliability, he went on to rely on the stereotype of a woman made vengeful when her advances were rejected. Razack (1998: 142) observes: "Familiar as the idea of a vengeful woman is, one wonders to what extent this line of argument is rendered more plausible by the assumption that a fat woman with a disability is inherently unrapeable and will stop at nothing to get the male attention usually denied to her. As Anne Finger notes, the stereotype of asexuality often applied to women with disabilities also has its opposite: people with disabilities are sometimes seen as 'diseased lusts' and, in the case of women, potential prostitutes." Razack goes on to note that the defence's "vengeful woman" would have had to have been smart enough to "cry rape," a position at odds with the earlier assertion that the complainant was not intelligent enough to understand an oath.

In *R. v. R.Y.* (1996) the judge, commenting adversely on the thirteen-year-old complainant's credibility, noted that she was "precocious. She was combative with defence counsel. She scowled at him. She glared at him. She showed impatient disdain.... She engaged in semantic duels.... She was as vigorous at the end of her testimony as she was at the beginning. I must confess to a feeling of unease with respect to [her] facile manner." The complainant's failure to maintain the docile demeanour expected of a real victim had a clear influence on the outcome of the case. The judge concluded that the defendant "may very well have committed the offences with which he is charged. Indeed, I believe that the accused probably did commit the offences. However, on the totality of the evidence, I am not convinced beyond a reasonable doubt that he did."

iii. Effectiveness of Bill C-49

The work of Meredith, Mohr, and Cairns Way (1997) on the first three years of Bill C-49's operation presents a bleak picture of its effectiveness in preventing even more intensive questioning on sexual history by defence counsel. Applications to have sexual history admitted are made in 10 to 20 percent of sexual violence cases and, it appears, they are often successful.[5] Meredith, Mohr, and Cairns Way's review of the case law indicates that judges, particularly appeal court judges, find the evidence to be relevant if it "might, under any circumstances, have some potential connection" to issues of credibility, bias or motive, or mistaken belief. The study also found that judges have "little or no understanding of the impact of the 'twin myths' and the likelihood that a jury will be unable to 'disabuse' its mind of those myths when presented with such evidence" (Meredith, Mohr, and Cairns Way 1997: 16). The Supreme Court of Canada's prediction that the evidence would be admitted only rarely and that judges were free of the old biases has not been realized even with the Bill C-49 requirements, which are more stringent and explicit than the *Seaboyer* guidelines.

For example, in *R*. v. *Ecker* (1995), the complainant and the defendant first met, at the bar where the complainant worked, sometime in the two-week period before they met again at a party on the night of the events in question. The defendant was charged with break and enter and sexual assault after entering the complainant's home in the middle of the night, taking off his clothes, climbing into her bed, and awakening her. The Saskatchewan Court of Appeal overturned the convictions and ordered a new trial because the trial judge had not admitted evidence that, on the occasion of their first meeting, the complainant sat on the defendant's lap and placed her hands on his genitals. This evidence was relevant, according to the appeal court, because it might have influenced his interpretation of events or made him believe that she would welcome the late-night visit two weeks later. The decision makes no mention of the Bill C-49 provisions on consent or mistaken belief.

In another case, *R. v. Majid* (1995), the Supreme Court of Canada affirmed a Saskatchewan Court of Appeal decision overturning a conviction of sexual assault. Both appeal courts ordered admittance of a letter the complainant had written to a former lover (not the defendant) as relevant to the issue of motive or bias. The letter expressed disappointment at the failure of their relationship and also described other unhappy sexual encounters. The Saskatchewan court held that "the fact that she had past sexual experiences did not indicate that she was less likely to be truthful, but the fact that she recounted them in this fashion made her testimony less reliable." Such letters, though, are not uncommon, and both the appeal and Supreme Court of Canada decisions do not make obvious or explain the basis for this determination.

In some cases, defence counsel seeks evidence of prior sexual abuse (which is conflated with sexual history) to show that, because the complainant has been proven in a criminal court to have been abused, she has a disordered sexual perception that could lead to misinterpretations, overreactions, and false criminal accusations. Alternatively, the defence seeks such evidence to be entered to show that the complainant has made allegations of prior abuse that did not result in a criminal conviction. The absence of a conviction respecting such allegations, goes the faulty inference, indicates that she has a tendency to lie. Thus, argues defence counsel, any evidence of the prior sexual abuse should be used to compromise a complainant's credibility. The Crown could adduce evidence of prior sexual abuse to contextualize, for example, a mentally disabled complainant's particular responses to sexual aggression, a strategy Razack (1998) suggests. This strategy has not been pursued because if the Crown puts the complainant's sexual history at issue, the door is opened wide to a defence cross-examination of her complete sexual history, an ordeal no complainant should have to endure.

As we have seen in the case of character evidence and similar fact evidence, courts exclude evidence that could lead to improper inferences when its probative value is low. Ironically, most people in Canada believe that a complainant cannot be questioned about her sexual history—

and celebrate this legal breakthrough. Yet, notwithstanding the Supreme Court of Canada's prediction and Parliament's clear intent that sexual history evidence should only be used rarely because it is not relevant and it supports improper inferences, such evidence is frequently used in one way or another in sexual violence proceedings. In light of the heavy burden placed on the Crown (proof beyond a reasonable doubt), defence use of sexual history evidence is a powerful tool to undermine the credibility of their chief (and, often, only) witness, the complainant.

Access to personal records
Despite Bill C-49's limited effectiveness, most defence lawyers were of the view that Bill C-49 went too far in restricting their ability to represent clients in sexual assault trials (Meredith, Mohr, and Cairns Way 1997). They lost little time in developing a tactic to counter the bill: if they could not intimidate or undermine complainants by dragging their sexual lives into court, they would seek access to any personal records about a complainant that might contain other embarrassing or discrediting information, on the ground that such information was necessary to make a full answer and defence. Access to personal records was virtually unheard of before 1992. The defence most commonly seeks sexual assault counselling records and child welfare records, but every imaginable personal record has been the object of a defence application.[6]

i. The *O'Connor* case
In 1995 the Supreme Court of Canada (by a bare majority of five judges) issued the infamous *O'Connor* decision, which raised personal records access to the status of a defendant's constitutional right to a fair trial. (In contrast, a minority of four judges held that records could be obtained in "the rarest of cases.") Defence lawyers now believe that the standard practice should be to seek every possible record on a complainant in all sexual violence cases.

O'Connor was charged with having committed various sexual offences in the early 1960s against four Aboriginal women. At the time of the offences, the women were students or former students employed at the residential school where O'Connor was priest, teacher, and principal. O'Connor's defence was that two of the women had consented to have sex with him and that nothing had happened between him and the two others.

A judge ordered the women to authorize the release to O'Connor of their entire residential school records (academic, medical, and employment) and all therapy and medical records since the time they had left the school. None of these records were in the Crown's possession, and, as the records covered a period of twenty to thirty years, compliance with the order was difficult. Consequently, O'Connor applied to have the proceedings stayed, and ultimately the trial judge ordered the proceedings stayed for failure to produce. The stay was appealed to the Supreme Court of Canada. While the Court overturned the stay, finding that the Crown's actions were not an abuse of process, it gave exceptionally large scope to defence access to complainants' personal records held by third parties.

The majority decision in *O'Connor* paid lip service to notions of protecting a complainant's privacy "interests," but unlike the minority decision, it utterly failed to comprehend that the production of personal records was the latest manifestation of laws that reflect and perpetuate women's and children's inequality. For example, the judges accepted—without comment on this double standard—that records are sought in sexual violence cases, but not others. They failed to note that the Court has been quick to protect against access to the records of a witness in other criminal cases, yet, in sexual violence cases, has been satisfied with baseless and highly prejudicial rationales for access to records. The Court also failed to notice that the practice—which it has now elevated to a constitutional right—was barely three years old and an obvious backlash to Bill C-49. The judges disregarded the fact, as frankly admitted by defence counsel in other settings, that production orders were sought not for information that would be relevant to the criminal proceedings but, rather, with the intent to intimidate complainants into refusing to continue to participate in the process (Kelly 1997; Feldthusen 1996).

The Court simply ignored the fact that O'Connor was seeking residential school records. Thus it avoided having to consider whether records created in a system designed to destroy Aboriginal cultures have any place in being used now to discredit those people subjected to that system. The Court refused to consider how records applications would have a disproportionate impact on women who have been subject to extensive record-keeping in contexts characterized by multiple inequalities, such as prisons, psychiatric hospitals, or the child welfare system. They also avoided having to consider whether records written by the defendant himself (as the residential school records almost certainly were in *O'Connor*) are inherently unreliable. They paid scant heed to the effects of the release of records on counselling relationships or the willingness of complainants to report sexual violence crimes to the police.

Every one of these issues was squarely before the Court on the facts of the *O'Connor* case, and various intervenors fully argued for constitutional equality rights. Yet the majority of members of the Court failed to deal with these issues. They do not even mention the equality rights section of the *Charter*. In contrast, the Court did refer to the newest rape mythologies—the beliefs that women falsely conjure up sexual abuse histories and then lay charges against innocent men and that counsellors use therapy to improperly influence complainants' memories—even though there was no evidence before the Court on such influences and none of the prosecutions in *O'Connor* involved recovered memories. Law's Official Version decides when and to whom it will be accountable; and judges ignore constitutional equality rights simply because they choose to do so, even when these rights plainly arise on the face of the case.

ii. Bill C-46

Well in advance of the Court's 1995 *O'Connor* ruling, feminist organizations had been attempting to deal with the crisis engendered by defendants' burgeoning disclosure demands. One strategy adopted by some record-keepers, particularly sexual assault counsellors, was to alter note-taking practices (remembering always that the defendant himself might read the record) and revise record retention policies. Another strategy was to engage in consultations with the federal Department of Justice to develop legislation to end the practice, a process that began months before the *O'Connor* decision was released. Some sixteen months after *O'Connor* was heard, Bill C-46 passed into law.

By Bill C-46, Parliament requires judges to take into account the issue on which the Supreme Court of Canada maintained a deafening silence in *O'Connor*: a reconciliation and accommodation of women's constitutional equality rights with the defendant's right to a fair trial. By this bill, records cannot even be considered for release if the defence cannot establish that they are "likely relevant," and Parliament sets out examples of rationales that would *not* meet this test, including the fact of the person in question having seen a counsellor or the possibility that the record may contain information about the acts giving rise to the charge. Even records that cross the likely relevance threshold cannot be released either to the judge or to the defendant unless that judge has weighed a number of factors, including effects on counselling relationships or the potential for biases to operate. Complainants and record-holders have the right to be represented by counsel at the hearing of these applications, and some provinces have programs to ensure that lawyers will be made available to complainants who cannot afford to pay for them.

While Bill C-46 will not prohibit all records production applications, it is designed to significantly reduce situations in which personal records can be released to a judge and lead to even fewer cases in which they will be ordered released to defendants. It is too early to say whether the spirit of the bill will be reflected in lower court decisions. Within months, the bill was subject to numerous constitutional challenges, one of which the Supreme Court of Canada was scheduled to hear in the 1998–99 session (*R. v. Mills* 1997).

CONCLUSION

The combined effect of the legal principles applicable to all criminal cases and the specific rules applicable only to sexual violence cases makes it very difficult to obtain a conviction. A conviction is even less likely in historic cases, and in recovered memory cases it is all but impossible unless it can be established that the memory is not false, the defendant (if he testifies) is not credible, and there is very strong confirmatory evidence. Many journalists and criminal defence would have us believe that criminal cases founded on recovered memories (which they conflate with false memories) are clogging up the criminal justice system and that innocent men have been wrongfully convicted (Makin 1998). But criminal prosecutions of recovered memory cases are rare, and at least one appeal court has strongly discouraged them. Even women whose memories of abuse are intact are scrutinized. The Supreme Court of Canada has assumed that such women's memories are "influenced" by therapists, and *The Globe and Mail* asserts that "some complainants sporting recovered memories have reacted to legal scepticism by disguising the purported origins of their recollections.... Instead they portray these memories as having been there all along" (Makin 1998: A7).

The trial process does little to affirm women's stories of male violence or to call into question the larger social forces that sustain a rape culture. As Carol Smart (1989: 35) states:

> The whole rape trial is a process of disqualification (of women) and celebration (of phallocentrism). It is true that not all women

are disqualified and some men are convicted and punished but these instances never challenge the basic ritual which reaffirms the phallocentric view of sex. This is not a question of whether some judges are progressive enough to restrain the defence's cross-examination of a raped woman, nor a question of the introduction of carpeted interview suites in police stations. Certainly it is possible to mitigate some of the worst horrors of the process of disqualification. But whether the disqualification is done nicely or not, it is still achieved.

In the *Adams* case the trial judge lifted the publication ban on the complainant's name after finding the defendant not guilty. While the first judgment expresses the traditional view that the benefit of the doubt had to go to the defendant, a second judgment (to justify lifting the ban) stated that the publication ban should not apply when the complainant is "a liar" and "a prostitute." As noted by the Supreme Court of Canada, the trial judge went on to state, "This woman went into the beer parlour as a predator, and this fellow says he lost $900.... Don't we owe society a duty to tell the next person who goes into the beer parlour for a beer and may be looking for a prostitute, that this is a dangerous one?" The trial judge's reasons are surprising, because the complainant was not on trial for assault, soliciting, extortion, or perjury and had none of the protections afforded a criminal defendant. Yet while the Supreme Court of Canada reinstated the publication ban, they did not comment on the impropriety of the trial judge's findings respecting the complainant in lifting the ban in the first place.

Moreover, some judges forget altogether that the criminal trial is partial to the defendant. In *R.* v. *Hill* (1997), for example, the defendant was charged with a number of offences against his daughter during a ten-year period (1981–91). The charges were laid soon after the complainant left the family home. The jury convicted the defendant on some counts but not on others, in particular the sexual assault charges. A Court of Appeal judge reviewing the case commented, "It was clear that [the jury] did not accept that any of these events took place." It is troubling that a judge would assume that an acquittal means that nothing occurred— rather than that it was not proved beyond a reasonable doubt. It is also possible that the jury was confused about what conduct amounted to a criminal offence, especially given that the *Criminal Code* was frequently amended during the time period of the events. The *R.* v. *D. (E.)* (1995)

case provides an even more insidious example of how sexual violence allegations come to be construed as false. The judge refers to previously disposed allegations of sexual abuse by the complainant against her uncle, but the judge does not say what happened to that charge; that is, whether it resulted in a conviction, a stay, or an acquittal. Even if an acquittal had been entered, this fact would not support an inference that a false complaint was made, given the reasonable doubt standard. Yet, the editors who provided a summary of the case, relying only on the reasons, *assumed* both that no conviction had been entered and that the prior allegations were false. The summary twice notes "the complainant's false allegations against an uncle." In a subsequent case, *R. v. L.J.S.* (1996), a different judge perpetuated this error by referring to the *D. (E.)* case as one where a complainant had made false allegations.

The law even has trouble finding a term for women who have been sexually assaulted. Some defence lawyers, academics, and journalists have recently started using the inflammatory term "accuser." This term is only used in sexual violence cases, not for other prosecutions. While "complainant" is not perfect, it is the least problematic term and the most widely used in legal writing. While most people who are directly hurt by crimes are called "victims," the double standard endemic to sexual violence cases finds its way into terminology as well. Again, as the Supreme Court of Canada stated, in a sexual assault case "One is not a victim until a conviction is entered," and use of the term "victim" is inconsistent with the presumption of innocence (*R. v. Seaboyer* 1991).

As the *Adams, H.K., L.D.(E.), L.J.S.,* and *Seaboyer* cases illustrate, many judges and others are willing to jump to the conclusion that allegations are false and the events did not happen if a conviction is not obtained. The complainant risks, among other things, that those around her will perceive that what legal "truth" has deemed to be incapable of supporting a criminal conviction amounts to actual, objective truth that no wrongdoing occurred, especially now that judges and defence lawyers repeat, mantra-like, "she is not a victim until a conviction is entered." The harm to the complainant is completely discounted if the criminal processes cannot render a guilty verdict.

If the original allegation is now seen as false, a complainant runs the additional risk of being turned into the wrongdoer, as happened in *Adams, H.K.L.,* and *D.E.*. Many people wrongly assume that significant breakthroughs to sexual violence law have also led to changes in courtroom practices, "ironically strengthening the view that men acquitted thereafter had most definitely been falsely accused" (Smart 1989: 49). Yet there are very few cases of false allegations (Busby 1995). The partiality and incompleteness engendered by the criminal fact-finding process, which is exacerbated by the judicial biases and other inequalities, including practices like the use of sexual history or personal records, are quickly forgotten. Instead, the Official Version congratulates itself on proving, once more, that a woman or a child has lied about sexual violence.

Notes

1. There has been a significant and steady increase in the number of reports made and the number of charges laid in Canada in the last decade. Using statistics gathered from the Uniform Crime Reporting System, Roberts (1994) determined that the number of sexual assaults reported to the police each year in Canada increased by an average of 12 percent per year between 1983 and 1992. Further, the percentage of cases where charges were laid also steadily increased during this period from 43 percent to 50 percent. However, according to the Statistics Canada National Violence Against Women Survey (as reported in Roberts at Table 4; see also Johnson 1996), only 6 percent of all sexual assaults reported in the survey were also reported to the police in 1993.
2. Note that most of the cases described in this essay were decided by appeal courts and therefore have significant precedential value.
3. Because it is, overwhelmingly, men who commit acts of sexual violence, I use male pronouns to describe defendants. I use female pronouns to describe complainants, as most criminal prosecutions in sexual violence cases involve female complainants and the rules specific to sexual violence prosecutions develop out of beliefs about women and girls.
4. While many feminists criticize the term "victim" because it promotes the myth of women as passive and helpless, this reasoning is very different from that stated by the Supreme Court of Canada.
5. Meredith, Mohr, and Cairns Way (1997) based this finding on a survey of a small number of Crown attorneys and defence lawyers across Canada. Crown attorneys said that applications to admit sexual history were made in 10 to 25 percent of the cases; defence lawyers said they were made in 0 to 20 percent of the cases. Crown attorneys said the applications to admit were not granted in 30 to 50 percent of the cases, although one Crown had never successfully opposed an application. Defence lawyers reported that their applications were refused in 0 to 25 percent of cases. It is not clear why there are such discrepancies between the figures; it may be a result of regional differences, limited experiences of interviewees, or the inherent frailties of anecdotal information.
6. Defendants have sought access not only to counselling, therapy, and psy-

chiatric records but also to records from abortion and birth control clinics, child welfare agencies, adoption agencies, residential and public schools, drug and alcohol abuse recovery centres, other doctors, employers, the military, psychiatric hospitals, victim/witness assistance programs, criminal injuries compensation boards, prisons and youth detention centres, social welfare agencies, immigration offices, and the Crown on unrelated charges against the complainant, and personal diaries, reporters' notes, and criminal and Young Offender records (Busby 1997).

Obscenity, Gender, and the Law

© Kirsten Johnson[1]

In 1992 the Supreme Court of Canada gave its decision in *R. v. Butler* (1992). The events that precipitated the *Butler* case began in August 1987, when Winnipeg police seized the entire inventory of a pornography video store. The store's owner, Donald Victor Butler, along with a female employee, was charged with about 250 violations of the *Criminal Code* for possessing and exposing "obscene" material (videos, magazines, and sex aids) for the purposes of distribution and sale. Butler was subsequently convicted on eight of those charges and acquitted on the remaining charges.

In 1989, following the Crown's appeal of this ruling, the Manitoba Court of Appeal overturned the original decision and convicted Butler on all counts. At this juncture Butler's lawyers appealed to the Supreme Court, arguing that section 163 of the *Criminal Code* infringes on freedom of expression, thereby violating section 2(b) of the *Charter of Rights and Freedoms*, which "guarantees freedom of thought, belief, opinion and expression, including freedom of the press and other media communication." The Supreme Court rejected the ruling by the Court of Appeal, provided a new comprehensive interpretation of section 163(8) of the *Criminal Code* based on the equality provisions in the *Charter*, and ordered a new trial for Butler. Butler was subsequently found guilty in 1993 of possessing and distributing obscene material, and he was sentenced to a few months in jail.

Given its import for the governance of pornographic material in Canada, the Supreme Court ruling in *Butler* opened a new chapter in the long-standing political debate among feminist legal scholars and activists, civil libertarians, and various religious groups over the issue of pornography and the corresponding efforts by the Canadian state to regulate it. Indeed, the Canadian legal history of pornography—both before and after *Butler*—has been a narrative about the criminalization of certain kinds of sexual representations—and not others. My main purpose here is to summarize the evolution of obscenity legislation in Canada in order to contextualize the Supreme Court decision in *R. v. Butler* (1992). This review of Canadian legal practices will illustrate how law socially legitimizes certain kinds of pornography and, in the process, takes for granted gendered (and, depending on the context, class-based and racist) notions of sexuality.

Since before Confederation, the Canadian state has regulated pornography on the basis of its perceived threat to established power. Authorities often justified regulation by referring to religious morals and the threat of the breakdown of society. With *Butler*, certain forms of violent pornography have been deemed obscene and therefore criminalized on the basis of harm to society and to women and children in particular. Nevertheless, in the months and years following the decision in *Butler*, enforcement of the *Criminal Code* obscenity provisions continues to take gendered notions of sexuality for granted. For instance, Canada Customs officials have repeatedly used *Criminal Code* provisions to justify the detention (and often destruction) of sexually explicit materials imported by gay and lesbian bookstores.[2] It would appear that what has been described as "state-enforced heterosexual hegemony through moral regulation" (Kinsman 1987) is a subtext of the Canadian legal narrative on pornography. By locating the analysis in the context of the mainly repressive history of Canadian prosecutions of pornography cases, therefore, we can better address questions about the limits of criminal law to promote sexual freedom or ideas about sexual subjectivity that challenge the status quo.

DEFINING PORNOGRAPHY

Nearly every discussion of pornography begins with the challenge of definition. The difficulty of defining pornography is, in part, due to its main purpose: sexual stimulation and gratification. The term "pornography" is inherently subjective, because it is an interpretive experience. One person might view a certain sex publication as "disgusting pornography," while another might be looking forward to the next issue. It is a misconception, then, to believe we can search for a foundational basis upon which to determine what counts as a monolithic definition of pornography. Invariably, we end up with a description of pornography that privileges certain cultural values over others. For example, people tend to underwrite their definitions of "great" or "disgusting" pornography with such values as sexual freedom, cultural convention, religious conviction, feminist ethics, and/or outright sexism. As a result, most attempts—legal or otherwise—to define pornography have failed to gain consensus despite their appeal to abstract philosophical principles such as undue exploitation, degradation, or harm. To be offended by a particular image is one thing, but to claim that it causes social harm because it offends you is another.

Pornography has long been around in a great variety of cultural forms, and it appears in a vast array of imagery. Since at least the sixteenth century, pornography has been used by political dissidents to criticize both church and state, by writers to challenge the status quo, and by entrepreneurs for financial gain. Hunt (1993b) demonstrates, for example, that French revolutionaries used pornography as a political tool to undermine the legitimacy of the ancien régime as a social and political system of rule.

The various contexts in which sexually explicit materials appear also play a role in the interpretation of the material as pornographic. Pictures of naked children on a wilderness camping trip displayed on parents' bookshelves become child pornography when found in the wallet of a paedophile. Excerpts of a book written by a nun about her sexual experiences and desires become pornography when published in *Penthouse Forum* (Valverde 1985). Moreover, the intentions of the producers of sexual representations play a role in the definition. Almost all mainstream pornography (mostly heterosexual) is produced for a whopping profit—estimated to be in the billions of dollars each year—while other sexual representations (including gay and lesbian) are produced with theoretical or artistic intent.[3] Finally, feminist definitions examine pornography as a form of deployment of power in which politics becomes central (Smart 1993: 185). Thus, perhaps the only accurate statement that can be made about pornography is this: pornography is about the representation of sex for pleasure and profit, and the debates surrounding its production and regulation are always political.

THE HISTORICAL BACKDROP

Historically, obscenity laws have been justified on the basis of Victorian-era morality. Typically, the regulation of the "obscene" was linked to the power of the church and later to the state. For instance, in British feudal society, literacy was a privilege available only to the clergy, and as a result the majority of the population was illiterate. According to Kuhn (1985: 24): "When the term pornography first came into use, virtually the only medium in which representations could be reproduced in very large numbers was print. The printed word demands literacy, and not everyone was able to read. As a written medium, pornography was consequently limited as to the audience it could reach, and seems to have been something of a gentleman's pastime."

In addition, most of the literature available was theological in nature and subject to ecclesiastical authorization (Chaster and Wilson 1984). Taylor (1984: 3) argues: "Attempts at the legal definition and regulation of obscene material have a long history in the United Kingdom. Some form of licensing of literature existed from the time of Henry VIII (1509–47), although the preoccupations of such censorship were more frequently political and religious than they were directly moralistic." Material censored in British feudal society tended to be prohibited for reasons of blasphemy. Sexual materials were therefore banned on the basis of heresy rather than strictly sex[4]—a condition for censorship that continued until the seventeenth century (Lacombe 1988).

By the end of the seventeenth century the capitalist expansion of the printing industry ensured the removal of religious restrictions on printing, but the state had not relinquished its control over the production and distribution of published material. Publications were regulated by a number of common-law (civil and criminal) prohibitions and restrictions against libel, slander, defamation, and sedition. Not surprisingly, then, during this time materials considered seditious rather than blasphemous were linked to immorality and therefore banned. "Obscene" materials drew little attention unless the materials were critical of the state.

Throughout the eighteenth century and until the mid-nineteenth century, when the state began to prosecute pornographic materials more vigorously, pornography continued to be defined as obscene on the basis of blasphemy and sedition rather than of so-called immoral sexuality alone. During the latter part of this period, described as an era of "moral panic," legislation was passed and court precedents were set in an attempt to deal with obscenity or, more precisely, to regulate sexuality. The passage of legislation coincided with changing forms of government, the printing revolution, and legislators' growing concern with controlling access to sexual information to protect society from "evil." The state expressed concern over harms caused to society in the form of legislation meant to prohibit mass access to sexually explicit materials. Judges rationalized their decisions to find certain sexually explicit materials obscene on the basis of criminal justice theory's explanation that pornography caused certain classes of people to commit sex crimes. In the early nineteenth century, a number of laws were passed to regulate pornography.

Earlier, in *R.* v. *Curl* (1727), Edmund Curl was prosecuted for publishing *Venus in the Cloister* or *Nun in Her Smock*, marking the first time British common law recognized the crime of obscene libel. According to Cossman and Bell (1997: 11–13), "This crime of obscene libel was intended to prohibit conduct that 'tends to corrupt the morals of the King's subjects.'" With the emergence of the moral reform movement in Britain, and in particular the activities of The Society for the Suppression of Vice, the state more vigorously pursued prosecutions against those who produced and distributed so-called obscene materials. The Society was also the driving force behind the passage of a number of acts aimed at reducing the "poisonous" effects of obscenity. Still, none of these acts contained a specific definition of the term "obscene," the determination of which was to become established through legal precedent with the test established in *R. v. Hicklin* (1868).

The passage of the Vagrancy Act (1824), the Customs Consolidation Act (1853) and the Obscene Publications Act (1857), along with the common-law legal precedents set in *Curl* and *Hicklin,* illustrates how British (and later Canadian) obscenity laws were rooted in class-based, gendered, and racist exclusions. Cossman and Bell (1997: 2) note: "It was not the possession of obscene materials by the educated upper classes that was of concern, but the possibility of the circulation of these materials among those who were morally vulnerable to its poisonous influences. The *Hicklin* test was intended to protect the morals of the lower classes and other vulnerable groups, and thereby promote a public morality that was based on the Victorian discourse of sexuality as a dangerous force to be controlled and repressed." According to Kuhn (1985: 24), widespread concern came with the eventual development of cheap, mass-produced pornography that opened up the market to the less well-off, foreign immigrants, the illiterate, and the working classes. Sexually explicit materials that fell into the hands of the so-called immigrant foreigner[5] or the working-class man or woman were defined as a "vice" that would inevitably lead to the moral breakdown of society.

English Canada governed itself according to the common law of Britain, and with the adoption of the Draft Criminal Code (1892) the common-law principles established in *Curl* and *Hicklin* to regulate obscene libel became the foundation of Canadian obscenity law.

The Hicklin *test*
In *R. v. Hicklin* (1868), a man named Scott was indicted for writing and distributing an anti-Catholic pamphlet, *The Confessional Unmasked,* in

which he fictionally described the methods used by priests to extricate erotic confessions from repentant women (Taylor 1984). In the judgment, Lord Cockburn rendered his method for determining the existence of obscenity in a given publication, delivering what was to become the threshold model for obscenity in Canada: "I think the test of obscenity is this, whether the tendency of the matter charged as obscenity is to deprave or corrupt those whose minds are open to such immoral influences, and into whose hands a publication of this sort may fall" (*R.* v. *Hicklin* 1868: 372).

Inappropriate sexual arousal and its effect on "weak" minds or those who are more susceptible to "corrupting" influences became the first legal rationale for criminalizing sexually explicit material. The underlying rationale for the *Hicklin* test was the control and repression of sexuality, especially among the so-called lesser classes. Although met with considerable judicial and academic criticism (Boyd 1984), the *Hicklin* test informed Canadian common and codified law until 1959, when the federal government added a new definition of obscenity to the *Criminal Code*.

Following the codification of the *Hicklin* test in 1892, only five obscenity cases were reported between 1900 and 1940, all of them concerned with the corruption of morals resulting from exposure to "obscene" material.[6] All cases followed the *Hicklin* precedent, and in all cases the intentions of the authors were of little regard to the court's determination of obscenity (Boyd 1984; Lacombe 1988). Cossman and Bell's (1997: 12) work further illustrates how the *Hicklin* test was an effect of nineteenth-century gender relations: "The gendered moral discourse was part of a more general Victorian discourse on women's sexuality. Criminal regulation of obscenity coincided not only with the extension of laws against prostitution ... but also with the emergence of the cult of domesticity and the reconstitution of the family. Women's sexuality was to be contained within the boundaries of marriage and the family. And the family had to be protected from moral corruption that might permeate it from dangerous external forces."

The justification for the criminal regulation of obscenity relied, too, on class-based and racist notions of the human subject. At the same time, pornographic materials were themselves riddled with narratives of race, class, and gender and often deployed as a means of differentiating between the white bourgeois womanhood promoted by British laws and the racialized subjects of the British colonial empire. Stoler (1995: 128) argues that nineteenth-century racial discourses came in various forms, including sexually explicit imagery and texts, that were inseparable from class-based and gendered discourses: "It [racial discourse] came loaded with a barrage of colonial representations of savagery, licentiousness, and basic truths about human nature that joined early visions of the 'others' of empire with the 'others' within Europe itself." For example, Stoler cites the sexual model of the promiscuous working-class woman of nineteenth-century industrial Britain as a creature forged from a myth of the "wild woman." This image stood in stark contradistinction to the morally pure, sexually restrained, middle-class British woman, who was a model for civility.

Like the law in Britain in earlier centuries, Canadian law promoted the idea that pornography was a vice to be controlled, along the lines of drugs and alcohol, because its consumption by those socially defined as morally inferior—based on class and race associations—would have a dangerous effect on the morally proper functioning of society. Not only were obscenity laws intended to limit sexuality to the confines of the procreative family unit, but they were also championed as a means of reducing criminality among the so-called dangerous classes.[7]

Bill C-58: Defining obscene

The years between 1944 and 1959 in Canada saw a number of significant changes made to the *Hicklin* test in common law. Most notably, in 1944 the test was altered with the addition of criminal intent or *mens rea* (*R. v. Conway* 1944; Lacombe 1988). In 1953 the court affirmed the idea that certain members of society could be morally corrupted by obscenity (*R. v. National News* 1953; Lacombe 1988). In 1954 two new qualifications were made to the *Hicklin* test: the notion of "contemporary standards" and the requirement that the material must be considered in its entirety (*R. v. Martin Secker & Warburg Ltd.* 1954). This decision altered *Hicklin* in two significant ways: by establishing in common law the idea that community standards will change over generations, and the idea that sexually explicit works must be considered as a whole. In 1957, among heated criticism of the *Hicklin* test, a Special Committee of the Senate, created in 1952 and headed by E.D. Fulton, gave its recommendations to the House of Commons (Boyd 1984; Lacombe 1988). These recommendations eventually took the form of Bill C-58, introduced to Parliament by E.D. Fulton (by then the Conservative justice minister), and became law in 1959. According to Cossman and Bell (1997: 15),

"The 1950s witnessed a return of gendered moral discourses circulating around the purity signifiers of wife, mother and family." This bill, meant not to displace the *Hicklin* test but to expand and clarify its intent (Boyd 1984), "resulted in the amendment of section 159 of the *Criminal Code* and in the addition of subsection (8) which defined the word 'obscene'" (Lacombe 1988: 36). Subsection (8)—which remains unchanged to date (except for its section number)—states: "For the purposes of the Act, any publication a dominant characteristic of which is the undue exploitation of sex, or of sex and any one or more of the following subjects, namely, crime, horror, cruelty and violence, shall be deemed to be obscene" (Lacombe 1988: 36).

The campaign to toughen Canadian obscenity law may have harkened back to the social purity campaigns of the late-nineteenth and early twentieth centuries, but it had little impact on the law itself. Mahoney (1984: 58) argues, however: "By enacting the legislation, Parliament appeared to depart from the common law traditional emphasis on the immorality of explicit sex. Parliament enlarged the definition of obscenity to include the portrayal of certain forms of violence if accompanied by the undue exploitation of sex. Violence could not by itself be obscene. This became known as the 'sex plus' requirement and its effect was to limit the reach of the obscenity law to sexual depictions." In its revised form, the concept of undue exploitation became the governing test for obscenity. A slight shift occurred, with sex now considered exploitative when coupled with violence, and the beginning of a liberal harms-based test of obscenity emerged in law.

The first obscenity case to be heard before the Supreme Court of Canada following the passage of Bill C-58 introduced the community standard test for obscenity—now defined as "undue exploitation"—in an attempt to correct the subjective evaluation of the materials by providing an objective standard—a standard of obscenity that the community would tolerate (*R. v. Brodie* 1962). In a decision that dealt with the sexual content of D.H. Lawrence's *Lady Chatterley's Lover*, Judson J. noted: "There does exist in any community at all times—however the standard may vary from time to time—a general instructive sense of what is decent and what is indecent, of what is clean and what is dirty, and when the distinction has to be drawn, I do not know that there is any better tribunal than a jury to draw it" (Boyd 1984: 25–26).

This judgment did recognize the relevance of artistic and literary merit of a work in determining whether or not there is "undue exploitation." Mahoney (1984: 58) argues that this decision rendered the *Hicklin* test obsolete—that the foundation of the definition became the undue exploitation of sex rather than depravity or corruption. Now it was up to the community to determine what kinds of sexual expression constituted undue exploitation.[8] In a subsequent case (*R. v. Dominion News and Gifts* 1963), the court determined that the community standard of tolerance test is a test of national community standards rather than standards of a specific community. Before then, jurisprudence had dictated that community standards would change from one generation to another and that they were not to be considered national standards. Accordingly, this decision marked a significant departure from the *Hicklin* rationale. The explicit concern of the Court appeared to be no longer the corrupting influences of obscenity on dangerous classes. Rather, the focus shifted to a consideration of the prevailing "tolerance" of the community, which nonetheless amounted to the same practice expressed in different legal language. The terms corruption and degradation of morals had begun to be translated into conventional liberal legal language, which couched the same ideas in universalist language. In other words, the courts renovated the notion of corruption into a fresh notion of "undue exploitation," meaning that which offends community standards of tolerance and, therefore, causes harm to society as a whole. These community standards of tolerance continued to be defined by an elite that allowed the perpetuation of limited formal notions of sexuality. The community standards test, in effect, gave judges—a small and conservative percentage of the population—the authority to determine what an entire community would consider obscene on the basis of an undefined notion of "undue exploitation." In practice, judges, customs agents, and police would deliver the united concepts of undue exploitation that violate community standards to justify criminal prosecutions of any sexually explicit material that failed to conform to their individual notions of decency. Moreover, they would do so without any appeal to scientific evidence or expert opinion—which is deemed unnecessary.

This shift in obscenity law towards considerations of tolerance and intolerance, of decency and indecency, in the community standards test illustrates the functionalism underlying the rationale for Canadian obscenity law. To operate effectively, community standards tests must assume that society agrees on a particular notion of undue exploitation and reinforces the idea through law when implemented by individual agents of the state. The underlying assumption in the community standards test for undue exploitation is the theory that individual members of a jury represent a consensual moral order and are thus able to articulate a unified view on what kinds of sexual representations pose a threat to the proper functioning of society by causing harm. The notion of harm, or risk of harm, in the *Butler* decision is the idea that pornography leads to vice by causing individuals to act in an anti-social manner (*R. v. Butler* 1992: 454). The fact that almost no obscenity cases are tried before a jury did not seem to matter. This Durkheimian world view expressed in the rationale for the criminal regulation of pornography effectively gives judges the authority to determine what counts as undue exploitation.

Before the *Butler* decision, Canadian courts relied for many years on the community standards test established in *R. v. Brodie* (1962) and *R. v. Dominion News and Gifts Ltd.* (1963). Case law established that obscenity was to be adjudicated on the basis of "undue exploitation of sex," with "undueness" measured in accordance with a judicial determination of "community standards." These standards were to be taken as an assumed fact rather than a fiction, or construct, of liberal criminal justice theory. Even though Sopinka J. and others have rejected legal moralism (the idea that a majority can decide what values should inform individual lives and then coercively impose those values on minorities), when judges determine community standards of tolerance on the basis of an abstract notion of undue exploitation, the act amounts to just that. Judges decide what is tolerable or intolerable (in the old language, decent or indecent) and impose their decisions on the rest of us through law.

Judicial interpretations of the community standards test have resulted in distorted views of society and heterosexist applications of law precisely because the determination of community standards is an exercise in judicial discretion. Given that the community standards are still very much influenced by heterosexist notions (wherein traditional notions of family and religious morality supersede all others), the law continues to authorize particular ideas about gender and sexuality, giving individual police officers, customs agents, and judges repressive authority to censor. In the process, pornography is abstracted from the conditions in which it is produced and consumed so as to advance a political and/or legal position that has practically nothing to do with the mundane uses to which pornography is actually put (Juffer 1998: 1).

In the 1960s, amid the liberalization of divorce laws, the decriminalization of birth control, and the partial decriminalization of abortion and homosexuality, a feminist and gay liberation movement emerged to challenge the sexual conservatism of the 1950s (Cossman and Bell 1997; Lacombe 1994). According to Lacombe, their fight to repeal obscenity laws was part of a larger movement to confront patriarchal rule over sexuality. Early feminists, gays, and lesbians embraced pornography as a means of challenging the sexual status quo and saw it as a tool for promoting sexual freedom.[9]

CHALLENGING OBSCENITY LAW IN THE 1980s

In the 1970s and 1980s, pornography itself, along with the outright censorship and repression of gay and lesbian sexual materials, precipitated considerable outrage and action on the part of feminist organizations and gay and lesbian activists. Certain groups argued that it was the responsibility of the state to promote women's equality (see, for example, Cole 1989), while others argued that the state—and repressive criminal law in particular—could not possibly be relied upon to promote women's equality (see, for example, Burstyn 1985). As a reflection of their political beliefs, certain feminist groups turned to the state to advance egalitarian ideals, while others were highly critical of any reliance on the state given its repressive history. Nevertheless, the terms of the debate came to be framed by the anti-pornography feminists, such as U.S. legal scholar Catharine MacKinnon, who argued that pornography was a practice of sex discrimination harming women both in its production and in the messages it advocated about women's role in society. Feminists opposed to legal remedies and censorship argued that the obscenity provisions in the *Criminal Code* tend to be used to control women's sexuality (Burstyn 1985). Even anti-pornography feminists, such as Canadian feminist journalist Susan Cole (1989: 70), acknowledged that the history of criminal enforcement of obscenity laws is a history of the control of women's sexual self-determination. *Criminal Code* provisions had been used to control access to birth control and abortion and to criminalize gay and lesbian sexual practices along with many other dissident views on sexuality.

Prior to the *Butler* case in the mid-1980s, gays and lesbians (such as the owners of both Glad Day Books in Toronto and Little Sister's Bookstore and Art Emporium in Vancouver), informed by their experiences with Customs Canada, launched court challenges to limit Customs officers' discretionary power to censor. The lessons from history, coupled with the state's ongoing and blatant suppression of gay, lesbian, and feminist materials and its implicit support of heterosexual pornography in the 1980s, contributed to the growing dissatisfaction among many progressive organizations. In particular, the formal criminal charges against the owner of Pages Bookstore in Toronto for a window display created by a feminist art collective in 1985, the Customs seizure of *The Joy of Gay Sex*[10] in 1986, and similar seizures of materials headed for Little Sister's in Vancouver demonstrated that the regulations governing Canada Customs seizures were inherently homophobic. For example, as Fuller and Blackley (1995) demonstrate, Customs exercised prior restraint on depictions of homosexual sex, specifically anal penetration, on the basis of undue exploitation of sex. Sexually explicit materials that depicted anal intercourse (especially those imported by Glad Day and Little Sister's) were subject to seizure by Customs officials according to Memorandum D9-1-1, which outlined concrete guidelines for enforcing Tariff Code 9956.[11]

Meanwhile, throughout the 1980s, feminist organizations formed to lobby the government to take action to deal with a perceived harm to women's equality caused by the proliferation of heterosexual pornography and its concomitant exploitation of women, while the owners of both Glad Day and Little Sister's (with the support of the B.C. Civil Liberties Association) launched costly court cases challenging the authority of Customs to arbitrarily censor material bound for their stores. At the time of the suit, Customs had the power to seize "books, printed paper, drawings, paintings, prints, photographs or representations of any kind" deemed to be "obscene, hate propaganda, treasonous and seditious" and child pornography. Customs legislation incorporates the obscenity provision of the *Criminal Code*. Busby (1993: 185, fn 44) notes, "Until 1985, Customs legislation prohibited any materials that were 'immoral and indecent,' but this standard was struck down as too vague to be enforced." Customs officers enjoy prior restraint privileges of any materials imported into Canada. As well, the onus is on the importer to challenge a Customs seizure (Fuller and Blackley 1995: 7). Not surprisingly, for many Customs officers, depictions of gay and lesbian sex, and anal penetration in particular, "counts" as the undue exploitation of sex and have been described as immoral and disgusting (Fuller and Blackley 1995). Even though jurisprudence had evolved to the point at which sexually explicit materials were tolerated so long as they did not couple sex with violence or degradation and dehumanization (as in *Butler*), Customs officials continued to discriminate between heterosexual and homosexual materials when they seized *Bad Attitude* (a lesbian erotic pornography magazine) from Glad Day Bookshop shortly after the *Butler* decision.

In the 1980s the Canadian government made two attempts to rewrite the obscenity law. The first, Bill C-51, was introduced in 1981 by the Liberals and eventually withdrawn. Between 1983 and 1985, two major federal committees issued their reports investigating pornography and prostitution. The Badgely Committee submitted its report to Parliament in 1984, and the Fraser Committee in 1985. In 1986 Bill C-114 was introduced by the Conservatives in response to the findings of the committees, but it also failed due to the condemnation of civil libertarians, feminists, librarians, artists, and fundamentalist Christians (Fuller and Blackley 1995). The following year, the Conservative government introduced yet another amendment, Bill C-54, without overcoming the problems associated with the earlier versions. Bill C-54 died on the order paper when an election was called before the bill could properly pass.

Meanwhile, back in the courtrooms, judges were beginning to absorb the anti-pornography position argued by certain feminist groups, both in Canada and the United States, who viewed pornography as causing real harm to women in the form of sexual abuse. For example, in 1983, in *R. v. Doug Rankine and Act III Video* (1983), the pornography was examined, according to Mahoney (1984:62), from the point of view of victims of sexual abuse. Cole (1989) described the case as a real shift in perspective that made a significant difference in how pornography was interpreted from the bench. Similarly, the finding in *R. v. Ramsingh* (1984) characterized the recognition of harm rather than sexual explicitness as obscene. Soon after, *R. v. Wagner* (1985) again articulated the general principles set forth in *Rankine* and *Ramsingh,* but with significant new considerations. The judgment defined three types of sexually explicit materials. According to Judge Shannon of the Alberta Court of Queen's Bench, three types of sexually explicit materials exist: violent, non-violent but degrading and dehumanizing, and erotica. According to Mahoney (1984: 62–63), the judge "described the three categories in detail, providing examples of each, and held that the Canadian community will tolerate erotica, but not material falling into the other two categories. Unlike Borins J. in *Rankine*, Shannon J. was of the opinion that explicit sex *per se* is not obscene. He said that '[i]t is the message that counts, not the degree of explicitness.' By emphasizing 'the message,' the Court is saying that the context of the sexual depictions is the paramount consideration."

Moreover, the judge held that, due to the social harm caused by sexually violent or degrading and/or dehumanizing pornography, the *Criminal Code* provisions proscribing "obscenity" do not infringe upon the freedom of expression guarantee recently adopted in The *Charter of Rights and Freedoms* (Mahoney 1984). According to Women's Legal Education and Action Fund (LEAF 1991: 8), in *R. v. Towne Cinema Theatres* (1985), the court acknowledged that the violence in—and therefore the harm of—pornography constituted "undue exploitation of sex" without concern for community standards, thereby implicitly stating that the objective of section 163(8) is the avoidance of harm. While, according to Mahoney (1984: 63), judicial acknowledgement of violence in obscenity was rare, it appears that, by this point in the development of Canadian case law, the existence of violence in pornography constituted harm and therefore obscenity. As such, pornography became obscenity when sex was coupled both with outright violence and degradation or dehumanization. Depictions such as these were to be considered undue exploitation of sex. They violate the community standards test for tolerance because they harm women.

Conservative, liberal, and radical-feminist notions of harm
From a conservative point of view, sexually explicit materials are intrinsically immoral because they undermine the social values of procreation within the institution of the family, and they are judged harmful on that basis. The assumption underlying the inherent immorality of sexually explicit material "is an assessment of whether or not the material poses a threat to the organizational structure of society and its institutions" (Mahoney 1984: 37). Hence the conservative approach to obscenity regulation focuses on the preservation of society in general from the corrupting influences of sexually explicit material. According to Mahoney (1984: 44): "The conservative morality creates and advocates what is to many an unacceptable sexual ethic, one that asks the law to subordinate sex to procreation and condemn all sexual interaction outside marriage. Sexual morality is seen by conservatives as the 'glue' holding together the rest of the structure of society." Rather than the content of the sexual interaction depicted, it is the expression of sexuality itself that threatens the moral integrity of the members of society. Thus, conservatives would place legal restrictions on sexually explicit material because of the harm

it causes to the proper functioning of the social order.

The liberal approach to harm is similar in that it has a concern with the harm caused to a democratic society. But, according to the liberal perspective, the censorship of obscene or, for that matter, any materials causes harm to individual liberty or freedom. Unlike the conservative approach, the liberal values underlying a conception of harm are not concerned with the inherent sexual nature of the material to be banned, "but rather asks whether more harm will be caused by banning it than by permitting its publication" (Mahoney 1984: 37–38). The liberal position focuses on the suppression of any material as harmful because of its potential for eroding the fundamental freedom of expression (right to political dissent) upon which a democratic society is based. The harm caused by censorship is weighed against the harm the expunged materials cause to an individual. So long as the material in question does not cause direct harm to the individual, liberal ethics encourage its unrestricted expression (Mahoney 1984: 38).

From a liberal perspective, harm is caused to society when the state interferes with individual freedom. The only grounds upon which the state is justified in interfering with individual liberty are to *prevent* harm to others. The harm principle is, thus, the basis upon which law allows censorship of sexual representations deemed to be indecent or obscene. Unfettered freedom of expression is the linchpin of a liberal value system, or morality, which underlies the regulation of obscenity. Canadian courts have consistently interpreted obscenity law in conjunction with *Charter* provisions as congruent with democratic principles. For example, in *R. v. Red Hot Video Ltd.* (1985), a B.C. court held that the obscenity provision does not violate freedom of expression in subsection 2(b) of the *Charter*. In *R. v. Ramsingh* (1985), a Manitoba court held that the obscenity provision amounted to a justifiable limit on freedom within the meaning of section 1 of the *Charter*.

Both the conservative and liberal notions of harm differ from the notion of harm contained in the radical anti-pornography feminist position advanced by legal scholars who advocate legal remedies for pornography. By focusing on the harm caused by pornography to the social order or on the direct injury caused to individuals' freedom, respectively, both conservative and liberal perspectives overlook three specific ways in which, according to the radical-feminist position, pornography causes harm: to society; to women and children generally; and to the participants in pornography. Certain feminist legal scholars have developed a distinct understanding of the concept of harm, as a concept rooted in women's experience of harm (Howe 1990; Mahoney 1984). The concept of harm flows as a common theme throughout feminist writing on pornography and is a concept that feminist organizations such as LEAF struggled to have legally recognized in Butler.[12] Underlying this feminist philosophy of harm is a feminist conception of morality, a concept informed by the principles of equality, non-violence, and women's right to self-determination. From this feminist point of view, sexual explicitness per se is not inherently immoral. Like the liberal perspective, the defining characteristic of immorality is the causation of harm to women's status as equal members of society. LEAF advanced this position in its intervention in the *Butler* case.

LEAF's legal position

For LEAF, working within the law meant having few options with respect to a feminist legal argument. Busby (1994: 173) argues that LEAF participated in litigation on pornography because it provided the opportunity to "deliver an important social and political message" and to voice a feminist legal opinion "on the relationship between sexual subordination, sexual violence and the laws that legitimate this violence." According to Busby (1994: 172), LEAF's legal subcommittee,[13] responsible for developing the arguments presented to the Supreme Court, had four options in the *Butler* case:

> [It] could have accepted the law as it had been interpreted; supported a position that could have eliminated any criminal regulation of pornography; asked the court to strike down the *Criminal Code* provision and to invite Parliament to introduce new legislation; or, asked the court to redefine the rationale for the *Criminal Code* obscenity provisions by focusing on its equality implications for women and children. Each option was assessed in light of its implications for women's equality and its effects on substantive equality claims of men who are part of historically disadvantaged communities.

After careful consideration of social-scientific and legal scholarship, the committee rejected the first three options in favour of arguing that the Supreme Court interpret the existing obscenity provision to promote constitutionally guaranteed equality.

Informed by MacKinnon's analysis of pornography, the members of the legal subcommittee sought to have the Court recognize that pornography is a practice of sex discrimination that harms women. In 1984 Catharine MacKinnon and Andrea Dworkin, at the request of the city of Minneapolis, drafted a civil ordinance that has come to be known as the Minneapolis Ordinance. This ordinance defines pornography as an act of sexual discrimination against women on the basis of sex, which would give women the right to sue pornographers for the harm done to them through pornography. According to MacKinnon (1986: 45), their "argument is simple: tolerance of such practices is inconsistent with any serious mandate of equality and with the reasons speech is protected." With MacKinnon participating in drafting the LEAF factum, the organization's submissions to the Supreme Court argued for a conceptual framework viewing pornography as an expressive form of inequality, and one that harms women.

MacKinnon (1985: 23) argued that defining "pornography as a practice of sex discrimination combines a mode of portrayal that has a legal history—the sexually explicit—with an active term central to inequality of the sexes—subordination." Pornography is thus defined as discrimination because it is a subordinating activity—the opposite of equality—which is not protected by a freedom of expression guarantee (MacKinnon 1991b). Busby (1993: 1) argues that this harms-based equality approach to pornography asserts that the *Charter*'s freedom of expression guarantee must be interpreted in view of the *Charter*'s equality guarantees, with a focus on pornography's harm to women. Because Canada constitutionally guarantees equality, LEAF sought to counter the *Charter* challenge of the obscenity statute on harms-based equality grounds. MacKinnon (1991b: 810) argues, "Any nation that has a constitutional guarantee of equality can potentially defend a group defamation statute that is challenged as a violation of freedom of expression on equality grounds." This is precisely what LEAF proposed within the Canadian context. However, LEAF members realized that, for such an argument to proceed, the equality provisions must be purposively interpreted to promote, in MacKinnon's (1991b: 810, n. 46) words, "equality in the application and formulation of the law, including promoting a society in which all of its members are recognized at law as equally deserving of concern, respect and consideration."

Members of the committee sought to connect this conceptualization of pornography with women's powerlessness to illustrate that subordination is the opposite of equality. According to MacKinnon (1993b: 100–1): "LEAF argued that if Canada's obscenity statute ... prohibiting 'undue exploitation of sex, or sex and violence, cruelty, horror, or crime,' was interpreted to institutionalize some people's views about women and sex over others it would be unconstitutional. But if the community standards applied were interpreted to prohibit harm to women as harm to the community, it was constitutional because it promoted sex equality." Accordingly, pornography is conceived as a harm of gender inequality, a harm outweighing any social interest in its protection under the freedom of expression guarantee (MacKinnon 1985: 25).

Because this case invoked the *Charter* to challenge the constitutional validity of the obscenity clause of the *Criminal Code*, LEAF intervened specifically because of the potential impact on women's equality of a Supreme Court ruling in favour of constitutionally protecting pornography under the freedom of expression guarantee of the *Charter*. In brief, LEAF presented an argument to the Supreme Court that addresses the substantive harm(s) engendered in and through pornography. LEAF argued that equality is a constitutional edict that compels the Court to uphold obscenity legislation. Indeed, the goal of obscenity legislation is to promote equality for women. Placing limitations on misogynist speech not only provides space for the voices of those who have been historically disadvantaged in this area, but also promotes women's equality by recognizing pornography as an inimical practice analogous to hate propaganda; that it is a practice systematically subordinating women (and children) on the basis of sex. LEAF argued that equality is a constitutional value and mandate; that the obscenity law, properly interpreted, is intended to promote equality. In short, LEAF demanded that the Supreme Court take equality seriously (MacKinnon 1993b).

It should be noted that many other feminist positions expressed during this period did not see pornography in the same ways as LEAF did. Instead, socialist feminists and sex radicals were more concerned about the effects of criminal regulation on women's sexual freedom than the actual harms caused by pornography (see, for example, Burstyn 1985; Cossman, Bell, Gotell, and Ross 1997; Johnson 1995; Lacombe 1994; Segal and McIntosh 1993).

THE SUPREME COURT DECISION

In February 1992 the Supreme Court of Canada determined, by virtue of section 1 of the *Charter*, that the state is constitutionally authorized to criminalize the distribution and sale of particular categories of porno-graphic materials. While section 163 of the *Criminal Code* was found to violate section 2(b) of the *Charter*, its violation is constitutionally justi-fied in accordance with the principles of a free and democratic society. Section 163(8) remains the exclusive statutory prohibition against ob-scenity, which is defined in terms of what the Canadian community would tolerate others being exposed to on the basis of the degree of harm that may flow from such exposure. This ruling recognizes that a link exists between pornography and attitudes and beliefs; and that depictions of sex coupled with violence and sex that is degrading and/or dehumaniz-ing are harmful to the extent that they promote anti-social behaviour towards women (and, arguably, men). As a result, the Supreme Court did not strike down the obscenity section of the *Criminal Code*. Post-*Butler*, the text of sub-section (8) remains in its original 1959 form, while the judicial interpretation has changed.

In its unanimous ruling, the Court noted that, historically, courts have sought to establish tests for the existence of undue exploitation as a domi-nant characteristic of pornographic materials. Therefore the Court be-gins its discussion in *Butler* by reviewing the judicial interpretations of section 163(8) employed pre-*Butler* to determine if the dominant char-acteristic of materials is the undue exploitation of sex. In a statement that significantly clarifies the common-law definition of pornography, Sopinka, J., writing for the Court, refers to three tiers of pornographic material: (1) explicit sex with violence; (2) explicit sex without violence but which subjects people to treatment that is degrading or dehumaniz-ing; and (3) explicit sex without violence that is neither degrading nor dehumanizing. Violence in this context includes both actual physical vio-lence and threats of physical violence (*R. v. Butler* 1992:36).

From the Court's review of the case law emerges three tests for the existence of undue exploitation of sex: the community standard of toler-ance test, the degradation and/or dehumanization test, and the internal necessities test (or the artistic defence). The first of these tests is a test of our tolerance for obscenity, which must be measured against the extent to which the contemporary Canadian community as a whole "would not tolerate *other* Canadians being exposed to" the materials in question (1992: 28; emphasis in original). The second test, the degrading and dehumanizing test, is a test for the undue exploitation of sex which, if found to exist, would exceed the community standards test of tolerance (1992: 28). The Court (1992: 29–30) states:

> Among other things degrading or dehumanizing materials place women (and sometimes men) in positions of subordination, servile submission or humiliation. They run against the principles of equality and dignity of all human beings. In the appreciation of whether material is degrading or dehumanizing the appearance of consent is not necessarily determinative. Consent cannot save materials that otherwise contain degrading and dehumanizing scenes. Sometimes the very appearance of consent makes the depicted acts even more degrading or dehumanizing.

Further, the Court (1992: 30) asserted, "This type of material would fail the community standards test not because it offends against morals but because it is perceived by public opinion to be harmful to society, particularly to women ... and therefore to society as a whole." The third test, the artistic defence, is the last step in a determination of the undue exploitation of sex. The Court (1992: 33) stated, "Even material which by itself offends community standards will not be considered 'undue,' if it is required for the serious treatment of a theme." In addition, the Court (1992: 38) noted, "Artistic expression rests at the heart of freedom of expression values and any doubt in this regard must be resolved in favour of freedom of expression." Consequently, the Court (1992: 37) concluded that these three tests would enable the courts to determine:

> as best they can what the community would tolerate others being exposed to on the basis of the degree of harm that may flow from such exposure. Harm in this context means that it predisposes persons to act in an anti-social manner as, for example, the physical or mental mistreatment of women by men, or what is perhaps debatable, the reverse. Anti-social conduct for this purpose is conduct which society formally recognizes as incompatible with its proper functioning. The stronger the inference of a risk of harm the lesser the likelihood of tolerance. The inference may be drawn from the material itself or from the material and other evidence. Similarly evidence as to the community standard is desirable but not essential.

Finally, a number of questions were relevant to the Court's application of the section (1) tests of the *Charter*. The Court determined that the definition of obscenity in section 163(8) provided an "intelligible standard" upon which to judge the impugned materials, and that the objective of section 163(8) is to prevent harm to society; that such an objective is valid and consequently justifies infringement upon the right of freedom of expression. The Court also considered the violation of freedom of expression in section 163(8) in proportion to the legislative objective of the law. In its application of the proportionality test, the Court affirmed that section 163(8) is directly related to and addresses the goal of protecting society from harm; that its infringement upon the freedom of expression is minimal and therefore justifiable and congruent with legislative objectives to protect society from harm.

POST-*BUTLER*: OBSCENITY LAW IN THE 1990S

In *Butler* the Supreme Court essentially ignored LEAF's equality argument and affirmed the common-law precedents of the 1980s. Nevertheless, the decision was considered a victory by some feminists, particularly those who saw a change of legal reasoning away from the Victorian-era moral regulatory practices towards a feminist understanding of how pornography harmed women's equality. MacKinnon (1993b: 103) later argued:

> Fundamentally, the Supreme Court of Canada recognized the reality of inequality in the issues before it: this was not big bad state power jumping on poor powerless individual citizen, but a law passed to stand behind a comparatively powerless group in its social fight for equality against socially powerful and exploitative groups. This positioning of forces—which makes the … obscenity law of Canada (properly interpreted) into equality [law], although neither was called such by Parliament—made the invocation of a tradition designed to keep government off the backs of people totally inappropriate.

Also, in an article published in the *Canadian Journal of Women and the Law*, U.S. feminist law professor Ann Scales (1994) declared that the *Butler* decision meant that Canadian obscenity law was now rooted in equality principles, even though others remained more critical of the underlying rationale of the *Butler* decision. For example, Cossman (1997) argues that the decision is a subtle joining of the anti-pornography feminist equality claims onto the courts' traditional moral conservative sexual morality underlying the legal definition of obscenity. Indeed, as proof that the rationale in *Butler* would have little effect, Customs officials seized a small-press lesbian erotic fiction magazine, *Bad Attitude*, which the courts judged to be obscene following the *Butler* standard.

That the *Butler* decision recognized harm to women is often mistakenly interpreted as the only feminist conception of harm. However, Cossman (1997), in particular, has demonstrated that the *Butler* decision simply added women into the courts' long-standing structural functionalist notion of harm to society. As members of society, women were included in the consensual moral order and seen as being harmed by obscenity. Because obscenity is pornography that is either violent or degrading and dehumanizing, it promotes certain ideas that undermine the proper functioning of society. This notion of obscenity is not dissimilar to the earlier nineteenth century notion of vice, which was concerned with the effects of the consumption of obscene materials on the moral turpitude of women, children, and persons of colour. Today the concern is broadened to include all members of society, even though, in practice, this rationale has been directed towards sexual representations of gay and lesbian sexuality. In its convoluted rationale, the Supreme Court placed the proper functioning of society front and centre, only acknowledging the equality argument advanced by LEAF to the extent that threats to equality undermine the social order. To this extent, feminists who advocated legal remedies for pornography succeeded in transforming a feminist argument for equality into functionalist conservative legal language.

Obscenity and indecency cases that followed the *Butler* decision and incorporated its rationale illustrate, among other things, the limits of law for addressing broader questions of gender and sexual freedom. For example, in the Supreme Court decision in *R. v. Mara,* which addressed the so-called indecency[14] of lap-dancing, the Court considered whether or not the theatrical performance in question was obscene and if the defendant "knowingly" allowed an indecent live performance.[15] On the question of the indecency of lap-dancing, Supreme Court Justice John Sopinka agreed with the Appeal Court that the performances in question were indecent according to community standards because of the social harm in the form of attitudinal harm to those watching the performance as perceived by the community as a whole.[16] The decision referred to women fondling themselves and being fondled in an intimately sexual manner, including mutual masturbation and cunnilingus in a public tavern. According to Sopinka, this conduct was indecent because it took place in public. "In effect, men, along with drinks, could pay for a public, sexual experience for their own gratification and those of others." For Sopinka the public nature of the sexual activity was, not surprisingly, the sticking point:

> Any finding of indecency must depend on all the circumstances. I am satisfied that the activities in the present case were indecent insofar as they involved sexual touching between dancer and patron. Thus, the fondling and sucking of breasts, as well as contact between the dancer and the patron and the other person's genitals, in circumstances such as the present case gave rise to an indecent performance. It is unacceptably degrading to women to permit such use of their bodies in the context of a public performance in a tavern. Insofar as the activities were consensual ... this does not alter their degrading character. Moreover, as I stated in *Butler* at p. 479, '[s]ometimes the very appearance of consent makes the depicted acts even more degrading or dehumanizing.' *(R. v. Mara 1997: para. 35)*

In this pointedly paternalistic decision, Sopinka takes it upon himself to protect society from the social harm caused by lap-dancing (which takes us back to the earlier discussion of the community standards test for tolerance). He also notes that the risk of harm to the women themselves in the form of sexually transmitted diseases and the harms associated with prostitution is relevant only insofar "as that risk exacerbates the social harm resulting from the degradation and objectification of women" (*R. v. Mara* 1997: 553). In other words, the women's working conditions are *irrelevant* to indecency, and the laws are concerned solely with the public nature of the performance and with the resultant harm caused to men who are subjected to lap-dancing. In Sopinka's view, lap-dancing is indecent and violates community standards because of its negative effect on *men*:

> The relevant social harm to be considered pursuant to s. 167 is the attitudinal harm on those watching the performance as perceived by the community as a whole. In the present case, as outlined in the facts, the patrons of Cheaters could, for a fee,

fondle and touch women and be fondled in an intimately sexual manner, including mutual masturbation and apparent cunnilingus, in a public tavern. In effect, men, along with drinks, could pay for a public, sexual experience for their own gratification and those of others. In my view, such activities gave rise to a social harm that indicates that the performances were indecent. (*R. v. Mara* 1997: 2)

But lap-dancing is also harmful to society because, according to Sopinka: "It degrades and dehumanizes women and publicly portrays them in a servile and humiliating manner as sexual objects, with a loss of their dignity. It dehumanizes and desensitizes sexuality and is incompatible with the recognition of the dignity and equality of each human being. It predisposes persons to act in an antisocial manner, as if the treatment of women in this way is socially acceptable and is normal conduct, and as if we live in a society without any moral values" (*R. v. Mara* 1997: 2)

Both men and women, then, are constructed as *victims* rather than as rational sexual agents engaged in consensual activity. Men first, because they are the hapless victims of women who perform indecent acts that inevitably cause the men to act in an anti-social manner; and women second, because they are the victims of lap-dancing itself, which "portrays them in a servile and humiliating manner as sexual objects." This approach does not see women as rational sexual agents, capable of making the decision to lap-dance for money, and I doubt that the Court ever asked any of these women (or any other women for that matter) if they felt humiliated or degraded on payday.

Ultimately, the Court acquitted Patrick Mara, the owner of the tavern, and allowed his appeal on the grounds that Mara did not possess the requisite *mens rea* for the crime, because he did not "knowingly" allow an indecent live performance to take place in his tavern. The Supreme Court allowed a similar acquittal in *R. v. Jorgensen* (1995) on the grounds that Jorgensen did not "knowingly" sell obscene material. In this case, obscenity was of peripheral concern. However, relying on the earlier Court of Appeal decision (which relied on *Butler),* the Supreme Court declared obscene a few heterosexual pornography videos (*Bung Ho Babes, Made in Hollywood,* and *Dr. Butts*), because each video showed a woman or women being spanked during intercourse (producing visible red marks on the buttocks). According to both the Appeal and Supreme Court judges, this constituted undue exploitation of sex because the pornography coupled sex with violence (*R. v. Jorgensen* 1995). Prosecutions of heterosexual pornography have tended to result in acquittals with the sexual content deemed "sex-for-fun" (*R. v. Hawkins* 1993: 246), leaving small bookstores and presses to defend their mostly gay and lesbian and/or artistic sexual materials.

These prosecutions of pornography and eventual court decisions illustrate the limits of criminal law. In the acquittals of *Mara* and *Jorgensen*, the courts found the material to be indecent and obscene, but certainly not for the reasons advanced by feminist legal scholars who advocate legal remedies for pornography. In both cases, the judges were concerned with the harmful effects on men first, and women second. But, more importantly, the courts continually position men as victims of both pornography and women. Troubling, too, is the underlying rejection of any notion of women as rational sexual agents. The law blames pornography itself for violence and for the broader social relations that place certain women (the young, the poor, the uneducated, and the racialized) at the end of the sharpest point of the patriarchal stick.

CONCLUSION

Obscenity law, then, is complicit in constructing gendered notions of sexuality and sexual freedom. The law may be used to promote specific feminist moral principles, but only when those principles elide with traditional conservative or liberal moral legal principles (as in much of the rationale in the *Butler* decision). The feminist principles adopted are extremely limited, particularly given the nature of criminal law. While the *Butler* decision did not reject the idea that sex-for-fun was okay (and therefore decent and clean), the criminal law can't be expected to promote sexual freedom or ideas about sexual subjectivity that challenge socially constructed gender norms, particularly given its repressive history. Questions about the sexual subordination of women in strip clubs and pornography call for a broader discussion of the relations that put those women there in the first place. Moreover, as dancers and porn stars are quick to point out, many other jobs performed by women—for example, waitressing, domestic, and secretarial services—can be far more degrading and dehumanizing given their lack of autonomy and low wages. This is not to glorify sex work, but to acknowledge, indeed, that a good deal of the work that women perform is degrading and dehumanizing—not because of sexual content—but because of low wages and abysmal working conditions. In recent cases the courts have been more concerned with the harmful effects that sexual representations and practices have on men than with the social relations that provide women with job opportunities in pornography and lap-dancing clubs.

NOTES

1. Many thanks to Karen Busby, Dorothy Chunn, and Elizabeth Comack for reading and commenting on an earlier version of this essay.
2. The Customs Tariff Act, which regulates the importation of obscene materials into Canada, incorporates *Criminal Code* provisions. In addition, individual film censor boards and the various provincial human rights codes regulate pornography provincially.
3. See, for example, Shannon Bell (1997) and consider the performance art of Annie Sprinkle, entitled "Post-Post Porn Modernist."
4. It is unclear if the church objected to depictions of sexuality because women's sexuality was considered *inherently* heretical or if particular materials were banned because they questioned the legitimacy of the church. It is possible to surmise that any depictions of sexuality not sanctioned by the church, such as homosexuality and/or sex outside of marriage, would have been viewed as a threat to its authority.
5. In Canada the term "foreigner" was later used to differentiate between people of colour who were deemed morally inferior to Canada's predominantly white British citizenry.
6. Karen Busby pointed out to me that there may have been many more obscenity cases, because very few criminal cases give reported reasons for their decisions. It is likely that there were many more prosecutions for obscenity than reported during this period.
7. This debate resurfaced in the twentieth century during the trial of serial sex killer Paul Bernardo when Judy Steed, features writer for *The Toronto Star* (1995: A1), argued that Bernardo was "one of us, a product of his culture, conditioned in the shadowy underworld of porn, where the dark side of the human psyche emerges in sadomasochism and sexual torture, in heroes who are rapists and serial killers." According to this theory, pornography is a public health hazard that turns seemingly normal, healthy men into sexual sadists who will inevitably rape, torture, and kill women. In the *Star* report, Staff Sergeant Bob Matthews, head of Project P, the Ontario Provincial Police agency established in 1975 to investigate and prosecute pornography, suggested that pornography is like an addictive drug. Once men get hooked on it, "They spend all their money on it, and some of them start doing what they see. They learn what to do from what they see."
8. The liberal notion of "tolerance" was advanced by Fulton who, in a House of Commons debate, suggested that the concept of "undue exploitation" referred to "generally something going beyond what men of good will and

common sense would tolerate" (Lacombe 1988: 37). This notion of "undue" exploitation begins to legally establish the distinction between soft-core and hard-core pornography, signifying that certain varieties of pornography that exploit women are not undue because they are tolerated by the community.

9. If anti-pornography feminists shared an uncomfortable ideological space with the religious right-wing moralists, it is here that feminists, gays, and lesbians advocating sexual freedom through pornography shared an uncomfortable ideological space with publishers of mainstream heterosexual pornography magazines, such as Hugh Hefner (*Playboy*) and Larry Flynt (*Hustler*). Both Hefner and Flynt advocated sexual freedom for both men and women through the publication, distribution, and consumption of their magazines.

10. At the time of the seizure, *The Joy of Gay Sex* had been readily available in dozens of other bookstores in Canada for ten years and had never been banned. Yet in 1986 Customs detained only those volumes imported by Glad Day.

11. Under Tariff Code 9956, Canada Customs is given prior restraint to block entry of any "books, printed paper, drawings, paintings, prints, photographs or representation of any kind" it considers "obscene, hate propaganda, treasonous and seditious" or child pornography (*R. v. Martin Secker Warburg Ltd. and Others* 1954). "Anal penetration" remained part of this checklist of prohibited activities until 1994, well after *Butler* (implicitly) and *Jorgensen* (explicitly) established that same-sex depictions were not of themselves obscene (personal communication with Karen Busby, August 1998).

12. The Women's Legal Education and Action Fund (LEAF) is a national feminist organization that participates in litigation to educate and compel Canadian courts to interpret and apply *Charter* provisions to promote equality. LEAF and other equality-seeking organizations argue that the *Charter* must be interpreted in accordance with the purposes of sections 15 and 28. In addition, it is important to note that LEAF's strategy in *R. v. Butler*—similar to many of its other cases—was a reactive response to a situation in which the *Charter* was being used to erode women's equality rather than to protect it. LEAF's intervention was not a proactive attempt to alter obscenity legislation. The case was initiated by Donald Victor Butler when his lawyers appealed the lower court decisions to the Supreme Court.

13. The LEAF factum in *R. v. Butler* was co-authored by Kathleen Mahoney, Catharine MacKinnon, and Linda Taylor in consultation with LEAF's National Legal Committee. A broad consultation with equality-seeking groups, such as that undertaken in *Keegstra* and *Taylor*, was unrealistic given the limited time frame (three weeks) that LEAF members had to research and write the *Butler* factum.

14. The terms "indecency" and "obscenity" have distinct legal traditions in

Canada, a discussion of which is beyond the scope of this chapter. However, I discuss the *Mara* decision here since it incorporates the legal tenets of *Butler*.

15. The community standards test is the same in indecency cases as in obscenity cases but, according to the decision, indecency, unlike obscenity, requires an assessment of the surrounding circumstance or context within which the indecent act takes place *(R. v. Mara* 1997).

16. Sopinka argued that *men* were caused attitudinal harm by watching lap-dancers perform *(R. v. Mara* 1997: 551).

References

Abel, Richard. 1985a. "Informalism: A Tactical Equivalent to Law?" *Clearinghouse Review* 19: 375–83.

———. 1985b. "Law Without Politics: Legal Aid Under Advanced Capitalism." *UCLA Law Review* 32: 474–642.

———. 1979. "Socializing the Legal Profession: Can Redistributing Lawyers' Services Achieve Social Justice?" *Law and Policy Quarterly* 1: 5–51.

Abell, Jennie. 1993. "Ideology and the Emergence of Legal Aid in Saskatchewan." *Dalhousie Law Journal* 15: 125–68.

Abella, I., and H. Troper. 1983. *None Is Too Many: Canada and the Jews of Europe, 1933–1948*. Toronto: Lester and Orpen Dennys.

Acker, Joan. 1988. "Class, Gender and the Relations of Distribution." *Signs* 12: 473–97.

Adamson, Nancy, Linda Briskin, and Margaret McPhail. 1988. *Feminist Organizing for Change: The Contemporary Women's Movement in Canada*. Toronto: Oxford University Press.

Andrew, Caroline. 1984. "Women and the Welfare State." *Canadian Journal of Political Science* 17: 667–83.

Andrew, Caroline and Sandra Rodgers (eds.). 1997. *Women and the Canadian State*. Montreal: McGill-Queen's University Press.

Arat-Koc, Sedef. 1997. "From 'Mothers of the Nation' to Migrant Workers." In Abigail Bakan and Daiva Stasiulis (eds.), *Not One of the Family: Foreign Domestic Workers in Canada*. Toronto: University of Toronto Press.

———. 1993. "Politics of the Family and Politics of Immigration in the Subordination of Domestic Workers in Canada." In Bonnie Fox (ed.), *Family Patterns and Gender Divisions*. Toronto: Oxford University Press.

———. 1992. "Immigration Policies, Migrant Domestic Workers and the Definition of Citizenship in Canada." In Vic Satzewich (ed.), *Deconstructing a Nation: Immigration, Multiculturalism and Racism in '90s Canada*. Halifax: Fernwood Publishing.

———. 1990. "Importing Housewives: Non-Citizen Domestic Workers and the Crisis of the Domestic Sphere in Canada." In M. Luxton et al., *Through the Kitchen Window: The Politics of Home and Family* (2nd edition). Toronto: Garamond Press.

Arat-Koc, Sedef and Fely Villasin. 1990. "Report and Recommendations on the Foreign Domestic Movement Program." Submitted to the Ministry of Employment and Immigration on behalf of INTERCEDE (Toronto Organization for Domestic Workers' Rights).

Armstrong, Pat. 1996. "The Feminization of the Labour Force: Harmonizing down in a Global Economy." In I. Bakker (ed.), *Rethinking Restructuring:*

Gender and Change in Canada. Toronto: University of Toronto Press.

Armstrong, Pat and Hugh Armstrong. 1994. *The Double Ghetto: Canadian Women and Their Segregated Work* (3rd edition). Toronto: McClelland & Stewart.

———. 1990. *Theorizing Women's Work.* Toronto: Garamond Press.

———. 1984. *The Double Ghetto* (2nd edition). Toronto: McClelland and Stewart.

Arnup, Katherine. 1989. "'Mothers Just Like Others': Lesbians, Divorce and Child Custody in Canada." *Canadian Journal of Women and the Law* 3: 18–32.

Austin R. and S. Dietrich. 1990. "Employer Abuse of Low-Status Workers: The Possibility of Uncommon Relief from the Common Law." In D. Kairys (ed.), *The Politics of Law: A Progressive Critique.* New York: Pantheon.

Ayres, I. and J. Braithwaite. 1992. *Responsive Regulation: Transcending the Deregulation Debate.* New York: Oxford.

Bacchi, Carol Lee. 1983. *Liberation Deferred? The Ideas of the English-Canadian Suffragists, 1877–1918.* Toronto: University of Toronto Press.

Backhouse, Constance. 1992. "Married Women's Property Law in Nineteenth-Century Canada." In B. Bradbury (ed.), *Canadian Family History: Selected Readings.* Toronto: Copp Clark Pitman Ltd.

———. 1991. *Petticoats and Prejudice: Women and Law in Nineteenth-Century Canada.* Toronto: The Women's Press.

Bailey, Martha J. 1989. *"Pelech, Caron,* and *Richardson."* *Canadian Journal of Women and the Law* 3(2): 615–33.

Baines, Carol, Patricia Evans, and Sheila Neysmith (eds.). 1998. *Women's Caring: Feminist Perspectives on Social Welfare* (2nd edition). Toronto: Oxford University Press.

Bakan, Abigail and Daiva Stasiulis. 1997. "Foreign Domestic Worker Policy in Canada and the Social Boundaries of Modern Citizenship." In Abigail Bakan and Daiva Stasiulis (eds.), *Not One of the Family: Foreign Domestic Workers in Canada.* Toronto: University of Toronto Press.

——— (eds.). 1997. *Not One of the Family: Foreign Domestic Workers in Canada.* Toronto: University of Toronto Press.

Bakker, Isabella and Katherine Scott. 1997. "From the Postwar to the Post-Liberal Keynesian Welfare State." In Wallace Clement (ed.), *Understanding Canada: Building on the New Canadian Political Economy.* Montreal & Kingston: McGill-Queen's University Press.

Bannerji, Himani (ed.). 1993. *Returning the Gaze: Essays on Racism, Feminism and Politics.* Toronto: Sister Vision Press.

Barber, Marilyn. 1991. *Immigrant Domestic Servants in Canada.* Ottawa: Canadian Historical Association.

———. 1987. "The Servant Problem in Manitoba, 1896–1930." In Mary Kinnear (ed.), *First Days, Fighting Days: Women in Manitoba History.* Regina:

References

Canadian Plains Research Centre, University of Regina.

Bardach, E. and R.A. Kagan. 1982. *Going by the Book: The Problem of Regulatory Unreasonableness*. Philadelphia: Temple University Press.

Barrett, Michele and Mary McIntosh. 1982. *The Anti-Social Family*. London: Verso and NLB.

Basran, G.S. 1983. "Canadian Immigration Policies and Theories of Racism." In P.S. Li and B.S. Bolaria (eds.), *Racial Minorities in Canada*. Toronto: Garamond Press.

Battiste, Marie and Jean Barman. 1995. *First Nations Education in Canada: The Circle Unfolds*. Vancouver: University of British Columbia Press.

Battle, Ken. 1998. "Poverty and the Welfare State." In L. Samuelson and W. Antony (eds.), *Power and Resistance: Critical Thinking About Canadian Social Issues* (2nd edition). Halifax: Fernwood Publishing.

———. 1994. "Myths, Misconceptions and Half-Truths." In Andrew F. Johnson and Stephen McBride (eds.), *Continuities and Discontinuities: The Political Economy of Social Welfare and Labour Market Policy in Canada*. Toronto: University of Toronto Press.

Becker, Howard. 1963. *The Outsiders*. New York: The Free Press.

Beirne, Piers and Robert Sharlet (eds.). 1980. *Pashukanis: Selected Writings on Marxism and Law*. London: Academic Press.

Bell, D. 1996. "Regulators' Perspectives." In M. Mehta (ed.), *Regulatory Efficiency and the Role of Risk Assessment*. Kingston: Queen's University School of Policy Studies (Environmental Policy Unit).

Bell, Shannon. 1997. "On ne Peut pas Voir L'image (The Image Cannot be Seen)." In Brenda Cossman et al. (eds.), *Bad Attitudes: Pornography, Feminism, and the Butler Decision*. Toronto: University of Toronto Press.

Bertoia, Carl and Janice Drakich. 1993. "The Fathers' Rights Movement: Contradictions in Rhetoric and Practice." *Journal of Family Issues* 14(4): 592–615.

Bienen, L. 1983. "A Question of Credibility: John Henry Wigmore's Use of Scientific Authority." *California Western Law Review* 19.

Bindman, Stephen. 1995. "Doesn't Deserve Protection: Judge Strips "Prostitute" of Publication Ban." *Law Times* March 5, 1995.

Blackstone, Sir William. 1979. *Commentaries on the Laws of England*. Chicago: University of Chicago Press.

Bliss, M. 1974. *A Living Profit: Studies in the Social Organization of Canadian Business*. Toronto: McClelland and Stewart.

Bolaria, B. Singh and Peter S. Li (eds.). 1988. *Racial Oppression in Canada* (2nd edition.). Toronto: Garamond Press.

Bonacich, E. 1980. "Class Approaches to Ethnicity and Race." *The Insurgent Sociologist* X (2) : 9–23.

———. 1976. "Advanced Capitalism and Black/White Race Relations in the United States: A Split Labor Market Interpretation." *American Sociologi-*

cal Review 41 (February): 34–51.

———. 1972. "A Theory of Ethnic Antagonism: The Split Labor Market." *American Sociological Review* 37 (October): 547–59.

Bourque, Dawn. 1994. "'Reconstructing' the Patriarchal Nuclear Family: Recent Developments in Child Custody and Access in Canada." *Canadian Journal of Law and Society* 10(1): 1–24.

Box, S. 1983. *Power, Crime and Mystification.* London: Tavistock Publications.

Boyd, Neil. 1984. "Sexuality and Violence, Imagery and Reality: Censorship and the Criminal Control of Obscenity." *Working Papers on Pornography and Prostitution*, Report No. 16. Ottawa: Ministry of Justice.

Boyd, Susan. 1998. "Lesbian (and Gay) Custody Claims: What Difference Does Difference Make?" *Canadian Journal of Family Law* 15(1): 131–52.

———. 1997a. "Looking Beyond *Tyabji*: Employed Mothers, Lifestyles, and Child Custody Law." In S.B. Boyd (ed.), *Challenging the Public/Private Divide.* Toronto: University of Toronto Press.

——— (ed.). 1997b. *Challenging the Public/Private Divide: Feminism, Law, and Public Policy.* Toronto: University of Toronto Press.

———. 1996. "Can Law Challenge the Public/Private Divide? Women, Work, and Family." *Windsor Yearbook of Access to Justice* 15:161–85.

———. 1989a.. "Child Custody, Ideologies and Employment." *Canadian Journal of Women and the Law* 3(1): 111–33.

———. 1989b. "Child Custody Law and the Invisibility of Women's Work."*Queen's Quarterly* 96(4): 831–58.

Boyd, Susan B. and Elizabeth A. Sheehy. 1986. "Feminist Perspectives on Law." *Canadian Journal of Women and the Law* 2(1): 1–51.

Braithwaite, J. 1995. "Corporate Crime and Republican Criminological Praxis." In F. Pearce and L. Snider (eds.), *Corporate Crime: Contemporary Debates.* Toronto: University of Toronto Press.

———. 1985a. "White Collar Crime." *American Review of Sociology* II: 1–25.

———. 1985b. *To Punish or Persuade: The Enforcement of Coal Mine Legislation.* Albany: State University of New York Press.

———. 1984. *Corporate Crime in the Pharmaceutical Industry.* London: Routledge and Kegan Paul.

Brand, Dionne. 1994. "'We Weren't Allowed to Go into Factory Work Until Hitler Started the War': The 1920s to the 1940s." In Peggy Bristow et al. (eds.), *'We're Rooted Here and They Can't Pull Us Up': Essays in African Canadian Women's History.* Toronto: University of Toronto Press.

———. 1991. *No Burden to Carry: Narratives of Black Women in Ontario, 1920s–1950s.* Toronto: Women's Press.

Brewer, Rose M. 1997. "Theorizing Race, Class, and Gender: The New Scholarship of Black Feminist Intellectuals and Black Women's Labour." In R. Hennessy and C. Ingraham (eds.), *Materialist Feminism.* London: Routledge.

References

Brickey, Stephen and Elizabeth Comack. 1987. "The Role of Law in Social Transformation: Is a 'Jurisprudence of Insurgency' Possible?" *Canadian Journal of Law and Society.* 2: 97–120.

———. 1986. *The Social Basis of Law: Critical Readings in the Sociology of Law* (1st edition). Toronto: Garamond Press.

British Columbia Civil Liberties Association. 1992. "Factum of the Intervenor." *R. v. Butler.* Supreme Court of Canada.

Brodie, Janine. 1995. *Politics on the Margins: Restructuring and the Canadian Women's Movement.* Halifax: Fernwood Publishing.

——— (ed.). 1996. *Women and Canadian Public Policy.* Toronto: Harcourt Brace and Company.

Brophy, Julia and Carol Smart (eds.). 1985. *Women-in-Law.* London: Routledge and Kegan Paul.

Burstyn, Varda (ed.). 1985. *Women Against Censorship.* Vancouver: Douglas and McIntyre.

Busby, Karen. 1997. "Discriminatory Uses of Personal Records in Sexual Violence Cases." *Canadian Journal of Women and the Law/ Revue "Femme et Droit"* 9.

———. 1995. "Rape Crisis Backlash and the Spectre of False Rape Allegations." (unpublished).

———. 1993. "LEAF and Pornography: Litigating on Equality and Sexual Representations." *Canadian Review of Law and Society* 9(1): 165–92.

Busby, Karen, Lisa Fainstein, and Holly Penner (eds.). 1990. *Equality Issues in Family Law.* Winnipeg: Legal Research Institute of the University of Manitoba.

Cain, Maureen. 1994. "The Symbol Traders." In Maureen Cain and Christine B. Harrington (eds.), *Lawyers in a Postmodern World.* New York: New York University Press.

———. 1983. "The General Practise Lawyer and the Client: Towards a Radical Conception." In R. Dingwall and P. Lewis (eds.), *The Sociology of Professions: Doctors, Lawyers, and Others.* London: Macmillan.

Calavita, K., H. Pontell, and R. Tillman. 1997. *Big Money Crime.* Berkeley: University of California Press.

Calliste, Agnes. 1993/4. "Race, Gender and Canadian Immigration Policy: Blacks from the Caribbean, 1900–1937." *Journal of Canadian Studies* 28(4): 131–48.

———. 1991. "Canada's Immigration Policy and Domestic Blacks from the Caribbean: The Second Domestic Scheme." In Elizabeth Comack and Stephen Brickey (eds.), *The Social Basis of Law* (2nd edition). Halifax: Garamond Press.

———. 1989. "Canada's Immigration Policy and Domestics from the Caribbean: The Second Domestic Scheme." In Jesse Vorst et al. (eds.), *Race, Class, Gender: Bonds and Barriers.* Toronto: Garamond Press and The

Society for Socialist Studies.

Canada. 1996. *Report of the Royal Commission on Aboriginal Peoples*. Volume 4. Ottawa: Minster of Supply and Services Canada.

Canada. 1994. *Improving Social Security in Canada: A Discussion Paper.* Ottawa: Department of Human Resources.

Canada. 1992. *House of Commons Debates.* 3rd Session, 34th Parliament, June 22.

Canada. 1970. *Report of the Royal Commission on the Status of Women*. Ottawa: Queen's Printer.

Canada, Bureau of Competition Policy. 1989. *Competition Policy in Canada: The First Hundred Years.* Ottawa: Consumer and Corporate Affairs.

Canada, Environment Canada. 1995. *It's About Our Health: Towards Pollution Prevention.* Report of the House of Commons Standing Committee on the Environmental and Sustainable Development. Ottawa: House of Commons, #81. (CEPA Review).

Canada, Industry Canada. 1998. *Annual Report of the Director of Investigation and Research, Competition Act* (for the year ending March 31, 1997). Ottawa.

————. 1997. *Annual Report of the Director of Investigation and Research, Competition Act* (for the year ending March 31, 1996). Ottawa.

Canada, Royal Commission on Aboriginal Peoples. 1995. *Accommodating the Concerns of Aboriginal People Within the Existing Justice System.* John Giokas, Chair. Ottawa: Ministry of Supply and Services.

Canadian Advisory Council on the Status of Women. 1988. "Pornography: An Analysis of Proposed Legislation (Bill C-54)." A Brief presented to the Hon. Ray Hnatyshyn, Minister of Justice.

————. 1984. "On Pornography and Prostitution: Brief Presented to The Special Committee on Pornography and Prostitution." Ottawa.

CEIC. 1992. Immigrant Regulations, 1978. As amended by SOR/92-214, P.C. 1992–685.

Canadian Forum. 1997. "Index on Global Corporate Power." (January/February): 48.

Canadian Immigration Act. 1989. R.S. 1985, c.I-2-November.

Cappon, P. 1975. "The Green Paper: Immigration as a Tool of Profit." *Canadian Ethnic Studies* 7: 50–54.

Caragata, W. 1992. "Immigration Changes Play to the Right." *Toronto Star*, June 17.

Carby, Hazel V. 1997. "White Woman Listen! Black Feminism and the Boundaries of Sisterhood." In R. Hennessy and C. Ingraham (eds.), *Materialist Feminism.* London: Routledge.

Carey, Ruth. 1992. "Useless" (UOCLAS) v. The Bar: The Struggle of the Ottawa Student Clinic to Represent Battered Women." *Journal of Law and Social Policy* 10: 54–81.

Carson, W. 1980. "The Institutionalization of Ambiguity: Early British Factory Acts." In G. Geis and E. Stotland (eds.), *White Collar Theory and Research.* Beverly Hills: Sage.

———. 1970. "White Collar Crime and the Enforcement of Factory Legislation." *British Journal of Criminology* 10: 383–98.

Chambliss, William. 1986. "On Lawmaking." In S. Brickey and E. Comack (eds.), *The Social Basis of Law* (1st edition). Toronto: Garamond Press.

———. 1975. "Toward a Political Economy of Crime." *Theory and Society* 2 (2)(Summer): 149–70.

———. 1964. "A Sociological Analysis of the Law of Vagrancy." *Social Problems* 12(Summer): 67–77.

Chartrand. Mark. 1984. "The First Canadian Trade Union Legislation: An Historical Perspective." *Ottawa Law Review* 16: 267–96.

Chaster, Sally and Mary Wilson. 1985. "The Politics of Obscenity: Pornography and Canadian Legal Systems." Paper presented to the Western Association of Sociology and Anthropology Annual Conference, February 16.

———. 1984. "Pornography and Law Enforcement." Paper presented to the Western Association of Sociology and Anthropology Annual Conference, February 11.

Chernier, Nancy M. 1982. *Reproductive Hazards at Work: Men, Women and the Fertility Gamble.* Ottawa: Advisory Council on the Status of Women.

Christie, Nils. 1978. "Conflicts as Property." In Charles E. Reasons and Robert M. Rich (eds.), *The Sociology of Law: A Conflict Perspective.* Toronto: Butterworths.

Chunn, Dorothy. 1992. *From Punishment to Doing Good: Family Courts and Socialized Justice in Ontario 1880–1940.* Toronto: University of Toronto Press.

———. 1990. "Boys Will Be Men, Girls Will Be Mothers: The Regulation of Childhood in Vancouver and Toronto." *Sociological Studies in Childhood Development* 3: 87–110.

Chunn, Dorothy and Dany Lacombe (eds.). 1999. *Law as a Gendering Practice.* Toronto: Oxford University Press.

Cicourel, Aron. 1968. *The Social Organization of Juvenile Justice.* New York: John Wiley and Sons.

Citizenship and Immigration Canada. 1996. *Annual Report to Parliament.* Ottawa: Citizenship and Immigration.

Clarke, Lorenne and Debra Lewis. 1977. *Rape: The Price of Coercive Sexuality.* Toronto: The Women's Press.

Clarke, M. 1990. *Business Crime.* Cambridge: Polity Press.

Clinard, M.B. and P. Yeager. 1980. *Corporate Crime.* New York: Free Press.

Cohen, Marjorie Griffen. 1997. "From the Welfare State to Vampire Capitalism." In P.M. Evans and G.R. Werkle (eds.), *Women and the Canadian Welfare State.* Toronto: University of Toronto Press.

————. 1988. *Women's Work, Markets, and Economic Development in Nineteenth–Century Ontario.* Toronto: University of Toronto Press.

Cohen, Marjorie Griffin with Judy Morrison and Darcian Smith. 1995. "Dismantling Social Welfare: Chronology of Federal Government Cutbacks, 1985–1995." *Canadian Centre for Policy Alternatives Monitor* (November): 9–12.

Cohen, Rina. 1987. "The Work Conditions of Immigrant Women Live-in Domestics: Racism, Sexual Abuse and Invisibility." *Resources for Feminist Research* 16(1).

Cole, Susan G. 1989. *Pornography and the Sex Crisis.* Toronto: Amanita Press.

————. 1987. "Pornography and Harm." Paper prepared for the Metro Action Committee on Public Violence Against Women and Children, Toronto.

————. 1986. "The Minneapolis Ordinance: Feminist Law Making." *Resources for Feminist Research* 14: 30–31.

Coleman, J.W. 1987. "Toward an Integrated Theory of White-Collar Crime." *American Journal of Sociology* 93: 406–39.

————. 1985. *The Criminal Elite: The Sociology of White Collar Crime.* New York: St. Martin's Press.

Comack, Elizabeth. 1996a. *Women in Trouble: Connecting Women's Law Violations to Their Histories of Abuse.* Halifax: Fernwood Publishing.

————. 1996b. "Women and Crime." In R. Linden (general editor), *Criminology: A Canadian Perspective* (3rd edition). Toronto: Harcourt Brace.

————. 1993. *The Feminist Engagement with the Law: The Legal Recognition of the 'Battered Woman Syndrome.'* The CRIAW Papers no. 31. Ottawa: Canadian Research Institute for the Advancement of Women.

————. 1991. "'We Will Get Some Good out of This Riot Yet': The Canadian State, Drug Legislation and Class Conflict." In E. Comack and S. Brickey (eds.), *The Social Basis of Law: Critical Readings in the Sociology of Law* (2nd edition). Toronto: Garamond Press.

Comack, Elizabeth and Stephen Brickey (eds.). 1991. *The Social Basis of Law: Critical Readings in the Sociology of Law* (2nd edition). Halifax: Garamond Press.

Comish, Shaun. 1993. *The Westray Tragedy: A Miner's Story.* Halifax: Fernwood Publishing.

Commission on Systemic Racism in the Ontario Criminal Justice System. 1998. "Racism in Justice: Perceptions." In Vic Satzewich (ed.), *Racism and Social Inequality in Canada: Concepts, Controversies and Strategies of Resistance.* Toronto: Thompson Educational Publishing.

Cook, Shantu and Juliet Watt. 1987. "Women, Racism and Poverty." In C. Glendinning and J. Millar (eds.), *Women and Poverty in Britain.* Brighton: Wheatsheaf Books.

Cook-Lynn, Elizabeth. 1996. *Why I Can't Read Wallace Stegner and Other Essays.* Madison: The University of Wisconsin Press.

References

Correctional Service of Canada. 1990. *Creating Choices: Report of the Task Force on Federally Sentenced Women*. Ottawa: Solicitor General.

Corrigan, Phillip and Derek Sayer.1985. *The Great Arch: English State Transformation as a Cultural Revolution*. Oxford: Blackwell.

———. 1981. "How the Law Rules: Variation on Some Themes in Karl Marx." In B. Fryer et al. (eds.), *Law, State and Society*. London: Croom Helm.

Cossman Brenda. 1997. "Feminist Fashion or Morality in Drag? The Sexual Subtext of the *Butler* Decision." In Brenda Cossman, Shannon Bell, Lise Gotell, and Becki L. Ross (eds.), *Bad Attitude/s: Pornography, Feminism, and the Butler Decision*. Toronto: University of Toronto Press.

Cossman, Brenda and Shannon Bell. 1997. "Introduction." In Brenda Cossman, Shannon Bell, Lise Gotell and Becki L. Ross (eds.), *Bad Attitude/s: Pornography, Feminism, and the Butler Decision*. Toronto: University of Toronto Press.

Cossman, Brenda, Shannon Bell, Lisa Gotell, and Becki L. Ross (eds.). 1997. *Bad Attitude/s: Pornography, Feminism, and the Butler Decision*. Toronto: University of Toronto Press.

Cossman, Brenda and Carol Rodgerson. 1997. "Case Study in the Provision of Legal Aid: Family Law." In the *Report of the Ontario Legal Aid Review: A Blueprint for Publicly Funded Legal Services*. Volume 3. Toronto: Queen's Printer.

Cotterrell, R. 1992. *Sociology of Law: An Introduction* (2nd edition). London: Butterworths.

Cox, O.C. 1948. *Caste, Race and Class*. New York: Modern Reader Paperbacks.

de Silva, A. 1992. *Earnings of Immigrants: A Comparative Analysis*. A Study Prepared for the Economic Council of Canada. Ottawa: Supply and Services Canada.

Craven, Paul. 1984. "Workers' Conspiracies in Toronto, 1854–72." *Labour/ Le Travail* 14: 49–70.

———. 1981. "The Law of Master and Servant in Mid-Nineteenth Century Ontario." In D. Flaherty (ed.), *Essays in the History of Canadian Law*. Toronto: University of Toronto Press.

Creese, Gillian. 1991. "Sexual Equality and the Minimum Wage in B.C." *Journal of Canadian Studies* 26: 120–40.

Cressey, D. 1953. *Other People's Money: A Study in the Social Psychology of Embezzlement*. Glencoe, Illinois: Free Press.

Culhane, Dara. 1998. *The Pleasure of the Crown: Anthropology, Law and First Nations*. Burnaby: Talonbooks.

Cullen, F., W. Maakestadt, and G. Cavender. 1987. *Corporate Crime Under Attack: The Ford Pinto Case and Beyond*. Cincinnati: Anderson.

Cunningham, Nicola. 1991. *Seduced and Abandoned: The Legal Regulation of Domestic Workers in Canada from 1867 to 1940*. Unpublished LL.M thesis, York University.

Currie, Dawn. 1992. "Feminist Encounters with Postmodernism: Exploring the Impasse of Debates on Patriarchy and Law." *Canadian Journal of Women and the Law.* 5: 63–86.

Daenzer, Patricia M. 1993. *Regulating Class Privilege: Immigrant Services in Canada, 1940s–1990.* Toronto: Canadian Scholars Press.

Dale, Jennifer and Peggy Foster. 1986. *Feminists and State Welfare.* London: Routledge and Kegan Paul.

Danys, Milda. 1986. *DP: Lithuanian Immigration to Canada.* Toronto: Multicultural Historical Society of Ontario.

Das Gupta, Tania. 1996. *Racism and Paid Work.* Toronto: Garamond Press.

Dei, George J. Sefa. 1998. "The Politics of Educational Change: Taking Anti-Racism Education Seriously." In Vic Satzewich (ed.), *Racism and Social Inequality in Canada: Concepts, Controversies and Strategies of Resistance.* Toronto: Thompson Educational Publishing.

DeMara, Bruce. 1992. "New Immigration Rules Racist Domestic Workers Rally Told." *Toronto Star,* February 3: A3.

Dion Stout, Madeleine and Catherine R. Bruyere. 1997. "Stopping Family Violence: Aboriginal Communities Enspirited." In J. Rick Ponting (ed.), *First Nations in Canada: Perspectives on Opportunity, Empowerment, and Self-Determination.* Toronto: McGraw-Hill Ryerson.

Dobbin, Murray. 1998. "Unfriendly Giants." *Report on Business Magazine* July 15: 73–80.

Domestics Cross Cultural News (monthly newsletter of the Toronto Organization for Domestic Workers' Rights).

Domhoff, William. 1970. *The Higher Circles.* New York: Random House.

Donzelot, Jacques. 1980. *The Policing of Families.* New York: Pantheon.

Drakich, Janice. 1989. "In Search of the Better Parent: The Social Construction of Ideologies of Fatherhood." *Canadian Journal of Women and the Law* 3(1): 69–87.

Duclos, Nitya. 1991. "Some Complicating Thoughts on Same-Sex Marriage." *Law and Sexuality* 1: 31–62.

Dummett, A. 1973. *A Portrait of English Racism.* Harmondsworth: Penguin.

Durkheim, Emile. 1964. *The Division of Labor in Society.* New York: The Free Press.

Edelhertz, H. 1970. *The Nature, Impact and Prosecution of White-Collar Crime.* Washington, D.C.: National Institute for Law Enforcement and Criminal Justice, Department of Justice.

Eichler, Margrit. 1997. *Family Shifts: Families, Policies, and Gender Equality.* Toronto: Oxford University Press.

———. 1991. "The Limits of Family Law Reform, or the Privatization of Female and Child Poverty." *Canadian Family Law Quarterly* 7: 59–83.

Eisenstein, Zillah R. 1989. *The Female Body and the Law.* Berkeley: University of California Press.

———. 1979. "Developing a Theory of Capitalist Patriarchy and Socialist Feminism." In Zillah R. Eisenstein (ed.), *Capitalist Patriarchy and the Case for Socialist Feminism.* New York: Monthly Review Press.

Elliott, J.E. and A. Fleras. 1996. *Unequal Relations: An Introduction to Race and Ethnic and Aboriginal Dynamics in Canada* (2nd edition). Scarborough: Prentice-Hall Canada.

———. *Unequal Relations: An Introduction to Race and Ethnic Dynamics in Canada.* Scarborough: Prentice-Hall Canada.

Ellsworth, Randall. 1997. "Squandering Our Inheritance: Re-Forming the Canadian Welfare State in the 1990s." *Journal of Law and Social Policy* 12: 259–90.

Employment and Immigration Canada. 1996. *Foreign Domestic Workers in Canada: Facts for Domestics and Employers* (Pamphlet). Ottawa: Ministry of Supply and Services, Cat. No. MP23-61/1986.

———. 1991. "Admission to Canada—Immigrants (General)." *Immigration Manual—Selection and Control, Volume 1.* Ottawa: Supply and Services Canada (looseleaf insert).

Epstein, Rachel. 1983. "Domestic Workers: The Experience in B.C." In L. Briskin and L. Yanz (eds.), *Union Sisters.* Toronto: Women's Press.

Ericson, Richard M. and Patricia M. Baranek. 1982. *The Ordering of Justice.* Toronto: University of Toronto Press.

Ericson R. and K. Haggerty. 1997. *Policing the Risk Society.* Toronto: University of Toronto Press.

Ermine, Willie. 1995. "Aboriginal Epistemology." In Marie Battiste and Jean Barman (eds.), *First Nations Education in Canada: The Circle Unfolds.* Vancouver: University of British Columbia Press.

Evans, Patricia. 1998. "Gender, Poverty, and Women's Caring." In C. Baines et al. (eds.), *Women's Caring: Feminist Perspectives on Social Welfare* (2nd edition). Toronto: Oxford University Press.

———. 1991. "The Sexual Division of Poverty: The Consequences of Gendered Caring." In Carol Baines, Patricia Evans, Sheila Newsmith (eds.), *Women's Caring: Feminist Perspectives on Social Welfare.* Toronto: McClelland and Stewart.

Evans, Patricia and Norene Pupo. 1993. "Parental Leave: Assessing Women's Interests." *Canadian Journal of Women and the Law* 6(2): 402–18.

Evans, Patricia and Gerda Wekerle (eds.). 1997. *Women and the Canadian Welfare State: Challenges and Change.* Toronto: University of Toronto Press.

Ewart, Doug. 1997. "Parkdale Community Legal Services: A Dream That Died." *Osgoode Hall Law Journal* 35 (3&4): 475–84.

Feldberg, Georgina. 1997. "Defining the Facts of Rape: The Uses of Medical Evidence in Sexual Assault Trials." *Canadian Journal of Women and the Law/Revue "Femme et Droit"* 9.

Feldthusen, Bruce. 1996. "The Best Defence Is a Good Offence: Access to the Private Therapeutic Records of Sexual Assault Complainants under the *O'Connor* Guidelines and Bill C-46." *Canadian Bar Review* 75.

Ferguson, Evelyn. 1998. "The Child-Care Debate: Facing Hopes and Shifting Sands." In C.T. Baines et al. (eds.), *Women's Caring: Feminist Perspectives on Social Welfare* (2nd edition). Toronto: Oxford University Press.

Fine, Bob. 1984. *Democracy and the Rule of Law: Liberal Ideals and Marxist Critiques.* London: Pluto Press.

———. 1979. "Law and Class." In Bob Fine et al. (eds.), *Capitalism and the Rule of Law.* London: Hutchinson.

Foucault, Michel. 1990. *The History of Sexuality* (Vols. I, II, III). New York: Vintage Books Edition.

———. 1979a. *Discipline and Punish.* New York: Vintage Books.

———. 1979b. "Governmentality." *Ideology & Consciousness* 6: 5–21.

———. 1978. *The History of Sexuality, Volume I.* (Translated by Robert Hurley). New York: Pantheon Books.

Fowler, H.W. and F.G. Fowler (eds.). 1974. *The Concise Oxford Dictionary.* Oxford: Clarendon Press.

Fox, Alan. 1974. *Beyond Contract: Work, Power and Trust.* London: Faber.

Fraser, Paul, Susan Clark, Mary Eberts, Jean-Paul Gilbert, John McLaren, Andree Ruffo, and Joan Wallace. 1985. (The Special Committee on Pornography and Prostitution). *Pornography and Prostitution in Canada*, Volumes 1 and 2. Ottawa: Minister of Supply and Services.

Frideres, James. 1988. "Institutional Structures and Economic Deprivation: Native People in Canada." In S. Bolaria and P. Li (eds.), *Racial Oppression in Canada* (2nd edition). Toronto: Garamond Press.

Friedman, Lawrence. 1977. *Law and Society: An Introduction.* New Jersey: Prentice Hall.

Fudge, J. 1998. "Corporate Campaigns Against Labour Abuse: Consumers to the Rescue?" Paper presented at *(Ab)Using Power: The Canadian Experience.* Conference held at Simon Fraser University, Vancouver, B.C., May 7–9.

———. 1997. "Little Victories and Big Defeats: The Rise and Fall of Collective Bargaining Rights for Domestic Workers in Ontario." In Abigail Bakan and Daiva Stasiulis (eds.), *Not One of the Family: Foreign Domestic Workers in Canada.* Toronto: University of Toronto Press.

———. 1996a. "Fragmentation and Feminization: The Challenge of Equity for Labour-Relations Policy." In J. Brodie (ed.), *Women and Canadian Public Policy.* Toronto: Harcourt Brace.

———. 1996b. "Rungs on the Labour Law Ladder: Using Gender to Challenge Hierarchy." *Saskatchewan Law Review* 60 (2): 237–63.

———. 1991a. "Reconceiving Employment Standards Legislation: Labour Law's Little Sister and the Feminization of Labour." *Journal of Law and*

Social Policy 7: 73–89.

———. 1991b. "Marx's Theory of History and a Marxist Analysis of Law." In R. Devlin (ed.), *Canadian Perspectives on Legal Theory*. Toronto: Emond Montgomery.

———. 1989. "The Privatization of the Costs of Reproduction." *Canadian Journal of Women and the Law* 3: 246–55.

Fudge, Judy and Harry Glasbeek. 1992. "The Politics of Rights: A Politics with Little Class." *Socio-Legal Studies* 1: 45–70.

Fuller, Janine and Stuart Blackley. 1995. *Restricted Entry: Censorship on Trial.* Vancouver: Press Gang Publishers.

Furlong, J. and C. Schmitz. 1995. "Lawyers Fear Legal Aid Crisis Could Wipe Them Out." *The Lawyers' Weekly* September 22: 2.

Galliher, G.F. and F. Walker. 1978. "The Politics of Systematic Research Error: The Case of the Federal Bureau of Narcotics as a Moral Entrepreneur." *Crime and Social Justice.* 29–33.

Gallon, G. 1996. "Ontario Government Backsliding on Environment." *Canadian Environmental Business Letter: The Gallon Report* 11 (46), November 20.

Gallup Report. 1992. *Economic Difficulties Preoccupy Canadian Public.* May 7.

Garland, David. 1985. *Punishment and Welfare.* Brookfield, Vt.: Gower.

Gathercole, Richard J. 1982. "Legal Services and the Poor." In R.G. Evans and M.J. Trebilcock (eds.), *Lawyers and the Consumer Interest: Regulating the Market for Legal Services*. Toronto: Butterworths.

Gavigan, Shelley A.M. 1998. "Legal Forms, Family Forms, Gender Norms: What Is a Spouse?" North York, Ontario: Osgoode Hall Law School, York University.

———. 1997. "Twenty-five Years of Dynamic Tension: The Parkdale Community Legal Services Experience." *Osgoode Hall Law Journal* 35 (3&4): 443–74.

———. 1995. "A Parent(ly) Knot: Can Heather Have Two Mommies?" In D. Herman and C. Stychin (eds.), *Legal Inversions: Lesbians, Gay Men and the Politics of Law*. Philadelphia: Temple University Press.

———. 1993. "Paradise Lost, Paradox Revisited: The Implications of Familial Ideology for Feminist, Lesbian and Gay Engagement to Law." *Osgoode Hall Law Journal* 31 (3): 589–624.

———. 1988. "Law, Gender and Ideology." In Anne F. Bayefsky (ed.), *Legal Theory Meets Legal Practice*. Edmonton: Academic Printers and Publishing.

———. 1981. "Marxist Theories of Law: A Survey, with Some Thoughts on Women and Law." *Canadian Criminology Forum* 4: 1–12.

Glasbeek, Harry. 1995. "Preliminary Observations on Strains of, and Strains in, Corporate Law Scholarship." In F. Pearce and L. Snider (eds.), *Corporate*

Crime: Contemporary Debates. Toronto: University of Toronto Press.

———. 1989. "Why Corporate Deviance Is Not Treated as a Crime: The Need to Make Profits a Dirty Word." In T. Caputo et al. (eds.), *Law and Society: A Critical Perspective*. Toronto: Harcourt Brace Jovanovich.

———. 1982. "The Contract of Employment at Common Law." In J. Anderson and M. Gunderson (eds.), *Union-Management Relations in Canada*. Toronto: Addison-Wesley.

Goff, Colin and Charles Reasons. 1978. *Corporate Crime in Canada: A Critical Analysis of Anti-Combines Legislation*. Scarborough, Ontario: Prentice Hall.

Goldman, C. 1989. "The Impact of the Competition Act of 1986." Address given to the National Conference on Competition Law and Policy in Canada, Toronto, October 24–25.

Gordon, Linda. 1994. *Pitied but Not Entitled: Single Mothers and the History of Welfare*. New York: The Free Press.

——— (ed.). 1990. *Women, the State and Welfare*. Madison, Wis.: University of Wisconsin Press.

Gramsci, Antonio. 1971. *Selections from the Prison Notebooks*. New York: International Publishers.

Green, G. 1994. *Occupational Crime*. Chicago: Nelson-Hall.

Green, A. 1976. *Immigration and the Postwar Canadian Economy*. Toronto: Macmillan.

Guillaumin, C. 1980. "The Idea of Race and Its Elevation to Autonomous Legal Status." In UNESCO's *Sociological Theories: Race and Colonialism*. Paris: UNESCO.

Gunningham, N. 1984. *Safeguarding the Workers*. Sydney: Law Book Co.

Hamilton, A.C. and C.M. Sinclair. 1991. *Report of the Aboriginal Justice Inquiry of Manitoba: The Justice System and Aboriginal People*, Volume 1. Winnipeg: Queen's Printer.

Harper, T. 1992. "Immigration Plan: Is Canada Getting Meaner?" *Toronto Star,* September 14, A1 and A24.

Hart, H.L.A. 1961. *The Concept of Law*. Oxford: Clarendon Press.

Hartmann, Heidi. 1981. "The Unhappy Marriage of Marxism and Feminism: Toward a More Progressive Union." In L. Sargent (ed.), *Women and the Revolution*. Boston: South End Press.

Hawkins, F. 1989. *Critical Years in Immigration: Canada and Australia Compared*. Montreal: McGill-Queen's University Press.

———. 1988. *Canadian Immigration: Public Policy and Public Concern* (2nd edition). Montreal: McGill-Queen's University Press.

Hennessy, Rosemary. 1993. "Women's Lives/Feminist Knowledge: Standpoint as Ideology Critique." *Hypatia: A Journal of Feminist Philosophy 8* (1): 14–34.

Henry, F., C. Tator, W. Mattis, and T. Rees. 1995. *The Colour of Democracy:*

Racism in Canadian Society. Toronto: Harcourt Brace and Company.

Henry, Frances and Effie Ginzberg. 1985. *Who Gets the Work: A Test of Racial Discrimination in Employment*. Toronto: The Urban Alliance on Race Relations and the Social Planning Council of Metropolitan Toronto.

Herman, Didi. 1994. *Rights of Passage: Struggles for Lesbian and Gay Legal Equality*. Toronto: University of Toronto Press.

———. 1988. "AIDS as a Poverty Law Issue." Paper submitted in partial fulfilment of the requirements of the Intensive Program in Poverty Law at Parkdale Community Legal Services. Toronto: York University, Osgoode Hall Law Schoool.

Hobbes, Margaret. 1985. "'Dead Horses' and 'Muffled Voices': Protective Legislation, Education and the Minimum Wage for Women in Ontario." Unpublished M.A. thesis, University of Toronto.

Hook, Nancy. 1978. *Domestic Service Occupation Study: Final Report*. Ottawa: Canada Manpower and Immigration.

hooks, bell. 1981. *Ain't I a Woman? Black Women and Feminism*. Boston: South End Press.

House of Commons (HC). 1992. *Minutes of Proceedings and Evidence of the Legislative Committee on Bill C-86* (Issue #4- July 29; Issue #5- July 30; Issue #8- August 12; Issue #10- September 15).

Howe, Adrian. 1990. "The Problem of Privatized Injuries: Feminist Strategies for Litigation." *Studies in Law, Politics and Society* 10: 119–42.

———. 1987. "'Social Injury' Revisited: Towards a Feminist Theory of Social Justice." *International Journal of the Sociology of Law* 15: 423–38.

Hunt, Alan. 1993. *Explorations in Law and Society: Toward a Constitutive Theory of Law*. London: Routledge.

———. 1991a. "Marxism, Law, Legal Theory and Jurisprudence." In Peter Fitzpatrick (ed.), *Dangerous Supplements: Resistance and Renewal in Jurisprudence*. London: Pluto Press.

———. 1991b. "Postmodernism and Critical Criminology." In B. MacLean and D. Milovanovic (eds.), *New Directions in Critical Criminology*. Vancouver: Collective Press.

———. 1976. "Law, State and Class Struggle." *Marxism Today* 20 (6): 178–87.

Hunt, Lynn. 1993a. "Pornography and the French Revolution." In Lynn Hunt (ed.), *The Invention of Pornography: Obscenity and the Origins of Modernity 1500—1800*. New York: Zone Books.

——— (ed.). 1993b. *The Invention of Pornography: Obscenity and the Origins of Modernity 1500–1800*. New York: Zone Books.

Iacovetta, Franca. 1986. "'Primitive Villagers and Uneducated Girls': Canada Recruits Domestics from Italy, 1951–52." *Canadian Woman Studies* 7(4): 14–18.

Immigration Canada. 1992. *Managing Immigration: A Framework for the 1990's*. Ottawa: Supply and Services Canada.

Iyer, Nitya. 1997. "Some Mothers Are Better Than Others: A Re-examination of Maternity Benefits." In S.B. Boyd (ed.), *Challenging the Public/Private Divide*. Toronto: University of Toronto Press.

Jackel, Susan. 1982. *A Flannel Shirt and Liberty: British Emigrant Gentlewomen in the Canadian West, 1880–1914*. Vancouver: University of British Columbia Press.

Jakubowski, Lisa Marie. 1997. *Immigration and the Legalization of Racism*. Halifax: Fernwood Publishing.

James, Carl E. 1998. "'Up to No Good': Blacks on the Streets and Encountering Police." In Vic Satzewich (ed.), *Racism and Social Inequality in Canada: Concepts, Controversies and Strategies of Resistance*. Toronto: Thompson Educational Publishing.

Jamieson, Kathleen. 1978. *Indian Women and the Law in Canada: Citizens Minus*. Ottawa: Canadian Advisory Council on the Status of Women.

Jobb, Dean. 1998. "Westray: A Deadly Misuse of Power." Paper presented at *(Ab)Using Power: The Canadian Experience*. Conference held at Simon Fraser University, Vancouver, B.C., May 7–9.

Johansen, Bruce E. 1993. *Life and Death in Mohawk Country*. Golden, Colorado: North American Press.

Johnson, Holly. 1996. *Dangerous Domains: Violence Against Women in Canada*. Toronto: Nelson.

Kelly, Katharine. 1997. "'You Must Be Crazy If You Think You Were Raped': Reflections on the Use of Complainants' Personal and Therapy Records in Sexual Assault Trials." *Canadian Journal of Women and the Law/Revue "Femme et Droit"* 9.

Johnson, Kirsten. 1996. "The Socio-Legal Governance of Obscenity in Canada, Britain and the United States." *Canadian Journal of Law and Society* 11 (1): 255–71.

———. 1995. *Undressing the Canadian State: The Politics of Pornography from Hicklin to Butler*. Halifax: Fernwood Publishing.

Juffer, Jane. 1998. *At Home with Pornography: Women, Sex and Everyday Life*. New York: New York University Press.

Katz, M.B. 1989. *The Undeserving Poor: From the War on Poverty to the War on Welfare*. New York: Pantheon.

Kealey, Linda. 1998. *Enlisting Women for the Cause: Women, Labour and the Left in Canada, 1890–1920*. Toronto: University of Toronto Press.

———. 1987. "Women and Labour during World War II: Women Workers and the Minimum Wage in Manitoba." In M. Kinnear (ed.), *First Days, Fighting Days: Women in Manitoba History*. Regina: Canadian Plains Research Centre.

Keeshig-Tobias, Lenore. 1983. "(a found poem)." In Beth Brant (Degonwadonti) (ed.), *A Gathering of Spirit: Writing and Art by Native American Women*. Berkeley: Sinister Wisdom.

References

Keet, Jean. 1990. "The Law Reform Process, Matrimonial Property, and Farm Women: A Case Study of Saskatchewan, 1980–1986." *Canadian Journal of Women and the Law* 4 (1): 166–89.

Kieran, Sheila. 1986. *The Family Matters: Two Centuries of Family Law and Life in Ontario*. Toronto: Key Porter.

Kinsman, Gary. 1987. *The Regulation of Desire: Sexuality in Canada*. Montreal: Black Rose Books.

Kirkham, D. 1998. "The Reform Party of Canada: A Discourse on Race, Ethnicity and Equality." In V. Satzewich (ed.), *Racism and Social Inequality in Canada*. Toronto: Thompson Educational Press.

Kline, Marlee. 1994. "The Colour of Law: Ideological Representations of First Nations in Legal Discourse." *Social and Legal Studies* 3: 451–76.

Knowles, V. 1997. *Strangers at Our Gates: Canadian Immigration and Immigration Policy, 1540–1997* (revised edition). Toronto: Dundurn Press.

Krosenbrink-Gelissen, Lilianne E. 1991. *Sexual Equality as an Aboriginal Right: The Native Women's Association of Canada and the Constitutional Process on Aboriginal Matters*. Germany: Breitenbach Publishers.

Kuhn, Annette A. 1985. *The Power of Image: Essays on Representation and Sexuality*. London: Routledge.

———. 1978. "Structures of Patriarchy and Capitalism in the Family." in Annette Kuhn and AnnMarie Wolpe (eds.), *Feminism and Materialism: Women and Modes of Production*. London: Routledge.

Lacelle, Claudette. 1987. *Urban Domestic Servants in Nineteenth-Century Canada*. Ottawa: National Historic Parks and Sites, Environment Canada.

Lacombe, Dany. 1997. "Review of Carol Smart's *Law, Crime and Sexuality: Essays in Feminism*." *Social and Legal Studies* 6 (1): 145–57.

———. 1994. *Blue Politics: Pornography and the Law in the Age of Feminism*. Toronto: University of Toronto Press.

———. 1988. *Ideology and Public Policy: The Case Against Pornography*. Toronto: Garamond Press.

Ladner, Kiera. 1996. "*Nit-acimonawin oma acimonak ohci*: This is My Story About Stories." *Native Studies Review* 11 (2): 103–15.

Law Union of Ontario. 1981. *The Immigrant's Handbook*. Montreal: Black Rose Books.

Laxer, James. 1998. *The Undeclared War: Class Conflict in the Age of Cyber Capitalism*. Toronto: Penguin Books.

Leatch, Dorothy. 1997. "Reflections on 22.2 Years as Receptionist at Parkdale Community Legal Services." *Osgoode Hall Law Journal* 35 (3&4): 663–73.

Legislative Review Advisory Group (LRAG). 1997. *Not Just Numbers: A Canadian Framework for Future Immigration*. Ottawa: Minister of Public Works and Government Services Canada.

Lenskyj, Helen. 1981. "A 'Servant Problem' or a 'Servant-Mistress Problem'?

Domestic Service in Canada, 1890–1930." *Atlantis* 7 (1): 3–11.

Leslie, Genevieve. 1974. "Domestic Service in Canada, 1880–1920." In Janice Acton (ed.), *Women at Work, 1850–1930*. Toronto: Women's Press.

Light, Beth and Ruth R. Pierson. 1990. *No Easy Road: Women in Canada, 1920s to 1960s*. Toronto: New Hogtown Press.

Lilles, Heino. 1992 "A Plea for More Human Values in Our Justice System." *Queen's Law Journal* 15: 327–434.

Lindstrom-Best, Varpu. 1986. "'I Won't Be a Slave'—Finnish Domestics in Canada, 1911–1930." In Jean Burnett (ed.), *Looking into My Sister's Eyes: An Exploration in Women's History*. Toronto: Multiculturalism Historical Society of Ontario.

———. 1988. *Defiant Sisters: A Social History of Finnish Immigrant Woman in Canada*. Toronto: Multicultural History Society of Ontario.

Little, Margaret Hillyard. 1994. "Manhunts and Bingo Blabs: The Moral Regulation of Ontario Single Mothers." *Canadian Journal of Sociology* 19: 233–47.

Los, Maria. 1994. "The Struggle to Redefine Rape in the Early 1980s." In Renate M. Mohr and Julian V. Roberts (eds.), *Confronting Sexual Assault: A Decade of Legal and Social Change*. Toronto: University of Toronto Press.

Luxton, Meg (ed.). 1997. *Feminism and Families: Critical Policies and Changing Practices*. Halifax: Fernwood Publishing.

———. 1980. *More Than a Labour of Love: Three Generations of Women's Work in the Home*. Toronto: Women's Press.

Luxton, Meg and Ester Reiter. 1997. "Double, Double, Toil and Trouble ... Women's Experience of Work and Family in Canada, 1980–1995." In P.M. Evans and G.R. Wekerle (eds.), *Women and the Canadian Welfare State*. Toronto: University of Toronto Press.

Luxton, Meg, Harriet Rosenberg, and Sedef Arat-Koc. 1990. *Through the Kitchen Window: The Politics of Home and Family*. Toronto: Garamond Press.

Mackenzie, Ian R. 1988. "Early Movements of Domestics from the Caribbean and Canadian Immigration Policy: A Research Note." *Alternate Routes* 8: 124–43.

MacKinnon, Catharine. 1993a. *Visionary Lecture Series*. Toronto: University of Toronto, November 20.

———. 1993b. *Only Words*. Cambridge: Harvard University Press.

———. 1992. "Does Sexuality Have a History?" In Donna C. Stanton (ed.), *Discourses of Sexuality: From Aristotle to AIDS*. Ann Arbor: The University of Michigan Press.

———. 1991a. "Reflections on Sex Equality under Law." *The Yale Law Journal* 100:1281–328.

———. 1991b. "Pornography as Defamation and Discrimination." *Boston University Law Review* 71: 793–815.

———. 1990. "Sexuality, Pornography, and Method: 'Pleasure under Patriarchy'." In Cass R. Sunstein (ed.), *Feminism and Political Theory*. Chicago: University of Chicago Press.

———. 1989. *Toward a Feminist Theory of the State*. Cambridge: Harvard University Press.

———. 1987. *Feminism Unmodified: Discourses on Life and Law*. Cambridge: Harvard University Press.

———. 1986. "Pornography: Social Science, Legal, and Clinical Perspectives." *Law and Inequality* 4 (17): 17–39.

———. 1985. "Pornography, Civil Rights, and Speech." Harvard Civil Rights—*Civil Liberties Law Review* 20: 1–70.

———. 1983. "Feminism, Marxism, Method and the State: Toward Feminist Jurisprudence." *Signs* 8: 635–58.

———. 1982. "Feminism, Marxism, Method, and the State: An Agenda for Theory." *Signs* 7 (3): 515–44.

Macklin, Audrey. 1994. "On the Inside Looking In: Foreign Domestic Workers in Canada." In Wenona Giles and Sedef Arat-Koc (eds.), *Maid in the Market: Women's Paid Domestic Labour*. Halifax: Fernwood Publishing.

———. 1992. "*Symes* v. *M.N.R.*: Where Sex Meets Class." *Canadian Journal of Women and the Law* 5(2): 498–517.

Maclean's. 1993. "Voices of Canada: Maclean's/CTV poll." January 4.

MacLeod, Linda. 1987. *Battered but Not Beaten: Preventing Wife Battering in Canada*. A Report for the Canadian Advisory Council on the Status of Women. Ottawa.

Mahoney, Kathleen E. 1984. "Obscenity, Morals and the Law: A Feminist Critique." *Ottawa Law Review* 17 (1): 33–71.

Maine, Sir Henry. 1963. *Ancient Law: Its Connection with the Early History of Society and Its Relation to Modern Ideas*. Edited by R. Firth. Boston: Beacon Press.

Makin, Kirk. 1988. "False Memory's Victims Languish in Jail: Syndrome Discredited but Convictions Still Stand." *Globe and Mail* May 9: A1.

Malarek, V. 1987. *Haven's Gate: Canada's Immigration Fiasco*. Toronto: Macmillan.

Mandel, Michael. 1986. "Democracy, Class and Canadian Sentencing Law." In S. Brickey and E. Comack (eds.), *The Social Basis of Law: Critical Readings in the Sociology of Law* (1st edition). Toronto: Garamond Press.

Mannette, Joy. 1992. *Elusive Justice: Beyond the Marshall Inquiry*. Halifax: Fernwood Publishing.

Manpower and Immigration Canada. 1974. *The Immigration Program*. Ottawa: Information Canada.

Marcus, S. 1974. *Engels, Manchester and the Working Class*. New York: Random House.

Martin, Dianne L. 1992. "Passing the Buck: Prosecution of Welfare Fraud; Preservation of Stereotypes." *Windsor Yearbook of Access to Justice* 12: 52–97.

Marx, Karl and Friedrich Engels. 1998. *The Communist Manifesto*. Halifax: Fernwood Publishing.

———. 1968. *Selected Works*. Moscow: Progress Press.

Matsudi, Mari. 1988. "Affirmative Action and Legal Knowledge: Planting Seeds in Plowed-Up Ground." *Harvard Women's Law Journal* 11: 1–17.

Matthews, Nancy. 1994. *Confronting Rape: The Feminist Anti-Rape Movement and the State*. New York: Routledge.

McCallum, Margaret. 1996. "Labour and the Liberal State: Regulating the Employment Relationship, 1867–1920." *Manitoba Law Journal* 23: 574–93.

———. 1986. "Keeping Women in their Place: The Minimum Wage in Canada." *Labour/Le Travaill* 17: 29–56.

McClung, Nellie. 1976. "What Will They Do with It?" In Ramsay Cook and Wendy Mitchinson (eds.), *The Proper Sphere*. Toronto: University of Toronto Press.

McCormack, Thelma. 1991. *Politics and the Hidden Injuries of Gender: Feminism and the Making of the Welfare State*. Ottawa: CRIAW/ICREF.

McGillivray, Anne. 1998. "*R. v. Bauder*: Seductive Children, Safe Rapists, and Other Justice Tales." *Manitoba Law Journal* 25.

McGillivray, Anne and Brenda Comaskey. 1996. *Intimate Violence, Aboriginal Women and Justice System Response: A Winnipeg Study*. Winnipeg: Manitoba Research Centre on Family Violence and Violence Against Women.

McIntosh, Mary. 1978. "The State and the Oppression of Women." In Annette Kuhn and Ann Marie Wolpe (eds.), *Feminism and Materialism: Women and Modes of Production*. London: Routledge and Kegan Paul.

McIntosh, Robert. 1993. "Sweated Labour: Female Needleworkers in Industrializing Canada." *Labour/ Le Travail* 32: 105–38.

McIntyre, Sheila. 1994. "Redefining Reformism: The Consultations That Shaped Bill C-49." In Renate M. Mohr and Julian V. Roberts (eds.), *Confronting Sexual Assault: A Decade of Legal and Social Change*. Toronto: University of Toronto Press.

McMurtry, The Honourable R. Roy., C.J.O. 1997. "Celebrating a Quarter Century of Community Legal Clinics in Ontario." *Osgoode Hall Law Journal* 35 (3&4): 425–30.

———. 1982. "Notes for a Statement to the Ontario Legislature Standing Committee on the Administration of Justice." In M.J. Mossman, "Community Legal Clinics in Ontario." *Windsor Yearbook Access to Justice* 3: 375–402.

McNeil, Kent. 1998. "Defining Aboriginal Title in the 90's: Has the Supreme Court Finally Got It Right?" Unpublished lecture. Toronto: York University, March 25.

McQuaig, Linda. 1998. *The Cult of Impotence: Selling the Myth of Powerlessness in the Global Economy*. Toronto: Viking Press.

———. 1993. *The Wealthy Banker's Wife: The Assault on Equality in Canada*.

Toronto: Penguin Books.

Mehta, M. 1997. "Risk Assessment and Sustainable Development: Towards a Concept of 'Sustainable Risk'." *Risk: Health Safety and Environment.* Kingston: School of Policy Studies, Queen's University.

———. (ed.). 1995. *Regulatory Efficiency and the Role of Risk Assessment.* Kingston: School of Policy Studies, Queen's University.

Meredith, Colin, Renate Mohr, and Rosemary Cairns Way. 1997. "Implementation Review of Bill C-49." *TR1997-1e.* Ottawa: Department of Justice, February.

Mihesuah, Devon A. 1998. "Commonalty of Difference: American Indian Women and History." In Devon A. Mihesuah (ed.), *Natives and Academics: Researching and Writing about American Indians.* Lincoln and London: University of Nebraska Press.

Miles, R. 1989. *Racism.* London: Routledge.

———. 1984. "Marxism versus the Sociology of 'Race Relations'?" *Ethnic and Racial Studies* 7 (2): 217–37.

Miliband, Ralph. 1969. *The State in Capitalist Society: An Analysis of the Western System of Power.* London: Basic Books.

Miller, Bruce (ed.). 1992. *B.C. Studies* 95 (Autumn).

Miller, Christine and Patricia Chuchryk. 1996. *Women of the First Nations: Power, Wisdom, and Strength.* Winnipeg: University of Manitoba Press.

Milner, B. 1998. "Competition Cops Flex Muscle." *The Globe and Mail Report on Business* March 30: B1 and B3.

Miyoshi, M. 1993. "A Borderless World? From Colonialism to Transnationalism and the Decline of the Nation-State." *Critical Inquiry* 20(3): 726–51.

Montour, Martha. 1987. "Iroquois Women's Rights with Respect to Matrimonial Property on Indian Reserves." *Canadian Native Law Reporter* 4(3).

Monture, Patricia. 1989. "A Vicious Circle: Child Welfare and the First Nations." *Canadian Journal of Women and the Law* 3(1): 1–17.

———. 1993. "I Know My Name: A First Nations Woman Speaks." In Geraldine Finn (ed.), *Limited Edition: Voices of Women, Voices of Feminism.* Halifax: Fernwood Publishing.

Monture-Angus, Patricia A. 1997. "Resisting the Boundaries of Academic Thought: Aboriginal Women, Justice and Decolonization." *Native Studies Review 12 (1).*

———. 1995. *Thunder in My Soul: A Mohawk Woman Speaks.* Halifax: Fernwood Publishing.

Monture-Okanee, P.A. and M.E. Turpel. 1992. "Aboriginal Peoples and Canadian Criminal Law: Rethinking Justice." *U.B.C. Law Review* (special edition): 239–79.

Morris, Allison. 1987. *Women, Crime and Criminal Justice.* Oxford: Basil Blackwell.

Morton, Mary E. 1993. "The Cost of Sharing, the Price of Caring: Problems in the Determination of 'Equity' in Family Maintenance and Support." In J. Brockman and D.E. Chunn (eds.), *Investigating Gender Bias in Law: Socio-Legal Perspectives*. Toronto: Thompson Educational Publishing.

———. 1988. "Dividing the Wealth, Sharing the Poverty: The (Re)formation of 'Family' in Law in Ontario." *Canadian Review of Sociology and Anthropology* 25 (2): 254–75.

Moscovitch, Allan and Jim Albert (eds.). 1987. *The 'Benevolent' State: The Growth of Welfare in Canada*. Toronto: Garamond Press.

Mosher, Janet. 1997. "Poverty Law—A Case Study." In the *Report of the Ontario Legal Aid Review: A Blueprint for Publicly Funded Legal Services*. Volume 3. Toronto: Queen's Printer.

Mossman, Mary Jane. 1993. "Gender Equality and Legal Aid Services: A Research Agenda for Institutional Change." *Sydney Law Review* 15: 30–58.

———. 1983. "Community Legal Clinics in Ontario." *Windsor Yearbook Access to Justice* 3: 375–402.

Mossman, Mary Jane and Morag MacLean. 1997. "Family Law and Social Assistance Programs: Rethinking Equality." In P.M. Evans and G.R. Wekerle (eds.), *Women and the Canadian Welfare State*. Toronto: University of Toronto Press.

———. 1986. "Family Law and Social Welfare: Toward a New Equality." *Canadian Journal of Family Law* 5: 79–110.

Murray, M. 1998. "Immigrants Set to Battle Rule Changes." *Toronto Star* March 3, B1 and B5.

Naffine, Ngaire. 1990. *The Law and the Sexes: Explorations in Feminist Jurisprudence*. Sydney: Allen and Unwin.

National Council of Welfare (NCW). 1998a. *Poverty Profile 1996*. Ottawa: Minister of Public Works and Government Services Canada.

———. 1998b. *Profiles of Welfare: Myths and Realities*. Ottawa: Minister of Public Works and Government Services Canada.

———. 1997–98. *Welfare Incomes 1996*. Ottawa. Minister of Public Works and Government Services Canada.

———. 1997. *Poverty Profile 1995*. Ottawa: Minister of Supply and Services Canada.

———. 1995. *Legal Aid and the Poor*. Ottawa: Minister of Supply and Services Canada.

———. 1991. *Poverty Profile Update for 1991*. Ottawa: Minister of Supply and Services Canada.

———. 1976. *One in a World of Twos: A Report on One Parent Families*. Ottawa: National Council of Welfare.

National Association of Women and the Law (NAWL). 1985. "Response of NAWL to the Recommendations in Regard to Pornography in the Fraser Report and to the Government's Discussion Paper on the Report of the Special Committee on Pornography and Prostitution." Ottawa.

References

National Task Force on the Definition and Measurement of Poverty in Canada. 1984. *Not Enough: The Meaning and Measure of Poverty in Canada.* Ottawa: Canadian Council on Social Development.

National Film Board of Canada. 1995. *Who Gets In?*

National Action Committee on the Status of Women (NACSW). 1988. "Brief to the House of Commons Justice Committee on Bill C-54." Prepared by Kate Andrew and Debra J. Lewis, Toronto.

Native Women's Association of Canada. 1986. *Guide to Bill C-32: An Explanation of the 1985 Amendments to the Indian Act.* Ottawa.

Ng, Roxanna. 1993. "Racism, Sexism and Immigrant Women." In Sandra Burt, L. Code and L. Dorney (eds.), *Changing Patterns: Women in Canada* (2nd edition). Toronto: McClelland and Stewart.

———. 1989. "Sexism, Racism, Nationalism." In J. Vorst (ed.), *Race, Class, Gender: Bonds and Barriers.* Socialist Studies/Etudes Socialistes: A Canadian Annual 5: 10–25.

———. 1986. ""Immigrant Women in Canada: A Socially Constructed Category." *Resources for Feminist Research* 15: 13–16.

Nikiforuk, A. 1997. *The Nasty Game: The Failure of Environmental Assessment in Canada.* Toronto: Walter and Duncan Gordon Foundation.

Noble, C. 1995. "Regulating Work in a Capitalist Society." In F. Pearce and L. Snider (eds.), *Corporate Crime: Contemporary Debates.* Toronto: University of Toronto Press.

O'Connor, James. 1973. *The Fiscal Crisis of the State.* New York: St. Martin's Press.

Oberle, P.R. 1993. *The Incidence of Family Poverty on Canadian Indian Reserves.* Ottawa: Indian and Northern Affairs Canada.

Ontario Family Law Tariff Sub-Committee to the Legal Aid Committee of the Law Society of Upper Canada. 1992. *Equal Justice for Women and Children: A Report.* Toronto: unpublished.

Ontario Legal Aid Review. 1997. *Report of the Ontario Legal Aid Review: A Blueprint for Publicly Funded Legal Services.* (3 volumes). Toronto: Queen's Printer.

Ontario. 1988. *Report of the Social Assistance Review Committee: Transitions.* (Chair: G. Thomson). Toronto: Queen's Printer.

———. 1995. *Report of the Commission on Systemic Racism in the Ontario Criminal Justice System.* (Margaret Gittens and David Cole, Co-Chairs). Toronto: Queen's Printer.

Orton, Helena. 1990. "Litigating for Equality: LEAF's Approach to Section 15 of the *Charter.*" In Karen Busby, Lisa Fainstein, and Holly Penner (eds.), *Equality Issues in Family Law: Considerations for Test Case Litigation.* Winnipeg: Legal Research Institute, Faculty of Law, University of Manitoba.

Owens, Rosemary. 1995. "The Peripheral Worker: Women and the Legal Regulation of Outwork." In M. Thornton (ed.), *Public and Private: Feminist*

Legal Debates. Melbourne: Oxford University Press.

Palmer, Bryan. 1992. *Working Class Experience; Rethinking the History of Canadian Labour, 1800–1991* (2nd edition). Toronto: McClelland & Stewart.

Panitch, Leo. 1977. "The Role and Nature of the Canadian State." In L. Panitch (ed.), *The Canadian State: Political Economy and Political Power.* Toronto: University of Toronto Press.

——— (ed.). 1977. *The Canadian State: Political Economy and Political Power.* Toronto: University of Toronto Press.

Parkdale Community Legal Services (PCLS). 1997. "Poverty Law and Community Legal Clinics: A View from Parkdale Community Legal Services." *Osgoode Hall Law Journal* 35: 595–603.

Parkdale Community Legal Services, et al. (PCLS). 1989. *Brief in Response to the "Draft Discussion Paper on Changes to the Employment Standards Act by the Ontario Advisory Council on Women's Issues.* Toronto: unpublished.

Parr, Joy. 1980. *Labouring Children: British Immigrant Apprentices to Canada, 1869–1924.* Montreal/Kingston: McGill-Queen's University Press.

Parsons, Talcott. 1980. "The Law and Social Control." In Wm. Evan (ed.), *The Sociology of Law: A Social-Structural Perspective.* New York: The Free Press.

Pashukanis, Evgeny. 1978. *Law and Marxism: A General Theory.* (Edited by C. Arthur.) London: Ink Links.

Paulus, I. 1974. *The Search for Pure Food: A Sociology of Legislation in Britain.* London: Martin Robertson.

Pearce, Diana. 1985. "Welfare Is Not for Women: Toward a Model of Advocacy to Meet the Needs of Women In Poverty." *Clearinghouse Review* 19: 412–18.

Pearce, Frank. 1993. "Corporate Rationality as Corporate Crime." *Studies in Political Economy* 40 (Spring): 135–62.

———. 1990. *The Second Islington Crime Survey*. Middlesex: Middlesex University Centre of Criminology.

———. 1989. *The Radical Durkheim*. London: Unwin Hyman.

———. 1976. *Crimes of the Powerful*. London: Pluto Press.

Pearce, F. and S. Tombs. 1998. *Toxic Capitalism: Corporate Crime and the Chemical Industry*. Aldershot: Ashgate/Dartmouth.

Pearce, F. and L. Snider. 1995. "Regulating Capitalism." In F. Pearce and L. Snider (eds.), *Corporate Crime: Contemporary Debates*. Toronto: University of Toronto Press.

Peikoff, Tannis and Stephen Brickey. 1991. "Creating Precious Children and Glorified Mothers: A Theoretical Assessment of the Transformation of Childhood." In E. Comack and S. Brickey (eds.), *The Social Basis of Law* (2nd edition). Halifax: Garamond Press.

Petchesky, Rosalind P. 1985. *Abortion and Woman's Choice: The State, Sexual-*

ity and Reproductive Freedom. Boston: Northeastern University Press.

Phillips, Paul and Erin Phillips. 1993. *Women & Work* (Revised edition). Toronto: Lorimer.

Picchio, Antonella. 1992. *Social Reproduction: The Political Economy of the Labour Market*. Cambridge: Cambridge University Press.

Picciotto, Sol. 1979. "The Theory of the State, Class Struggle and the Rule of Law." In Bob Fine (ed.), *Capitalism and the Rule of Law*. London: Hutchinson.

Piliavin, S. and S. Briar. 1964. "Police Encounters with Juveniles." *American Journal of Sociology* 70: 206–14.

Platt, Anthony. 1969. *The Child Savers: The Invention of Delinquency*. Chicago: University of Chicago Press.

Ponting, J. Rick. 1997. *First Nations in Canada: Perspectives on Opportunity, Empowerment, and Self-Determination*. Toronto: McGraw-Hill Ryerson.

Portes, A. 1978. "Migration and Underdevelopment." *Politics and Race* 8(1): 1–48.

Poulantzas, Nicos. 1975. *Classes in Contemporary Capitalism*. London: New Left Books.

Prentice, Alison et al. 1988. *Canadian Women: A History*. Toronto: Harcourt Brace and Jovanovich.

Pulkingham, Jane. 1994. "Private Troubles, Private Solutions: Poverty among Divorced Women and the Politics of Support Enforcement and Child Custody Determination." *Canadian Journal of Law and Society* 9(2): 73–97.

Pulkingham, Jane and Gordon Ternowetsky (eds.). 1996. *Child and Family Policies: Struggles, Strategies and Options*. Halifax: Fernwood Publishing.

Punch, M. 1996. *Dirty Business: Exploring Corporate Misconduct*. London: Sage.

Quinney, Richard. 1975. "Crime Control in a Capitalist Society." In I. Taylor, P. Walton, and J. Young (eds.), *Critical Criminology*. London: Routledge and Keagan Paul.

Ramirez, Judith. 1983/84. "Good Enough to Stay." *Currents* 1(4).

Ratner, Robert and John McMullan (eds.). 1987. *State Control: Criminal Justice Politics in Canada*. Vancouver: University of British Columbia Press.

Razack, Sherene. 1998. *Looking White People in the Eye: Gender, Race, and Culture in Courtrooms and Classrooms*. Toronto: University of Toronto Press.

———. 1991. *Canadian Feminism and the Law: The Women's Legal Education and Action Fund and the Pursuit of Equality*. Toronto: Second Story Press.

Reeves, F. 1983. *British Racial Discourse: A Study of British Political Discourse about Race and Race-Related Matters*. Cambridge: Cambridge University Press.

Regush, N. 1991. "Health and Welfare's National Disgrace." *Saturday Night* April: 9–18; 62–63.

Reiman, J. 1994. *The Rich Get Richer and the Poor Get Prison* (4th edition). Toronto: Allyn and Bacon.

Reimers, D.M. and H. Troper. 1992. "Canadian and American Immigration Policy Since 1945." In B.R. Chiswick (ed.), *Immigration, Language and Ethnicity*. Washington: The AEI Press.

Reiss, A. 1992. "The Institutionalization of Risk." In J. Short and L. Clarke (eds.), *Organizations, Uncertainties and Risk*. Boulder: Westview Press.

Reiss, A. 1984. "Selecting Strategies of Social Control over Organizational Life." In K. Hawkins and J. Thomas (eds.), *Enforcing Regulation*. Boston: Kluwer-Nijoff.

Rex, J. 1983. *Race Relations and Sociological Theory*. London: Routledge and Kegan Paul.

Richard, Justice K. Peter (Commissioner). 1997. *The Westray Story: A Predictable Path to Disaster*. Report of the Westray Mine Public Inquiry. Halifax: Province of Nova Scotia.

Ristock, Janice and Joan Pennell. 1996. *Community Research as Empowerment: Feminist Links, Postmodern Interruptions*. Toronto: Oxford University Press.

Roberts, Dorothy. 1996. "Welfare and the Problem of Black Citizenship." *Yale Law Journal* 105: 1563–602.

Roberts, Julian. 1994. "Criminal Justice Processing of Sexual Assault Cases." *Juristat* 14.

Roberts, Barbara. 1979. "A Work of Empire: Canadian Reformers and British Female Immigration." In Linda Kealey (ed.), *A Not Unreasonable Claim: Women and Reform in Canada, 1880s–1920s*. Toronto: Women's Press.

———. 1988. *Whence They Came: Deportation from Canada, 1900–1935*. Ottawa: University of Ottawa Press.

Roberts, Wayne. 1979. "'Rocking the Cradle for the World': The New Woman and Maternal Feminism, Toronto, 1877–1914." In L. Kealey (ed.), *A Not Unreasonable Claim*. Toronto: Women's Press.

Rollins, Judith. 1985. *Between Women: Domestics and Their Employers*. Philadelphia: Temple University Press.

Rosenberg, Harriet. 1990. "The Home Is the Workplace: Hazards, Stress and Pollutants in the Household." In M. Luxton et al., *Through the Kitchen Window*. Toronto: Garamond Press.

Rosnes, Melanie. 1997. "The Invisibility of Male Violence in Canadian Child Custody and Access Decision-Making." *Canadian Journal of Family Law* 14(1): 31–60.

Ross, Becki L. 1995. *The House That Jill Built: A Lesbian Nation in Formation*. Toronto: University of Toronto Press.

Ross, David P., E.R. Shillington, and C. Lochead. 1994. *The Canadian Fact*

References

Book on Poverty—1994. Ottawa: Canadian Council on Social Development.

Ross, Rupert. 1996. *Returning to the Teachings: Exploring Aboriginal Justice.* Toronto: Penguin.

Rothman, D. 1995. "More of the Same: American Criminal Justice Policies in the 1990s." In T. Blomberg and S. Cohen (eds.), *Punishment and Social Control.* New York: Aldine de Gruyter.

Russell, Bob. 1991. "A Fair or Minimum Wage? Women Workers, the State, and the Origins of Wage Regulation in Western Canada." *Labour/Le Travail* 28: 59–88.

Sage, Barbara. 1987. "B.C. Lesbian Mother Denied Custody of Daughter." *The Lawyers' Weekly* 6 (38): 1, 8.

Samuel, T.J. 1990. "Third World Immigration and Multiculturalism." In S. Halli, F. Trovato, and L. Driedger (eds.), *Ethnic Demography: Canadian Immigrant, Racial and Cultural Variations.* Ottawa: Carleton University Press.

Satzewich, Vic. 1989. "Racism and Canadian Immigration Policy: The Government's View of Caribbean Immigration, 1926–66." *Canadian Ethnic Studies* 21(1): 77–97.

Scales, Ann. 1994. "Avoiding Constitutional Depression: Bad Attitudes and the Fate of *Butler.*" *Canadian Journal of Women and the Law* 7 (2): 349–92.

Schmitz, C. 1995. "Veteran Criminal Lawyer Disbands Firm; Accuses Ontario Government of 'Fraud.'" *The Lawyers' Weekly* September 22: 1.

Scott, The Honourable Ian, Q.C. 1985. "Legal Aid Statement." Unpublished statement.

Scott, Jennifer, and Sheila McIntyre. 1997. "Women's Legal Education and Fund (LEAF) Submissions to the Standing Committee on Justice and Legal Affairs Review of Bill C-46." Unpublished, March.

Seccombe, Wally. 1974. "The Housewife and Her Labour under Capitalism." *New Left Review* 83: 3–24.

Segal, Lynn and Mary McIntosh (eds.). 1993. *Sex Exposed: Sexuality and the Pornography Debate.* New Jersey: Rutgers University Press.

Seward, Shirley and K. McDade. 1988. *Immigrant Women in Canada: A Policy Perspective* (Background Paper 1988). Ottawa: Canadian Advisory Council on the Status of Women.

Shapiro, S. 1990. "Collaring the Crime, Not the Criminal: Considering the Concept of White-Collar Crime." *American Sociological Review* 55(June): 346–65.

———. 1985. "The Road Not Taken: The Elusive Path to Criminal Prosecution for White Collar Offenders." *Law and Society Review* 19(2): 179–217.

———. 1984. *Wayward Capitalists.* New Haven: Yale University Press.

Shields, John and B. Mitchell Evans. 1998. *Shrinking the State: Globalization and Public Administration "Reform."* Halifax: Fernwood Publishing.

Shime, Pamela. 1994. "AIDS and Poverty Law: Inaction, Indifference, and Ignorance." *Journal of Law and Social Policy* 10: 155–81.

Silvera, Makeda, 1989. *Silenced.* Toronto: Sister Vision.

———. 1983. Silenced. Toronto: Williams-Wallace Publishers Inc.

———. 1981. "Immigrant Domestic Workers: Whose Dirty Laundry?" *Fireweed* 9.

Simmons, A.B. 1992. "Canadian Migration in the Western Hemisphere." Paper prepared for the workshop *Canada's Role in the Hemisphere: Setting the Agenda.* University of Miami: North-South Centre, March 27–28.

———. 1990. "'New Wave' Immigrants: Origins and Characteristics." In S. Halli, F. Trovato, and L. Driedger (eds.), *Ethnic Demography: Canadian Immigrant, Racial and Cultural Variations.* Ottawa: Carleton University Press.

Smandych, Russell. 1991. "The Origins of Canadian Anti-Combines Legislation, 1890–1910." In E. Comack and S. Brickey (eds.), *The Social Basis of Law: Critical Readings in the Sociology of Law* (2nd edition). Halifax: Garamond Press.

Smart, Carol. 1995. *Law, Crime and Sexuality: Essays in Feminism.* London: Sage Publications.

———. 1993. "Unquestionably a Moral Issue: Rhetorical Devices and Regulatory Imperatives." In Lynne Segal and Mary McIntosh (eds.), *Sex Exposed: Sexuality and the Pornography Debate.* New Jersey: Rutgers University Press.

———. 1992. "The Woman of Legal Discourse." *Social and Legal Studies* 1 (1): 29–44.

———. 1990. "Law's Power, the Sexed Body, and Feminist Discourse." *Journal of Law and Society* 7 (2) (Summer): 194–210.

———. 1989. *Feminism and the Power of Law.* London, Routledge.

———. 1986. "Feminism and the Law: Some Problems of Analysis and Strategy." *International Journal of the Sociology of Law* 14(2): 109–23.

———. 1984. *The Ties That Bind: Law, Marriage and the Reproduction of Patriarchal Relations.* London: Routledge and Kegan Paul.

Smith, D. 1987. *The Everyday World as a Problematic: A Feminist Sociology.* Toronto: University of Toronto Press.

Snell, James G. 1991. *In the Shadow of the Law: Divorce in Canada, 1900–1939.* Toronto: University of Toronto Press.

Snider, Laureen. 1998a. "Understanding the Second Great Confinement." *Queen's Quarterly* (Spring): 29–49.

———. 1998b. "Towards Safer Societies: Punishment, Masculinities and Violence Against Women." *British Journal of Criminology* 38(1): 1–39.

———. 1997. "Nouvelle Donne Legislative et Causes de la Criminalite 'Corporative'." *Criminologie* XXX (1): 9–34.

———. 1996. "Options for Public Accountability." In M. Mehta (ed.), *Regulatory Efficiency and the Role of Risk Assessment.* Kingston: School of Policy

References

Studies, Queen's University.

———. 1994. "Feminism, Punishment and the Potential for Empowerment." *Canadian Journal of Law and Society* 9(1) (Spring): 75–104.

———. 1993. *Bad Business: Corporate Crime in Canada.* Scarborough, Ontario: Nelson.

———. 1991. "The Regulatory Dance: Understanding Reform Processes in Corporate Crime." *International Journal of Sociology of Law* 19: 209–36.

———. 1989. "Ideology and Relative Autonomy in Anglo-Canadian Criminology." *Journal of Human Justice* 1(1) (Fall):27–42.

———. 1987. "Towards a Political Economy of Reform, Regulation and Corporate Crime." *Law and Policy* 9(1): 37–68.

———. 1978. "Corporate Crime in Canada: A Preliminary Report." *Canadian Journal of Criminology* 20(2): 142–68.

Social Planning Council of Metropolitan Toronto. 1986. *Living on the Margin: Welfare Reform for the Next Decade.* Toronto.

Stanbury, W. 1995. "Public Policy Towards Individuals Involved in Competition Law Offences in Canada." In F. Pearce and L. Snider (eds.), *Corporate Crime: Contemporary Debates.* Toronto: University of Toronto Press.

———. 1988. "A Review of Conspiracy Cases in Canada, 1965–66 to 1987–88." *Canadian Competition Policy Record* 10 (1): 33–49.

———. 1986–87. "The New Competition Act and Competition Tribunal Act: Not with a Bang but a Whimper?" *Canadian Business Law Journal* 12: 2–42.

———. 1977. *Business Interests and the Reform of Canadian Competition Policy 1971–75.* Toronto: Carswell/Methuen.

Statistics Canada. 1998. *National Census.* Ottawa: Supply and Services.

———. 1997. *Income Distributions by Size in Canada.* Ottawa: Ministry of Supply and Services.

———. 1996. *Death and Injury Rates on the Job.* (Catalogue # 75-001-XPE). Ottawa: Ministry of Supply and Services.

———. 1992. *The Canadian National Child Care Study: Parental Work Patterns and Child Care Needs.* Ottawa: Supply and Services.

———. 1990. *Women in Canada: A Statistical Report* (2nd edition). Ottawa: Supply and Services.

Statutes of Canada. 1992. *Bill C-86: An Act to Amend the Immigration Act.* Chapter 49.

Steel, Freda M. 1985. "The Ideal Marital Property Regime—What Would It Be?" In E. Sloss (ed.), *Family Law in Canada: New Directions.* Ottawa: Advisory Council on the Status of Women.

Stoler, Ann Laura. 1995. *Race and the Education of Desire: Foucault's History of Sexuality and the Colonial Order of Things.* Durham: Duke University Press.

Stolenberg, John. 1989. *Refusing to Be a Man: Essays on Sex and Justice.* New

York: Penguin Books.

Strong-Boag, Veronica. 1979. "The Girl of the New Day: Canadian Working Women in the 1920s." *Labour/Le Travail* 4: 31–64.

———. 1979. "'Wages for Housework': Mothers' Allowances and the Beginnings of Social Security in Canada." *Journal of Canadian Studies* 14 (1): 24–34.

Struthers, James. 1994. *The Limits of Affluence: Welfare in Ontario, 1920–1970.* Toronto: University of Toronto Press.

Sumner, C. 1983. "Rethinking Deviance: Toward a Sociology of Censures." *Research in Law, Deviance and Social Control* 5: 187–204.

Sunahara, A.G. 1981. *The Politics of Racism: The Uprooting of Japanese-Canadians during the Second World War.* Toronto: James Lorimer and Company.

Sutherland, Edwin. 1977. "White-Collar Criminality." In G. Geis and R. Meier, (eds), *White Collar Crime.* New York: Free Press.

———. 1961. *White Collar Crime.* New York: Holt, Rinehart and Winston.

———. 1949. *White Collar Crime.* New York: Dryden.

———. 1940. "White-Collar Criminality." *American Sociological Review* 5 (February): 1–12.

Taylor, Georgina, Jan Barnsley, and Penny Goldsmith. 1996. *Women and Children Last: Custody Disputes and the Family Justice System.* Vancouver: Vancouver Custody and Access Support and Advocacy Association.

Taylor, Ian. 1984. "The Development of Law and Public Debate in the United Kingdom in Respect of Pornography and Obscenity." *Working Papers on Pornography and Prostitution*, Report No. 14. Ottawa: Department of Justice.

Taylor, Ian, Paul Walton, and Jock Young. 1973. *The New Criminology.* London: Routledge and Keagan Paul.

The Task Force on Child Care. 1986. *Report of the Task Force on Child Care.* Ottawa: Ministry of Supply and Services.

The Task Force on Immigration Practices and Procedures. 1981. "Domestic Workers on Employment Authorizations Report." Ottawa: Employment and Immigration.

Thompson, A. 1993. "Closing the Door." *Toronto Star* January 13: B1 and B7.

Thompson, E.P. 1975. *Whigs and Hunters: The Origins of the Black Act.* Middlesex: Penguin.

Tombs, S. Forthcoming. "Health and Safety Crimes: (In)Visibility and the Problems of Knowing."

———. 1996. "Injury, Death and the Deregulation Fetish: The Politics of Occupational Safety Regulation in United Kingdom Manufacturing Industries." *International Journal of Health Services* 26(2): 309–29.

———. 1995. "Corporate Crime and New Organizational Forms." In F. Pearce and L. Snider (eds.), *Corporate Crime: Contemporary Debates.* Toronto:

University of Toronto Press.

Toughill, Kelly. 1986. "Domestic Workers Praise Rule Change." *Toronto Star* September 22: C2.

Tucker, Eric. 1995. "Labour Law and Fragmentation before Statutory Collective Bargaining ." In M. Steedman, P. Suschnigg, and D. Bose (eds.), *Hard Lessons: The Mine Mill Union in the Canadian Labour Movement.* Toronto: Dundurn.

———. 1995a. "The Westray Mine Disaster and Its Aftermath." *Canadian Journal of Law and Society* 10 (1): 92–123.

———. 1995b. "And Defeat Goes On: An Assessment of Third Wave Health and Safety Regulation." In F. Pearce and L. Snider (eds.), *Corporate Crime: Contemporary Debates.* Toronto: University of Toronto Press.

———. 1991. "'That Indefinite Zone of Toleration': Criminal Conspiracy and Trade Unions in Ontario, 1837–1877." *Labour/ Le Travail* 27: 15–54.

———. 1990. *Administering Danger in the Workplace: The Law and Politics of Occupational Health and Safety Regulation in Ontario, 1850–1914.* Toronto: University of Toronto Press.

Turk, Austin. 1980. "Law as a Weapon in Social Conflict." In Wm. Evan (ed.), *The Sociology of Law: A Social-Structural Perspective.* New York: The Free Press.

———. 1969. *Criminality and Legal Order.* Chicago: Rand-McNally.

Turkel, Gerald. 1988. "The Public/ Private Distinction: Approaches to the Critique of Legal Ideology." *Law and Society Review* 22: 801–23.

Turpel, Mary Ellen. 1991. "Home/Land." *Canadian Journal of Family Law* 10(1): 17–40.

Ujimoto, V.K. 1988. "Racism, Discrimination and Internment: Japanese in Canada." In S. Bolaria and P. Li (eds.), *Racial Oppression in Canada.* Toronto: Garamond Press.

United Nations. 1996. *Human Development Report.* New York: Oxford University Press.

Ursel, Jane. 1992. *Private Lives, Public Policy: 100 Years of State Intervention in the Family.* Toronto: Women's Press.

Valverde, Mariana. 1991. *The Age of Light, Soap and Water: Moral Reform in Canada, 1885–1925.* Toronto: McClelland and Stewart.

———. 1985. *Sex, Power and Pleasure.* Toronto: The Women's Press.

Valverde, M., L. MacLeod and K. Johnson (eds.). 1995. *Wife Assault and the Canadian Criminal Justice System.* Toronto: University of Toronto Press.

Varrette, S.E., C. Meredith, P. Robinson, and D. Huffman, ABT Association of Canada. 1985. *White Collar Crime: Exploring the Issues.* Ottawa: Ministry of Justice.

Villasin, Felicita and M. Anne Phillips. 1994. "Falling through the Cracks: Domestic Workers and Progressive Movements." *Canadian Women Studies* 14(2): 87–90.

Walters, V., W. Lewchuk, J. Richardson, L. Moran, T. Haines, and D. Verma. 1995. "Judgments of Legitimacy Regarding Occupational Health and Safety." In F. Pearce and L. Snider (eds.), *Corporate Crime: Contemporary Debates*. Toronto: University of Toronto Press.

Webber, Jeremy. 1995. "Labour and Law." In P. Craven (ed.), *Labouring Lives: Work and Workers in Nineteenth-Century Ontario*. Toronto: University of Toronto Press.

Weber, Gloria Valencia and Christine Zuni. 1995. "Domestic Violence and Tribal Protection of Indigenous Women in the United States." *Women's Rights and Human Rights Law Journal* 69 (1–2): 69–170.

Weber, Max. 1968. *Economy and Society*. (Eds. Guenther Roth and Claus Wittich). New York: Bedminster Press.

———. 1958. *The Protestant Ethic and the Spirit of Capitalism*. New York: Charles Scribner's Sons.

Weisburd, D., E.F. Chayet, and E.J. Waring. 1990. "White Collar Crime and Criminal Careers: Some Preliminary Findings." *Crime and Delinquency* 36(3): 342–55.

Wells, C. 1993. *Corporations and Criminal Responsibility*. Oxford: Oxford University Press.

Wendell, Susan. 1996. *Rejected Body: Feminist Philosophical Reflections on Disability*. New York: Routledge.

Wexler, Stephen. 1970. "Practicing Poverty Law for Poor People." *Yale Law Journal* 79: 1049–67.

Wheeler, S., D. Weisburd, and N. Bode. 1982. "Sentencing the White-Collar Offender: Rhetoric and Reality." *American Sociological Review* 47: 641–59.

White, Julie. 1993. *Sisters and Solidarity: Women and Unions in Canada*. Toronto: Thompson Educational Press.

Wigmore, John. 1970. *Evidence in Trials at Common Law* (revised edition). J.C. Chadbourne (ed.), Boston: Little Brown and Co.

Wing, Adrien Katherine. 1997. *Critical Race Feminism: A Reader*. New York: New York University Press.

Women, Immigration and Nationality Group (WING). 1985. *Worlds Apart: Women under Immigration and Nationality Law*. London: Pluto Press.

Women's Legal Education and Action Fund (LEAF). 1991. "Factum of the Intervenor in R. v. Butler." *Equality and the Charter: Ten years of Feminist Advocacy before the Supreme Court of Canada*. Toronto: Edmond Montgomery.

Wood, Ellen Meiksins. 1998. "The Agrarian Origins of Capitalism." *Monthly Review* 50: 14–31.

———. 1981. "The Separation of the Economic and Political in Capitalism." *New Left Review* 127: 66–95.

Woodiwiss, Anthony. 1990. *Social Theory after Post-Modernism: Rethinking*

Production, Law and Class. London: Pluto Press.

Workman, Thom. 1996. *Banking on Deception: The Discourse of Fiscal Crisis.* Halifax: Fernwood Publishing.

Yeager, P. 1995. "Management, Morality, and Law: Organizational Forms and Ethical Deliberations." In F. Pearce and L. Snider (eds.), *Corporate Crime: Contemporary Debates.* Toronto: University of Toronto Press.

———. 1991. *The Limits of Law: The Public Regulation of Private Pollution.* Cambridge: Cambridge University Press.

York, Geoffrey. 1990. *The Dispossessed: Life and Death in Native Canada.* London: Vintage Books.

Young, M. 1997. *Canada's Immigration Program (Background Paper).* Ottawa: Library of Parliament Research Branch.

———. 1992. *Bill C-86: An Act to Amend the Immigration Act (Legislative Summary).* Ottawa: Library of Parliament Research Branch.

———. 1991a. *Canada's Immigration Program (Background Paper).* Ottawa: Library of Parliament Research Branch—Law and Government Division, February.

———. 1991b. *Canada's Refugee Determination System (Background Paper).* Ottawa: Library of Parliament Research Branch, February.

Zaretsky, Eli. 1976. *Capitalism, the Family and Personal Life.* New York: Harper and Row.

Zemans, Frederick H. and Patrick J. Monahan with Aneurin Thomas. 1997. *From Crisis to Reform: A New Legal Aid Plan for Ontario.* North York: York University Centre for Public Law and Public Policy.

Zey, M. 1993. *Banking on Fraud: Drexel, Junk Bonds and Buyouts.* New York: Aldine de Gruyter.

Legislation and Case Law Cited

Attorney General of Canada v. *Bliss.* 1979. 1 Supreme Court Reports 183.

Attorney General of Canada v. *Lavell*; *Isaac et al.* v. *Bedard.* 1973. 38 Dominion Law Reports (3d) (Supreme Court of Canada).

Bill C-54. The House of Commons of Canada, Second Session, Thirty-Third Parliament, 1986-87, First Reading May 4, 1987.

Bill C-114. The House of Commons of Canada, First Session, Thirty-Third Parliament, 1984-85-86, First Reading June 10, 1986.

Delgamuukw v. *British Columbia.* 1998. 1 Canadian Native Law Reporter 21 (Supreme Court of Canada).

Derrickson v. *Derrickson.* 1986. 2 Canadian Native Law Reporter 45 (Supreme Court of Canada).

Falkiner v. *Ontario* (Attorney General). 1996. 94 Ontario Appeal Cases. 109 (Ontario Court General Division, Divisional Court).

Glad Day Bookshop Inc. v. *Deputy Minister of National Revenue for Customs and Excise.* 1992. O.J. (Q/L) No. 1466 (Ontario Court General Division).

LiSanti v. *LiSanti.* 1990. 24 Reports on Family Law (3d) 178 (Ontario Provincial Court).

Little Sister's Book and Art Emporium v. *Canada (Minister of Justice).* 1996. British Columbia Judgments No. 71, 19 January.

M. v. *H.* 1997. 25 Reports on Family Law (4th) 116 (Ontario Court of Appeal).

Masse v. *Ontario* (Ministry of Community and Social Service. 1996. 134 Dominion Law Reports(4th) 20 (Ontario Court General Division, Divisional Court).

Maw v. *Maw.* 1985. 44 Reports on Family Law (2d) 364 (British Columbia Supreme Court).

Moge v. *Moge.* 1992. 3 Supreme Court Reports 813.

Murdoch v. *Murdoch.* 1973. 41 Dominion Law Reports (3d) 367 (Supreme Court of Canada).

Murdoch v. *Murdoch.* 1975. 1 Supreme Court Reports 423.

Paul v. *Paul.* 1986. 2 Canadian Native Law Reporter 74 (Supreme Court of Canada).

R. v. *A.J.G.* 1998. Ontario Judgments (Q/L) No. 1742 (Court of Justice).

R. v. *Adams.* 1995. 4 Supreme Court Reports 707.

R. v. *Bauder.* 1997. Manitoba Judgments (Q/L) No. 270 (Court of Appeal).

R. v *Brodie.* 1962. Supreme Court Reports 681.

R. v. *Brown.* 1994. Nova Scotia Judgments (Q/L) No. 269 (Court of Appeal).

R. v. *Burke.* 1996. 1 Supreme Court Reports 474.

R. v. *Butler.* 1989. 60 Manitoba Reports (2d) 82 (Manitoba Queen's Bench); (1990) 73 Manitoba Reports (2d) 197 (Court of Appeal); (1992) 78 Manitoba Reports (2) 1 (Supreme Court of Canada); retrial (March 31, 1993) 88-01-04647 (Manitoba Queen's Bench).

R. v. *C.(M.H.).* 1991. 1 Supreme Court Reports 763.

R. v. *Carosella.* 1997. 1 Supreme Court Reports 80.

R. v. *Charland.* 1996. 110 Canadian Criminal Cases (3d) 300 (Alberta Court of Appeal).

R. v. *Chase.* 1984. 55 New Brunswick Reports (2d) 97 (Court of Appeal), reversed (1987), 37 Canadian Criminal Cases (3d) 97 (Supreme Court of Canada).

R. v. *Conway.* 1944. 2 Dominion Law Reports 530.

R. v. *Curl.* 1727. 93 English Reports 849 (King's Bench).

R. v. *D.(E.).* 1995. 32 Alberta Law Reports 109 (Queen's Bench).

R. v. *Darrach.* 1998. Ontario Judgments (Q/L) No. 397 (Court of Appeal).

R. v. *Dominion News and Gifts (1962).* 1964. 2 Supreme Court Reports 251.

R. v. *Dominion News and Gifts (1962).* 1963. 2 Canadian Criminal Cases 103 (Manitoba Court of Appeal).

R. v. *Doug Rankine and Act III Video.* 1983. 9 Canadian Criminal Cases (3d) 53 (Ontario County Court).

R. v. *E.F.H.* 1994. Ontario Judgments (Q/L) No. 452 (General Division), affirmed (1996) Ontario Judgments (Q/L) No. 553 (Court of Appeal) (leave to appeal to the Supreme Court of Canada denied).

R. v. *Ecker.* 1995. 128 Saskatchewan Reports 161 (Court of Appeal).

R. v. *Ewanchuk.* 1998. Alberta Judgments (Q/L) No. 150 (Court of Appeal). (On appeal to the Supreme Court of Canada).

R. v. *Finley.* 1998. Ontario Judgments (Q/L) No. 974 (Court of Justice).

R. v. *Hawkins.* 1993. 86 Canadian Criminal Cases (3d) 246 (Ontario Court of Appeal).

R. v. *Hicklin.* 1868. 3 Law Reports Queen's Bench 360.

R. v. *Jorgensen.* 1995. 4 Supreme Court Reports 55.

R. v. *Khan.* 1996. 110 Manitoba Reports (2d) 241 (Court of Appeal).

R. v. *L.J.S.* 1996. Alberta Judgments (Q/L) No. 73 (Queen's Bench).

R. v. *Lifchus.* 1997. Supreme Court Judgments (Q/L) No. 77.

R. v. *Majid.* 1995. 128 Saskatchewan Reports 248 (Court of Appeal), affirmed [1996] 1 Supreme Court Reports 472.

R. v. *Mara.* 1997. 2 Supreme Court Reports (Q/L) 630.

R. v. *Martin Secker & Warburg Ltd.* 1954. 1 W.L.R. 1138.

R. v. *Mills.*1997. Alberta Judgments (Q/L) No. 891 and 1036 (Queen's Bench). (On appeal to the Supreme Court of Canada).

R. v. *Moreau.* 1986. 26 Canadian Criminal Cases (3d) 359 (Ontario Court of Appeal).

R. v. *National News.* 1953. 106 Canadian Criminal Cases 26 (Ontario Court of Appeal).

R. v. *O'Connor.* 1998. British Columbia Judgments (Q/L) No. 649 (Court of

Appeal).

R. v. *O'Connor*. 1995. 4 Supreme Court Reports 411.

R. v. *P.(M.B.)*. 1994. 89 Canadian Criminal Cases (3d) 289 (Supreme Court of Canada).

R. v. *R.Y.* 1996. Ontario Judgments No. 2134 (Q/L) (Court of Justice).

R. v. *Ramsingh*. 1984. 14 Canadian Criminal Cases (3d) 230 (Manitoba Queen's Bench).

R. v. *Red Hot Video*. 1985. 18 Canadian Criminal Cases (3d) 1 (British Columbia Court of Appeal).

R. v. *Ronish*. 1993. 26 C.R. (4th) 165 (Ontario Court of Appeal).

R. v. *Ronish*. 1992. 18 C.R. (4th) 75 (Ontario Provincial Division per Cole J.).

R. v. *S.F.* 1997. Ontario Judgments (Q/L) No. 4116 (Court of Justice).

R. v. *Sansregret*. 1985. 1 Supreme Court Reports 570.

R. v. *Scott*. 1997. Manitoba Judgments (Q/L) No. 239 (Court of Appeal).

R. v. *Scythes*. 1993. Ontario Judgments (Q/L) No. 537 (Provincial Division).

R. v. *Seaboyer*. 1991. 2 Supreme Court Reports 577.

R. v. *Smith*. 1915. 84 Law Journal King's Bench (New Series) 2153 (England) Chancery Court of Appeal).

R. v. *Sparrow*. 1990. 3 Canadian Native Law Reporter 160 (Supreme Court of Canada).

R. v. *Stillman*. 1997. 1 Supreme Court Reports 607.

R. v. *Towne Cinema Theatres*. 1985. 1 Supreme Court Reports 494.

R. v. *W.(D.)*. 1991. Supreme Court Reports 742.

R. v. *Wagner*. 1985. 36 Alberta Law Reports (2d) 301 (Queen's Bench).

Weeks v. *Weeks*. 1955. 3 Dominion Law Reports 704 (British Colombia Court of Appeal).